Richard J. Howard

901 Livingston
Columbia University
New York City

Shakespeare's Use of the Arts
of Language

number 165
COLUMBIA UNIVERSITY STUDIES IN ENGLISH
AND COMPARATIVE LITERATURE

Shakespeare's Use of the Arts of Language

BY SISTER MIRIAM JOSEPH, C.S.C.

NEW YORK · MCMXLVII

COLUMBIA UNIVERSITY PRESS

To SISTER M. MADELEVA, c.s.c.

Poet and Educator

PREFACE

T HE RHETORICAL and logical theory current during the Renaissance and its influence on the literature of the time have engaged the attention of many scholars interested in the period, among whom the following may relevantly be mentioned here. William Lowes Rushton, in *Shakespeare and 'The Arte of English Poesie'* (Liverpool, 1909), pointed out parallels between passages in Shakespeare and definitions and illustrations in the *Arte*. Gladys Doidge Willcock and Alice Walker edited a reprint of Puttenham's *Arte of English Poesie* (Cambridge, 1936) with an illuminating introduction and notes. Miss Willcock has also written essays on Shakespeare's use of rhetoric. Veré L. Rubel selected certain figures of speech from Puttenham's *Arte* and in her *Poetic Diction in the English Renaissance* (New York, 1941) illustrated their use in the work of the poets from Skelton through Spenser, after some preliminary notice of their use by Chaucer. Frank P. Wilson, in "Shakespeare and the Diction of Common Life," *Proceedings of the British Academy*, Vol. XXVI (1941), examined Shakespeare's use of three figures: paronomasia (a form of pun), the image, and the proverb. William G. Crane, in *Wit and Rhetoric in the Renaissance* (New York, 1937), particularly noted the relation of the rhetorical figures of thought to the logical topics of invention and emphasized the importance of both logic and rhetoric in developing the "wit" deemed necessary for the composition of all forms of Renaissance literature. Rosemond Tuve, in "Imagery and Logic: Ramus and Metaphysical Poetics," *The Journal of the History of Ideas*, III (October, 1942), 365–400, showed the intimate connection of logic and rhetoric with poetic composition in the work of Elizabethan writers and cited examples from Spenser, Sidney, Marlowe, and Donne. Hardin Craig, in "Shakespeare and Formal Logic" (*Studies in English Philology; a Miscellany in Honor of Frederick Klaeber* (Minneapolis, 1929, pp. 380–96), demonstrated Shakespeare's knowledge and use of the terms and processes of formal logic, and Allan H. Gilbert, in "Logic in the Elizabethan Drama," *Studies in Philology*, XXXII (October, 1935), 527–45, illustrated the use of logic by other Elizabethan dramatists from Lyly to Shirley. T. W. Baldwin, in *William Shakspere's Small Latine and Lesse Greeke* (Urbana, 1944), adduced evidence to prove not only that Shakespeare had a thorough and systematic knowledge of rhetoric and logic but also that he gained this knowledge from the Latin textbooks regularly studied in the Tudor grammar schools and that he employed in the composition of his plays and poems both techniques and materials derived from these Latin texts. Baldwin illustrates Shakespeare's use of particular forms of composition, as for example various forms of the oration described in the *Rhetorica ad C. Herennium* and in Quintilian's *Institutio oratoria.*

The contribution of the present work is to present in organized detail essentially complete the general theory of composition current during the Renaissance (as contrasted with special theories for particular forms of composition) and the illustration of Shakespeare's use of it. A few examples from the work of other Elizabethan writers are included for the sake of comparison. There are in Shakespeare's works many comments on the arts of language, that is, on grammar, rhetoric, and logic. Most of them are assembled at the beginning of Chapter II, a few at the opening of other chapters and sections of chapters. Remarks which are virtually definitions of figures of speech or obvious references to them are placed where the given figure is treated. The Renaissance classification of puns among highly esteemed figures may be mentioned as one instance in which the sixteenth-century theory sheds light on Shakespeare's work, for he uses puns in the most serious contexts, a fact which surprises and even offends many modern readers. The expository intention of the present study precludes the omission of any part of the general theory of composition, however unimportant, although it permits emphasis of the more significant parts. It also precludes continuous treatment of any one play and necessitates the use of scattered quotations from all of them. There is, however, a somewhat sustained treatment of particular plays at the close of sections in Chapters III, IV, and V.

Quotations from Renaissance works, except Shakespeare's, reproduce the spelling and punctuation of the time, but mere typographical peculiarities, such as the interchange of *u* and *v* and the use of *i* for *j*, have been modernized. The quotations from Shakespeare follow the text of George Lyman Kittredge's edition of *Shakespeare's Complete Works* (Ginn and Company, 1936).

My indebtedness to scholars to whose work mine is related at many points is acknowledged specifically in the footnotes and generally in the bibliography. For facilities necessary to carry on this study, particularly the use of rare books, and for their unfailing courtesy I desire to thank staff members of the libraries of Columbia University (including the main library, the law library, special collections, the Plimpton Library, and the library of Teachers College), the New York Public Library, the Library of Congress, the libraries of the University of Chicago, and the Newberry Library. I thank the authorities of the Huntington Library for permission to quote from Fenner's *The Artes of Logike and Rhetorike*, and the following publishers for permission to incorporate copyrighted material: Oxford University Press and the Clarendon Press for passages from Hardin Craig, *The Enchanted Glass*, George Stuart Gordon, S.P.E. Tract 29, C. S. Lewis, *The Allegory of Love*, Frank P. Wilson, "Shakespeare and the Diction of Common Life," from *The Works of Aristotle Translated into English*, and from the Oxford editions of Spenser, Lyly, Jonson, Thomas Wilson, *The Arte of Rhetorique*, Mulcaster, *Elementarie*, *The Pilgrimage to Parnassus*, and *Elizabethan Critical Essays*; the Cambridge University Press, for passages from E. E. Kellett, *Suggestions*, and from Cambridge editions of Puttenham's *The Arte of English Poesie* and the works of Sidney; Yale University Press for passages from Hoskyns, "Direccions for Speech and Style"; and the University of Illinois Press for passages from T. W. Baldwin, *William Shakspere's Small Latine and Lesse Greeke*.

I wish to express my sincere gratitude to Professor Harry Morgan Ayres, Professor Oscar James Campbell, and Professor Donald Lemen Clark, of Columbia University, for their direction of this work and for their helpful criticism.

I am deeply grateful to Mother M. Rose Elizabeth, superior general of the Congregation of the Sisters of the Holy Cross, to Mother M. Una, provincial, to Mother M. Vincentia, former superior general, to Mother M. Verda, former provincial (now deceased), and to Sister M. Madeleva, president of Saint Mary's College, Notre Dame, for the opportunity to pursue the studies which led to the writing of this book. To my colleague Sister Maria Teresa I owe thanks for typing the manuscript and for friendly criticism.

S. M. J.

Saint Mary's College, Notre Dame
Holy Cross, Indiana
Sept. 15, 1947

CONTENTS

KEY TO REFERENCES

THEORETICAL WORKS

Blundeville — Thomas Blundeville, *The Arte of Logick* [1599], London, 1617.

Day — Angel Day, *The English Secretorie, with a Declaration of Tropes, Figures and Schemes* [1592], London, 1635.

Fenner — Dudley Fenner, *The Artes of Logike and Rhetorike*, Middelburg, 1584.

Fraunce, *AR* — Abraham Fraunce, *The Arcadian Rhetorike*, London, 1588.

Fraunce, *LL* — Abraham Fraunce, *The Lawiers Logike*, London, 1588.

Hoskyns — John Hoskyns, *Direccions for Speech and Style* [wr. *ca.* 1599], printed from MS Harley 4604 in *The Life, Letters, and Writings of John Hoskyns*, pp. 114–166, by Louise Brown Osborn, New Haven, 1937.

Lever — Raphe Lever, *The Arte of Reason, Rightly Termed, Witcraft*, London, 1573.

Peacham, 1577 — Henry Peacham, *The Garden of Eloquence*, London, 1577.

Peacham — Henry Peacham, *The Garden of Eloquence*, London, 1593.

Puttenham — George Puttenham, *The Arte of English Poesie* [1589]; ed. by Gladys Doidge Willcock and Alice Walker, Cambridge, 1936.

Sherry — Richard Sherry, *A Treatise of Schemes & Tropes*, London, 1550.

Sherry, 1555 — Richard Sherry, *A Treatise of the Figures of Grammer and Rhetorike*, London, 1555.

Wilson, *AR* — Thomas Wilson, *The Arte of Rhetorique* [1553]; ed. by G. H. Mair, Oxford, 1909.

Wilson, *RR* — Thomas Wilson, *The Rule of Reason, Conteining the Art of Logike* [1551], London, 1567.

SHAKESPEARE'S PLAYS

A & C — The Tragedy of Antony and Cleopatra

AW — All's Well That Ends Well

AYLI	As You Like It
CE	The Comedy of Errors
Cor.	The Tragedy of Coriolanus
Cym.	Cymbeline
Ham.	The Tragedy of Hamlet, Prince of Denmark
1H4	The First Part of King Henry the Fourth
2H4	The Second Part of King Henry the Fourth
H5	The Life of King Henry the Fifth
1H6	The First Part of King Henry the Sixth
2H6	The Second Part of King Henry the Sixth
3H6	The Third Part of King Henry the Sixth
H8	The Famous History of the Life of King Henry the Eighth
JC	The Tragedy of Julius Caesar
KJ	The Life and Death of King John
Lear	The Tragedy of King Lear
LLL	Love's Labour's Lost
MA	Much Ado about Nothing
Mac.	The Tragedy of Macbeth
MM	Measure for Measure
MND	A Midsummer Night's Dream
MV	The Merchant of Venice
MWW	The Merry Wives of Windsor
Oth.	The Tragedy of Othello, the Moor of Venice
Per.	Pericles, Prince of Tyre
R2	The Tragedy of King Richard the Second
R3	The Tragedy of King Richard the Third
R & J	The Tragedy of Romeo and Juliet
RL	The Rape of Lucrece
Son.	Sonnets
T & C	The Tragedy of Troilus and Cressida
Tem.	The Tempest
TGV	The Two Gentlemen of Verona
Tim.	The Life of Timon of Athens
Tit.	The Tragedy of Titus Andronicus
TN	Twelfth Night; or, What You Will
TNK	The Two Noble Kinsmen
TS	The Taming of the Shrew
V & A	Venus and Adonis
WT	The Winter's Tale

PART ONE

INTRODUCTION

CHAPTER I

THE GENERAL THEORY OF COMPOSITION AND OF READING IN SHAKESPEARE'S ENGLAND

SCHOLARS have endeavored, especially in recent years, to show by historical studies how Shakespeare's plays were influenced in form and content by such matters as stage conventions and conditions of production,[1] by current doctrines of science, philosophy, and physiology,[2] or even by something apparently as remote as the bishops' order of June 1, 1599, prohibiting the printing of satires and epigrams.[3] If such historical studies illuminate for the modern reader certain plays of Shakespeare, as many agree they do, then the recovery of the current theory of composition, which enters into the very form and texture of all Shakespeare's plays and was the common idiom of his time, should likewise be of value.

The extraordinary power, vitality, and richness of Shakespeare's language are due in part to his genius, in part to the fact that the unsettled linguistic forms of his age promoted to an unusual degree the spirit of free creativeness, and in part to the theory of composition then prevailing. It is this last which accounts for those characteristics of Shakespeare's language which differentiate it most from the language of today, not so much in the words themselves as in their collocation. The difference in habits of thought and in methods of developing a thought results in a corresponding difference in expression principally because the Renaissance theory of composition, derived from an ancient tradition, was permeated with formal logic and rhetoric, while ours is not.

The purpose of this study is to present to the modern reader the general theory of composition current in Shakespeare's England. A general theory of composition, and correlatively of reading, is to be understood as one which underlies all special forms, such as the oration, the epic,

---

[1] As in the work of E. E. Stoll and E. K. Chambers.

[2] See Spencer, *Shakespeare and the Nature of Man*; Curry, *Shakespeare's Philosophical Patterns*; L. B. Campbell, *Shakespeare's Tragic Heroes, Slaves of Passion*.

[3] See O. J. Campbell, *Comicall Satyre and Shakespeare's 'Troilus and Cressida'*; also, his *Satire in Shakespeare*.

the drama, whether in prose or in verse. The Elizabethan critical essays unequivocally witness to the fact that the art of composition was then conceived as a body of precepts laid down in works on the three arts of language: grammar, rhetoric, and logic. Since grammar in its aesthetic aspects is treated in the works on rhetoric, the general theory of composition is to be sought in the works on rhetoric and logic which circulated in Tudor England. These include the *Rhetorica ad C. Herennium*, treatises by Cicero, Quintilian, and Aristotle, and Renaissance works directly or indirectly derived from them and often designed to lead into them. The Renaissance rhetoricians may be considered for the moment in two classes: those who in addition to a work on rhetoric, treating comparatively few figures of speech, wrote a companion work on logic; and those who deal only with the figures of speech, distinguishing from about ninety to one hundred and eighty figures, and who may therefore be called the figurists. A concordance of the Tudor figures approximates two hundred.

This study undertakes to establish four points: first, that the general theory of composition and of reading current in Shakespeare's England is to be found in one form in the contemporary works on logic and rhetoric combined; second, that it is to be found in another form in the work of the figurists which, surprisingly, treats of approximately the same matter as do the logic and rhetoric texts combined; third, that these two forms, though outwardly different, are fundamentally alike; fourth, that the theory in its entire scope, whether in the one form or in the other, is, with two or three negligible exceptions, illustrated in Shakespeare's plays and poems, where it contributes to the power and richness of his language and even of his thought, while it accounts for certain peculiar differences between the characteristic mode of expression of his time and of ours. Included also in this study are the vices of language, treated by the figurists in connection with the figures of grammar, and the fallacies and captious arguments, treated by the logicians in connection with correct forms of reasoning. Shakespeare makes capital use of them to create humor and to depict villainy and low life.

In the light of this theory it becomes evident, first, that Shakespeare's development of his subject matter and his mode of expression in his plays and poems are characteristic of his time; secondly, that he utilized every resource of thought and language known to his time; thirdly, that his genius, outrunning precept even while conforming to it, transcends that of his contemporaries and belongs to all time.

1. The Concept of Art in Renaissance England

In the late sixteenth century the Renaissance in England, no longer occupied primarily in making the acquaintance of ancient classics or in translating them or in composing imitations in Latin, was well advanced in its third phase: the later Elizabethan writers were eagerly and patriotically bent on creating literature in the vernacular inspired not only by the ancient classics but also by the new vernacular literatures of Italy and France. Spenser's simultaneous devotion to Aristotle, Plato, Theocritus, Bion, Vergil, Ariosto, Tasso, Mantuan, Marot, the French Pléiade, and Chaucer, and above all his desire to enrich English poetry by art comparable to that of other nations, exemplified the spirit of the time. The Elizabethan literary critics and poets, no less than the rhetoricians and logicians, insisted on the importance of precepts and theory in the creation of literature. Richard Mulcaster, Spenser's teacher at the Merchant Taylors school in London, with a robust faith in the artistic capacities of English, confidently asserted that "our natural tung" is "as readie to anie rule of Art, as anie other is." [4] George Puttenham conceived of art as "a certaine order of rules prescribed by reason, and gathered by experience." [5] Undertaking to write an *Arte of English Poesie* (1589) he reasoned:

Then as there was no art in the world till by experience found out: so if Poesie be now an Art, & of al antiquitie hath bene among the Greeks and Latines, & yet were none, untill by studious persons fashioned and reduced into a method of rules & precepts, then no doubt may there be the like with us. (p. 5)

Artificial was accordingly, as Puttenham pointed out, a word of praise.

Man also in all his actions that be not altogether naturall, but are gotten by study & discipline or exercise, as to daunce by measures, to sing by note, to play on the lute, and such like, it is a praise to be said an artificiall dauncer, singer, & player on instruments, because they be not exactly knowne or done, but by rules & precepts or teaching of schoolemasters. (p. 305)

In the Renaissance "to imitate the excellentest artificiality of the most renowned worke-masters that antiquity affourdeth" [6] was the ideal which

---

[4] Mulcaster, *Elementarie* (1582), ed. by E. T. Campagnac, p. 59.
[5] Puttenham, *The Arte of English Poesie*, ed. by Gladys Doidge Willcock and Alice Walker, p. 5.
[6] Gabriel Harvey, from *Pierce's Supererogation*, 1593, in *Elizabethan Critical Essays*, ed. with an introduction by G. Gregory Smith (hereafter cited as Smith), II, 277.

many of the greatest writers, such as Tasso and Spenser, sought to achieve. A lack of art was regarded as intolerable by Thomas Nashe: "Nothing is more odious to the Auditor then the artlesse tongue of a tedious dolt."[7] Nashe was quick to note, however, the even greater importance of experience:

Endevour to adde unto Arte Experience: experience is more profitable voide of arte then arte which hath not experience. Of it selfe arte is unprofitable without experience, and experience rashe withoute arte.[8]

Art, as Richard Rainolde explained, supplements and perfects the gifts of nature.

Nature hath indued every man, with a certain eloquence, and also subtilitee to reason and discusse, of any question or proposicion propounded, as *Aristotle* the Philosopher, in his Booke of *Rhetorike* dooeth shewe. . . . therefore Nature itself beyng well framed, and afterward by arte and order of science, instructed and adorned, must be singularlie furthered, helped, and aided to all excellencie, to exquisite invencion, and profound knowledge, bothe in *Logike* and *Rhetorike*. In the one, as a Oratour to pleate with all facilitee, and copious-lie to dilate any matter or sentence: in the other to grounde profunde and sub-till argument, to fortifie & make stronge our assercion or sentence, to prove and defende, by the force and power of arte, thinges passyng the compasse & reach of our capacitee and witte.[9]

In his "Apologie for Poetrie" Sir Philip Sidney expressed the current conviction that the arts are derived from nature and have nature for their object.

There is no Arte delivered to mankinde that hath not the workes of Nature for his principall object, without which they could not consist, and on which they so depend, as they become Actors and Players, as it were, of what Nature will have set foorth. So doth the Astronomer looke upon the starres, and, by that he seeth, setteth downe what order Nature hath taken therein. . . . The Grammarian speaketh onely of the rules of speech; and the Rethorician and Logitian, considering what in Nature will soonest prove and perswade, thereon give artificial rules. (Smith, I, 155)

The three arts of language, observed Puttenham, while derived from nature, bring it to perfection only through exercise.

---

[7] Nash, from "The Anatomie of Absurditee," 1589, Smith, I, 335.
[8] *Loc. cit.*
[9] Rainolde, *A Booke Called the Foundacion of Rhetorike*, fol. i[r].

But what else is language and utterance, and discourse & persuasion, and argument in man, then the vertues of a well constitute body and minde, little lesse naturall then his very sensuall actions, saving that the one is perfited by nature at once, the other not without exercise & iteration? . . . And yet I am not ignorant that there be artes and methodes both to speake and to perswade and also to dispute, and by which the naturall is in some sorte . . . relieved in his imperfection . . . in which respect I call those artes of Grammer, *Logicke*, and *Rhetorick* . . . by long and studious observation rather a repetition or reminiscens naturall, reduced into perfection, and made prompt by use and exercise. . . . Also in that which the Poet speakes or reports of another mans tale or doings, as *Homer* of *Priamus* or *Ulisses* . . . in that he speakes figuratively, or argues subtillie, or perswades copiously and vehemently, he doth as the cunning gardiner that using nature as a coadjutor, furders her conclusions & many times makes her effectes more absolute and straunge. (pp. 305 ff.)

Art, then, according to Tudor critics and poets, is assumed to rest on a body of precepts derived from nature, and both composition and reading are to be guided by the three ancient interrelated arts of language. Raphe Lever noted what every humanist considered a truism, that

artes are knit together in such a bande of knowledge, that no man can be cunning in anye one but he must have some knowledge in manye.[10]

Montaigne, well known in England, especially in Florio's translation, explained more specifically the interrelatedness of the liberal arts.

The Logitian referreth himselfe to the Grammarian for the signification of words: the Rethoritian borroweth the places of arguments from the Logitian: The Poet his measures from the Musitian. The Geometrician his proportion from the Arithmetician.[11]

Ben Jonson conceived the ideal poet as one in whom the gifts of nature are perfected by the knowledge and exercise particularly of the three arts of language, in addition to ethics.

I would leade you to the knowledge of our *Poet*, by a perfect Information, what he is, or should bee by nature, by exercise, by imitation, by Studie; and so bring him downe through the disciplines of Grammar, Logicke, Rhetoricke, and the Ethicks, adding somewhat, out of all, peculiar to himselfe, and worthy of your Admittance, or reception.[12]

[10] Raphe Lever, *The Arte of Reason, Rightly Termed Witcraft*, p. 90.
[11] "An Apologie of *Raymond Sebond*," in Montaigne, *Essayes*, tr. by John Florio, ed. by Thomas Seccombe, II, 307.
[12] Jonson, *Discoveries*, ed. by Maurice Castelain, p. 122.

It is clear that the men of Shakespeare's time, no less than those of classical antiquity and the Middle Ages, held the basic theory of composition and of reading to lie in the arts of grammar, logic, and rhetoric, which guide and govern all discourse. They believed that the poet, the orator, and the prose narrator, each having distinct and peculiar problems of his own, inevitably draw upon these wider arts of language for the general theory which must underlie all special forms of composition.

2. *Training in the Arts in Renaissance England*

A thorough training in the arts of language was the fundamental aim of the grammar schools of Tudor England.[13] These schools were patterned on Saint Paul's, London, re-founded in 1510 by Dean Colet, whose friend Erasmus, then in England, planned the curriculum and wrote or helped to write many of the textbooks, which continued to be used throughout the century. These textbooks, imbued with the literary spirit of Erasmus, exemplified the ideals and methods of studying the classics which he set forth systematically in his *De ratione studii*, composed at the end of the fifteenth century and published in 1512. It is no mere coincidence that the early leaders of the Renaissance in various countries were schoolmasters and authors of school texts which were used internationally: Erasmus, Agricola, Vives, Melanchthon, Sturm. They cultivated the ground from which flowered the great vernacular literatures. Ariosto, Ronsard, and Shakespeare learned through training in Latin to write superbly in their own tongues.

There is no external proof that Shakespeare attended grammar school. It may be presumed, however, that he did. Very likely after learning his ABC's and catechism in English in petty school he entered Stratford grammar school, about 1571, and followed the curriculum and texts which had become practically uniform by mid-century.

The aim of the grammar-school curriculum was to enable the student to read, write, and speak Latin, to acquaint him with the leading Latin classics and a few of the Greek, and to infuse into him sound moral and religious principles. The method prescribed unremitting exercise in grammar, rhetoric, and logic. Grammar dominated the lower forms, logic and rhetoric the upper. In all forms the order was first to learn precepts, then to employ them as a tool of analysis in reading, and finally to use them as a guide in composition. Much of the reading, especially in the lower

[13] See T. W. Baldwin, *William Shakspere's Small Latine and Lesse Greeke.*

forms, was selected with a view to furnishing moral and religious instruction.

The boy learning the rules of accidence bit by bit in Lily's Latin grammar would apply them first in construing *Sententiae pueriles,* *Catonis disticha moralia,* and a Latin version of Aesop's fables, and then in translating English into Latin. The making of Latins might begin with mottoes from the *Satellitium* of Vives or *Sententiae Ciceronis* dictated in English by the teacher; the boy's Latin rendering could then be compared with the original. The English Bible would furnish longer passages for translation into Latin, the favorites being the Psalms and the books of moral wisdom, Proverbs, Ecclesiasticus, Wisdom, and Ecclesiastes. To these might be added Job, Isaiah, and Genesis. Meanwhile colloquial Latin would not have been neglected. The *Linguae Latinae exercitatio* of Vives, with its typical conversations related to the various phases of school life, would prepare the boy to obey the rule requiring that all conversation, even at play, be carried on in Latin. The *Dialogi sacri* of Castalio and the colloquies of Erasmus would lead into Terence, the perfection of colloquial Latinity. Plautus and a Latin translation of Lucian might also be used. It was customary, in some schools at least, for the boys to take part in a Latin play at Christmas and just before Lent. The play might be by Terence or by Plautus or it might be composed by the schoolmaster himself. The study of poetry would begin with the Italian Renaissance poets Mantuan and Palingenius, who wrote in Latin.

In the upper forms a closely interrelated group of texts embodied the precepts of logic-rhetoric which were to guide the study of literature and composition. The boy must first be grounded in the topics of logic through Cicero's *Topica* before he could properly understand the one hundred and thirty-two figures of speech defined and illustrated in Susenbrotus' *Epitome troporum ac schematum et grammaticorum et rhetoricorum.* A mastery of the topics and figures was presupposed in *De duplici copia verborum ac rerum,* by Erasmus, which explained the two modes of varying in order to secure copiousness: first of diction, chiefly by means of the figures and a wide vocabulary, second of matter, by employing the topics of logic. In *Modus conscribendi epistolas* Erasmus applied these principles to letter writing. The boy would next observe these precepts exemplified in the classical authors and finally apply them to the composition of Latin epistles, first in prose and then in verse. Cicero's epistles furnished models for prose, those of Horace and the

Heroidum epistolae of Ovid for verse. The *Ars poetica* of Horace was both an epistle and a treatise on poetry supplementing the prosody, which constituted the fourth division of grammar. The epistle thus provided an easy transition from prose to verse, both in reading and in composition.

The poetry read would include Ovid's *Metamorphoses, Fasti, Tristia, Amores,* Vergil's *Eclogues, Georgics, Aeneid,* Lucan's *Pharsalia,* Horace's odes, and satires of Horace, Juvenal, and Persius. Pupil-teaching was a common device which impressed a lesson doubly upon the mind of the student. The boys would memorize Ovid's *Metamorphoses* at the rate of twelve lines a week, five hundred lines a year, for two or more years. A form would recite to the one next above it, which in turn would recite to the one higher. Thus were poetic rhythms, as distinguished from mere meter, fixed in the ears of the students as an aid in writing verse. Elizabethan poetry illustrates the results of this method. A customary exercise was to compose Latin prose and then turn it into one or more prescribed metrical forms. Accordingly Jonson, who said that he composed in prose and then turned the prose into verse, merely continued to do in English what he had learned to do in Latin grammar school. The method of studying poetry involved daily exercises in grammar, rhetoric, and logic. In a work like Melanchthon's *Erotemata dialectices* the boy learned the forms of propositions and the rules of the syllogism. In reading a poem he would construe, parse, scan, describe the metrical form, point out the topics and forms of logic and the figures of rhetoric, and then write verses of his own in imitation. The figures were particularly valued as an aid in the reading and writing of poetry.

Precepts for fourteen minor forms of prose themes preliminary to the oration were studied in Aphthonius' *Progymnasmata.* Sentential and moral matter valuable for writing such themes was furnished in the collections of Erasmus, *Adagia, Apophthegmata,* and *Parabolae* and in Pliny's *De historia naturali.* The histories of Livy, Sallust, Caesar, Justin, Valerius Maximus, and Lucius Florus provided further matter. From the *Rhetorica ad C. Herennium* and Quintilian's *Institutio oratoria* the student received instruction in reading and writing orations and thereby reached the summit of achievement in grammar school. Cicero's orations, his *Tusculanae disputationes, De officiis, Paradoxes, Somnium Scipionis, De amicitia,* and *De senectute* would be studied with attention to grammatical constructions, logical arguments, and rhetorical figures and forms. The three arts would then be applied to writing, in imitation, orations of the three recognized kinds—judicial, deliberative, and demonstrative—in which much of the moral matter from the reading was introduced.

Meanwhile the study of Greek grammar presented in Latin would also have begun, with accompanying construing and parsing in Latin of Greek sentences and the translation of Latin sentences into Greek. Next would follow the reading and writing of longer passages in prose and verse, with attention to constructions, topics, figures, and the changing of verse to prose and prose to verse. The Greek New Testament, Isocrates, and Homer were most often required for reading, but the curriculum might include Aesop, Lucian, Demosthenes, Hesiod, Pindar, Euripides, Xenophon, Dionysius of Halicarnassus, Plutarch, Theocritus, Heliodorus, Saint Basil's epistles.

This program of studies necessitated a strenuous routine. The order of the day in the Tudor grammar schools prescribed rising at five; class from six to nine; breakfast; class from nine-fifteen to eleven; dinner; class from one to five; supper. After supper, from six to seven, the pupils recited to their fellows what they had learned during the day. The lessons drilled on in the morning were regularly recited in the afternoon, and all the work of the week was reviewed in recitation on Fridays and Saturdays. A week devoted to repetitions tested the accomplishments of the thirty-six weeks of the school year. A sixteenth-century schoolmaster estimated that one hour of instruction would require at least six hours of exercise to apply the principles to writing and speaking.

T. W. Baldwin, upon whose recent work the preceding summary is based, has shown that an Elizabethan would understand Ben Jonson's ascription to Shakespeare of "small Latine and lesse Greeke" as meaning that Shakespeare had the regular grammar school education of the time. In the university the same authors were studied on a higher level, and others, including Aristotle, were added. Using sixteenth-century editions of annotated grammar-school texts along with such contemporary school aids as the Latin-English dictionaries of Withals, Baret, and Cooper and collections of quotations such as *Polyanthea* and Octavianus Mirandula's *Illustrium poetarum flores,* Baldwin finds internal evidence, some of it certain, some of it probable, that Shakepeare was acquainted in the original Latin with all of the books mentioned above except Cicero's orations, *De amicitia* and *De senectute,* the histories of Sallust, Caesar, Justin, and Valerius Maximus, Horace's satires, and Lucan's *Pharsalia.* Of the Greek readings, he finds some probability only for the New Testament. It is not unlikely, however, that Shakespeare knew at least some of the books which he did not use as sources of material or of techniques in his writing. Baldwin concludes:

William Shakspere was trained in the heroic age of grammar school rhetoric in England, and he shows knowledge of the complete system, in its most heroic proportions. He shows a grasp of the theory as presented by the various texts through Quintilian. He shows a corresponding grasp upon all the different compositional forms of prose for which the theory prepared. And this is true whether or not Shakspere ever went to school a day. Manifestly, the sensible thing to do is to permit him to complete Stratford grammar school, as there is every reason to believe that he did.[14]

Particularly interesting is Baldwin's demonstration that Shakespeare's famous lines on the seven ages of man, beginning "All the world's a stage," were derived primarily from Palingenius' *Zodiacus vitae* (which borrowed from Vives, Ovid, and Saint Chrysostom) and secondarily from Susenbrotus, Proclus, Horace, and Lambinus' notes on Horace. Palingenius was also a source, along with Saint Chrysostom, Job, and Isaiah, of a beautiful passage in *The Tempest* (4.1.152–58).[15] In *Love's Labour's Lost,* when Holofernes quotes the opening lines of the eclogues of Mantuan, his words would have awakened reminiscences of school days in Shakespeare's contemporaries.

> Fauste, precor, gelida, quando pecus omne sub umbra
> Ruminat, and so forth. Ah, good old Mantuan! (4.2.95)

Baldwin's study [16] throws light particularly on three characters: Holofernes, the schoolmaster, Sir Nathaniel, the text-parading curate, and Hamlet, the Wittenberg scholar. According to Baldwin an Elizabethan audience would easily have recognized the satirical rogue referred to by Hamlet (2.2.198) as Juvenal,[17] and the book Hamlet was reading (in the first version of the play) just before he began to dispute with himself, "To be or not to be—that is the question" (3.1.56), as Cicero's *Quaestiones Tusculanae,* "the first and fundamental text for a scholar's consolation in doubts of death." [18]

---

[14] *Ibid.,* II, 378.   [15] *Ibid.,* I, 652–77.

[16] In reviewing Baldwin's work, Tucker Brooke comments on its importance to students of Shakespeare: "Many passages in the plays and poems are either explained or given a fuller meaning by Baldwin's analysis of the techniques and textbooks through which Elizabethan schoolboys were trained; and this exegesis will hereafter be ignored by teachers at their peril." *Modern Language Notes,* LX (February, 1945), 126.

[17] T. W. Baldwin, *op. cit.,* II, 526.   [18] *Ibid.,* II, 607; 601–8.

After demonstrating that the Latin textbooks used in grammar school are not only the source of many passages in Shakespeare's works but also the basis of his conscious use of technicalities and of his "mastery of the system as a whole, not merely of a few chance definitions," [19] Baldwin observes: "It would be possible to show how he has used without pointing to the fact this great body of rhetorical knowledge, but that is beyond our present scope." [20] To show how Shakespeare used the whole body of logical-rhetorical knowledge of his time is essentially the undertaking of the present study. Although Baldwin justly maintains that "in these Latin texts is the main stream; the English rhetorics are only the eddies," [21] yet, because the English works on logic and rhetoric were translations and adaptations of the Latin textbooks used in the grammar schools of Tudor England, they can furnish an authentic contemporary account of Renaissance theory in language which, though slightly antiquated, has obviously an advantage in an investigation that aims, not at the discovery of specific sources, as Baldwin's does, but at the reconstruction of the general theory of the time. Furthermore, the English works had a wide circulation in Elizabethan England, and there is evidence that some of them were known to Shakespeare.

3. The English Works on Logic and Rhetoric

The following are the extant sixteenth-century works in English on logic and rhetoric, arranged in three groups. At the beginning of each group is at least one Renaissance Latin work to which the English works are closely related, usually through adaptation or translation.[22]

GROUP 1: THE TRADITIONALISTS

Aphthonius, *Progymnasmata;* tr. by Agricola and Cataneus, ed. by Lorichius; 1542.

Philippus Melanchthon, *Institutiones rhetoricae,* Haganoa, 1521.

—— *Elementa rhetorices,* Wittenberg, 1531.

—— *Erotemata dialectices,* Basel, 1521.

Leonard Cox, *The Arte or Crafte of Rhethoryke,* London, *ca.* 1530.

Thomas Wilson, *The Rule of Reason, Conteining the Art of Logike,* London, 1551.

—— *The Arte of Rhetorique,* London, 1553.

Richard Rainolde, *A Booke Called the Foundacion of Rhetorike,* London, 1563.

---

[19] *Ibid.,* II, 237.   [20] *Ibid.,* II, 238.   [21] *Ibid.,* II, 175.

[22] The dates are those of the first editions. The editions or reprints used in this study are listed in the bibliography. For key to abbreviations used for references see p. xiii.

Raphe Lever, *The Arte of Reason, Rightly Termed Witcraft*, London, 1573.
Thomas Blundeville, *The Arte of Logick*, London, 1599.

GROUP 2: THE RAMISTS

Petrus Ramus, *Dialecticae institutiones*, Paris, 1543.
Audomarus Talaeus, *Rhetorica*, 1544?
Dudley Fenner, *The Artes of Logike and Rhetorike*, Middelburg, 1584.
Abraham Fraunce, *The Lawiers Logike*, London, 1588.
—— *The Arcadian Rhetorike*, London, 1588.
Charles Butler, *Rhetoricae libri duo*, London, 1598.
—— *Oratoriae libri duo*, Oxford, 1629.
John Hoskyns, *Direccions for Speech and Style*, Harley MS 4604, written
    ca. 1600.

GROUP 3: THE FIGURISTS

Joannes Susenbrotus, *Epitome troporum ac schematum et grammaticorum et
    rhetoricorum*, Zurich, 1540.
Richard Sherry, *A Treatise of Schemes and Tropes*, London, 1550.
—— *A Treatise of the Figures of Grammer and Rhetorike*, London, 1555.
Henry Peacham, *The Garden of Eloquence*, London, 1577.
—— *The Garden of Eloquence*; corrected and augmented by the first author;
    London, 1593.
George Puttenham, *The Arte of English Poesie*, London, 1589.
Angel Day, *The English Secretorie* [1586]: with a declaration of tropes,
    figures, and schemes [this later part is added in the second edition]; London,
    1592.

These English works had in Tudor times a popularity, a vitality, and
an importance astonishing to us today, due in part to the use of illustrations
from matter of intense interest to the readers for whom the books were
designed. The Latin works were school texts, but the English books
circulated among adults, especially among those of the court and of the
upper and middle classes. From 1551 to 1595 there were at least seven
editions of Wilson's *Rule of Reason* and eight of his *Arte of Rhetorique*
which was written, so the title page informs us, "for the use of all such
as are studious of Eloquence"—as who in intellectual circles in Tudor
England was not? Puttenham explicitly stated that he wrote his *Arte*
for courtiers, and particularly for ladies, to assist them in composing and
in appreciating polite verse. He drew his illustrations chiefly from the
best English poets of his time, such as Wyatt, Surrey, Sidney, and Dyer.
Fraunce, too, capitalized on the lively interest in the new literature of
the vernaculars by illustrating the topics of logic and the various forms

of the syllogism from Spenser's *Shepheardes Calender;* the figures of rhetoric from Sidney's *Arcadia* and his songs and sonnets, from Tasso's *Gerusalemme liberata, Aminta,* and *Torrismondo,* from Du Bartas' *Judith* and *La Semaine,* from the sonnets and eclogues of Boscan and Garcilasso. Fraunce's illustrations from these leading English, Italian, French, and Spanish writers, along with examples from Homer's *Iliad* and *Odyssey* and from Vergil's *Eclogues, Georgics,* and *Aeneid* emphasized the likeness of Renaissance literature to the classics which inspired it, a likeness dear to the literary hearts of the time. Angel Day's work, which went through eight editions before 1626, appealed especially to the middle class by adapting the figures of rhetoric to the practical needs of letter writing. In an age ardently devoted to the reading of the Bible, Peacham, like his countryman the Venerable Bede eight centuries earlier,[23] assured his readers that a knowledge of the figures of rhetoric "helpeth much for the better understanding of the holy Scriptures," [24] from which he drew most of his examples. Fenner, in the three editions of his work, took all of the illustrations for both his logic and his rhetoric from the Bible. Blundeville, like Rabanus Maurus seven centuries earlier, valued logic as a means to find the truth in Scripture and to perceive and confute the subtle deceits of heretics. On his title page he asserted that logic is very necessary to all students in any profession in order to know "how to defend any Argument against all subtill Sophisters, and cavelling Schismatikes, and how to confute their false Syllogismes, and captious arguments." The religious controversies of the sixteenth century are reflected in many of the illustrations in Wilson's *Rule of Reason.*

Thus the Tudor rhetoricians and logicians enhanced the universally recognized merit of the arts they treated by illustrating their application to matters of vital interest among men of their own time: to the understanding of the ancient classics and of the new vernacular literatures, to composition, to the reading of the Scriptures, and to religious controversy. It is quite natural, therefore, that Elizabethan literature should reflect the current zestful interest in rhetoric and logic. As Hardin Craig has observed:

Elizabethan literature is alive with debate. . . . It is no wonder that drama flourished, which is itself an art of contest, dialogue and debate, agreement and disagreement. The reason for this preoccupation with controversial utterance . . . arises from the conception of logic (or rather dialectic) as an in-

23 The Venerable Bede illustrated his *Liber de schematibus et tropis* wholly from the Bible.
24 Peacham, *The Garden of Eloquence,* 1577, title page.

strument for the discovery of truth. . . . The syllogism, supplemented by an acute knowledge of the fallacies, was the chosen and obvious instrument for the discovery of truth—by deduction and induction. . . . every question has two sides, and . . . the acutest minds would habitually see both sides. Now, drama itself, as just said, is debate, and the issues it loves to treat are debatable issues. Shakespeare, the acutest of Renaissance thinkers, has . . . an ability to see both sides of a question, and a sympathy with all sorts and conditions of men. . . . No one can tell whether Bolingbroke or Richard II is in the right. Is it not fair, then, to regard Shakespeare as an exemplification of controversial broadmindedness in an age of advocacy? [25]

It is only in their choice of illustrations, and often not even in that, that the works of the Tudor rhetoricians and logicians can claim any originality or independence; their sources were principally Latin works of the Renaissance scholars, Erasmus, Agricola, Melanchthon, Ramus, Talaeus, Mosellanus, Susenbrotus, used singly or in combination and derived in their turn from earlier works reaching back through Quintilian, Cicero, and the *Ad Herennium* ultimately to Aristotle and Gorgias.

There are among the English authors of the Renaissance, as among the Latin, obvious differences that dispose them into the three groups which in the present study are called the traditionalists, the Ramists, and the figurists.

Thomas Wilson is eminently the traditionalist. His *Arte of Rhetorique* presents the whole of the classical tradition of rhetoric with its five parts: invention, disposition, elocution, memory, and delivery. The opinion, however, that it is the only English work of Tudor times which does so, requires qualification. Wilson is also a traditionalist in his work on logic. In treating of invention, he depends directly on Agricola,[26] whose work is in the main Aristotelian tradition. Lever and Blundeville follow Aristotle even more closely, but, like Wilson, admit accretions and modifications contributed in the intervening ages. Leonard Cox's rhetoric, the earliest one in English, is mostly a translation of that part of Melanchthon's which treats of invention, and is admittedly incomplete. Cox belonged to the circle of Erasmus and Sir Thomas More. Rainolde's book is a school text which explains how the topics of invention are to be applied in the composition of fourteen kinds of "Oracions" and illustrates each by example. Except for the illustrations, some of which are probably

---

[25] Craig, *The Enchanted Glass*, pp. 156 f.
[26] See Crane, *Wit and Rhetoric in the Renaissance*, p. 54.

original, it is derived from Aphthonius, whose *Progymnasmata* in Latin was a standard text in the sixteenth-century schools of England and of the continent and had been used in schools for centuries.[27]

The Ramists—as Ramus and his collaborator Talaeus and their English adapters, Fenner, Fraunce, Butler, and, to some degree, Hoskyns, may be called—depart from the Aristotelian tradition not so much in content as in pedagogical method and to a slight degree in terminology. Ramus and Talaeus insist that they follow Aristotle but do not hesitate to improve upon him and more especially upon the Aristotelians, whose sterile method of teaching they sought to vitalize by relating logic to literature and to the discourse of life and to clarify by making a clean-cut division between the functions of logic and rhetoric. To logic the Ramists assign invention, disposition, and memory inasmuch as it is aided most by method, a subdivision of disposition; to rhetoric they assign elocution and delivery. Thus the five parts of the classical tradition are embodied in their logic and rhetoric texts when taken together, as the Ramists explicitly asserted they must be, since the two supplement each other. To logic belong the two essential processes of composition, namely, the investigation of the desired subject by means of the topics of invention, and the organization of the material thus derived into appropriate logical forms by means of a suitable method. This they call genesis. The same principles employed to apprehend the meaning of what one reads or hears is analysis. For the Ramists the functions of rhetoric are but two: to beautify composition and make it emotionally effective by means of a comparatively few figures of speech and to contribute the graces of good voice and gesture in the delivery of a speech.

The figurists, as Susenbrotus, Sherry, Peacham, Puttenham, and Day may be named, appear on superficial examination to treat only of elocution and to omit the four other traditional parts of classical rhetoric. A closer examination of their work, however, shows that their concept of figures is so inclusive as to omit little of what has ever been included in a theory of composition, for the approximately two hundred figures of speech

---

[27] See Johnson, "Two Renaissance Textbooks of Rhetoric: Aphthonius' *Progymnasmata* and Rainolde's *A Booke Called the Foundacion of Rhetorike*," *The Huntington Library Quarterly*, VI (August, 1943), 427–44. Hermogenes, a second century Greek rhetorician, devised rules for twelve orations or elementary exercises in composition. Aphthonius, a fourth-century Greek rhetorician, increased the exercises to fourteen and added an illustrative example of each. In the sixteenth century Lorich's Latin edition of Aphthonius became the most widely used textbook of Latin composition; even Priscian's Latin translation, (*ca.* 500 A.D.) of Hermogenes yielded to it. Rainolde's book is adapted from Lorich. See also Crane, *op. cit.*, pp. 62–69.

which they distinguish represent an analysis of practically every aspect of grammar, logic, and rhetoric.

One of the conclusions to which the present study leads is that in the works of all three of these groups of Renaissance writers there is a fundamental likeness despite obvious differences, for in all of them are discernible, to a degree not hitherto adequately recognized, the dominant features of Aristotle's rhetoric.[28] The present study stresses the likenesses of the Tudor works to one another, not their differences, and the important features in which they are at one with the classical tradition, whether they drew their theory of composition directly from the ancient treatises, which were eagerly studied, or indirectly through contemporary works ultimately derived from them.

4. The Tradition

Gabriel Harvey, writing to Spenser, speaks of "the best Philosophers, and namely Aristotle, that poynt us . . . to the very fountaines and head springes of Artes and Artificiall preceptes" (Smith, I, 103). From Aristotle came the most important and influential treatises on the intimately related arts of logic, rhetoric, and poetic. Logic and rhetoric are concerned with the communication of ideas directly from mind to mind through words; poetic, with the communication of experience indirectly by the creation of illusion, into which the reader may enter imaginatively to share the experience vicariously. Aristotle defines poetic as imitation, the kind of composition whereby the writer speaks to the reader not directly but mediately through the interposed creations of his imagination, such imitation as we describe today as creative or imaginative writing. Poetic employs, but subordinates, the arts of logic and rhetoric and of course presupposes grammar as necessary to the intelligibility of any kind of verbal communication. In the *Poetics* Aristotle distinguishes six elements of tragedy: plot, characters, dianoia, diction, music, and spectacle. Where dianoia, or thought, rather than action determines the course of events, logic, rhetoric, and poetic are fused, functioning simultaneously, as in Plato's dialogues, which Aristotle regarded as poems.

In his works on logic Aristotle distinguishes three divisions: scientific demonstration, treated in his *Analytics,* its matter necessary premises true and primary, its instrument the demonstrative syllogism, its result knowledge through formal causes, that is, true and universal knowledge; dialectic, treated in the *Topics,* its matter probable premises discussed

---

[28] This is shown in detail in Part Three.

in the spirit of inquiry, its instrument the dialectical syllogism and induction, its result opinion probable, but not certain or strictly demonstrable; and sophistic, treated in *De sophisticis elenchis*, its matter premises that seem to be generally accepted or appropriate, but really are not, discussed by "those who argue as competitors and rivals to the death" [29] seeking by whatever means to refute the opponent, its instrument the sophistic syllogism, apparent reasoning either fallacious or inappropriate, its result apparent refutation of the opponent, refutation not absolute but only relative, in order thereby at all costs to gain the victory and to appear wise. Rhetoric, Aristotle says, is the counterpart of dialectic: like dialectic, it has for its matter the probable, for its aim persuasion. But as instruments of persuasion it employs the enthymeme as the counterpart of the dialectical syllogism, and the example as the counterpart of induction. Precisely because their proper subject matter is opinion, that is, the probable, rhetoric and dialectic have the capacity to generate arguments on both sides of a question. Hence rhetoric is sometimes, and dialectic always, a form of disputation. But in the oration, its most characteristic form, and in the debate, which is a series of orations on opposite sides, rhetoric advances by continued discourse, whereas dialectic, as illustrated in Plato's dialogues, advances by interrupted discourse, the give and take of question and answer, of objection and counter-objection. Rhetoric, as Aristotle defines it, is the faculty of observing in any given case the available means of persuasion, and since the orator addresses a popular audience including untrained thinkers, his appeal is threefold: to their reason (*logos*), to their feelings (*pathos*), and to their confidence in his character, that is, in his virtue, competence, courtesy, good sense, good will (*ethos*). It thus appears, says Aristotle, that rhetoric is an offshoot of dialectic (*logos*) and also of ethical studies (*ethos* and *pathos*).[30]

By the wholeness and balance of this well-constructed system, Aristotle corrected the one-sidedness and superficiality of Gorgias and Protagoras, which Plato had exposed, particularly in his *Gorgias*.

The tradition was transmitted to later ages principally through Cicero,[31] who modified and developed it in both theory and practice, drawing eclectically on Aristotle, on Isocrates, and to a relatively slight degree on his own teacher Hermagoras. Cicero subordinated logic to

---

[29] Aristotle *De sophisticis elenchis* 3.165^{b} 13, in *Works*, Vol. I, translated into English under the editorship of W. D. Ross. All citations from Aristotle are from this edition.

[30] Aristotle *Rhetoric* 1.2.1356^{a} 25. He treats of the emotions and passions in his *Ethics* and his *Rhetoric*; today these are regarded as primarily within the province of psychology.

[31] Cicero's work takes no account of the *Analytics* or the *Poetics* of Aristotle.

rhetoric and incorporated a great part of it in his rhetorical treatises. Every careful method of arguing, according to Cicero, has two parts: invention and judgment.[32] Aristotle, he says, seems to have been the chief discoverer of each; the Stoics diligently pursued the latter but disregarded the former. Cicero followed Isocrates rather than Aristotle in emphasizing the graces of style and the value of figures, and in his orations he employed the three styles—the lofty, the intermediate, and the plain. In his rhetorical treatises he gave rules for memory and for delivery. Therefore, in Cicero's work and through it, the division of rhetoric into five parts—invention, disposition, elocution, memory, and pronunciation—a division which he attributed to numerous writers before him,[33] became firmly established in the tradition.[34] It was primarily through his youthful *De inventione* and his orations that Cicero affected the rhetoric of the Middle Ages; and through these and his more mature works on rhetoric, especially the *De oratore*, which later became available, he continued to be a dominant influence in the Renaissance. The *Rhetorica ad C. Herennium*, probably by Cornificius, but wrongly attributed throughout the Middle Ages to his younger contemporary Cicero and owing its great influence in part to Cicero's name, was the first Latin work which treated the rhetorical figures stressed by Gorgias and his pupil Isocrates and became the principal link in transmitting them to its own and later ages. Quintilian's *Institutio oratoria*, based mainly on Cicero and recovered by scholars in the fifteenth century, strengthened the classical tradition. Aristotle, the *Ad Herennium*, Cicero, and Quintilian were studied directly in the schools during the Renaissance and were the chief ultimate sources of the works on rhetoric and logic, whether in Latin or in the vernaculars.

The sixteenth-century texts on rhetoric and logic make frequent explicit reference to Tully and Quintilian and also to Aristotle, though often these references, especially to the last, represent intermediary rather than direct acquaintance. Unquestionably there had been in the course of centuries shifts of emphasis and other distortions of the tradition, as

[32] Cicero *Topica* ch. 2. This division became standard in treatises on logic. Abraham Fraunce, in *The Lawiers Logike*, fol. 5ᵛ, notes that Aristotle himself commends this division in 8 *Topics* [ch. 1] and 3 *Rhet.* [ch. 1].

[33] Cicero *De inventione* 1.7.

[34] Richard McKeon, in "Rhetoric in the Middle Ages," *Speculum*, XVII (January, 1942), 1–32, p. 4, comments: "Whatever the estimate critics and historians are disposed to make of Cicero's achievement, originality, and consistency, his choices and emphases fixed the influence and oriented the interpretation of ancient thought, Greek as well as Latin, at the beginning of the Middle Ages and again in the Renaissance."

scholars have pointed out.[35] Yet the tradition persisted, and its features are discernible in all the works which circulated in Shakespeare's England. Despite obvious differences, the Renaissance works are essentially alike and at one with the classical tradition. They recognize as important the traditional five parts of rhetoric—invention, disposition, elocution, memory, and utterance—even when they do not explicitly treat all of them.

Two of these parts, memory and utterance, because they relate only to the oral delivery of a speech, may be passed over here with a brief notice. In his *Arte of Rhetorique* Wilson, the traditionalist, gives the lengthiest treatment of memory in the Tudor works. The Ramists held that memory is assisted most by method, the proper disposition or ordering of ideas in accordance with logical principles, and that it is therefore a part of logic. Wilson and the Ramists, following Cicero and the *Ad Herennium* in their treatment of delivery, which they called utterance, pronunciation, or action, divided it into two parts, voice and gesture.[36] The figurists did not deal with memory, but they took into account voice and gesture. By the figure mimesis, explained Peacham,

we counterfeit not only what one sayd, but also utteraunce and gesture, immitating everything as it was . . . cutting it shorte, or drawing it out a long, with stammering, with loude or loe voyce, lisping, nodding the head, wincking, frowning, smiling . . . (1577 ed., sig. O iiii ᴿ)

A pittifull pronunciation is of great force: and moveth affections wonderfully, in expressing a wofull case, for the apte bending of the voyce to the quallity of the cause, is a Godly ornament in an Oratour. (*Ibid.*, sig. P iii ᵛ) . . . likewyse, that which the Oratoure hath uttered in whole and vehemente speech, he may repeate agayne with cold and quyet words. (*Ibid.*, sig. Q i ᴿ)

In their attitude toward invention, disposition, and elocution, the traditionalists, Ramists, and figurists apparently differ, but the differences

---

[35] Among them are the following: C. S. Baldwin, *Ancient Rhetoric and Poetic; Medieval Rhetoric and Poetic; Renaissance Literary Theory and Practice*; Clark, *Rhetoric and Poetry in the Renaissance*; Crane, *Wit and Rhetoric in the Renaissance*; Hultzen, "Aristotle's 'Rhetoric' in England before 1600," an unpublished dissertation presented to Cornell University, 1932; Herrick, *The Poetics of Aristotle in England*; Spingarn, *A History of Literary Criticism in the Renaissance*; Abelson, *The Seven Liberal Arts; a Study in Medieval Culture*; McKeon, "Rhetoric in the Middle Ages," *Speculum*, XVII (January, 1942), 1–32; Faral, "Les Arts poetiques du XIIᵉ et du XIIIᵉ siècle," in *Bibliothèque de l'École des Hautes Etudes*; Haskins, *The Renaissance of the Twelfth Century*; Paetow, *The Arts Course at Medieval Universities; with Special Reference to Grammar and Rhetoric*.
[36] Shakespeare takes account of voice and gesture in Hamlet's advice to the players (2.1.1–39).

on closer examination are seen to be superficial rather than fundamental. Consequently these three parts need to be examined in more detail.

5. Invention and Disposition

Aristotle treated invention in the first seven of his eight books of *Topics,* or dialectic, and also in his *Rhetoric,* especially in Book II, Chapter 23, where he enumerates twenty-eight topics [37] from which a speaker or writer may draw matter for whatever discourse he wishes to develop. Cicero wrote his *Topica* in response to the request of his friend the lawyer Trebatius, who said he could not understand Aristotle's *Topics* and wished for a clearer and simpler statement of its substance. Cicero presented his list of the topics of invention with great clarity as complete and exhaustive.

Every rule necessary for the finding of arguments is now concluded; so that when you have proceeded from definition, from division, from the name, from conjugates, from genus, from species, from similarity, from difference, from contraries, from adjuncts, from consequents, from antecedents, from things incompatible with one another, from causes, from effects, from a comparison with things greater or less or equal—there is no topic of argument whatever remaining to be discovered.[38]

To these sixteen topics internal to the subject of inquiry he added a seventeenth, testimony, which does not depend on the art of the investigator, but requires recourse to external aids such as laws, contracts, witnesses, tortures, oaths, prophecies, divinations, and oracles. Testimony evokes belief if it proceeds from authority such as that derived from a man's character, knowledge, experience, age, or position.

Cicero's *Topica,* probably the clearest and most concise treatment of invention, was the standard text for beginning this study in the grammar schools of Tudor England. Regarded sometimes as a work on rhetoric, more often as one on logic, it became basic to all later studies of the kind.

Whether the topics or places of invention belong to rhetoric, to logic,

---

[37] In the *Rhetoric,* Bk. III, ch. 15, Aristotle further enumerates sixteen lines of argument designed to allay prejudice. Their purpose is to promote *ethos* and *pathos;* their method, disputation: excuse, counterattack, admission of facts while denying alleged evil motives, etc. In Book II, ch. 24, Aristotle enumerates ten lines of spurious argument employed by the sophists.

[38] Perfecta est omnis argumentorum inveniendorum praeceptio, ut, cum profectus sis a definitione, a partitione, a notatione, a coniugatis, a genere, a formis, a similitudine, a differentia, a contrariis, ab adiunctis, a consequentibus, ab antecedentibus, a repugnantibus, a causis, ab effectis, a comparatione maiorum minorum parium, nulla praeterea sedes argumenti quaerenda sit. (*Topica,* 18.71)

or to both was a moot question. Aristotle had not clearly defined the relation between dialectical and rhetorical investigation; many of the topics
in his *Rhetoric* were the same as those treated also in his *Topics*, or dialectic. According to Cicero, Hermagoras made the important distinction
between thesis, the general or theoretical question, and hypothesis, the
particularized or practical question, but then wrongly assigned both to
the orator, whereas, remarks Cicero, the first belongs properly to the
philosopher.[39] Accepting Cicero's view, Boethius in his *De differentiis
topicis* came nearest to stating a clear distinction between dialectical and
rhetorical investigation, but he admitted that the two tend to overlap;
for, if the dialectician takes up a dispute as of persons or deeds, he will
bring it under a general or philosophical question, which is his proper
concern; likewise, if the rhetorician takes up a general question, he will
treat it with reference to certain persons, times, deeds, circumstances, for
such particularized questions are his proper concern.[40] The allocation of
the topics of invention was the primary question dividing the traditionalists and the Ramists.

a. The Traditionalists.—The traditionalists held that the topics of invention belong to both logic and rhetoric. Thomas Wilson, in his *Arte
of Rhetorique*, agreed with Boethius that while both the logical and
rhetorical forms of investigation have their proper subject matter, they
tend to overlap.

Thinges generally spoken without all circumstaunces, are more proper unto
the *Logician*, who talketh of thinges universally, without respect of person,
time, or place. And yet notwithstanding, *Tullie* doth say, that whosoever will
talke of particular matter must remember, that within the same also is comprehended a general. (p. 2)

Cox, following Melanchthon, who had taken the position of Hermagoras, added to the generally recognized three kinds of orations—
the deliberative, the judicial, and the demonstrative—a fourth kind, the
logical, which deals with a general question, either simple, as what justice
is, or compound, as whether justice be a virtue. It must be developed, says
Cox, according to the precepts of logic, and set forth with the graces
of rhetoric.

[39] Cicero *De inventione*, 1.6. Cf. *De partitione oratoriae*, ch. 18. Also compare Aristotle,
Topics, Bk. III, ch. 6, where he treats of the definite and indefinite thesis.
[40] Boethius (480?–524?) *De differentiis topicis*, in Migne *Patrologia Latina*, LXIV,
1177, 1205–6, 1216.

Nothinge can be perfectly and propryely knowen but by rules of Logike, whiche is nothynge but an observacyon or a diligent markynge of nature . . . so then the sure Judgement of argumentes or reasons muste be lernyd of the Logicyan but the crafte to set them out with plesaunte fygures and to delate the matter longith to the Rhetorycian.[41]

In *The Arte of Rhetorique* Wilson lists as places or topics of rhetorical inquiry such practical and particularized questions as what was done, who did it, where, with whose help, how, when. In a deliberative oration the investigation would turn on whether the proposed action would be honest, profitable, possible, necessary, difficult, easy, pleasant, safe, just, prudent, honorable, according to custom. Most suited to a demonstrative oration eulogizing a man, especially one dead, says Wilson, are the places of persons, that is, gifts of mind, body, and fortune. He lists ten: ancestrie, the Realme, the Shire, or Towne, the sexe or kinde, education, inclination of nature, attempts worthie, wise counsaile given, time of departing this worlde, his Tombe and all such honours as are used in Funeralles (*AR*, p. 120). A judicial oration in particular would employ various forms of testimony, such as laws, contracts, witnesses.

Wilson points out, however, the superiority even in rhetoric of the more general topics of logic because they are more searching, more fundamental.

I wish that every man should desire, & seeke to have his *Logique* perfit, before he looke to profite in *Rhetorique,* considering the ground and confirmation of causes, is for the most part gathered out of *Logique.* (*AR*, p. 113)

Places to confirme things are fower: Things honest, Profitable, Easie to be done, Hard to be done. Many learned will have recourse to the places of *Logicke* in steede of these fower places, when they take in hand to commend any such matter. . . .

The places of *Logicke* are these. Definition, Causes, Parts, Effects, Things adjoyning, Contraries. . . . I thinke these of *Logicke* must first bee minded, ere the other can well be had. For what is he, that can cal a thing honest, and by reason prove it, except he first know what the thing is: the which he cannot better doe, then by defining the nature of the thing. Againe, how shall I know whether mine attempt be easie or hard if I knowe not the efficient cause, or be assured how it may be done. In affirming it to bee possible, I shall not better knowe it then by searching the ende, and learning by *Logicke*, what is the finall cause of every thing. (p. 23)

---

[41] Cox, *The Arte or Crafte of Rhethoryke,* ed. by F. I. Carpenter, pp. 45–48.

The traditionalists Wilson, Cox, and Rainolde do not attempt in their works on rhetoric a general or systematic treatment of invention in one place. Instead, following their sources, they list for each kind of oration the topics best suited to it, sometimes combining the general topics of logic with the more particularized topics of rhetoric related to persons and circumstances. The pattern which Rainolde prescribes for composing a "Confirmacion" is limited to rhetorical topics.

1. It shall behove you first, for the entring of the oracion, to induce a reprehension againste those, whiche have confuted as a truthe, that which you will confirme.
2. In the seconde parte, place the exposicion and meanyng of the aucthours sentence.
3. Shewe the matter to be manifest.
4. Credible.
5. Possible.
6. Agreying to the truthe.
7. Shewe the facte comelie.
8. Profitable.[42]

For gnome, or sentence, "an oracion in fewe wordes, shewyng a godlie precept of life, exhorting, or diswayding," [43] he combines rhetorical and logical topics. The latter are marked with asterisks, supplied by the present writer.

1. The praise of the aucthour.
2. The Exposicion of the sentence.
* 3. A Confirmacion in the strength of the cause.
* 4. A conference, of the contrarie.
* 5. A similitude.
6. The example.
* 7. The testimonie of aucthours, shewing the like.
8. Then adde the conclusion.[44]

[42] Rainolde, *A Booke Called the Foundacion of Rhetorike*, fol. xxviii[v]. [43] *Ibid.*, fol. xx[r].
[44] That Shakespeare used these forms as presented by Aphthonius, whose work Rainolde adapted, is noted by T. W. Baldwin. When Malvolio, wearing yellow stockings crossgartered, comes before Olivia, he confirms his hopes by checking with four of the rules of confirmation her reactions and the letter which he thinks she wrote to him: the matter is manifest (he has "limed" Olivia); it is credible and possible (he finds "no incredulous or unsafe circumstance"); it agrees with the truth ("concurs directly with the letter . . . everything adheres together.") (*TN*, 3.4.71–92.) King Henry IV concludes his apostrophe to sleep with the gnome, or sentence, "Uneasy lies the head that wears a crown" (*2H4*, 3.1.4–31). The matter of this speech is adapted from the annotations of the sixteenth-

Notwithstanding the clarity of Cicero's *Topica* and the wide use of his book as a school text and despite his claim that the seventeen topics of invention he treats are complete and exhaustive, a desire for more minute distinctions resulted in some diagreement among the traditionalists as to their number. Thomas Wilson, in *The Rule of Reason*, lists twenty-four places of logic; these are his translation into English of Agricola's re-working of the seventeen topics of Cicero and the twenty-four of Themistius, which Boethius had set side by side in his *De differentiis topicis*. Raphe Lever, while remaining within the traditional boundaries, attempted an avowedly original treatment by appointing the ten categories of Aristotle as places and adding and interlacing others which could not conveniently be referred to them, making in all twenty-four places, which he later subdivided to make forty-four. Furthermore, some of the logicians among the traditionalists entered territory usually assigned to rhetoric and grammar. Thus, Thomas Blundeville, in his table, lists seventeen places of persons as well as thirty-five places of things; [45] the latter include figurative speech and grammatical comparison of the positive, comparative, and superlative degrees.

Disposition, or arrangement of a speech, was explicitly discussed by only one of the Tudor rhetoricians. In *The Arte of Rhetorique* Wilson defined disposition as the ordering of the parts of an oration. He distinguished two kinds. The first is merely the traditional sequence: exordium, narration, confirmation, confutation, peroration. The second admits a variation from that order to gain certain desired effects, principally through the weighing of reasons and the placing of the strongest reasons at the beginning and at the end, the weakest in the middle. In his *Rule of Reason*, Wilson, like the other logicians of the traditionalist group, treated disposition or judgment in terms of definition, division, method, propositions, and the syllogism.

b. The Ramists.—The Ramists differed from the traditionalists in ignoring the rhetorical topics—such as the credible, the profitable, the difficult—and in considering only the logical topics. In opposition to the traditionalists they flatly denied that invention and disposition are common to both logic and rhetoric. They insisted that they belong only to

---

century editors of Aphthonius, and the framework is that of an illustration from Priscian which they added. *Op. cit.*, II, 322–27.

[45] Melanchthon, in his "Erotemata dialectices," also treats *loci personarum* (11) in addition to *loci rerum* (28). See *Opera, Corpus reformatorum*, ed. by Bretschneider and Bindseil, XIII, 659–63.

logic.[46] Abraham Fraunce states this position forcefully in *The Lawiers Logike*.

What precepts soever the common Rhetoricians put downe for ordering of *Exordiums* and framing and disposing of the whole course of their speeche fitly and according to cause, auditors, time, place, and such like circumstances; all these I say, are altogether Logicall, not in any respect perteining to Rhetoricke, but as a Rhetor may bee directed by Logicall precepts of judgement and disposition. (fol. 115ʳ)

The Ramists asserted that neither the distinction between necessary propositions and those merely contingent or probable nor that between true propositions and false demands such separate treatment according to subject matter as Aristotle had given in his *Analytics*, his *Topics* and *Rhetoric*, and his *De sophisticis elenchis*. Fraunce reasons thus:

Because of these two kinds of conceipts, *Aristotle* woulde needes make two Logikes, the one for Science, the other for Opinion: wherein (if so it may be sayde of so great a Philosopher) it seemeth hee was but an *Opinator*. For although among thinges conceaved and knowne, some bee necessary and unfallible, some doubtfull and contingent, yet the Arte of Knowing and Reasoning of the same (I meane Logike) is only one and the same, as the sight of the eye in perceyving all colours, bee they chaungeable or not chaungeable. And as well might a man say there must bee two arts of Grammer (if Grammer bee a distinct Art, one for courtly speeche, an other for country talke: or two distinct arts of making of cups, one for golden cuppes, an other for cuppes of silver, as two Logikes, one for unfallible Argumentes, and another for Contingent. Therefore one Logike suffiseth to dispute of all thinges, necessary or contingent whatsoever. Yet this one Logike her selfe in respect of her preceptes is always necessary and never contingent, for otherwise it were no Art, but the application of it may bee in contingent causes as well as necessary. (5ᵛ)
. . . as for the third kinde of Logike, which they call *Elenchticall*, seeing it is no Logike at all, but rather the abuse and perversion of Logike, I see no cause why it should be taught in Logike: yet if any man thinke that the true preceptes of Logike once knowne, will not be sufficient to descry the falsenesse of sophisticall argumentations, he may for his contentation seeke for a full discourse

---

[46] Thus Gabriel Harvey, in true Ramist fashion, divided the twelve books of Quintilian's *Institutio oratoria*: "The first two bookes, preparative. The five next, Logique for Invention, and disposition. The fower following, Rhetorique for Elocution, & pronunciation: Logique for memory: an accessary, and shaddow of disposition. The last, A supplement, and discourse of such appurtenaunces, as may otherwyse concerne an Orator to knowe and practise." Moore-Smith, *Gabriel Harvey's Marginalia*, p. 110. For a clear outline of the Ramist theory on this point see p. 380, below.

thereof out of some commentarie, and not overcharge the Art it selfe with unnecessary institutions. (6 ʳ) . . . Artificiall Logike then is the polyshing of natural wit, as discovering the validitie of everie reason, bee it necessary, whereof cometh science: or contingent, whence proceedeth opinion. (5 ʳ)

If, then, as the Ramists held, there is only one art of reasoning which includes both the necessarily true and the probable, it follows that there is only one art concerned with the invention and disposition of arguments, the art of logic. On these premises the Ramists allocated to rhetoric only style and delivery. Yet while insisting on this strict division, they, even more than the traditionalists, emphasized the close relationship of logic and rhetoric and the necessity of using both together as tools of analysis or reading and of genesis or composition. For this reason the Ramist texts are in pairs.[47] William Kempe and John Brinsley, schoolmasters who wrote on education during Shakespeare's lifetime, were Ramists. In *The Education of Children* (1588) Kempe describes the vital integration of the three arts of language in grammar school practice.

First the scholler shal learne the precepts concerning the divers sorts of arguments in the first part of Logike, (for without them Rhetorike cannot be well understood) then shall followe the tropes and figures in the first part of Rhetorike, wherein he shall employ the sixth part of his studie, and all the rest in learning and handling good authors: as are *Tullies Offices,* his Orations, *Caesars Commentaries, Virgils Aeneis, Ovids Metamorphosis,* and *Horace.* In whom for his first exercise of unfolding the Arte, he shall observe the examples of the hardest poynts in Grammar, of the arguments in Logike, of the tropes and figures in Rhetorike, referring every example to his proper rule, as before. Then he shall learne the two latter parts also both of Logike and Rhetorike. . . . And by this time he must observe in authors all the use of the Artes, as not only the words and phrases, not only the examples of the arguments; but also the axiome, wherein every argument is disposed; the syllogisme, whereby it is concluded; the method of the whole treatise, and the passages, whereby the parts are joyned together. Agayne he shall observe not only every trope, every figure, aswell of words as of sentences; but also the Rhetoricall pronunciation and gesture fit for every word, sentence, and affection.

And so let him take in hand the exercise of all these three Artes at once in making somewhat of his owne, first by imitation . . . then let him have a

[47] Hultzen, in his "Aristotle's 'Rhetoric' in England before 1600," finds Fraunce's *Lawiers Logike* and *Arcadian Rhetorike,* taken together, the nearest approach, and that not very close, to Aristotle's *Rhetoric.* Butler in his *Oratoriae libri duo,* treats invention as the other Ramists do in their logic texts. And under disposition, he treats the proposition and syllogism; but he subordinates logic to oratory in the manner of Cicero and Quintilian.

like theame to prosecute with the same artificiall instruments, that he findeth in his author.[48]

Brinsley explains in greater detail just how the precepts of logic and rhetoric were applied in composition.

For the manner of writing downe the Theames by schollers of judgement, it may not be amisse where leisure will serve, to cause the schollers to write them thus: In the first Margent towards the left hand, together with the severall parts of the Theame (as *Exord. Narratio, Confirmatio, Confutatio, Conclusio,* being set in great letters over against each part) to set also the heads of the severall arguments; chiefly against the Confirmation: as *Causa, Effectum:* like as *Apthonius* doth set his places, à *Causa,* à *Contrario.* And in the latter side of the page, towards the right hand, to set the severall tropes or figures, but in two or three letters. As for *Metonymia Efficientis,* no more but *Met. Effic.* or the like . . .[49]

In *The Scholemaster* Roger Ascham tells of the happy effects achieved by his royal pupil in applying the precepts of logic and rhetoric to her reading of the classics.

And a better, and nerer example herein, may be, our most noble Queene *Elizabeth* . . . the mynde by dailie marking, first, the cause and matter: than, the wordes and phrases: next, the order and compos[it]ion: after the reason and argumentes: than the formes and figures of both the tonges [Greek and Latin]: lastelie, the measure and compas of everie sentence, must nedes, by litle and litle drawe unto it the like shape of eloquence, as the author doth use, which is red.[50]

As to the number of topics, Brinsley had his pupils distinguish ten.

The following of those tenne first and chiefe heads of reasoning; to wit, from Causes, Effects, Subjects, Adjuncts, Disagreeable things, Comparisons, Notations, Distributions, Definitions, Testimonies, (to one of which each of *Apthonius* or *Tullies* places do belong) is farre the easiest, surest, and plainest way. (p. 183)

In addition to these ten, Ramus himself had listed conjugates. Merely by further subdivision, Butler showed twenty topics on his table, and Fraunce treated nineteen; both of these writers rejected notation and conjugates. All of the Ramists omitted antecedents and consequents.

[48] Kempe, *The Education of Children,* sig. G2ᵛ.
[49] Brinsley, *Ludus literarius; or, The Grammar Schoole,* ed. by E. T. Campagnac, p. 185.
[50] Ascham, *The Scholemaster,* fol., 35ʳ. Upton edition, p. 105.

With these exceptions their list of topics is, as Brinsley remarked, the same as Cicero's.

Nothwithstanding the variety of opinion as to the number of topics or places, there was complete unanimity among all Renaissance groups as to their nature, use, and importance. The traditionalist Wilson expresses the common judgment of the time in *The Rule of Reason* when he asserts:

A place is, the resting corner of an argument (fol. 37 ʳ) . . . [the orator] may have arguments at will, if he search the places which are none other thing, but the store house of reason and the fountaine of all wisedome. (fol. 61 ᵛ)

Thus we see how large the use is of these places, for not only shall any one bee able to speake right aptly, and very well to the purpose, whensoever he shal seeke out the trueth of any cause by diligent search, and raunging in these corners, but also hee shall largely set out his matter, with much delite, and orderly tel his tale, with singular profite, and passing gaine. And therefore I would wish that Logike were alwaies the square to rule our talke, and made the very touch stone to trie our reasons, such as in weightie matters, full ofte are alledged, and then I would not doubt, but that folly should the sooner bee espied, and wise mens sayinges the better estemed. (fol. 61 ʳ)

The practical use of logic [51] and rhetoric in the affairs of life is insisted on by Fraunce even more ardently than by Wilson.

Logike is an art of teaching . . . whose vertue is seene not onely in teaching others, but also in learning thy selfe, in discoursing, thinking, meditating, and framing of thine owne, as also in discussing, perusing, searching and examining what others have either delivered by speach, or put downe in writing; this is called *Analysis*, that *Genesis*, and in them both consisteth the whole use of Logike.

As farre then as mans reason can reach, so farre extendeth it selfe the use and vertue of this art of reasoning, . . . Men reason in schooles as Philosophers, in Westminster as Lawyers, in Court as Lords, in Countrey as worldly

---

[51] The most accessible Ramist work on logic is Milton's expansion of Ramus's *Dialectica*, entitled *Artis logicae plenior institutio, ad Petri Rami methodum concinnata*, ed. and tr. by Allan H. Gilbert, in *The Works of John Milton*, Vol. XI. In *The Pilgrimage to Parnassus* (*ca.* 1597) is a contemporary comment on the clarity of the Ramist method. Even Stupido can learn logic as Ramus presented it: "I have (I pray God prosper my labours!) analised a peece of an hommelie according to Ramus, and surelie in my minde and simple opinion Mr. Peter maketh all things verie plaine and easie. As for Setons *Logique*, trulie I never looke on it but it makes my head ache!" (lines 324–29). The Ramists made a special point of illustrating the principles of logic by examples from literature. Fraunce, for instance, uses Spenser's *Shepheardes Calender*. See Part Three.

husbands . . . the true use of Logike is as well apparant in simple playne and easie explication, as in subtile, strict, and concised probation. Reade *Homer,* reade *Demosthenes,* reade *Virgill,* read *Cicero,* reade *Bartas,* reade *Torquato Tasso,* reade that most worthie ornament of our English tongue, the *Countess of Penbrookes Arcadia* and therein see the true effectes of natural Logike which is the ground of artificiall . . . (fol. 3 $^{r-v}$) Let no day passe without some practice, either in making, framing, and inventing of our selves, or in resolving & dissolving of things doone by others, for the triall of their skil, and confirmation of our owne. Neither would I have this practise continued onely in reading, or writing, but in every civill assembly or meeting: wherein yet I will not bee so severe a censor, as to exact every speech to the formall rules of axiomes, syllogismes, &c. It shall be sufficient for us to folow a more easie and elegant kinde of disputation, joyning Rhetorike with Logike, and referring that precise straitnesse unto Philosophicall exercises.

Neyther let any man thinke, that because in common meetings and assemblies the woordes and tearmes of Logike bee not named, therefore the force and operation of Logike is not there used and apparent. For, as in Grammer wee name neyther Noune, Pronoune, Verbe, nor any other parte of speech: and as in Rhetorike, we make mention neyther of *Metonymia, Synecdoche, Exclamatio,* nor any other Rhetoricall figure or trope: yet use in our speech the helpe of the one in speaking grammatically, and the direction of the other in talking eloquently: so, although in common conference wee never name syllogismes, axiomes, propositions, assumptions, & other woords of art, yet doo wee secretly practise them in our disputations, the vertue whereof is, to make our discourses seeme true to the simple, and probable to the wise. (120 ^{r})

Despite differences as to the allocation of the topics of invention and their precise number, the traditionalists and Ramists clearly agreed on their importance and their vital function in providing matter for discourse. Both groups considered the general topics of logic the more fundamental, even for rhetorical use, and with minor exceptions and divergences accepted Cicero's seventeen topics.

6. Elocution or Style

The rhetoricians of the sixteenth century agreed in conceiving elocution or style as concerned mainly with the figures of speech, but they differed as to the scope of the figures and their number. The figures have a long history. Plato and Aristotle reprehended the excessive ornateness of Gorgias. Isocrates, the pupil of Gorgias, reduced this extravagance of ornament and used figures with more art. In the third book of his *Rhetoric* Aristotle took up the discussion of style, for, as he remarked,

The arts of language cannot help having a small but real importance, whatever it is we have to expound to others: the way in which a thing is said does affect its intelligibility. (1404 ª 8)

With regard to style Aristotle was concerned principally with lucidity, vividness, appropriateness, structure, and prose rhythm, but he devoted some attention to figures. He did not name many of those which he described, but he favored metaphor, simile, synecdoche, prosopopoeia, antonomasia, periphrasis, all of which tend to promote vividness; likewise antithesis, isocolon, homoioteleuton, anaphora, epistrophe, polysyndeton, and asyndeton, figures which emphasize balance in periodic structure and affect prose rhythm. He counseled the avoidance of zeugma, parenthesis, and in general whatever tends to ambiguity and obscurity, although he liked antanaclasis and paronomasia, which are figures of deliberate ambiguity. Nearly half of the *Rhetorica ad C. Herennium,* contemporary with Cicero and influential as a school text throughout the Middle Ages and the Renaissance, was devoted to style, chiefly the figures. Cicero treated the same elements of style as did Aristotle, but he was more hospitable to the figures, enumerating them in *De oratore* and again, reducing their number, in *Orator.* He used them extensively in his orations, especially those which rise to the lofty style. Quintilian reviewed Cicero's presentation of the figures before giving his own more detailed treatment, and he told why he excluded some which Cicero had included. He stated clearly his own concept of figures.

Consider what we are to understand by the word figure; for it is used in two senses; signifying, in the one, any form of words, whatever it may be, as bodies, of whatever they be composed, have some certain shape; in the other, in which it is *properly* termed a figure, any deviation, either in thought or expression, from the ordinary and simple method of speaking, as our bodies assume different postures when we sit, lie, or look back. . . . If we adopt the first and general sense, then, there will be no part of language that is not *figured.* . . . But if particular habits, and, as it were, gestures of language, are to receive this designation, that only must here be regarded as a figure, which deviates, by poetical or oratorical phraseology, from the simple and ordinary modes of speaking. Thus we shall be right in saying that one sort of style is . . . destitute of figures, (and this is no small fault) and another . . . diversified with figures. . . . Let the definition of a figure, then, be *a form of speech artfully varied from common usage.*[52]

[52] Quare primum intuendum est, quid accipere debeamus figuram. Nam duobus modis dicitur: uno qualiscunque forma sententiae, sicut in corporibus, quibus, quoquo modo sunt

This definition was accepted by the Tudor rhetoricians of all three groups. For example, Puttenham analyzes the purpose and scope of figurative language.

Figurative speech is a noveltie of language evidently (and yet not absurdly) estranged from the ordinarie habite and manner of our dayly talke and writing and figure it selfe is a certaine lively or good grace set upon wordes, speaches and sentences to some purpose and not in vaine, giving them ornament or efficacie by many maner of alterations in shape, in sounde, and also in sence, sometime by way of surplusage, sometime by defect, sometime by disorder, or mutation, & also by putting into our speaches more pithe and substance, subtiltie, quicknesse, efficacie or moderation, in this or that sort tuning and tempring them, by amplification, abridgement, opening, closing, enforcing, meekening or otherwise disposing them to the best purpose. (p. 159)

With the exception of Hoskyns, the rhetoricians of the three Renaissance groups employed the traditional division of figures into tropes and schemes, and the further division of schemes into those that are grammatical and those that are rhetorical. A trope, such as a metaphor, turns the significance of a word or sentence from its proper meaning to another not proper, but yet near it in order to increase its force. Grammatical schemes were subdivided into orthographical and syntactical schemes; rhetorical schemes, into figures of words and figures of sentence or thought. The rhetorical figures of words were figures of repetition. Some authors gave the name figures of amplification to a certain group of the figures of thought. In *The Arcadian Rhetorike* Fraunce remarked that tropes confer on language a certain grace, figures of words a kind of delicacy fit to delight, and figures of thought a majesty and force apt to persuade. (Sig. E 4 ᵛ)

The table on page 35 shows how the figures in the Renaissance works [53] compare in number with those in the *Rhetorica ad C. Herennium*,[54] in Cicero's *De oratore*, and in Quintilian's *Institutio oratoria*.

composita, utique habitus est aliquis; altero, quo proprie schema dicitur, in sensu vel sermone aliqua a vulgari et simplici specie cum ratione mutatio, sicut nos sedemus, incumbimus, respicimus. . . . In quo ita loquimur, tanquam omnis sermo habeat figuram. . . . Sed si habitus quidam et quasi gestus sic appellandi sunt, id demum hoc loco accipi schema oportebit, quod sit a simplici atque in promptu posito dicendi modo poetice vel oratorie mutatum. Sic enim verum erit, aliam esse orationem . . . carentem figuris, quod vitium non inter minima est, aliam . . . est figuratam. . . . Ergo figura sit arte aliqua novata forma dicendi. (*Institutio oratoria*, 9.1.10–14 [Loeb Classical Library]. Translation by J. S. Watson [Bohn's Classical Library], II, 146.)

[53] Rainolde gives almost no attention to figures; Cox, none at all.

[54] Faral, *op. cit.*, pp. 52–54, presents a table showing the degree of correspondence of the

According to the number of figures dealt with, the Ramists represent one extreme and the figurists the other. Yet they are not so far apart as the difference in number might suggest, for the figurists incorporated in their figures much of what the Ramists treated in their logic texts, since, as the former often remarked, many of the figures are derived from the topics of invention. The figurists, like the traditionalists and the Ramists, had a high regard for invention. Sherry included a brief but pointed section on invention and proofs in his *Treatise of Schemes and Tropes* (1550). Angel Day speaks of

invention first, wherein plentifully is searched and considered, what kinde of matter, how much variety of sentences, what sorts of figures, how many similitudes, what approbations, diminutions, insinuations, and circumstances are presently needfull, or furthering to the matter in handling. (p. 14)

It would be a mistake to regard the treatises of the figurists as limited to a discussion of style in the narrow sense.[55] Puttenham, eager to bestow upon the poet the right to use the rhetorical figures of thought, which he considered pre-eminent, declared the poet to be the most ancient orator (p. 196). Peacham emphasized the value of the figures as means of persuasion, considering

the knowledge of them so necessary, that no man can read profytably, or understand perfectlye eyther Poets, Oratours, or the holy Scriptures, without them: nor any Oratoure able by the waight of his wordes, to perswade his hearers, having no helpe of them. (Epistle dedicatory, A. iii ʳ, 1577 edition)

In terms of the three-fold means of persuasion basic in Aristotle's *Rhetoric,* namely, *logos, pathos,* and *ethos,* and of the aesthetic aspects of grammar such as are touched on in his discussion of style, the fundamental likeness among the three groups of sixteenth-century works becomes clear. When the approximately two hundred figures which the Tudor theorists distinguished are arranged under these four headings, it becomes evident that the work of the figurists covered practically the

---

figures in nine leading rhetorical works of the twelfth and thirteenth centuries to those in the *Rhetorica ad C. Herennium.*

[55] All the Renaissance groups valued the figures as means to enhance style. In the words of Puttenham's recent editors: "The figures are the sum of all the resources (other than metrical) by which poetry conveys its special overplus of excitement or stimulation; they are the sum, expressed in Elizabethan terms, of the types of ambiguity, the obliquities, the transferences, the echoes and controlled associations, which lift poetry above mere statement and by which the poet lets odd and unexpected lights into his subject, 'drawing it,' says Puttenham, 'from plainnesse and simplicitie to a certaine doublenesse.' " (p. lxxx)

FIGURES OF SPEECH [a]

	I. TROPES		II. SCHEMES GRAMMATICAL		III. SCHEMES RHETORICAL		TOTAL	VICES
	Of Words	Of Sentences	Orthographical	Syntactical	Of Words	Of Thought and Amplification		
1. *Rhet. ad. Her.*	10				35	20	65	
2. *Cic. De or.*	4				41	46	91	
3. Quintilian	14	1(5)		8	29	38	89	14
4. Wilson	8		6		24	41	80	
5. Talaeus	4				9	10	23	
6. Fenner	4(8)				9	10	23(27)	
7. Fraunce	4(8)		13		9	10(11)	23(28)	2
8. Butler	4(11)				8(10)	10(31)	22(65)	21
9. Hoskyns	6			3	13	28	50	
10. Susenbrotus	9	10	15	32	14	60	132	
11. Sherry 1550	7	8	11	12	41	25	104	16
12. Sherry 1555	7	8	12	12	20	60	119	22
13. Peacham 1577	9	10	14	42	24	85	184	10
14. Peacham 1593	8	10		18	24	123	165	15
15. Puttenham	10	12	6		9	52	107	
16. Day	7	9		21	12	44	93	

[a] Because some authors list separately figures which others treat as subdivisions, a comparison of mere numbers is misleading. The same figure is sometimes treated in more than one section of a work and counted each time. For example, Wilson names five tropes of sentences but prefers to treat four of them under other classifications. In his table of figures Butler agrees with the other Ramists, but in his text he introduces additional figures which bring the number up to the totals indicated in parentheses. Similar additions of other writers are similarly indicated. Because Hoskyns uses a different and original classification, his figures have been reclassified here in the traditional groupings for purposes of comparison. The classification by Puttenham is novel in words rather than in meaning. He himself says (pp. 160, 163) that his auricular figures are orthographical and syntactical, his sensable figures are tropes, and his sententious figures, with some exceptions, are figures of thought. (For a more precise comment on Puttenham's classification in relation to the traditional one, especially Quintilian's, and for parallels with Quintilian see La Rue Van Hook, "Greek Rhetorical Terminology in Puttenham's 'The Arte of English Poesie,'" in *Transactions of the American Philological Association*, XLV [1914], 113, note 9). The vices of speech are listed above only where they are distinguished from the figures, not where they themselves are called figures, as in the work of Susenbrotus, of Day, and of Peacham in 1577.

same ground as the combined works on logic and rhetoric, whether traditionalist or Ramist. The figures under *logos*, constituting by far the most numerous and the most important group, best illustrate the parallel between the works of the logicians and the figurists, for many of the examples cited by the logicians to illustrate the topics and forms of logic are exactly parallel to those cited by the figurists as figures. Some of the figures are identical with logical forms, for example, the dilemma, which was regarded as both a figure and a form of reasoning. That the figures of thought were understood to function under *logos* is clear from the fact that the Ramists treated the substance of them in their logic texts and the figurists frequently mentioned the topics and forms of logic on which they are based. The tropes likewise function under *logos*, as the Ramists recognized, for although they treated them in their rhetoric texts, they related them strictly to the logical topics from which they are derived.[56] The figures may accordingly be reorganized as follows:

Grammar: schemes of words; of construction
           the vices of language
           figures of repetition

Logos: the figures related to
           (*a*) logical topics: testimony, definition, division, genus, species, adjunct, contrary, contradictory, similarity, dissimilarity, comparison, cause, effect, antecedent, consequent, notation, conjugates
           (*b*) logical forms, as the syllogism, enthymeme, sorites, dilemma
           (*c*) the devices of disputation

Pathos: the figures of affection and vehemence

Ethos: the figures revealing courtesy, gratitude, commendation, forgiveness of injury

This reorganization makes the numerous figures more significant by ordering them in groups fulfilling four fundamental functions, somewhat as the periodic table makes the chemical elements more significant by ordering them in families having similar properties. By thus correlating the figures with the whole body of theory in logic and in the parts of rhetoric other than elocution this reorganization emphasizes the completeness of the pattern and the interdependence of its parts, for

[56] The Ramists admitted four tropes. They distinguished metonymy of cause, of effect, of subject, of adjunct; synecdoche of genus, of species, of the whole, of the parts. They explained that irony is based on the contrary; metaphor, on similitude.

every part gains meaning from its relation to the other parts and to the whole.

The essential general theory of composition and of reading current in Shakespeare's England, as expressed in the definitions, illustrations, and comments of the Tudor logicians and rhetoricians, is presented at the end of this volume in an eclectic handbook constructed by selecting each item from the author who seems to have treated it best and by arranging the whole in the pattern outlined above. The entire theory, with a few negligible exceptions, is illustrated from Shakespeare's plays and poems in the following chapters.[57]

The Renaissance figures seem to us remarkable for their inclusiveness. They deal with words, in the figures of orthography; with grammar, in such matters as interrogation, exclamation, the unfinished sentence, the periodic sentence, ellipsis, rhythm, and the means of varying through them; with coherence, through figures of conjunction and transition; with emphasis, through word order and the figures of repetition; with clarity and obscurity; with amplification and condensation; with beauty, through exergasia and all the figures of exornation; with force, through vehemence (*pathos*); with proof, through *logos*; with *ethos;* even with gesture (mimesis and mycterismus), and voice (pathopopoeia and tasis). The Tudor rhetoricians were tireless in their distinctions, unflagging in their faith in art and artifice, eager to assist in transplanting to the vernacular the adornments of Latin, Greek, and Hebrew literatures assiduously noted in the grammar schools and the universities. They anatomized composition and reading in an age that delighted in anatomies, as of wit, of flattery, of absurdity, and they showed composition interpenetrated with logic.

The Tudor rhetoricians classified the figures in the traditional manner indicated by the table on page 35, not under grammar, *logos, pathos,* and *ethos.* There is warrant for the present reclassification, however, in Aristotle, who furnished the pattern, and in the Renaissance rhetoricians, who implicitly adapted it. Aristotle, discussing style in his *Rhetoric,* gave some attention to the figures of grammar and, in relation to them, to

---

[57] The reader may study the theory in Part Three (Chapters VI–IX) either a section at a time or a chapter at a time before he reads the illustration of it from Shakespeare in Part Two (Chapters II–V). He may even want to read all of Part Three before beginning Chapter II. The headings of sections and the order of topics within sections in Parts Two and Three are identical to facilitate reference. The reader who is not interested in the theory either for proof or for flavor may disregard Part III entirely, since the chapters on Shakespeare are intelligible without it.

figures of repetition. In discussing the substance of rhetorical discourse he emphasized its function to effect an interrelated threefold persuasion: by *logos*, the speaker convinces his hearers of the truth of his argument by appealing to their reason; by *pathos* he puts them into a favorable, not a hostile, frame of mind by appealing to the emotions which color their judgment; by *ethos* he inspires their confidence in his own character and trustworthiness by convincing them of his honesty and goodness, his competence and judgment, and above all his good will toward them. The importance which Aristotle attached to *ethos*, *logos*, and *pathos* is indicated by the fact that his final words on the art of rhetoric emphasize the necessity of including this threefold persuasion in the epilogue of an oration:

The Epilogue has four parts. You must (1) make the audience well-disposed towards yourself and ill-disposed towards your opponent, (2) magnify or minimize the leading facts, (3) excite the required state of emotion in your hearers, and (4) refresh their memories. (*Rhetoric*, 19, 1419 ᵇ 10)

Renaissance rhetoricians, although accepting the traditional classification of figures under schemes of grammar, tropes, rhetorical figures of words, and rhetorical figures of thought, nevertheless did take account of these three modes of persuasion. For example, in his revised and improved work of 1593 Peacham subdivided his figures into those whose function is: repetition, omission, conjunction, and separation (grammatical); distribution, description, comparison, collection (*logos*); the stirring of affection and vehemence (*pathos*); nor is the hearer's impression of the speaker (*ethos*) left out of account, for some figures are directly designed to win good will and a favorable hearing. In other words, Peacham divides his figures of thought according to their functions into those of amplification (*logos*) and those of affection (*pathos*). Some promote *ethos*. In his *Elementa rhetorices* (1531) Melanchthon classified approximately forty of the figures of thought under selected topics of logic (definition, division, cause, contraries, similitudes, genus, circumstances and signs). The studious reader, he says, will observe that these especially take their origin from the places of dialectic, for the same places, when they are applied to proving or disproving a matter are called sinews of argument; when they are applied to illuminating it, they are called ornaments and many times add weight to the argument.[58] We

---

[58] Melanchthon, *Opera*, XIII, 479–80: "Observet autem studiosus lector figuras omnes, praesertim has, quae augent orationem ex locis dialecticis oriri, ad quos si quis prudenter sciet eas referre, pleraque in causis subtiliter et acute iudicare, et definitas negotii regiones

should not, however, be too exact and superstitious in comparing the places of dialectic and the figures of elocution. It is enough to employ a moderate prudence and to see some relation between them.[59]

Peacham's subdivisions and Melanchthon's classification furnish contemporary evidence indicating that the Renaissance rhetoricians would regard the reorganization of the figures under grammar, *logos, pathos,* and *ethos* as a clarification of what is partly explicit and partly implicit in their work. The present study undertakes to reclassify not merely the figures of thought, which have long been recognized as related to dialectic, but all of the two hundred Tudor figures, in terms of these four functions, and that without resorting to a miscellaneous catch-all such as Melanchthon's circumstances and signs. This reclassification of the figures makes no claim to apodictic exactitude. Their classification, by whatever method, has always proved baffling, for one figure may fit into any one of a number of classes, and some figures may not fit precisely into any one. For instance, a figure of collection or summary does not precisely fit in with figures of division; yet it may reasonably be placed with them because it is understood in relation to division as a reverse process. In addition to making the figures more intelligible and significant, the reorganization here presented accentuates the basic agreement of the Renaissance rhetoricians and logicians among themselves and with the ancient tradition.

It is difficult for a modern to keep in mind the ancient and the Renaissance conception of ornament as something more integral than we conceive it to be. According to Aristotle,

Ornament is attained by induction and distinction of things closely akin . . . an instance of the kind of thing meant is . . . the distinction of sciences into speculative, practical, and productive. For everything of this kind lends additional ornament to the argument, though there is no necessity to say them, so far as the conclusion goes. (*Topics,* 8.1.157 [a] 7)

Hermogenes constantly spoke of the enthymeme and the epicheirema as embellishments. Cicero also delighted in them and recognized that even

---

melius videre poterit. Nam iidem loci cum confirmandi aut confutandi causa adhibentur, argumenta sunt ac nervi, ut vocant. Cum adhibentur illuminandi causa, dicuntur ornamenta. Ac pleraque non tantum ad pugnae speciem comparata sunt, sed argumentis pondus addunt."

[59] *Ibid.,* p. 483: "Utimur autem in hac comparatione locorum dialecticorum et figurarum elocutionis non nimis subtili ac superstitiosa ratione. Satis est enim ad eam rem adhibere mediocrem quandam prudentiam, et aliqua ex parte cognationem videre, ut fontes ornamentorum et negociorum regiones animadverti queant."

to discuss style and ornament apart from thought involves an unnatural separation.

It is impossible to achieve an ornate style without first procuring ideas and putting them into shape, and . . . no idea can possess distinction without lucidity of style.[60]

This is the reason why that genuine and perfect eloquence we are speaking of, has been yet attained by no one; because the art of *reasoning* has been supposed to be one thing, and that of *speaking* another; and we have had recourse to different instructors for the knowledge of things and words.[61]

The figures of thought evoked great enthusiasm in the Renaissance, an age that delighted in logical exercise. As Sherry remarked at the close of his *Treatise of the Figures of Grammer and Rhetorike* (1555), they were called

ornamentes of matter, because by them, not only the oration and wordes, but the body of the matter groweth and is increased. (fol. lvii ʳ)

Since the figures of thought bulk largest in both number and importance, logic emerges as the dominant factor in composition not only for the Ramists and the traditionalists but for the figurists as well. Elizabethan literature was produced by a technique which, while giving attention to patterns of sound and movement and heaping up a rich profusion of imagery, was deeply rooted in thought and emotion.

---

[60] ". . . tantum significabo brevi, neque verborum ornatum inveniri posse non partis expressisque sententiis, neque esse ullam sententiam illustrem sine luce verborum." (Cicero *De oratore* 3.6.24), tr. by E. W. Sutton and H. Rackham (Loeb Classical Library).

[61] ". . . quo fit ut veram illam et absolutam eloquentiam nemo consequatur, quod alia intelligendi alia dicendi disciplina est et ab aliis rerum ab aliis verborum doctrina quaeritur." (Cicero *Orator* 5.17); tr. by E. Jones, whose translation of this passage is preferable to that in the Loeb edition.

PART TWO

SHAKESPEARE'S USE OF THE THEORY

CHAPTER II

SHAKESPEARE'S USE OF THE SCHEMES OF GRAMMAR, VICES OF LANGUAGE, AND FIGURES OF REPETITION

IN THE POEM prefacing the 1623 folio edition of Shakespeare's plays Ben Jonson wrote of his friend:

> Nature her selfe was proud of his designes,
>   And joy'd to weare the dressing of his lines!
> Which were so richly spun, and woven so fit,
>   As, since, she will vouchsafe no other Wit.

But he was quick to add:

> Yet must I not give Nature all: Thy Art,
>   My gentle *Shakespeare*, must enjoy a part.
> For though the *Poets* matter, Nature be,
>   His Art doth give the fashion. . . .
>   For a good *Poet's* made, as well as borne.
> And such wert thou.

This is undoubtedly a truer estimate of the part art played in forming Shakespeare's genius than the one implied by Milton's lines in "L'Allegro" inviting us to the stage where we may hear

> sweetest Shakespeare, fancies childe,
> Warble his native Wood-notes wilde.

In *The Winter's Tale* Polixenes discourses on the relation of nature and art, reaching a conclusion that may fitly be applied to Shakespeare's own genius.

> Yet nature is made better by no mean
> But nature makes that mean. So, over that art
> Which you say adds to nature, is an art
> That nature makes. . . .
>   This is an art
> Which does mend nature—change it rather; but
> The art itself is nature. (4.4.89–97)

Only one gifted by nature can use art supremely.

If Shakespeare was a country schoolmaster before he came to London, as William Beeston, son of Christopher Beeston, a fellow actor in Shakespeare's company, reported to Aubrey,[1] his familiarity with the formal arts of language to which grammar school had accustomed him would have been intensified. Furthermore, there is reason to think that while he was writing plays his interest in theoretical works continued. For example, he apparently became acquainted with *The Orator*, translated from the French of Alexandre van den Busche (Le Silvayn) by Lazarus Pyott, almost as soon as it was published in 1596, for it is fairly certain that he drew on the ninety-fifth oration in that work for the order and the motives in Shylock's arguments in court (2.1.139–52) in *The Merchant of Venice*, which is believed to have been composed the same year.[2] Moreover, there is evidence that Shakespeare knew other English works on rhetoric and perhaps also on logic. H. C. Hart, in his edition of *Love's Labour's Lost* (The Arden Shakespeare), and W. L. Rushton, in *Shakespeare and 'The Arte of English Poesie,'* cite details indicating that Shakespeare was well acquainted with Puttenham's work.[3] That he was familiar with Peacham's *Garden of Eloquence* is suggested by a parallel which will be presented in the next chapter.[4] He is thought to have made some use of Fraunce's *Lawiers Logike* and *Arcadian Rhetorike*.[5] Hardin Craig considers it probable that he knew Wilson's *Rule of Reason* and perhaps also *The Arte of Rhetorique*, although his acquaintance with the latter has not yet been satisfactorily demonstrated.[6] Shakespeare's knowledge of formal logic is attested by the frequent use of logical terms and processes in his plays.[7]

---

[1] T. W. Baldwin regards this, even though it comes through Aubrey, as credible testimony, "the direct statement of a competent witness." *William Shakspere's Small Latine and Lesse Greeke*, I, 36.

[2] See *ibid.*, II, 44–49.

[3] George Stuart Gordon, in "Shakespeare's English," Society for Pure English, *Tract* 29, p. 260, writes concerning Puttenham's *Arte:* "It was read by Shakespeare when it came out, and has been classed, on the evidence of language, among his early favourites or books of reference by that excellent scholar the late Mr. H. C. Hart." See also W. B. Drayton Henderson, in "Montaigne's *Apologie of Raymond Sebond* and *King Lear*," *Shakespeare Association Bulletin*, XIV (October, 1939), 210. Harold S. Wilson, in "Nature and Art in 'Winter's Tale,' *Shakespeare Association Bulletin*, XVIII (1943), 114–19, points out that the immediate source of the discussion (4.4.88 ff.) was probably Puttenham's *Arte*.

[4] See p. 113, below.

[5] See T. W. Baldwin, *op. cit.*, II, 669. Baldwin does not regard the evidence as conclusive.

[6] Hardin Craig, "Shakespeare and Wilson's *Arte of Rhetorique*," *Studies in Philology*, XXVIII (October, 1931), 618–30.

[7] Hardin Craig, "Shakespeare and Formal Logic," in *Studies in English Philology: a Miscellany in Honor of Frederick Klaeber*, pp. 380–96.

Many passages in Shakespeare's works reveal his easy familiarity with the arts of language and the terms peculiar to them. In *The Taming of the Shrew* Tranio warns his young master Lucentio not to become too much engrossed in study

> Or so devote to Aristotle's checks
> As Ovid be an outcast quite abjur'd.
> Balk logic with acquaintance that you have,
> And practise rhetoric in your common talk. (*TS*, 1.1.32)

In *Titus Andronicus* Chiron recognizes at once the Latin verses on the scroll, as no doubt many of Shakespeare's audience also did.

> O, 'tis a verse in Horace. I know it well.
> I read it in the grammar long ago. (4.2.22)

Shakespeare's most delightful and lively reference to grammar is in *The Merry Wives of Windsor* (4.1), where Evans gives the boy William a lesson which, as H. R. D. Anders points out,[8] abounds in unmistakable echoes of Lily's Latin grammar, so familiar to Elizabethans. These echoes, combined with Mistress Quickly's ridiculous misapprehension of grammatical terms and Latin words and her confusion of them with like-sounding words familiar to her, demonstrate how even the most humdrum of school exercises can be transformed by genius into delightful foolery. Playing on technical terms of grammar, Falstaff boasts that Mistress Ford loves him.

I can construe the action of her familiar style, and the hardest voice of her behaviour (to be English'd rightly) is 'I am Sir John Falstaff's.' (*MWW*, 1.3.50)

The patrician Coriolanus is excited to a pitch of fury when the tribune of the people, whom he despises, uses "shall" with imperative force.

> Shall remain?
> Hear you this Triton of the minnows? Mark you
> His absolute 'shall'? (*Cor.*, 3.1.88)

The figures are frequently mentioned.

> What is the figure? What is the figure? (*LLL*, 5.1.67)
>
> He apprehends a world of figures here (*1H4*, 1.3.209)
>
> . . . there is figures in all things (*H5*, 4.7.35)
>
> I speak but in the figures and comparisons of it. (*H5*, 4.7.46)

---

[8] Anders, *Shakespeare's Books*, p. 14.

They were but sweet, but figures of delight (*Son. 98*)

What's in the brain that ink may character
Which hath not figur'd to thee my true spirit? (*Son. 108*)

Nay, you need not to stop your nose, sir. I spake but by a metaphor.
                                                    (*AW*, 5.2.11)

I do pity his distress in my similes of comfort, and leave him to your lordship.
                                                    (*AW*, 5.2.25)

In *As You Like It* Duke Senior asks:

> *Duke S.*   But what said Jaques?
>   Did he not moralize this spectacle?
> *1 Lord.* O, yes, into a thousand similes. (2.1.43)

Beatrice in *Much Ado* mockingly observes of Benedick:

He'll but break a comparison or two on me; which peradventure, not marked
or not laugh'd at, strikes him into melancholy; and then there's a partridge
wing saved, for the fool will eat no supper that night. (2.1.152)

Troilus vouches for his fidelity by declaring that his name will become
the very peak of comparison for true love.

> True swains in love shall in the world to come
> Approve their truth by Troilus. When their rhymes,
> Full of protest, of oath, and big compare,
> Want similes, truth tir'd with iteration—
> 'As true as steel, as plantage to the moon . . .
> As iron to adamant, as earth to th' centre'—
> Yet, after all comparisons of truth . . .
> 'As true as Troilus' shall crown up the verse
> And sanctify the numbers. (*T & C*, 3.2.180)

In *Love's Labour's Lost* Berowne promises henceforth to woo in simple
language, and forswears

> Taffeta phrases, silken terms precise,
>   Three-pil'd hyperboles, spruce affectation,
> Figures pedantical—   (5.2.406)

And Berowne's exclamation,

> Fie! painted rhetoric— O, she needs it not! (4.3.239)

echoes the theme of Sonnet LXXXII:

>   yet when they have devis'd
> What strained touches rhetoric can lend,

> . . . their gross painting might be better us'd
> Where cheeks need blood; in thee it is abus'd.

The language of logic, too, comes easily to Shakespeare's men and women. Celia tells Rosalind:

It is as easy to count atomies as to resolve the propositions of a lover.
(*AYLI*, 3.2.245)

Longaville protests to his lady:

> Did not the heavenly rhetoric of thine eye,
> 'Gainst whom the world cannot hold argument,
> Persuade my heart to this false perjury? (*LLL*, 4.3.60)

Holofernes complains of Nathaniel:

He draweth out the thread of his verbosity finer than the staple of his argument.
(*LLL*, 5.1.18)

Jaques remarks of the exiled duke:

> He is too disputable for my company. (*AYLI*, 2.5.36)

When Brabantio presents his charges against Othello, he asks for reasonable judgment.

> I'll have't disputed on.
> 'Tis probable, and palpable to thinking. (1.2.74)

Later, however, the duke has to check his vehemence and unreason.

> To vouch this is no proof. (1.3.106)

In *All's Well* the king agrees to grant Helena's request, if she cures him of his illness.

> Here is my hand. The premises observ'd,
> Thy will by my performance shall be serv'd. (2.1.204)

These instances, to which others could be added, show Shakespeare explicitly referring to grammar, logic, and rhetoric, and using terms peculiar to them. Much more important and more pervasive, however, is his implicit attention to them throughout his work. A few years ago, in his illuminating work *The Allegory of Love,* C. S. Lewis sought to assist modern readers to recapture the art of reading allegory, a form of composition familiar to medieval and Renaissance readers. He explained his own function as he conceived it.

It is the chief duty of the interpreter to begin analyses and to leave them unfinished. They are not meant as substitutes for the imaginative apprehension of the poem. Their only use is to awaken, first of all, the reader's conscious knowledge of life and books in so far as it is relevant, and then to stir those less conscious elements in him which alone can fully respond to the poem. (p. 345)

To awaken attention to features which characterized the art of composition and of imaginative apprehension in Shakespeare's day, the present work merely begins analyses which outline the intricate pattern of the arts of language taken for granted by Shakespeare and his contemporary audience.

1. The Schemes of Grammar

The schemes of grammar are concerned only with the more artistic aspects of grammar, with what we today call grammar for style. Schemes are patterns or fashionings of language which confer on it a character that distinguishes it from ordinary speech. They are employed by men of all walks of life when moved by excitement to adopt short cuts and turns of expression which give vividness and vitality not ordinarily found in their speech. The schemes of grammar are used today, as always, even though the nomenclature and the minute distinctions are unfamiliar to us.[9] The difference between the Elizabethan cognizance and ours is aptly described by Gladys Doidge Willcock and Alice Walker in their edition of Puttenham.

A well-educated modern reader may confess without shame to momentary confusion between *Hypozeuxis* and *Hypozeugma,* but to his Elizabethan prototype the categories of the figures were, like the multiplication-tables, a part of his foundations. . . . The comic dramatist expected rhetorical jest and allusion to be taken as readily as a music-hall joke about the loss of King John's clothing in the Wash would be today.

This brings us once more to the question of Elizabethan reading and listening . . . Poets who took so much trouble to follow Art would not wish this Art to be ignored in the reading and would expect their listeners, and still more their readers, to respond with aural and mental agility. The 'schemes' are nothing but the organization of patterning: this patterning contented the ear like rhyme and the identification of the patterns was a delight to the instructed mind. Such a response to poetry was never vague nor half-awake. . . . Shake-

---

[9] It is principally the nomenclature of the figures that makes them seem formidable to us. Yet efforts such as Puttenham's to Anglicize their names won no favor. We still prefer Greek names for the few figures we distinguish, such as metaphor. Many of the Tudor figures are employed today by writers and speakers who probably do not suspect that they are using them and are quite unaware of their names. Shakespeare's use of the figures, however, was not unconscious, as T. W. Baldwin has demonstrated.

speare had absorbed the Art of Rhetoric and his early plays, especially the
Chronicles, are often dubbed 'rhetorical' . . . in the Poems and Sonnets . . .
he approximates himself most closely to the courtly intelligentsia. . . . We are
all aware of the patterning in Elizabethan verse of this period, but we are generally content to name the *genus*—balance, antithesis, repetition, and so on.
The educated Elizabethan could give a name to every *species*. (pp. lxxv ff.)

Nashe's rogue, Jack Wilton, describes a disputant who was confident that
his auditors would appreciate his clever use of figures.

And ever when he thought he had cast a figure so curiously as he dived over
head and eares into his auditors admiration, hee would take occasion to stroke
up his haire, and twine up his mustachios twice or thrice over while they might
have leasure to applaud him.[10]

The schemes of grammar are divided into those of words and those
of construction.

a. Schemes of Words.—The orthographical schemes of words are
variations from the more usual forms of words, mainly for the sake of
meter or rhyme. To us they often appear to be mere metrical adaptations,
obsolete pronunciations, misspellings, or typographical errors. The
Elizabethans, however, regarded them as poetic adornments. Benedick
finds Claudio's use of them a sign that he has turned poetic as a result
of falling in love.

He was wont to speak plain and to the purpose, like an honest man and a
soldier; and now is he turn'd orthography; his words are a very fantastical
banquet—just so many strange dishes. (*MA*, 2.3.19)

When language was in a state of unusual flux, as in sixteenth-century
England, when it had, as George Stuart Gordon remarked, "no fixed
standard . . . no accepted grammar, or spelling, or pronunciation, or
accent," when poets were makers of language as well as of poems, these
figures of orthography could add their bit of encouragement to the
"experimental gusto" and to the "genuine and widespread feeling of
word-creation." [11]

One exhilarating result of the linguistic licence of the century was, in its latter
years at any rate, a period of almost complete linguistic freedom. . . . There
had never been such a time for the bold employers of words. . . . You tried
a thing to see what happened. . . . Even the failures played their part, as in

[10] Nashe, *The Unfortunate Traveller*, in *Works*, ed. by R. B. McKerrow, II, 250.
[11] George Stuart Gordon, "Shakespeare's English," in Society for Pure English, *Tract* 29,
pp. 255, 262.

genuine experiment they so often do. . . . It is in the plays of Shakespeare that
the general movement may best be studied. He was, by every sign—indeed the
evidence is overwhelming—in the first rank of the advance, and of all its
members the most exuberant; an experimenter always. . . . For the first
quality of Elizabethan, and therefore of Shakespearian English, is its power of
hospitality, its passion for free experiment, its willingness to use every form of
verbal wealth, to try anything. . . . Shakespeare was to do what he liked
with English grammar, and drew beauty and power from its imperfections.
In the rankness and wildness of the language he found his opportunity, and
exploited it royally, sometimes tyrannically. . . . The fertility and happy-go-
luckiness of Elizabethan English, and the linguistic vitality of its greatest master,
are apparent in . . . the making of words by derivation . . . those significant atoms, the prefix and the suffix . . . Shakespeare's . . . *enmesh, enfreedom,* and *ensky* . . . typical products of the new licence.[12]

The traditional schemes of words and of grammatical construction
probably contributed something to the creative use of language by
Shakespeare and his contemporaries. In his gloss to Spenser's *Shepheardes Calender* E. K. comments on the schemes of words as poetical
variations.

> Yblent) Y is a poeticall addition. ["Aprill"]
> Nas) is a syncope, for ne has, or has not: as nould, for would not.
> ["Maye"]
> Emprise) for enterprise. Per Syncopen. ["September"]

The schemes of words are modifications of words wrought by adding
or subtracting a syllable or letter at the beginning, middle, or end, and,
less frequently, by exchanging sounds. Regarded as embellishments, they
bestow on the poet or orator a measure of freedom in manipulating words.
Cicero gave them careful attention, Vergil used them, and they played
a part in the fashioning of Latin for literary expression. Susenbrotus and
other Renaissance rhetoricians cited examples of them from the Latin
classics. Sherry, Wilson, Peacham in his 1577 edition, Puttenham, and
Butler discussed and illustrated them. Although the schemes of words
served principally in meter, they were sometimes employed in prose.
Often they represented merely a selection by the poet of one form of a
word, a less generally accepted one, among a number of forms current
at the time. Sometimes, however, the poet coined new forms.[13] As E. K.'s

---

12 *Ibid., passim.*
13 George Gordon noted as probable coinages: Sidney's *endear*, Spenser's *embosom* and
enclosed, Shakespeare's *ensnare, enmesh, enfreedom, ensky, disbench, dispark, recall* and
reword. Ibid., p. 271.

gloss indicates, selections and coinages that exemplified the various schemes of words would have been recognized as such by Elizabethans.

The addition of a syllable at the beginning of a word was called prosthesis, as *embolden* for *bolden,* *berattle* for *rattle,* *ymade* for *made,* *adown* for *down.* These illustrations and all others employed in this section to explain the schemes of words come from the Tudor rhetoricians, who, it must be remembered, knew little about the history of the English language. The following are a few examples of prosthesis in Shakespeare:

> I hold you as a thing enskied and sainted (*MM,* 1.4.34)

> the female ivy so
> Enrings the barky fingers of the elm. (*MND,* 4.1.47)

> the grace of heaven . . . Enwheel thee round! (*Oth.,* 2.1.87)

> Old fond eyes, Beweep this cause again (*Lear,* 1.4.323)

> Nor, by my will, assubjugate his merit (*T & C,* 2.3.202)

The addition of a syllable or letter in the middle of a word was called epenthesis, as *meeterly* for *meetly.*

> Give Mutius burial with our bretheren (*Tit.,* 1.1.348)

> Lie blist'ring fore the visitating sun (*TNK,* 1.1.146)

> I have but with a cursorary eye O'erglanc'd the articles (*H5,* 5.2.77)

The addition of a syllable at the end of a word was called proparalepsis or paragoge, as *spoken* for *spoke,* *hasten* for *haste.* To us these seem merely the normal forms. Yet, taking Wilson's illustration *hasten,* we find that Shakespeare uses *haste* as a verb in his plays thirty-one times, while he uses *hasten* but six times and only once intransitively. It would seem that if *haste* was then the usual form, *hasten* may be regarded as an instance of this scheme.

> And bid her hasten all the house to bed (*R & J,* 3.3.156)

Climature may be another instance of this scheme. According to the *Oxford English Dictionary,* Shakespeare was the first to use it, combining *climate* and *temperature.*

> Have heaven and earth together demonstrated
> Unto our climature and countrymen (*Ham.,* 1.1.124)

The following epitaph on the death of a deer, which Holofernes composed extemporaneously in *Love's Labour's Lost,* parodies a number of figures, including this scheme proparalepsis, by adding the syllable *-el.*

The preyful princess pierc'd and prick'd a pretty pleasing pricket;
Some say a sore; but not a sore till now made sore with shooting.
The dogs did yell: put el to sore, then sorel jumps from thicket,
Or pricket sore, or else sorel. The people fall a-hooting.
If sore be sore, then L to sore makes fifty sores one sorel.
Of one sore I an hundred make by adding but one more L. (4.2.58)

This ridiculous piece gains a modicum of meaning if one perceives in it
not only the obvious travesty of excessive alliteration but also the carica-
ture of proparalepsis. *Love's Labour's Lost* has been aptly called "that
playground of the new language." [14]

The schemes of subtraction include aphaeresis, syncope, synaloepha,
and apocope. *'Twixt* for *betwixt* is an example of aphaeresis, subtracting
a syllable from the beginning. Shakespeare uses this scheme very freely.

Point against point, rebellious arm 'gainst arm (*Mac.*, 1.2.56)

Now spurs the lated traveller apace (*Mac.*, 3.3.6)

what 'cerns it you (*TS*, 5.1.77)

pale as any clout in the versal world (*R & J*, 2.4.218)

The King hath cause to plain (*Lear*, 3.1.39)

Then shall we hear their 'larum and they ours (*Cor.*, 1.4.9)

Syncope is the removal of a letter or syllable from the middle of a word,
as *prosprous* for *prosperous.*

Ignomy and shame Pursue thy life (*T & C.*, 5.10.33)

And whe'r he run or fly they know not whether (*V & A*, 304)

Pray heartly pardon me (*MWW*, 3.3.243)

O'ermaster't as you may (*Ham.*, 1.5.140)

You shall do marvell's wisely (*Ham.*, 2.1.3)

Let's make us med'cines of our great revenge (*Mac.*, 4.3.214)

When at the juncture of two vowels one is elided, the scheme is called
synaloepha, as *t'attain* for *to attain.* Perhaps it may have included the
elision of the only vowel, as *is't* for *is it.* The latter is very frequent in
Shakespeare's later plays. This scheme gives swiftness to the verse.

Take't; 'tis yours. What is't? (*Cor.*, 1.10.80)

Believe't not lightly (*Cor.*, 4.1.29)

star . . . had made his course t'illume that part (*Ham.*, 1.1.37)

14 *Ibid.*, p. 263.

Apocope, the omission of the last syllable of a word, as *bet* for *better*, Shakespeare employs with great freedom.

> With Clifford and the haught Northumberland (*3H6*, 2.1.169)
>
> As seld I have the chance (*T & C*, 4.5.150)
>
> this habitation where thou keep'st Hourly afflict (*MM*, 3.1.10)
>
> Season your admiration for awhile With an attent ear (*Ham.*, 1.2.192)
>
> To make inquire Of his behaviour (*Ham.*, 2.1.4)
>
> whose low sound Reverbs no hollowness (*Lear*, 1.1.156)
>
> the holy cords . . . Which are too intrinse t'unloose (*Lear*, 2.2.80)

Diastole, or eciasis, and systole, the lengthening and shortening of syllables, or rather in English the shifting of stress, are schemes difficult to recognize on account of the fluctuating pronunciation of Elizabethan English. Peacham, in 1577, listed *commendable* accented on the third syllable as an example of diastole, stating that necessity of meter occasions such a shift of accent. In some instances Shakespeare seems to have pronounced the word as we do today, but in the following line the shift of accent from the second to the third syllable illustrates both diastole and systole:

> And power, unto itself most commendable (*Cor.*, 4.7.51)

Of the two remaining schemes of words, metathesis, or transposition, was an exchange of letters in a word. Peacham gave as an example *brust* for *burst*. Shakespeare has *cestron* for *cistern*; *frevent* for *fervent*.

> to him that makes the camp a cestron
> Brimm'd with the blood of men (*TNK*, 5.1.46)
>
> With liver burning hot. Frevent . . . (*MWW*, 2.1.121)

The exchange of one sound for another in a word, as *wrang* for *wrong*, usually for the sake of rhyme, was called antisthecon.

> Which better than the first, O dear heaven, bless,
> Or, ere they meet, in me, O nature, cesse! (*AW*, 5.3.71)
>
> *Troilus.* But to the sport abroad! Are you bound thither?
> *Aeneas.* In all swift haste.
> *Troilus.*   Come, go we then togither. (*T & C*, 1.1.118)

Tasis is not precisely a figure, but Sherry and Puttenham presented it in close relation to the figures, defining it as a sweet and pleasant modulation or tunableness of the voice in pronunciation, and Shakespeare seems to have been aware of it. Cymbeline, recognizing the disguised Imogen by her voice, cries out with joy:

> . . . the tune of Imogen! (*Cym.*, 5.5.238)

The orthographical schemes encouraged liberties with words in the name of art. They added the sanction of literary tradition to the ebullient spirit of linguistic freedom which characterized the Elizabethan poets, and Shakespeare most of all.

b. Schemes of Construction.—The schemes of grammatical construction are refashionings of language for variety and force. They give a certain poise and balance, and differ from ordinary speech as dance steps or the movements of ceremony and ritual differ from a walk. The purpose of walking is the simple and practical one of reaching one's destination, but the movements of dance and ceremony have a virtue in themselves in that they are concerned with the grace and dignity of the action. The effective use of the schemes of grammar indicates that a speaker or writer has mastery and easy control over his medium quite beyond the ordinary. Shakespeare, above all writers of English, has this poise, balance, mastery, and easy control. Yet so absorbed are we in what he is saying that we are often unaware of the devices by which he achieves his art—as, indeed, we should be.

In English, where word order exercises an important grammatical function, the various forms of departure from the ordinary order, called in general hyperbaton, frequently confer both emphasis and distinction. The Tudor rhetoricians distinguished various species of hyperbaton: anastrophe, tmesis, hysteron proteron, hypallage.[15]

Shakespeare uses anastrophe, or unusual word order, throughout the plays, but especially in the later ones. It might almost be said to characterize the style of *The Tempest*. The following are a few instances of this figure:

> Jove's lightnings, the precursors
> O' th' dreadful thunderclaps, more momentary
> And sight-outrunning were not. (*Tem.*, 1.2.201)

> I'll resolve you . . . of every These happen'd accidents
> (*Tem.*, 5.1.248)

---

[15] For a fuller treatment the reader should consult Part Three, pp. 294–299, below, where the figures are explained and illustrated by quotations from the Tudor rhetoricians in the same order as that adopted here. Part Three is similarly correlated with succeeding chapters on Shakespeare.

Yet I'll not shed her blood,
Nor scar that whiter skin of hers than snow. (*Oth.*, 5.2.3)

Of something nearly that concerns yourselves (*MND*, 1.1.126)

that a swift blessing
May soon return to this our suffering country
Under a hand accurs'd! (*Mac.*, 3.6.47)

Whither indeed, before thy here-approach (*Mac.*, 4.3.133)

When words were put between the parts of a compound word, such as *however,* the scheme was called tmesis.

how heinous e'er it be,
To win thy after-love I pardon thee (*R2*, 5.3.34)

that man—how dearly ever parted (*T & C*, 3.3.96)

Hysteron proteron puts first that which occurs later. Shakespeare achieves a breathless effect by the striking use of this figure when Enobarbus reports the sudden about-face and flight of Cleopatra's ships, which proved so ruinous to Antony and to his fortunes.

Th' Antoniad, the Egyptian admiral,
With all their sixty, fly and turn the rudder. (*A & C*, 3.10.2)

In hypallage, the changeling, as Puttenham named it, the application of words is perverted and sometimes made absurd. Waking from the effects of the magic flower-juice, the bewildered Bottom tries to recall his most rare vision.

The eye of man hath not heard, the ear of man hath not seen, man's hand is not able to taste, his tongue to conceive, nor his heart to report what my dream was. (*MND*, 4.1.215)

By the use of hypallage in this instance Shakepeare achieves the tone of grotesque wonder suited to the situation without incurring the risk of mockery of the Scripture (1 Cor. 2:9) which might otherwise have resulted. Bottom seems to be addicted to this misplacing of words whether he speaks as Pyramus or for himself.

I see a voice. Now will I to the chink,
To spy an I can hear my Thisby's face. (5.1.194)

Will it please you to see the Epilogue, or to hear a Bergomask dance between two of our company? (5.1.359)

The magistrate's comment clearly indicates that Shakespeare is using hypallage with conscious intent to reveal the confusion of Elbow, the constable, who brings Pompey before Escalus and Angelo, sitting in judgment.

> *Elbow.* [*to Pompey*] Prove it before these varlets here, thou honourable man; prove it.
> *Escalus.* [*to Angelo*] Do you hear how he misplaces? (*MM*, 2.1.88)

Other examples indicate the mental condition of the speaker.

> *Stephano.* Every man shift for all the rest, and let no man take care for himself. (*Tem.*, 5.1.256)

> *Slender.* All his successors (gone before him) hath done't; and all his ancestors (that come after him) may. (*MWW*, 1.1.13)

> *Dogberry.* To be a well-favoured man is the gift of fortune, but to write and read comes by nature. (*MA*, 3.3.14)

Day spoke of a milder form of hypallage, rife in poesy, where the exchange of words is less violent, as "the wicked wound thus given," wherein it is the giver and not the wound that is wicked. This is equivalent to a transferred epithet. A memorable instance in Shakespeare is Antony's remark as he holds up Caesar's mantle before the crowd, showing them the rent through which the well-beloved Brutus stabbed.

> This was the most unkindest cut of all. (*JC*, 3.2.188)

Hypallage of this kind confers vitality and compression.

> Alas, what ignorant sin have I committed? (*Oth.*, 4.2.70)

> He rais'd the house with loud and coward cries (*Lear*, 2.4.43)

> And never brandish more revengeful steel (*R2*, 4.1.50)

> With Tarquin's ravishing strides . . . Moves like a ghost
> (*Mac.*, 2.1.55)

> this bird Hath made his . . . procreant cradle (*Mac.*, 1.6.7)

> Our Italy Shines o'er with civil swords (*A & C*, 1.3.44)

> Forgive my fearful sails! (*A & C*, 3.11.55)

> With rainy marching in the painful field (*H5*, 4.3.111)

> the treacherous feet
> Which with usurping steps do trample thee (*R2*, 3.2.16)

> I heard myself proclaim'd,
> And by the happy hollow of a tree Escap'd the hunt (*Lear*, 2.3.1)

> Or have we eaten on the insane root
> That takes the reason prisoner? (*Mac.*, 1.3.84)

Among the forms of hyperbaton, the generic figure that we have been considering, Sherry included parenthesis, which Shakespeare uses extensively, especially in his later plays. Thus in *Coriolanus* Menenius admonishes a citizen.

> If you'll bestow a small (of what you have little)
> Patience awhile . . . (1.1.129)

Here the parenthesis serves both to condense and to juxtapose ideas with sudden, striking effect. In *The Winter's Tale* the frenzied jealousy of Leonatus is emphasized by the parentheses.

> Ha' not you seen, Camillo
> (But that's past doubt; you have, or your eye-glass
> Is thicker than a cuckold's horn), or heard
> (For to a vision so apparent rumour
> Cannot be mute) or thought (for cogitation
> Resides not in that man that does not think)
> My wife is slippery? (1.2.267)

Iachimo's story of his villainy is often interrupted thus (*Cym.*, 5.5. 153 ff.), and so is Prospero's account of Caliban's early life (*Tem.*, 1.2.267 ff.). In *Measure for Measure* Angelo's parenthesis imitates the manner of Saint Paul (2 Cor. 11:21, 23).[16]

> Yea, my gravity,
> Wherein (let no man hear me) I take pride,
> Could I, with boot, change for an idle plume
> Which the air beats for vain. (2.4.9)

Similar to parenthesis in interposing explanatory matter is epergesis, or apposition. Sometimes appositive phrases are metaphors.

> Antiquity forgot, custom not known,
> The ratifiers and props of every word (*Ham.*, 4.5.104)
>
> the thunder, That deep and dreadful organ pipe (*Tem.*, 3.3.97)
>
> He, A most unbounded tyrant (*TNK*, 1.2.62)
>
> Her father and myself (lawful espials) . . . (*Ham.*, 3.1.32)
>
> Behold, these are the tribunes of the people,
> The tongues o' th' common mouth (*Cor.*, 3.1.21)

---

[16] Compare Peacham's citation of this passage, p. 295, below.

The grammatical figures of omission include eclipsis, zeugma, syllepsis, and diazeugma. Eclipsis, or ellipsis, the omission of a word easily understood, contributes to the compressed character of Shakespeare's later style, although it appears throughout his work.

> And he to England shall along with you (*Ham.*, 3.3.4)
>
> For what, alas, can these my single arms? (*T & C*, 2.2.135)
>
> Desire them home (*T & C*, 4.5.157)
>
> Haply you shall not see me more; or if,
> A mangled shadow. (*A & C*, 4.2.26)

Zeugma, one verb serving a number of clauses, is a favorite with Shakespeare. He places the one verb sometimes first, sometimes last.

> But passion lends them power, time means, to meet. (*R & J*, 2. Prol. 13)
>
> Our blood to us, this to our blood is born. (*AW*, 1.3.137)
>
> wishing clocks more swift? Hours, minutes? noon, midnight?
>   (*WT*, 1.2.289)
>
> How Tarquin wronged me, I Collatine. (*RL*, 819)
>
> As you on him, Demetrius dote on you! (*MND*, 1.1.225)

Syllepsis differs from zeugma in that a verb, expressed but once, lacks grammatical congruence with at least one subject with which it is understood.

> She has deceiv'd her father, and may thee. (*Oth.*, 1.3.294)
>
> Nor God nor I delights in perjur'd men. (*LLL*, 5.2.346)
>
> Love loving not itself, none other can. (*R2*, 5.4.88)
>
> I have no more to reckon, he to spend. (*Tim.*, 3.4.56)

In contrast to zeugma, hypozeuxis provides every clause in a series with its own subject and verb. This figure is used with comic effect in *Romeo and Juliet* when the servingman announces:

Madam, the guests are come, supper serv'd up, you call'd, my young lady ask'd for, the nurse curs'd in the pantry, and everything in extremity. (1.3.100)

Puttenham makes iteration an additional characteristic of this figure. Thus:

> Blessed are clouds, to do as such clouds do. (*LLL*, 5.2.204)
>
> What, I? I love? I sue? I seek a wife? (*LLL*, 3.1.191)

The use of one subject with many verbs, called diazeugma, gives cumulative force to Norfolk's account of Cardinal Wolsey's strange conduct.

> He bites his lip and starts,
> Stops on a sudden, looks upon the ground,
> Then lays his finger on his temple; straight
> Springs out into fast gait, then stops again,
> Strikes his breast hard, and anon he casts
> His eye against the moon. (*H8*, 3.2.113)

The omission of conjunctions between words, called brachylogia, emphasizes the grief and sense of loss felt by Paris and Capulet on discovering Juliet dead.

> *Paris*. Beguil'd, divorced, wronged, spited, slain! . . .
> *Capulet*. Despis'd, distressed, hated, marty'rd, kill'd!
> (*R & J*, 4.5.55,59)

It contributes an effect of piled-up derision to Enobarbus' description of Lepidus.

> Hoo! hearts, tongues, figures, scribes, bards, poets, cannot
> Think, speak, cast, write, sing, number—hoo!—
> His love to Antony. (*A & C*, 3.2.16)

Ariel's spirit-quality and his swift and ready obedience to Prospero are enhanced by his use of asyndeton, omitting conjunctions between clauses.

> All hail, great master! Grave sir, hail! I come
> To answer thy best pleasure; be't to fly,
> To swim, to dive into the fire, to ride
> On the curl'd clouds. (*Tem.*, 1.2.189)

In contrast is the measured deliberateness of polysyndeton, the use of a conjunction between each clause.

> 'Tis as I should entreat you wear your gloves,
> Or feed on nourishing dishes, or keep you warm,
> Or sue to you to do a peculiar profit
> To your person. (*Oth.*, 3.3.77)

The figure primarily concerned with rhythm is isocolon or parison in which phrases or clauses are of equal length and usually of corresponding structure, as in Nathaniel's euphuistic comments to Holofernes.

Your reasons at dinner have been sharp and sententious; pleasant without scurrility, witty without affection, audacious without impudency, learned without opinion, and strange without heresy. (*LLL*, 5.1.2)

Often the equal members are marked off by homoioteleuton, or like ending, as -*ly* in the following.

> How churlishly I chid Lucetta hence
> When willingly I would have had her here!
> How angerly I taught my brow to frown . . . (*TGV*, 1.2.60)

In the periodic sentence, called hirmus, the sense is suspended until the end.

> Tell my friends,
> Tell Athens, in the sequence of degree
> From high to low throughout, that whoso please
> To stop affliction, let him take his haste,
> Come hither ere my tree hath felt the axe,
> And hang himself. (*Tim.*, 5.1.210)

Metabasis is a figure of transition, telling what has been said and what is to follow. Dramatic transition, more vitally concerned with action, should include what has been done and what is next to be done, as in the following passage, where Hamlet, revealing emotion and resolution as well as his intentions, surveys the past and the future.

> Why, what an ass am I! This is most brave,
> That I, the son of a dear father murther'd,
> Prompted to my revenge by heaven and hell,
> Must (like a whore) unpack my heart with words
> And fall a-cursing like a very drab,
> A scullion!
> Fie upon't! foh! About, my brain! Hum, I have heard
> That guilty creatures, sitting at a play,
> Have by the very cunning of the scene
> Been struck so to the soul that presently
> They have proclaim'd their malefactions;
> For murther, though it have no tongue, will speak
> With most miraculous organ. I'll have these players
> Play something like the murther of my father
> Before mine uncle. I'll observe his looks;
> I'll tent him to the quick. If he but blench,
> I know my course. (2.2.610)

There remain four figures of grammatical exchange: enallage, hendiadys, Graecismus, and anthimeria. Enallage is the deliberate use of one case, person, gender, number, tense, or mood for another. Obviously, if this were done through ignorance, it would be a solecism. In departing from the ordinary, art often approaches the borderline of error or momentarily goes even beyond it. It is true that the Elizabethans, like some moderns, may have been uncertain about grammatical forms, particularly since the language was then to an exceptional degree in a state of flux. Yet the license sanctioned by enallage probably accounts for at least some of Shakespeare's variations from the normal. Each of the following represents a shift in person or case of the pronoun.

> With female fairies will his tomb be haunted,
> And worms will not come to thee [for *him*] (*Cym.*, 4.2.217)

> Is she as tall as me? (*A & C*, 3.3.14)

> So saucy will the hand of she here (*A & C*, 3.13.98)

> And hang more praise upon deceased I (*Son.* 72)

Sometimes the singular form of the verb is used with a plural subject.[17]

> Is there not wars? Is there not employment? (*2H4*, 1.2.85)

> Never was waves nor wind more violent (*Per.*, 4.1.60)

> But see where Somerset and Clarence comes! (*3H6*, 4.2.3)

> Whiles I threat, he lives;
> Words to the heat of deeds too cold breath gives. (*Mac.*, 2.1.60)

Similarly a plural form of the verb may be used with a singular subject.

> The posture of your blows are yet unknown (*JC*, 5.1.33)

> more than the scope Of these dilated articles allow (*Ham.*, 1.2.37)

> Equality of two domestic powers Breed scrupulous faction
> (*A & C*, 1.3.47)

Hendiadys, the use of two nouns for a noun with its modifier, gives increased emphasis.

> The heaviness and the guilt within my bosom
> Takes off my manhood. (*Cym.*, 5.2.1)

---

[17] Franz, in *Die Sprache Shakespeares in Vers und Prosa*, sec. 155, p. 157, remarks that the needs of rhyme, as in the example cited from *Macbeth*, often occasioned lack of congruence of subject and verb. See also sec. 671, p. 565. It may be added that a poet would invoke the privilege of enallage in just such circumstances.

The singular verb assists in yoking the nouns, and makes it more clear that *heavy guilt* is meant. Shakespeare has an especially striking phrase, surely figurative, since it noticeably refashions ordinary speech. It is a sort of hendiadys in reverse, and is used by Coriolanus.

> at once pluck out The multitudinous tongue (3.1.155)

Here Shakespeare's creative art fashioning something new and very effective outruns the precepts of the figurists, who, notwithstanding their minute analysis of language, did not describe a turn of words like this. *Multitudinous tongue* expresses far more vehemently than the *tongue of the multitude* could possibly do, the scornful contempt of Coriolanus.

Shakepeare's nearest approach to Graecismus, the use of a Greek idiom, seems to be by confusion of two constructions, such as:

> This is the greatest error of all the rest (*MND*, 5.1.250)
>
> York is most unmeet of any man (*2H6*, 1.3.167)
>
> Of all men else I have avoided thee (*Mac.*, 5.8.4)
>
> I do not like the Tower of any place (*R3*, 3.1.68)

E. A. Abbott, who quotes these examples, remarks with particular reference to the last: "This . . . is a thoroughly Greek idiom, though independent in English . . . The line is a confusion of two constructions. . . . 'I dislike the tower more than any place' and 'most of all places' becomes 'of any place'." [18]

Of all the schemes of grammar in Elizabethan English, anthimeria, the substitution of one part of speech for another, is perhaps the most exciting. More than any other figure of grammar, it gives vitality and power to Shakespeare's language, through its packed meaning, liveliness, and stir. In the following examples, adjectives are used as adverbs, prepositions as adjectives, adjectives as nouns, nouns as adjectives, nouns as adverbs, verbs as nouns.

> report That I am sudden sick. Quick and return! (*A & C*, 1.3.4)
>
> shap'd out a man Whom this beneath world (*Tim.*, 1.1.43)
>
> All cruels else subscrib'd (*Lear*, 3.7.65)
>
> his complexion is perfect gallows (*Tem.*, 1.1.32)
>
> Kingdom'd Achilles in commotion rages (*T & C*, 2.3.185)
>
> It more imports me Than all the actions that I have foregone
> Or futurely can cope. (*TNK*, 1.1.172)

[18] Abbott, *A Shakespearian Grammar*, 3d ed., p. 296.

betwixt too early and too late (*H8*, 2.3.84)

> goodness, growing to a plurisy,
Dies in his own too-much. (*Ham.*, 4.7.118)

And many such-like as's of great charge (*Ham.*, 5.2.43)

What you shall know meantime Of stirs abroad (*A & C*, 1.4.81)

To ransack Troy, within whose strong immures (*T & C*, Prol. 8)

I true? How now? What wicked deem is this? (*T & C*, 4.4.61)

Most striking are the verbs. As Alfred Hart, who recently made very careful and admirable studies of Shakespeare's vocabulary, observes:

Most Elizabethan and Jacobean authors use nouns freely as verbs, but they are not very venturesome. . . . The last plays of Shakespeare teem with daringly brilliant metaphors due solely to this use of nouns and adjectives as verbs. . . . they add vigour, vividness and imagination to the verse . . . almost every play affords examples of such happy valiancy of phrase.[19]

Shakespeare uses pronouns, adjectives, and nouns as verbs.

> If thou thou'st him some thrice, it shall not be amiss (*TN*, 3.2.48)

> the good mind of Camillo tardied My swift command (*WT*, 3.2.163)

> And that which most with you should safe my going,
Is Fulvia's death (*A & C*, 1.3.55)

> Shall dizzy with more clamour Neptune's ear (*T & C*, 5.2.174)

> Lord Angelo dukes it well (*MM*, 3.2.100)

> it hath ruffian'd so upon the sea [the wind] (*Oth.*, 2.1.7)

> a hand that kings Have lipp'd (*A & C*, 2.5.29)

> I'll unhair thy head! (*A & C*, 2.5.64)

> Julius Caesar, Who at Philippi the good Brutus ghosted (*A & C*, 2.6.12)

> Had our great palace the capacity To camp this host (*A & C*, 4.8.32)

> Wouldst thou be window'd in great Rome and see
Thy master . . . bending down His corrigible neck (*A & C*, 4.14.72)

> had I come coffin'd home (*Cor.*, 2.1.193)

> A mile before his tent fall down, and knee
The way into his mercy (*Cor.*, 5.1.5)

[19] Alfred Hart, "Shakespeare and the Vocabulary of *The Two Noble Kinsmen*," in his *Shakespeare and the Homilies*, p. 250.

a Jack guardant cannot office me from my son Coriolanus (*Cor.*, 5.2.67)

My affairs Are servanted to others (*Cor.*, 5.2.88)

Lov'd me above the measure of a father;
Nay godded me indeed (*Cor.*, 5.3.10)

my true lip Hath virgin'd it e'er since (*Cor.*, 5.3.47)

        and nature prompts them
In simple and low things to prince it much (*Cym.*, 3.3.84)

'Tis still a dream, or else such stuff as madmen
Tongue, and brain not (*Cym.*, 5.4.146)

the thunder would not peace at my bidding (*Lear*, 4.6.103)

Bosom up my counsel (*H8*, 1.1.112)

        give us the bones
Of our dead kings, that we may chapel them (*TNK*, 1.1.49)

they have skiff'd Torrents (*TNK*, 1.3.37)

In reading Shakespeare's work chronologically, one notices that his language grows in ease, range, and mastery, in its capacity to be vivid, sudden, condensed. These qualities of Shakespeare's later style result in no small measure from his consummate skill in using the schemes of grammatical construction.

2. *The Vices of Language*

The vices of language are closely related to the figures of grammar, for while a deliberate deviation from the grammatical norm for the sake of some desired aesthetic effect is a figure, the ignorant violation of grammatical rules is a vice.

Solecismus, a vice related to the grammatical figure enallage, is the ignorant misuse of cases, genders, tenses. Holofernes, the pedant, corrects Sir Nathaniel for this kind of error.

Nath. Laus Deo, bone intelligo.
Hol. 'Bone'?—'bone' for 'bene.' Priscian a little scratched; 'twill serve. (*LLL*, 5.1.30) [20]

Solecismus is a fault of which Mistress Quickly is frequently guilty.

And didst thou not. . . desire me to be no more so familiarity with such poor people . . . ? (*2H4*, 2.1.106)

[20] Cf. Puttenham's remark on Priscian, p. 300, below.

she gives you to notify that her husband will be absence from his house between ten and eleven. . . . He's a very jealousy man. (*MWW*, 2.2.85–93)

Barbarismus, mispronunciation of words, most often marks a foreigner. Dr. Caius, the French physician, combines barbarismus and solecismus in his speech.

I pray you bear vitness dat me have stay six or seven, two tree hours for him, and he is no-come. (*MWW*, 2.3.36)

So does Sir Hugh Evans, who mispronounces English in the Welsh manner.

Fery goot. I will make a prief of it in my notebook, and we will afterwards ork upon the cause with as great discreetly as we can. (*MWW*, 1.1.146)

Soraismus, the mingling of sundry languages ignorantly or affectedly,[21] is a characteristic of the pedant Holofernes.

> Most barbarous intimation! Yet a kind of insinuation, as it were, *in via*, in way, of explication; *facere*, as it were, replication, or rather, *ostentare*, to show, as it were, his inclination. (*LLL*, 4.2.13)

> He clepeth a calf 'cauf,' 'half' 'hauf,' neighbour vocatur 'nebour'
> . . . Ne intelligis, domine? (5.1.25–29)

> I do sans question. (5.1.91)

> Allons! we will employ thee! (5.1.159)

Listening to talk such as this between Holofernes and Sir Nathaniel, Moth comments to Costard, with patent reference to this vice:

They have been at a great feast of languages and stol'n the scraps. (5.1.39)

Other characters also indulge in this mingle-mangle, as Puttenham dubbed soraismus.

> *Armado.* But we will put it, as they say, to fortuna della guerra. (*LLL*, 5.2.533)

> *Caius.* Pray you go and vetch me in my closset un boitier vert—a box, a green-a box. (*MWW*, 1.4.46)

[21] In defining soraismus, Sherry and Puttenham mention Italian, French, Spanish, Dutch, Scottish, and Welsh among the languages which may be thus mingled with English. After quoting Puttenham, H. C. Hart remarks in his edition of *Love's Labour's Lost:* "Latin is deliberately omitted. Probably in Puttenham's mind it was so usual and needful that it never occurred to him that it was pedantic." (3d ed., The Arden Shakespeare, p. xl. The introduction is dated September, 1905.) Peacham, however, includes Latin. He defines soraismus as "a mingling together of divers Languages, as when there is in one sentence English, Lattine & French" (1577 edition, Sig. G iiiiʳ).

Heterogenium is the vice of answering something utterly irrelevant to what is asked. This vice is used with fine dramatic effect in the account given by Dromio of Ephesus to Adriana of his encounter with Antipholus of Syracuse whom he mistook for Antipholus of Ephesus, his master and her husband. The irrelevance occasioned by the confusion of the twin brothers is much more sharply pointed in this recital than it was in the encounter itself, and appears more ridiculous.

> But sure he is stark mad.
> When I desir'd him to come home to dinner,
> He ask'd me for a thousand marks in gold.
> ' 'Tis dinner time,' quoth I. 'My gold!' quoth he.
> 'Your meat doth burn,' quoth I. 'My gold!' quoth he.
> 'Will you come home?' quoth I. 'My gold!' quoth he.
> 'Where is the thousand marks I gave thee, villain?'
> 'The pig,' quoth I, 'is burn'd.' 'My gold!' quoth he. (*CE*, 2.1.59)

All sorts of irrelevancies clutter the nurse's replies to Juliet, who is beside herself to know Romeo's answer to her message:

> *Juliet.* No, no. But all this did I know before.
> What says he of our marriage? What of that?
> *Nurse.* Lord, how my head aches! What a head have I!
> It beats as it would fall in twenty pieces.
> My back o' t' other side—ah, my back, my back! . . .
> *Juliet.* I' faith, I am sorry that thou art not well.
> Sweet, sweet, sweet nurse, tell me, what says my love?
> *Nurse.* Your love says, like an honest gentleman, and a courteous,
> and a kind, and a handsome, and, I warrant, a virtuous— Where is
> your mother? (2.5.47–59)

It is the nurse's habit to inject adventitious details into any account she gives, as that of Juliet's birth and childhood (1.3.16–57).

Amphibology is ambiguity of grammatical structure, often occasioned by mispunctuation. The clown chooses to mis-hear Cassio in order to make a captious retort:

> *Cassio.* Dost thou hear, my honest friend?
> *Clown.* No, I hear not your honest friend. I hear you.
> (*Oth.*, 3.1.22)

By mispunctuation, Quince renders the prologue which he recites ridiculous and opposite in meaning.

> If we offend, it is with our good will.
>> That you should think, we come not to offend,
> But with good will. To show our simple skill,
>> That is the true beginning of our end.
> Consider then, we come but in despite.
>> We do not come, as minding to content you,
> Our true intent is. All for your delight,
>> We are not here. That you should here repent you,
> The actors are at hand: and by their show,
>> You shall know all, that you are like to know.
>
> <div align="center">(<i>MND</i>, 5.1.108) [22]</div>

Noting the error, the auditors comment, "This fellow doth not stand upon points . . . he knows not the stop . . . a sound, but not in government."

Tapinosis is the use of a base word to diminish the dignity of a person or thing. When Cressida declares that Achilles is a better man than Troilus, Pandar retorts:

> Achilles? A drayman, a porter, a very camel! (<i>T & C</i>, 1.2.270)

Holofernes addresses Moth:

> Quis, quis, thou consonant? (<i>LLL</i>, 5.1.55)

Sir Toby maintains that judgment and reason have been grand-jurymen in disputes "since before Noah was a sailor" (<i>TN</i>, 3.2.18). Fabian assures Sir Andrew that it was only to exasperate him and to awaken his "dormouse valor" that Olivia showed favor to Cesario. Since, however, he let this opportunity to show his mettle go by, his case is the worse.

> You are now sail'd into the North of my lady's opinion, where you will hang like an icicle on a Dutchman's beard, unless you do redeem it. (<i>TN</i>, 3.2.27)

Thinking Cesario has double-crossed him, the duke exclaims contemptuously:

> O thou dissembling cub! What wilt thou be
> When time hath sow'd a grizzle on thy case? (5.1.167)

---

[22] The prologue seems to be an imitation of the mispunctuated love letters in *Ralph Roister Doister*. Hardin Craig thinks that Shakespeare probably became acquainted with the letters in Wilson's *Rule of Reason*, where they are quoted in full and the play is ascribed to Nicholas Udall, for the reason that Wilson's book, which went through many editions, was easily available, while the play itself probably was not. "Shakespeare and Wilson's *Arte of Rhetorique*," *Studies in Philology*, XXVIII (October, 1931), p. 628. See p. 368, below.

Tapinosis is a favorite device with Rosalind. As Ganymede, she tells Orlando that she knows the marks of a man in love, "in which cage of rushes I am sure you are not prisoner" (*AYLI*, 3.2.389). She speaks slightingly to Phebe.

> I see no more in you than in the ordinary
> Of nature's sale-work. (3.5.42)

To torment Katharina, Petruchio berates the tailor.

> O monstrous arrogance! Thou liest, thou thread, thou thimble,
> Thou yard, three-quarters, half-yard, quarter, nail! . . .
> Brav'd in mine own house with a skein of thread?
> Away, thou rag, thou quantity, thou remnant. (*TS*, 4.3.107–12)

Cacemphaton, or aischrologia, is the vice of foul speech. It characterizes a buffoon or railing companion, whom the Latins called *scurra*. Scurrilous jests are plentifully illustrated in the remarks of Thersites and Lucio. Another form of cacemphaton is an unpleasing combination of sounds such as results from excessive alliteration. It is consciously illustrated in the opening line of the epitaph already quoted, which was composed extemporaneously by Holofernes, who announces that he "will something affect the letter."

> The preyful princess pierc'd and prick'd a pretty pleasing pricket.
> (*LLL*, 4.2.58)

Cacosyntheton is the ill placing of words, as when an adjective improperly follows a noun or when there is any other unpleasing order of words:

> A soul feminine saluteth us (*LLL*, 4.2.83)
>
> My name is Pistol call'd (*H5*, 4.1.62)

Common to a group of linguistic vices is the fault of employing many words to say little, or to repeat the same thing inanely, dilutedly, tediously, garrulously. These vices, which differ but slightly from each other, are the distinguishing marks of several of Shakespeare's characters. Tautology, vain repetition of the same idea, is used skillfully by Antony to mock drunken Lepidus.

> *Lepidus.* What manner o' thing is your crocodile?
> *Antony.* It is shap'd, sir, like itself, and it is as broad as it has breadth. It is just so high as it is, and moves with its own organs. It lives by that which nourisheth it, and the elements once out of it, it transmigrates.
> *Lepidus.* What colour is it of?

Antony. Of its own colour too.
Lepidus. 'Tis a strange serpent.
Antony. 'Tis so. And the tears of it are wet. (*A & C*, 2.7.46)

Perissologia, or macrologia, is the addition of a superfluous clause which adds nothing to the meaning.

Evans. I do despise a liar as I do despise one that is false, or as I despise one that is not true. (*MWW*, 1.1.68)

Parelcon is the addition of a superfluous word, as of *that* in the following:

When that I was and a little tiny boy (*TN*, 5.1.398)

Till that the wearer's very means do ebb? (*AYLI*, 2.7.73)

Pleonasmus, the needless telling of what is already understood, is a fault in Pistol which Sir Hugh Evans cannot tolerate:

Falstaff. Pistol!
Pistol. He hears with ears.
Evans. The tevil and his tam! What phrase is this? 'He hears with ear'? Why, it is affectations. (*MWW*, 1.1.149)

Juliet's nurse, reporting Tybalt's death, insists:

I saw the wound, I saw it with mine eyes. (*R & J*, 3.2.52)

Speaking of the asp he has brought her, the clown volubly warns Cleopatra:

His biting is immortal. Those that do die of it do seldom or never recover. (*A & C*, 5.2.247)

Homiologia, tedious and inane repetition, is the specific means by which Shakespeare characterizes Justice Shallow.

He hath wrong'd me; indeed he hath; at a word, he hath. Believe me! Robert Shallow, Esquire, saith he is wronged. (*MWW*, 1.1.107)

Where's the roll? Where's the roll? Where's the roll? Let me see, let me see, let me see. So, so, so, so, so—so, so. Yea, marry, sir. Ralph Mouldy! Let them appear as I call; let them do so, let them do so. Let me see. Where is Mouldy? (*2H4*, 3.2.106)

I will not excuse you; you shall not be excus'd; excuses shall not be admitted; there is no excuse shall serve; you shall not be excus'd. (*2H4*, 5.1.5)

Falstaff says that Shallow prates of the wildness of his youth and every third word a lie. But whatever tale he tells, it is with this same tedious repetitiousness.

When I lay at Clement's Inn,—I was then Sir Dagonet in Arthur's Show,—there was a little quiver fellow, and 'a would manage you his piece thus; and 'a would about and about, and come you in and come you in. 'Rah, tah, tah!' would 'a say; 'Bounce!' would 'a say; and away again would 'a go, and again would 'a come. I shall ne'er see such a fellow. (*2H4*, 3.2.299)

The vice of homiologia appears also in Falstaff, not characteristically as in Shallow, but occasionally for a purpose. Falstaff remarks to Prince Hal:

An old lord of the Council rated me the other day in the street about you, sir, but I mark'd him not; and yet he talk'd very wisely, but I regarded him not; and yet he talk'd wisely, and in the street too. (*1H4*, 1.2.93)

Juliet's nurse, Mistress Quickly, and Pandar add this vice to others which make up the sum of their garrulity. It is exemplified also in Fluellen's repeated "Look you," in Nym's "That's the humour of it," and in Pompey's "I hope here be truths . . . as I said . . . as I told you," in *Measure for Measure* (2.1.99–136).

Periergia is a vice not so much of superfluity of words as of overlabor to seem fine and eloquent, especially in a slight matter. Armado, making a request of the king which can be answered in two words, puts it thus:

Anointed, I implore so much expense of thy royal sweet breath as will utter a brace of words. (*LLL*, 5.2.523)

The princess comments on his pomposity: " 'A speaks not like a man of God his making." The circumlocution characteristic of this vice is carried to ridiculous excess by the player king in *Hamlet* when he reminds his queen: [23]

> Full thirty times hath Phoebus' cart gone round
> Neptune's salt wash and Tellus' orbed ground,
> And thirty dozen moons with borrowed sheen
> About the world have times twelve thirties been,
> Since love our hearts, and Hymen did our hands,
> Unite comutual in most sacred bands. (3.2.165)

Bomphiologia or bombastic speech characterizes the braggart. Falstaff, a prolific and incorrigible braggart, tells Prince Hal and Poins that a

---

[23] Compare Puttenham's example of this vice, p. 303, below. It seems not improbable that Shakespeare patterned this travesty of pretentious style on that.

hundred men attacked him and his three companions near Gadshill and robbed them of the thousand pounds they had taken.

I am a rogue if I were not at half-sword with a dozen of them two hours together. I have scap'd by miracle. I am eight times thrust through the doublet, four through the hose; my buckler cut through and through; my sword hack'd like a handsaw—ecce signum! I never dealt better since I was a man. . . . if I fought not with fifty of them, I am a bunch of radish! If there were not two or three and fifty upon poor old Jack, then am I no two-legg'd creature. (*1H4*, 2.4.182–208)

Falstaff declares that after having worsted these men, he was attacked by two rogues in buckram suits. As his story goes on, these two grow to four, then to seven, then to nine, and finally to eleven, seven of whom he himself valiantly paid off with his sword. Prince Hal mocks this bombast: "O monstrous! Eleven buckram men grown out of two!" (243). He then deflates the braggart, confronts him with his lies, tells him that he himself and Poins were the two in buckram who set upon the four of them, outfaced them, took their prize, witnessed Falstaff's cowardly running away and his roaring for mercy. Later he greets him with the gibe: "How now, my sweet creature of bombast?" (359).

Bombast is a characteristic of Glendower. When Hotspur tells him that King Henry IV grows pale at his name, he answers:

> I cannot blame him. At my nativity
> The front of heaven was full of fiery shapes
> Of burning cressets, and at my birth
> The frame and huge foundation of the earth
> Shak'd like a coward. (*1H4*, 3.1.13)

Cloten is another braggart. In high dudgeon he tells his lords that he will not debase himself by answering the challenge of an inferior whom he has deliberately and openly offended.

Whoreson dog! I give him satisfaction? Would he had been one of my rank! . . . I am not vex'd more at anything in th' earth. A pox on't! I had rather not be so noble as I am. They dare not fight with me, because of the Queen my mother. Every Jack-slave hath his belly full of fighting, and I must go up and down like a cock that nobody can match. (*Cym.*, 2.1.16–24)

He bombastically threatens Guiderius.

>   Thou injurious thief,
>   Hear but my name and tremble. . . .
>   To thy further fear,

> Nay, to thy mere confusion, thou shalt know
> I am son to th' Queen. . . . Art not afeard?
>   . . . Die the death!
> When I have slain thee with my proper hand,
> I'll follow those that even now fled hence
> And on the gates of Lud's Town set your heads.
> Yield, rustic mountaineer! (4.2.86–100)

Affected diction, especially the coining of fine words out of Latin, is a form of the vice cacozelia. Through it Shakespeare satirizes inkhornism. Sir Andrew Aguecheek, eager to acquire a fine vocabulary, notes high-sounding words that he hears.

Cesario. [*to Olivia*] Most excellent accomplish'd lady, the heavens rain odours on you! . . . My matter hath no voice, lady, but to your own most pregnant and vouchsafed ear.
Andrew. [*aside*] 'Odours,' 'pregnant,' and 'vouchsafed'—I'll get 'em all three all ready. (*TN*, 3.1.95–102)

Armado bids Costard deliver a letter to Jaquenetta, and gives him money, saying:

Armado. There is remuneration; for the best ward of mine honour is rewarding my dependents. . . . [*Exit*]
Costard. Now will I look to his remuneration. Remuneration—O, that's the Latin word for three farthings. (*LLL*, 3.1.132–39)

Armado's deliberate effort to employ fine diction wins the commendation of the pedant Holofernes.

Armado. Sir, it is the King's most sweet pleasure and affection to congratulate the Princess at her pavilion in the posteriors of this day, which the rude multitude call the afternoon.
Holofernes. The posterior of the day, most generous sir, is liable, congruent, and measurable for the afternoon. The word is well cull'd, chose, sweet, and apt. (*LLL*, 5.1.92)

Touchstone, speaking to William, parodies such pompous affectation.

Therefore, you clown, abandon (which is in the vulgar, leave) the society (which in the boorish is, company) of this female (which in the common is, woman); which together is, abandon the society of this female. (*AYLI*, 5.1.52)

Mercutio excoriates the affectedness of Tybalt:

O, he's the courageous captain of compliments. . . . Ah, the immortal pas-

sado! the punto reverso! . . . The pox of such antic, lisping fantasticoes——
——these new tuners of accents! (*R & J*, 2.4.20–30)

Cacozelia is Osric's characteristic vice. In delivering to Hamlet a message
from the king he thus dilates on Laertes.

Sir, here is newly come to court Laertes; believe me, an absolute gentleman,
full of most excellent differences, of very soft society and great showing. Indeed, to speak feelingly of him, he is the card or calendar of gentry; for you
shall find in him the continent of what part a gentleman would see. (5.2.110)

Hamlet scornfully travesties Osric's affectation of "true diction" by answering him in kind.

Sir, his definement suffers no perdition in you; though, I know, to divide him
inventorially would dozy th' arithmetic of memory, and yet but yaw neither in
respect of his quick sail. But, in the verity of extolment, I take him to be a soul
of great article, and his infusion of such dearth and rareness as, to make true
diction of him, his semblable is his mirror, and who else would trace him, his
unbrage, nothing more. . . . The concernancy, sir? Why do we wrap the
gentleman in our rawer breath? (117)

Horatio comments, "All's golden words are spent," but he is mistaken.
Osric has another golden word which Hamlet again openly derides.

Osric. The King, sir, hath wager'd with him six Barbary horses; against the
which he has impon'd, as I take it, six French rapiers and poniards, with their
assigns . . .
Hamlet. . . . that's the French bet against the Danish. Why is this all
impon'd, as you call it? (5.2.154–71)

Having stated the reply which Osric is to give the king, Hamlet remarks
mockingly, knowing that Osric will translate it into his own inflated style:

To this effect, sir, after what flourish your nature will. (187)

Pistol is a swaggerer whose talk combines cacozelia, bomphiologia, and
cacosyntheton, or objectionable word order. In addition to these vices,
and partly because of them, there is in Pistol's speech a strange bombastic
rhythm. The soaring note of *Tamburlaine* is burlesqued when, referring
to Doll Tearsheet, who has just called him many vile names and openly
scorned him, he angrily exclaims:

> These be good humours indeed. Shall packhorses,
> And hollow pamper'd jades of Asia,
> Which cannot go but thirty mile a day,

> Compare with Caesars, and with Cannibals,
> And Troyan Greeks? Nay, rather damn them with
> King Cerberus and let the welkin roar!
> Shall we fall foul for toys? (*2H4*, 2.4.177)

Doll Tearsheet aptly characterizes him.

Hang him, swaggering rascal! . . . I cannot endure such a fustian rascal. (76, 203)

Pistol snatches up his sword and cries out to Bardolph, who at the request of the others comes to thrust him downstairs.

> What? Shall we have incision? Shall we imbrue?
> Then death rock me asleep, abridge my doleful days!
> Why then, let grievous, ghastly, gaping wounds
> Untwine the Sisters Three! Come, Atropos, I say! (210)

Here classical allusions increase the braggadocio. In characteristic style Pistol challenges Sir Hugh Evans, who credits Slender's complaint that Pistol picked his pocket.

> Ha, thou mountain foreigner! Sir John and master mine,
> I combat challenge of this latten bilbo.
> Word of denial in thy labras here!
> Word of denial! Froth and scum, thou liest! (*MWW*, 1.1.164)

Pistol's bombastic tone is in evidence even when he seeks to borrow money from Falstaff.

> *Pistol*. I will retort the sum in equipage.
> *Falstaff*. I will not lend thee a penny.
> *Pistol*. Why, then, the world's mine oyster,
> Which I with sword will open. (*MWW*, 2.2.1)

Pistol mingles bomphiologia, soraismus, and cacosyntheton in his reply to Nym.

> *Nym*. Will you shog off? I would have you solus.
> *Pistol*. 'Solus,' egregious dog? O viper vile!
> The 'solus' in thy most mervailous face!
> The 'solus' in thy teeth, and in thy throat . . .
> I do retort the 'solus' in thy bowels;
> For I can take, and Pistol's cock is up,
> And flashing fire will follow. (*H5*, 2.1.47–56)

When Nym speaks of stealing, Pistol scorns his commonplace diction.

'Convey' the wise it call. 'Steal'? foh! a fico for the phrase! (*MWW*, 1.3.32)

It is only a short step from the affectation of high sounding words to their ignorant misapplication, another form of the vice cacozelia, which we call malapropism, and which sometimes achieves, as it were unconsciously, a happy hit through the misused word.

Elbow. [*to Escalus*] My wife, sir, whom I detest before heaven and your honour—(*MM*, 2.1.69)

Launcelot Gobbo. [*to Shylock*] My young master doth expect your reproach. (*MV*, 2.5.19)

Quince. . . . one must come in with a bush of thorns and a lantern, and say he comes to disfigure, or to present, the person of Moonshine. (*MND*, 3.1.60)

Feste. [*as Sir Topas*] Out, hyperbolical fiend! (*TN*, 4.2.29)

Sir Andrew. [*of Sebastian*] . . . he's the very devil incardinate. (*TN*, 5.1.185)

1. Watch. We have here recover'd the most dangerous piece of lechery that ever was known in the commonwealth. (*MA*, 3.3.179)

Bardolph. [*to Hal*] My lord, do you see these meteors? Do you behold these exhalations? (*1H4*, 2.4.351)

Host. [*to Caius*] I will be thy adversary toward Anne Page. (*MWW*, 2.3.98)

Bardolph. . . . the gentleman had drunk himself out of his five sentences. (*MWW*, 1.1.178)

Dull is quite confident that he is repeating exactly what Holofernes said.

Holofernes. Th' allusion holds in the exchange.
Dull. 'Tis true indeed; the collusion holds in the exchange.
Holofernes. God comfort thy capacity! I say th' allusion holds in the exchange.
Dull. And I say the polusion holds in the exchange. (*LLL*, 4.2.42)

Slender assures his cousin Justice Shallow that he is resolutely resolved to marry Anne Page, as Shallow has requested.

I will marry her, sir, at your request; but if there be no great love in the beginning, yet heaven may decrease it upon better acquaintance, . . . if you say, 'Marry her,' I will marry her. That I am freely dissolved, and dissolutely. (*MWW*, 1.1.253)

Speed explicitly comments on this vice.

> *Speed.* How now, Signior Launce? What news with your mastership?
> *Launce.* With my master's ship? Why it is at sea.
> *Speed.* Well, your old vice still—mistake the word. (*TGV*, 3.1.279)

As Speed observes, mistaking a word for another similar in sound was a characteristic fault of Launce.

> *Speed.* But, Launce, how sayst thou that my master is become a notable lover?
> *Launce.* I never knew him otherwise.
> *Speed.* Than how?
> *Launce.* A notable lubber, as thou reportest him to be. (*TGV*, 2.5.42)

This vice is especially amusing when a word of one language is understood amiss in another, as when Pistol demands ransom of a French soldier whom he encounters on the battlefield.

> *Pistol.* Yield, cur! . . . Art thou a gentleman? What is thy name? Discuss.
> *French.* O Seigneur Dieu!
> *Pistol.* O Signieur Dew should be a gentleman. . . .
>   O Signieur Dew, thou diest on point of fox,
>   Except, O signieur, thou do give to me
>   Egregious ransom. (*H5*, 4.4.1–11)

Similarly, Mistress Quickly mistakes Latin.

> *Will. Singulariter, nominativo, hic, haec, hoc.* . . .
> *Evans.* What is your genitive case plural, William? . . .
> *Will. Genitivo, horum, harum, horum.*
> *Quickly.* Vengeance of Jinny's case! Fie on her. Never name her, child, if she be a whore. . . . You do ill to teach the child such words. He teaches him to hick and to hack, which they'll do fast enough of themselves, and to call *horum.* Fie upon you! (*MWW*, 4.1.42–70)

Mistress Quickly confuses words in her own language as well.

> [*To Falstaff and Doll Tearsheet*] You cannot one bear with another's confirmities. (*2H4*, 2.4.63)

> [*Of Falstaff*] he is indited to dinner (*2H4*, 2.1.30)

> [*Of Anne Page*] But, indeed, she is given too much to allicholy and musing. (*MWW*, 1.4.165)

The ignorant misuse of words is characteristic of Bottom.

saying thus, or to the same defect (*MND*, 3.1.40)

The flowers of odious savours sweet (3.1.84)

I have an exposition of sleep come upon me (4.1.41)

Dogberry perhaps excels all of Shakespeare's other characters in this amusing vice.[24]

[*To Seacoal, whom he has appointed constable of the watch*] This is your charge: you shall comprehend all vagrom men. (*MA*, 3.3.25)

[*To Leonato*] I would have some confidence with you that decerns you nearly. (3.5.3)

Comparisons are odorous (19)

Our watch, sir, have indeed comprehended two aspicious persons (49)

Only get the learned writer to set down our excommunication, and meet me at the jail. (68)

Is our whole dissembly appear'd? (4.2.1)

[*To Conrade*] Dost thou not suspect my place? Dost thou not suspect my years? (76)

By this time our sexton hath reformed Signior Leonato of the matter. (5.1.261)

The clue to the peculiar humor in Dogberry, however, is the vice acyron, the use of a word repugnant or contrary to what is meant. This

[24] Hardin Craig, in "Shakespeare and Wilson's *Arte of Rhetorique,*" *op. cit.*, p. 620, remarks of Dogberry that his is "a form of humor which seems to be peculiarly Shakespearian. Clowns, of course, always misused their words; it is impossible to think of a clown who does not do so. But in this case there is a touch of pedantry. There is a certain amount of ridicule of pedantry in Lyly, but no humor derived from a misunderstanding or misuse of learned terms. There are excellent fantastically talking clowns in Greene, Peele, and Porter; but nowhere in early comedy have I been able to find a malaprop who directly suggests Bottom, Mistress Quickly, and Dogberry. On the other hand, the pedantical misuse of fine language is not a rare form of comicality, as Wilson's story [of the pedantic mayor, Mair's edition, p. 164] bears witness."

H. C. Hart, however, *op. cit.*, (1905), p. xxxvii, points out a misuse of legal terms in Whetstone's *Promos and Cassandra*, printed 1578: "In Act III, Sc. ii, of the second part, a clown says to a promoter or informer: 'You sqwade knave, yle burne yee, For *reforming* a lye, thus against mee.' 'Reform' for 'inform' here is perhaps the earliest stage example of mistaking law terms."

According to Louise D. Frasure ("Shakespeare's Constables," *Anglia*, LVIII [1934], 388), "In Dogberry, Shakespeare, for the first time in drama, presents a truly realistic English constable, with appropriate setting, word and deed and with an obvious and significant part in the action of the play."

vice appears but rarely in other characters, although there are a few instances of it in the talk of Dogberry's companions.

   2. *Watch.* [*to Borachio*] Never speak, we charge you. Let us obey you to go with us. (3.3.188)

   Verges. [*to Dogberry*] Yea; or else it were pity, but they should suffer salvation, body and soul. (3.3.2)

Dogberry himself is the master practitioner of this vice, and it contributes not a little to his peculiar and amusing ineptitude. Having assembled the watch, he asks, before giving them their charge:

First, who think you the most desartless man to be constable? (3.3.9)

Upon advice he chooses George Seacoal and tells him:

You are thought here to be the most senseless and fit man for the constable of the watch. (22)

When the watch give their account of Borachio's crime, he exclaims to the culprit:

O villain! thou wilt be condemn'd into everlasting redemption for this. (4.2.58)

He tells Conrade, who has called him an ass, that he shall not escape punishment, even though the sexton, who was recording the examination, had left before this insult was uttered.

No, thou villain, thou art full of piety, as shall be prov'd upon thee by good witness. (80)

Leonato, the governor, thanks him for his good service as constable, and discharges him of further care of the prisoner. Dogberry respectfully takes his leave thus:

I humbly give you leave to depart; and if a merry meeting may be wish'd, God prohibit it! (5.1.334)

   The vices of language were utilized to the full by Shakespeare to achieve satiric humor and to create ludicrous characters and comic incidents, especially from low life.

3. *The Figures of Repetition*

   Of all the figures of repetition so highly valued by the Elizabethans, alliteration or paroemion, as it was called, is the one which we today think of most readily as an embellishment of style. In *Pericles* alliteration effectually recalls the circumstances of Marina's birth during a storm at sea.

> For a more blusterous birth had never babe. (3.1.28)

The other figures of repetition involve not letters merely, but words. A number of them are intrinsically related to grammar, because by their position they tend to emphasize such constructions as parallel or antithetical clauses. The figures of repetition, which abound in Shakespeare's early plays and poems, proclaim his conscious and sophisticated approach to art. His later use of them in solemn and moving iteration marks the growth in his mastery of rhetoric which kept pace with his growth in the mastery of verse. He used all the figures of repetition, some persistently to the end of his work, some rarely in the later plays, but always with increased skill and effectiveness.

Shakespeare's early schematic use of anaphora, beginning a series of clauses with the same word, and of epistrophe, ending with the same, is illustrated in Margaret's recital of her woes in *Richard III* (4.4.92–104; 40–44) and in *3 Henry VI* (2.5), where King Henry, sitting alone on a hill, reflects that a shepherd's life is better than a king's.[25] Henry's meditation is interrupted by a son who drags in the body of his father, whom he has unwittingly killed in the civil war then going on, and a father who has likewise slain his son. One after another, they exclaim:

> *Son.* How will my mother for a father's death
> Take on with me, and ne'er be satisfied!
> *Father.* How will my wife for slaughter of my son
> Shed seas of tears, and ne'er be satisfied!
> *King Henry.* How will the country for these woful chances
> Misthink the King, and not be satisfied! (2.5.103)

Such a combination of anaphora and epistrophe was called symploce. In *King John,* when a citizen of Angiers proposes reasons for the Dauphin's marriage to Blanch in a speech marked by anaphora, epistrophe, and other palpable figures, the bastard comments derisively on the overwrought rhetorical style.

Our ears are cudgell'd . . . I was never so bethump'd with words. (2.1.464)

---

[25] In the opinion of Frank P. Wilson, this early soliloquy "with its elaborate examples of anaphora . . . is redeemed by the lyricism which cuts across the formalism of the rhetoric." "Shakespeare and the Diction of Common Life," *Proceedings of the British Academy,* XXVII, 11 (read April 23, 1941).

Anaphora and epistrophe, the most obvious of rhetorical devices, appear in the early plays in stiff profusion. Used but rarely in the later plays, the repetition is deeply moving, as when Othello, to whom Iago has shown the false but convincing evidence of the handkerchief, cries out:

> O, now for ever
> Farewell the tranquil mind! farewell content!
> Farewell the plumed troop, and the big wars
> That make ambition virtue! O, farewell! (3.3.347)

And when Thaisa asks:

> Are you not Pericles? Like him you spake;
> Like him you are. (*Per.*, 5.3.32)

Similar artistry appears in the later, rare use of epistrophe. Othello exclaims ironically of Desdemona:

> A fine woman! a fair woman! a sweet woman! (4.1.189)

And Desdemona's simple trust is somehow enhanced by the use of this figure, when she says to Othello:

> Why I should fear I know not,
> Since guiltiness I know not; but yet I feel I fear. (5.2.38)

Hamlet implores the ghost:

> If thou hast any sound, or use of voice,
> Speak to me.
> If there be any good thing to be done,
> That may to thee do ease, and grace to me,
> Speak to me. (1.1.128)

Repetition drives home to the audience the one thought that pounds in Shylock's mind.

> I'll have my bond! Speak not against my bond!
> I have sworn an oath that I will have my bond. (*MV*, 3.3.4)

Epanalepsis is the repetition at the end of a clause or sentence of the word with which it begins.

> Purpose so barr'd, it follows Nothing is done to purpose. (*Cor.*, 3.1.148)

> Blood hath bought blood, and blows have answer'd blows;
> Strength match'd with strength, and power confronted power.
> (*KJ*, 2.1.329)

Cassius from bondage will deliver Cassius. (*JC*, 1.3.90)

Remember March, the ides of March remember. (*JC*, 4.3.18)

Shakespeare shows continuing favor toward three figures of repetition related to logical processes: antimetabole, anadiplosis, and climax. Antimetabole is akin to logical conversion in that it turns a sentence around.

Plainly as heaven sees earth and earth sees heaven (*WT*, 1.2.315)

Grief joys, joy grieves, on slender accident. (*Ham.*, 3.2.209)

For 'tis a question left us yet to prove, Whether love lead fortune, or else fortune love. (*Ham.*, 3.2.212)

And give to dust that is a little gilt More laud than gilt o'erdusted. (*T & C*, 3.3.178–9)

The fool doth think he is wise, but the wise man knows himself to be a fool. (*AYLI*, 5.1.34–35)

After a sparring of words in which this figure has part, Feste comments on it.

Cesario. So thou mayst say, the king lies by a beggar, if a beggar dwell near him; or, the church stands by thy tabor, if thy tabor stand by the church.

Feste. You have said, sir. To see this age! A sentence is but a chev'ril glove to a good wit. How quickly the wrong side may be turn'd outward! (*TN*, 3.1.8)

Shakespeare's interest in this figure is revealed by the variations which he introduces in the repetition.

Elbow. Bless you, good father friar.
Duke. And you, good brother father. (*MM*, 3.2.12)

The goodness that is cheap in beauty makes beauty brief in goodness. (*MM*, 3.1.185)

till all graces be in one woman, one woman shall not come in my grace. (*MA*, 2.3.28)

When he is best, he is a little worse than a man; and when he is worst, he is little better than a beast. (*MV*, 1.2.94)

who . . . if he be not fellow with the best king, thou shalt find the best king of good fellows. (*H5*, 5.2.260)

Stanley. Richmond is on the seas.
Richard. There let him sink, and be the seas on him! (*R3*, 4.4.462)

When Timon shows Apemantus a jewel, the sudden change of emphasis through the turning of words makes Apemantus' reply pert, clever, characteristic.

>*Timon.* What dost thou think 'tis worth?
>*Apemantus.* Not worth my thinking. (*Tim.*, 1.1.218)

Quiet dignity and practical wisdom are expressed in the duke's neatly turned reply to Orlando's demand for food.

>What would you have? Your gentleness shall force
>More than your force move us to gentleness. (*AYLI*, 2.7.102)

Antimetabole aids in succinctly stating a situation and an emotional turn-about when Juliet exclaims:

>My husband lives, that Tybalt would have slain;
>And Tybalt's dead, that would have slain my husband.
>All this is comfort; wherefore weep I then? (*R & J*, 3.2.105)

Having killed Polonius by mistake, Hamlet aptly summarizes the situation.

>I do repent; but heaven hath pleas'd it so,
>To punish me with this, and this with me. (3.4.173)

Anadiplosis is the repetition of the last word of one clause or sentence at the beginning of the next. It often expresses the two premises of a syllogism, as where Richard III through its swift, compact logic shows himself a man of action and quick decision.

>Come! I have learn'd that fearful commenting
>Is leaden servitor to dull delay;
>Delay leads impotent and snail-pac'd beggary.
>Then fiery expedition be my wing. (*R3*, 4.3.51)

Anadiplosis accentuates Octavia's distress, her loyalty pulled both ways in the war between Antony and Octavius, the very war her marriage to Antony was designed to prevent:

>Husband win, win brother,
>Prays, and destroys the prayer; no midway
>'Twixt these extremes at all. (*A & C*, 3.4.18)

Used in dialogue, this figure often has an echo quality.

>*Othello.* What dost thou think?
>*Iago.*   Think, my lord?
>*Othello.*   Think, my lord?
>By heaven, he echoes me,
>As if there were some monster in his thought
>Too hideous to be shown. (3.3.105)

This quality, with a note of strong emotional excitement, appears in Cleopatra's frantic questions to the messenger who brings her news of Antony's marriage to Octavia.

> *Messenger.* Madam,
> She was a widow—
> *Cleopatra.* Widow? Charmian, hark!
> *Messenger.* And I do think she's thirty.
> *Cleopatra.* Bear'st thou her face in mind? Is't long or round?
> *Messenger.* Round even to faultiness. (*A & C*, 3.3.29)

In *Lear*, Cornwall, bent on punishing the disguised Kent, is echoed and outdone by the more cruel Regan, his wife.

> *Cornwall.* Fetch forth the stocks! As I have life and honour,
> There shall he sit till noon.
> *Regan.* Till noon? Till night, my lord, and all night too! (2.2.140)

Climax is a continued anadiplosis, inasmuch as it carries the same kind of repetition through three or more clauses. Shakespeare uses it in one instance to convey the impression of a mighty sweep of sound.

> And let the kettle to the trumpet speak,
> The trumpet to the cannoneer without,
> The cannons to the heavens, the heaven to earth.
> (*Ham.*, 5.2.286)

Polyptoton is the repetition of words derived from the same root, and as such is related to the logical argument from conjugates, as in the following examples:

> Which harm within itself so heinous is
> As it makes harmful all that speak of it. (*KJ*, 3.1.40)

> hardness ever Of hardiness is mother. (*Cym.*, 3.6.21)

> society is no comfort To one not sociable. (*Cym.*, 4.2.12)

> Unheedful vows may heedfully be broken (*TGV*, 2.6.11)

> that word 'grace' In an ungracious mouth is but profane (*R2*, 2.3.88)

> The Greeks are strong, and skilful to their strength,
> Fierce to their skill, and to their fierceness valiant (*T & C*, 1.1.7)

Sometimes, however, this figure is used rather for the sake of the sound, which is pleasing in itself, even while it enhances the meaning.

> But day doth daily draw my sorrows longer,
> And night doth nightly make grief's strength seem stronger. (*Son. 28*)

And so his knell is knoll'd. (*Mac.*, 5.8.50)

As ending anthem of my endless dolour (*TGV*, 3.1.240)

A king, woe's slave, shall kingly woe obey (*R2*, 3.2.210)

to the certain hazard Of all incertainties (*WT*, 3.2.169)

And Death once dead, there's no more dying then. (*Son. 146*)

That a ready facility in using the figures of repetition was regarded by the Elizabethans as a test of wit may be inferred from the following passage, in which polyptoton and antimetabole set the pattern:

Mercutio. Follow me this jest now till thou hast worn out thy pump, that, when the single sole of it is worn, the jest may remain, after the wearing, solely singular.
Romeo. O single-sol'd jest, solely singular for the singleness!
Mercutio. Come between us, good Benvolio! My wits faint. (*R & J*, 2.4.65)

Protesting that he will be brief and use no art at all in discussing Hamlet, Polonius nevertheless cannot refrain from employing figures of repetition in a manner he himself calls foolish.

> That he is mad, 'tis true: 'tis true 'tis pity;
> And pity 'tis 'tis true. A foolish figure!
> But farewell it, for I will use no art.
> Mad let us grant him then. And now remains
> That we find out the cause of this effect—
> Or rather say, the cause of this defect,
> For this effect, defective comes by cause.
> Thus it remains, and the remainder thus. (2.2.97)

Diaphora is the repetition of a common name so as to perform two logical functions: to designate an individual and to signify the qualities connoted by the common name, as when Desdemona remarks to Cassio of Othello's altered manner.

> My advocation is not now in tune.
> My lord is not my lord. (*Oth.*, 3.4.123)

And when Alcibiades reproaches Timon, turned misanthrope.

> Is man so hateful to thee That art thyself a man? (*Tim.*, 4.3.51)

According to Peacham and Day, the similar two-functional use of a proper name to designate a person and to signify his qualities was called ploce. It is exemplified in Hamlet's excuse to Laertes for having killed his father.

Was't Hamlet wrong'd Laertes? Never Hamlet.
If Hamlet from himself be ta'en away,
And when he's not himself does wrong Laertes,
Then Hamlet does it not, Hamlet denies it. (5.2.244)

Puttenham, however, gave the name ploce to the "speedie iteration of one word with some little intermission" (p.201.); others called this figure epanodos or traductio. Such iterance nettles Othello.

> *Othello.*   Thy husband knew it all.
> *Emilia.* My husband?
> *Othello.* Thy husband.
> *Emilia.* That she was false to wedlock? . . .
> My husband?
> *Othello.*   Ay, 'twas he that told me first. . . .
> *Emilia.* My husband?
> *Othello.* What needs this iterance, woman? I say, thy husband.
> (5.2.139–50)

Yet Othello resorts to this figure to heap up irony, when he bitterly inveighs against Desdemona in the presence of her kinsman Lodovico.

> Ay! You did wish that I would make her turn.
> Sir, she can turn, and turn, and yet go on,
> And turn again; and she can weep, sir, weep;
> And she's obedient; as you say, obedient.
> Very obedient. (4.1.263)

This form of ploce is employed with admirable effect in the later plays, often to express intense feeling.

> O, let me not be mad, not mad, sweet heaven! (*Lear*, 1.5.49)

> What shall I do? Say what! What shall I do? (*Tem.*, 1.2.300)

> Does not the stone rebuke me
> For being more stone than it? (*WT*, 5.3.37)

It is used with colloquial ease when Antony says to his servitors:

> Give me thy hand,
> Thou hast been rightly honest. So hast thou;
> And thou, and thou, and thou. You have serv'd me well.
> (*A & C*, 4.2.10)

Speaking of a new marriage for Henry VIII, Wolsey betrays aversion through this kind of repetition.

It shall be to the Duchess of Alençon,
The French king's sister. He shall marry her.
Anne Bullen? No! I'll no Anne Bullens for him.
There's more in't than fair visage. Bullen?
No, we'll no Bullens! (*H8*, 3.2.85)

Much against the grain, Coriolanus must follow custom and in the market place supplicate the citizens to give their voices for him as consul. His ill-concealed disdain is heightened by the repetition.

Here come moe voices.——
Your voices! For your voices I have fought;
Watch'd for your voices; for your voices bear
Of wounds two dozen odd; battles thrice six
I have seen and heard of; for your voices have
Done many things, some less, some more. Your voices!
Indeed I would be consul. (*Cor.*, 2.3.132)

This figure, used with utmost naturalness, marks the very turn of the tide of popular opinion shrewdly directed by the tribunes Sicinius and Brutus against Coriolanus, whose election Menenius has too hastily taken as assured.

Menenius.   Hear me speak.
As I do know the consul's worthiness,
So can I name his faults.
Sicinius.   Consul? What consul?
Menenius. The consul Coriolanus.
Brutus.   He consul?
All [*Plebeians*]. No, no, no, no, no! (3.1.277)

The repetition emphasizes the last ineffectual resolution of Coriolanus to restrain his proud, contemptuous spirit when he goes back to speak to the people.

Coriolanus. The word is 'mildly.' Pray you let us go.
Let them accuse me by invention; I
Will answer in mine honour.
Menenius.   Ay, but mildly.
Coriolanus. Well, mildly be it then—mildly. (3.2.142)

The two figures of repetition which Shakespeare uses most persistently throughout his work, diacope and epizeuxis, are noticeably fewer and less skillfully employed in those parts of *Pericles*, *Henry VIII*, and *The Two Noble Kinsmen* which have been assigned to some hand other than

Shakespeare's. Diacope, which often expresses deep feeling, is the repetition of a word with one or more between, usually in exclamation, as
in these examples from *Othello*:

Light, I say! light! (1.1.145)

Even now, now, very now. (1.1.88)

She swore, in faith, 'twas strange, 'twas passing strange;
'Twas pitiful, 'twas wondrous pitiful. (1.3.160)

Work on, My Medicine, work! (4.1.45)

But yet the pity of it, Iago! O Iago, the pity of it, Iago! (4.1.206)

In *The Winter's Tale* the shepherd, discovering the abandoned infant
Perdita, repeats:

A pretty one; a very pretty one. (3.3.71)

The exquisiteness of sleeping Imogen holds aloof the base-minded
Iachimo, gazing on her, who yet cannot forbear saying:

That I might touch!
But kiss; one kiss! (*Cym.*, 2.2.16)

Macbeth, deluded by the witches, disillusioned of his hopes of glory,
cynically sees life and time as but a meaningless succession of empty days.

Tomorrow, and tomorrow, and tomorrow . . . (5.5.19)

Epizeuxis, the repetition of words with none between, is a figure which
Shakespeare uses throughout his plays and songs and his narrative poems,
though seldom in his sonnets. Great variety of feeling and of movement
is created by the repeated words in the following:

O horror, horror, horror! Tongue nor heart
Cannot conceive nor name thee! (*Mac.*, 2.3.69)

Fly, good Fleance, fly, fly, fly! (*Mac.*, 3.3.17)

Out, out, brief candle! (*Mac.*, 5.5.23)

There is no tongue that moves, none, none i' th' world
So soon as yours could win me. (*WT*, 1.2.20)

O, I hope some god,
Some god hath put his mercy in your manhood. (*TNK*, 1.1.71)

'No, no!' quoth she. 'Sweet Death, I did but jest . . .' (*V & A*, 997)

To thee, to thee, my heav'd up hands appeal (*RL*, 638)

By heaven, I do not, I do not, gentlemen (*Oth.*, 5.2.232)

O Desdemona, Desdemona! dead! O! O! O! (*Oth.*, 5.2.281)

Blow, blow, thou winter wind. (*AYLI*, 2.7.174)

But why, why, why? (*A & C*, 3.7.2.)

Well, is it, is it? (*A & C*, 3.7.4)

Swift, swift, you dragons of the night (*Cym.*, 2.2.48)

[*Clock strikes*]. One, two, three. Time, time! (*Cym.*, 2.2.51)

O no, no, no! 'Tis true. (*Cym.*, 2.4.106)

In *Timon of Athens* the use of this figure is to Apemantus an occasion of cynical jest.

> *2. Lord.* Fare thee well, fare thee well.
> *Apemantus.* Thou art a fool to bid me farewell twice.
> *2. Lord.* Why, Apemantus?
> *Apemantus.* Shouldst have kept one to thyself, for I mean to give thee none.
> (1.1.272)

Epizeuxis, with diacope, expresses the bitter disillusionment of Troilus.

> O Cressid! O false Cressid! false, false, false! (5.2.178)

Lear cries out as he enters with the dead Cordelia in his arms:

> Howl, howl, howl, howl! O, you are men of stone. (5.3.257)

And shortly after, he hopelessly iterates the piercing sorrow of his desolate heart.

> Thou'lt come no more,
> Never, never, never, never, never! (5.3.307)

In his best work Shakespeare employs the figures of repetition with easy mastery to achieve varied artistic effects. Yet even in his early plays he seldom uses them merely as verbal embroidery. When they are so used, they usually serve by that very fact to characterize the speaker. The repetition often accentuates an idea dramatically significant, as in *2 Henry VI* (1.3), where the repetition of *Lord Protector* galls Queen Margaret, who wishes Henry to rule, and who accordingly schemes to get rid of the Lord Protector. In the scene in *King John* where Hubert, under orders from the king, comes to put out young Arthur's eyes with heated iron (4.1), *iron* becomes symbolic through repetition and acquires a quality of reflection and meditation, which joined to the repetition of *eyes, see,* and *look,* communicates both dignity and pathos.

Even in the more external phases of his art Shakespeare is pre-eminent. Writing at a time which invited to originality, distinction, and music of expression, he exhibits the ultimate in energy, verve, and daring creativeness. He uses every resource of language and imagination to give life, movement, and piquancy to his richly laden thought. Since the schemes of grammar owe much of their attractiveness to the very nearness of their approach to error, he likes to teeter on the brink of solecism and like a tight-rope walker or an acrobatic dancer to display in the precariousness of balance such sureness, poise, agility, and consummate skill as to awaken tense admiration in the prosaic onlooker with two feet squarely on the ground. And all this he does within the scope of an approved tradition which sanctioned such deviations from pedestrian style. The very vices of language he employs with fine dramatic effect to portray the ignorance, affectation, scurrility, garrulity, and ineptitude of certain characters in his plays. The figures of repetition in his later work give beauty, emphasis, and strength to the thought and feeling.

CHAPTER III

Logos: The Topics of Invention

THE ROLE which Shakespeare expected invention to play is evident in the sonnets.

> How can my Muse want subject to invent
> While thou dost breathe . . .
> For who's so dumb that cannot write to thee,
> When thou thyself dost give invention light? (*Son. 38*)

> how are our brains beguil'd,
> Which, labouring for invention, bear amiss (*Son. 59*)

> 'Fair, kind, and true,' is all my argument,
> 'Fair, kind, and true,' varying to other words;
> And in this change is my invention spent,
> Three themes in one, which wondrous scope affords. (*Son. 105*)

Shakespeare's characters, too, confronted with the problem of finding matter for speech or writing, consciously seek it in the processes of invention. "O, what excuse can my invention make?" Tarquin asks himself, mentally picturing his dear friend Collatine suddenly come to charge him with the black deed which he is now planning (*RL,* 225). When Lucrece prepares to write her lord of her heavy woe,

> Much like a press of people at a door,
> Throng her inventions. (1301)

In the course of a spirited conversation Desdemona asks Iago what he would write of her if he would praise her, and he replies:

> I am about it; but indeed my invention
> Comes from my pate as birdlime does from frieze—
> It plucks out brains and all. But my Muse labours,
> And thus she is deliver'd. (*Oth.,* 2.1.126)

Leonato, sad at the supposed death of his daughter Hero, bids Claudio:

> if your love
> Can labour aught in sad invention,
> Hang her an epitaph upon her tomb. (*MA,* 5.1.291)

Jaques apparently refers to the places of invention when he commends Touchstone:

> And in his brain . . . he hath strange places cramm'd
> With observation. (*AYLI*, 2.7.38–41)

Sir Toby prompts the bombastic but cowardly Sir Andrew to write a challenge to Cesario.

> Go write it in a martial hand. Be curst and brief; it is no matter how witty, so it be eloquent and full of invention. (*TN*, 3.2.45)

One character judges the invention of another. Rosalind remarks ironically of the love-sick letter Phebe has sent her by Silvius, who fears it is waspish and of an angry tenor:

> Women's gentle brain
> Could not drop forth such giant-rude invention,
> Such Ethiop words. (*AYLI*, 4.3.33)

Holofernes pronounces adverse judgment on Berowne's sonnet, misdirected to Jaquenetta.

> Here are only numbers ratified; but for the elegancy, facility, and golden cadence of poesy, caret. Ovidius Naso was the man. And why indeed 'Naso,' but for smelling out the odoriferous flowers of fancy, the jerks of invention? (*LLL*, 4.2.125)

Although he can thus good humoredly satirize the pedant, Shakespeare excels all his contemporaries in his skillful use of the topics of logic and the flowers of rhetoric, whether for comic or for serious purposes. When we speak of a topic sentence today and the methods, such as definition, contrast, or comparison, by which it may be developed into a paragraph, we hardly envision so systematic and objective a procedure as that by which Elizabethans as a matter of course amplified a subject by drawing it through the places of invention. Easy habituation to this method is apparent in a light and frivolous example of collective composition extemporaneously engaged in as a parlor sport, employing both rhetorical and logical places,[1] in *Cynthia's Revels* by Ben Jonson:

> *Phantaste.* Nay, we have another sport afore this, of *A thing done,* and, *Who did it, &c.*
> *Philautia.* I, good Phantaste, let's have that: Distribute the *places.*
> *Phantaste.* Why, I imagine, *A thing done;* Hedon thinkes, *Who did it;*

---

[1] See pp. 22, 24 f., above. See also pp. 342–344, below.

Moria, *With what it was done;* Anaides, *Where it was done;* Argurion, *When it was done;* Amorphus, *For what cause it was done;* you Philautia, *What followed upon the doing of it;* and this gentleman, *Who would have done it better.* What? is't conceiv'd about?

All. Yes, yes.

Phantaste. Then speake you, sir. *Who would have done it better?*

Each answers and then Phantaste begins to gather the answers together.

Phantaste. Then, *The thing done* was, An oration was made. Rehearse. An oration was made.

Hedon. By a travailer.

Moria. With a glyster.

Anaides. In a paire of pain'd slops.

Argurion. Last progresse.

Amorphus. For the delight of ladies.

Philautia. A few heat drops, and a moneths mirth followed.

Phantaste. And, this silent gentleman would have done it better. (4.3.160–201)

To the Elizabethan, invention meant finding matter for composition, which might or might not be invented by the writer in the modern sense of the word. Shakespeare accordingly did not hesitate to take over figures or arguments from Plutarch, Holinshed, or other sources if it so pleased him. This is particularly true of his use of the first of the topics of invention, inartificial arguments, which by their very nature are furnished to the writer or speaker by the testimony of others.

1. Inartificial Arguments or Testimony

Testimony, according to the Tudor logicians,[2] proceeds either from men or from supernatural powers. In Shakespeare's plays supernatural powers of both the pagan and the Christian order exert influence for good or evil. The testimony of oracles, soothsayers, augurs, prodigies, dreams, apparitions, ghosts, witches, prophecies is supernatural. The testimony of men includes proverbs, apothegms, pledges, oaths. Both kinds have the character of witnesses and the force of argument.

In *The Winter's Tale* Leontes, confident that he has grounds for his jealous suspicions of Hermione, wishes to secure decisive proof in order to convince his lords.

> Yet for a greater confirmation
> (For in an act of this importance 'twere

[2] See p. 309, below.

> Most piteous to be wild) I have dispatch'd in post
> To sacred Delphos, to Apollo's temple,
> Cleomenes and Dion, whom you know
> Of stuff'd sufficiency. Now from the oracle
> They will bring all, whose spiritual counsel had,
> Shall stop or spur me. (2.1.180)

Hermione also has implicit faith in the oracle and willingly rests her case on an appeal to its witness.

> I do refer me to the oracle.
> Apollo be my judge! (3.2.116)

The seals are broken and the officer reads the oracle.

'Hermione is chaste; Polixenes blameless; Camillo a true subject; Leontes a jealous tyrant; his innocent babe truly begotten; and the King shall live without an heir, if that which is lost be not found.' (3.2.133)

This oracle, unlike most, is unambiguous, specific, particular. After his first outburst of disbelief, Leontes accepts it, and his jealousy leaves him as suddenly as it had come upon him. He tries too late to make amends. The oracle, of central importance in the play, is frequently referred to, especially at the end. In *Cymbeline* Jupiter, appearing to Posthumus asleep in prison, gives him a book containing an oracle, which he on waking reads, but does not understand (5.4.138). It is an enigma interpreted only at the end of the play after its fulfillment. An oracle commands such strong belief that Ferdinand can make the weight of its testimony the measure of his faith in Miranda's excellence.

> I do believe it
> Against an oracle. (*Tem.*, 4.1.11)

Soothsayers and augurs testify regarding events to come. A soothsayer warns Julius Caesar: "Beware the ides of March" (1.2.18). Another warns Antony that in spite of superior abilities he cannot win against Octavius Caesar.

> If thou dost play with him at any game,
> Thou art sure to lose; and of that natural luck
> He beats thee 'gainst the odds. (*A & C*, 2.3.25)

Later Scarus reports the prognostication of the battle against Caesar.

> The augurers
> Say they know not, they cannot tell; look grimly
> And dare not speak their knowledge. (4.12.4)

A few moments later, Antony's cry "All is lost!" verifies the prognostication.

Disturbances and prodigies of nature are regarded as the testimony of supernatural powers that some evil threatens the state. Calphurnia, Caesar's wife, reports such prodigies seen by the watch: a lion whelped in the streets, graves yawned, ghosts shrieked about the streets, blood drizzled on the Capitol. She begs Caesar to remain at home, for, she declares,

> When beggars die there are no comets seen;
> The heavens themselves blaze forth the death of princes.
>
> *(JC, 2.2.30)*

Gloucester holds the same theory. He tells Edmund:

These late eclipses in the sun and moon portend no good to us. . . . Love cools, friendship falls off, brothers divide. In cities, mutinies; in countries, discord; in palaces, treason; and the bond crack'd 'twixt son and father. . . . the noble and true-hearted Kent banish'd! his offence, honesty! 'Tis strange. (*Lear*, 1.2.112)

Thereupon Edmund in soliloquy reveals his unorthodox views, accentuating his deliberate and self-reliant villainy by disbelief in the influence of the stars,

as if we were villains on necessity . . . and all that we are evil in, by a divine thrusting on. An admirable evasion of whoremaster man, to lay his goatish disposition to the charge of a star! (1.2.132)

Prodigies forbode the dire evil of Duncan's murder. An old man tells that a few days before, a falcon was hawked at and killed by a mousing owl. Ross asserts that he himself saw Duncan's horses break their stall and, turning wild in nature, eat each other. Lennox reports that the night has been unruly: chimneys were blown down; a clamor of birds, lamentings, and screams of death were heard; the earth shook. By the clock it is day, yet darkness entombs the earth. The obvious conclusion is:

> 'Tis unnatural,
> Even like the deed that's done. (2.4.10)

The testimony of dreams, frequent in Shakespeare, is invariably authenticated by subsequent events. Antigonus, having dreamed that Hermione appeared to him and bade him take the babe Perdita to Bohemia, remarks to himself:

> Dreams are toys;
> Yet for once, yea, superstitiously,
> I will be squar'd by this. (*WT*, 3.3.39)

He performs the behest and immediately after is devoured by a bear, whereby is fulfilled the prophecy of the same dream that he would never again see his wife, Paulina. Pericles is told by Diana in a dream (5.2.241) to go to her temple in Ephesus, if he would be happy. He goes and is reunited to his lost wife, Thaisa. Dreams are important in *Richard III*. The night before he is murdered Clarence is warned in a dream of his impending death and is upbraided for his misdeeds, that he may repent of them (1.4.66). Lord Hastings, who has rejected the warning of Stanley's dream (3.2.26), admits later, when he is about to be beheaded at Richard's command, that he deserves no pity, since he was "too fond" to heed the warning (3.4.80). On Bosworth field one after another appear the ghosts of those whom Richard has wronged. Each speaks to Richard and to Richmond asleep in opposite tents, moving the one to despair, assuring the other of victory. His dream so undermines Richard's usual strong reliance on rational mastery of a situation that he falters:

> O Ratcliff, I fear, I fear!. . .
> By the apostle Paul, shadows to-night
> Have struck more terror to the soul of Richard
> Than can the substance of ten thousand soldiers
> Armed in proof and led by shallow Richmond. (5.3.215)

Supernatural beings appear not merely to persons in dreams but also to those fully awake. The ghost of the murdered king is seen by the officers of the watch, by Horatio, and by Hamlet. Macbeth and Banquo encounter the weird sisters, whom they both recognize as evil beings. Evil also are the apparitions which the witches conjure up when Macbeth, grown desperate, comes to consult them about the future. On both occasions their prophecies are ambiguous, true in the letter, misleading in the implication, designed to delude and ruin. Banquo perceives their character clearly.

> oftentimes, to win us to our harm,
> The instruments of darkness tell us truths,
> Win us with honest trifles, to betray's
> In deepest consequence. (1.3.123)

The witch Margery Jourdain and her helpers by their incantations summon evil spirits who utter ambiguous prophecies (*2H6*, 1.4). For her part in this witchcraft Eleanor, Duchess of Gloucester, is publicly shamed and banished.

Authentic prophecies, mingled sometimes with curses, are uttered by persons of authority who have been wronged. In *Richard III* (1.3) Margaret curses those who have deposed and murdered Henry VI and the young Prince Edward. One after another suffers as she has predicted and recognizes the truth of her words. Buckingham, led to execution by Richard's order, acknowledges:

> Thus Margaret's curse falls heavy on my neck.
> 'When he,' quoth she, 'shall split thy heart with sorrow,
> Remember Margaret was a prophetess.' (5.1.25)

In the same play Richard is disturbed by the recollection of another prophecy.

> I do remember me Henry the Sixth
> Did prophesy that Richmond should be King
> When Richmond was a little peevish boy. (*R3*, 4.2.97)

Antony, indignant at dead Caesar's wrong, prophesies that it will be avenged.

> Woe to the hand that shed this costly blood!
> Over thy wounds now do I prophesy . . .
> And Caesar's spirit, ranging for revenge,
> With Ate by his side come hot from hell,
> Shall in these confines with a monarch's voice
> Cry 'Havoc!' and let slip the dogs of war. (*JC*, 3.1.258–73)

And on the field of Philippi, Cassius, resorting to suicide, cries out:

> Caesar, thou art reveng'd
> Even with the sword that kill'd thee. (5.3.45)

In another part of the field, Brutus prepares to die.

> The ghost of Caesar hath appear'd to me
> Two several times by night—at Sardis once,
> And this last night here in Philippi fields.
> I know my hour is come. (5.5.17)

Thus Caesar's revenging spirit spurs both Brutus and Cassius to suicide.

On the borderline between the supernatural and the human forms of testimony stands the medieval device of trial by combat, inasmuch as the outcome was regarded as the triumph of truth and right rather than of

mere might. In the opening scene of *Richard II* Bolingbroke and Mowbray, who have been summoned before Richard, vehemently accuse each
other of high treason and invoke trial by combat. The stage is set for the
encounter; the marshal gives the order, "Receive thy lance, and God
defend the right!" (1.3.101). The fact that just as the combatants are
about to set forward Richard halts the proceedings and decrees the exile
of both merely leaves unsettled the question of guilt which those present
would have considered proved by this form of testimony.

Circumstantial signs also are forms of testimony. That Perdita is
Leontes' lost daughter is most true, reports a gentleman,

if ever truth were pregnant by circumstance . . . there is such unity in the
proofs. The mantle of Queen Hermione's; her jewel about the neck of it; the
letters of Antigonus found with it, which they know to be his character. (*WT*,
5.2.33)

Probably the most striking instance of argument from circumstantial
evidence is that of the handkerchief, that tangible sign which the adroit
Iago made so convincing to jealous-wrought Othello.

Human testimony may be that of many or of one. The figure apodixis
grounds an argument on the experience of many. Gonzalo uses such an
argument to comfort Alonso, the shipwrecked king of Naples.

> Beseech you, sir, be merry. You have cause
> (So have we all) of joy; for our escape
> Is much beyond our loss. Our hint of woe
> Is common. Every day some sailor's wife,
> The master of some merchant, and the merchant,
> Have just our theme of woe; but for the miracle,
> I mean our preservation, few in millions
> Can speak like us. Then wisely, good sir, weigh
> Our sorrow with our comfort. (*Tem.*, 2.1.1)

The figure martyria, on the other hand, confirms a question by one's own
experience. Skeptical of the testimony of Marcellus and his companions
who declare that they have twice seen a ghost, Horatio assures them that
it was but a fantasy. When the ghost appears a third time, however,
Horatio trembles and turns pale. Convinced by his own experience, he
testifies:

> Before my God, I might not this believe
> Without the sensible and true avouch
> Of mine own eyes. (*Ham.*, 1.1.56)

Imogen, disguised as a boy, contrasts her experience of the kind courtesy shown her by the mountain huntsmen Belarius, Guiderius, and Arviragus with report.

> These are kind creatures. Gods, what lies I have heard!
> Our courtiers say all's savage but at court.
> Experience, O, thou disprov'st report! (*Cym.*, 4.2.32)

Proverbs or adages represent the testimony of many men; apothegms or maxims, often called sentences, the wisdom of one. The former, of popular origin, usually carry greater conviction, expressing as they do what generations have regarded as true. Yet since the people sometimes seize upon and popularize the wise sayings of one man, a sharp line cannot be drawn between these two types of generalization.[3] Shakespeare uses both. Shylock orders Jessica to go into the house.

> Do as I bid you; shut doors after you.
> Fast bind, fast find—
> A proverb never stale in thrifty mind. (*MV*, 2.5.53)

Prince Hal assures Poins that Falstaff will stand to his word,

for he was never yet a breaker of proverbs. He will give the devil his due. (*1H4*, 1.2.131)

Proverbs are neatly bandied back and forth by the Duke of Orleans and the Constable of France.

> *Orleans.* Ill will never said well.
> *Constable.* I will cap that proverb with 'There is flattery in friendship.'
> *Orleans.* And I will take up that with 'Give the devil his due.'
> *Constable.* Well plac'd! There stands your friend for the devil. Have at the very eye of that proverb with 'A pox of the devil!'
> *Orleans.* You are the better at proverbs, by how much 'a fool's bolt is soon shot.'
> *Constable.* You have shot over.
> *Orleans.* 'Tis not the first time you were overshot. (*H5*, 3.7.123)

---

[3] See, for example, Whiting, "The Nature of the Proverb," *Harvard Studies and Notes in Philology and Literature*, XIV (1932), 306; Tilley, *Elizabethan Proverb Lore*, p. 12; Katherine Lever, "Proverbs and *Sententiae* in the Plays of Shakspere," *Shakespeare Association Bulletin*, XIII (1938), 174. The last article points out that in Shakespeare's plays proverbs and sententious remarks are mainly used by certain characters and in certain situations which are by their very nature productive of them, and concludes: "It is part of Shakspere's timelessness that he, living in an age which loved proverbs and *sententiae* for their own sake, refused for the most part to cater to this audience at the expense of realism." (p. 228)

Lucio and Feste quote the same proverb, each with point.

Lucio. [*of Friar Lodowick*] 'Cucullus non facit monachum.' Honest in nothing but in his clothes. (*MM*, 5.1.263)

Feste. Lady, cucullus non facit monachum. That's as much to say as, I wear not motley in my brain. (*TN*, 1.5.62)

Dogberry, the constable, instructing the watch, introduces proverbs with bland incongruity.

Watch. If we know him to be a thief, shall we not lay hands on him?
Dogberry. Truly, by your office, you may; but I think they that touch pitch will be defil'd. The most peaceable way for you, if you do take a thief, is to let him show himself what he is, and steal out of your company. (*MA*, 3.3.57)

Shakespeare often recasts the proverbs he borrows, expressing them more attractively.[4] The prosaic "A gift is valued for the mind of the giver" (Tilley, No. 732) or "Gifts are not to be measured by the worth, but by the will" (Greene's *Pandosto*) is transmuted in Ophelia's reproach to Hamlet as she returns the gifts he had given her:

> Take these again; for to the noble mind
> Rich gifts wax poor when givers prove unkind. (3.1.100)

Proverbs and maxims, as Aristotle explained,[5] are potent in argument. Coriolanus bitterly describes the successful argument of the plebeians.

> They said they were anhungry; sigh'd forth proverbs—
> That hunger broke stone walls, that dogs must eat,
> That meat was made for mouths, that the gods sent not
> Corn for the rich men only. With these shreds
> They vented their complainings. (1.1.209)

In *Much Ado* Claudio argues from the proverb "When love puts in friendship is gone" (Tilley, No. 420). Having just heard the false tale that his friend the prince, who had promised to woo Hero in Claudio's name, intends to marry her himself that very night, Claudio soliloquizes:

> The prince wooes for himself.
> Friendship is constant in all other things
> Save in the office and affairs of love.
> Therefore all hearts in love use their own tongues.

---

[4] Katherine Lever, "Proverbs and *Sententiae* in the Plays of Shakspere," *Shakespeare Association Bulletin*, XIII, 236.
[5] See p. 358, below.

> Let every eye negotiate for itself,
> And trust no agent. (2.1.181)

Rosalind's observation, "Beauty provoketh thieves sooner than gold" (1.3.112) becomes the major premise for the decision to disguise, so important to the plot of *As You Like It*. Lady Macbeth argues against her husband's decision not to kill Duncan.

> Wouldst thou . . . live a coward in thine own esteem,
> Letting 'I dare not' wait upon 'I would,'
> Like the poor cat i' th' adage? (1.7.41)

A maxim clinches the argument by which Brutus convinces himself that he should put an end to Caesar.

> Fashion it thus: that what he is, augmented,
> Would run to these and these extremities;
> And therefore think him as a serpent's egg
> Which, hatch'd, would as his kind grow mischievous,
> And kill him in the shell. (*JC*, 2.1.30)

Angelo protests to Isabel, who has invoked maxims as arguments against his severity toward her brother:

> Why do you put these sayings upon me? (*MM*, 2.2.133)

Cressida soliloquizes on the advantage to a woman of holding off her lover and keeping him suing.

> Therefore this maxim out of love I teach:
> Achievement is command; ungain'd, beseech.
> Then, though my heart's content firm love doth bear,
> Nothing of that shall from mine eyes appear. (*T & C*, 1.2.318)

Nerissa admonishes Portia, who says she is aweary of this great world.

> *Nerissa.* They are as sick that surfeit with too much as they that starve with nothing. It is no mean happiness, therefore, to be seated in the mean. Superfluity comes sooner by white hairs, but competency lives longer.
> *Portia.* Good sentences, and well pronounc'd.
> *Nerissa.* They would be better if well followed. (*MV*, 1.2.6)

Sententious remarks, characteristic of King Henry VI, emphasize his piety and sometimes give him dignity; yet they contribute to the impression of futility, revealing him as a man of platitudinous words, not of action. The noble generalities which Iago utters cleverly instill belief in his own honesty and integrity; in the very act of insinuating false suspicion he asserts:

> Who steals my purse steals trash . . .
> But he that filches from me my good name
> Robs me of that which not enriches him
> And makes me poor indeed. (*Oth.*, 3.3.157–61)

The quality of thought which distinguishes *Hamlet* is due in part to the large number of proverbs and sentences in the play, more than in any other by Shakespeare.[6] The following are selected instances.

> Foul deeds will rise,
> Though all the earth o'erwhelm them, to men's eyes. (1.2.257–58)

> What to ourselves in passion we propose,
> The passion ending, doth the purpose lose. (3.2.204–5)

> For use almost can change the stamp of nature. (3.4.168)

> So full of artless jealousy is guilt
> It spills itself in fearing to be spilt. (4.5.19–20)

> There's a divinity that shapes our ends,
> Rough-hew them how we will. (5.2.10–11)

Diatyposis is a figure whereby one commends to another certain profitable rules and precepts. Polonius' advice to Laertes (*Ham.*, 1.3.58–80) is an outstanding example. Similar in vein is the parting advice which the countess gives to her son Bertram, called to the king's service.

> Love all, trust a few,
> Do wrong to none. Be able for thine enemy
> Rather in power than use, and keep thy friend
> Under thy own life's key. Be check'd for silence,
> But never tax'd for speech. (*AW*, 1.1.73)

An understandable reaction to such proffered advice is that of Leonato, who, distraught with grief, inveighs against those who

> Patch grief with proverbs . . .
> . . . counsel and speak comfort to that grief

---

[6] According to Katherine Lever, *op. cit.*, p. 176, there are forty-four. Shakespeare's pre-eminence in sententious utterance was recognized in his own day, for selections from his plays figured prominently in *Belvedere*, 1600, and in *England's Parnassus*, 1600, collections from contemporary poets similar to Mirandula's "flowers" from the ancient poets, used in the Tudor grammar schools. See T. W. Baldwin, *William Shakspere's Small Latine and Lesse Greeke*, I, 26.

> Which they themselves not feel;
> . . . give preceptial medicine to rage
> Fetter strong madness in a silken thread,
> Charm ache with air and agony with words. . . .
> For there was never yet philosopher
> That could endure the toothache patiently. (*MA*, 5.1.17–36)

In *Timon of Athens* this figure is perverted to convey the bitter pseudo-wisdom of too-munificent Timon, now turned misanthrope, bestowing his cynical, warped precepts as freely as formerly he had bestowed his goods: in his ironical prayer to the gods before his mock banquet, meant rather for the ears of his false friends and flatterers (3.6.80–85); in his advice to Alcibiades (4.3.108–28); and to Flavius, whom he urges to

> Go, live rich and happy,
> But thus condition'd: thou shalt build from men;
> Hate all, curse all, show charity to none,
> But let the famish'd flesh slide from the bone
> Ere thou relieve the beggar. Give to dogs
> What thou deniest to men. (4.3.532)

That those to whom Timon addresses his remarks understand them as precepts is clear from their replies. Alcibiades answers:

> I'll take the gold thou givest me,
> Not all thy counsel. (4.3.129)

And the two women who are with him beg:

> More counsel with more money, bounteous Timon. (167)

The figure apomnemonysis is a form of inartificial argument which quotes for authority the testimony of approved authors. The Archbishop of Canterbury employs it to assure King Henry V that he has a just claim to the French throne, through the female line, and that the French unfairly invoke against his claim the Salique law barring women's succession, for their own writers say that the Salique land is in Germany, not in France, and that Pepin, Hugh Capet, and Louis X all held their right and title from the female; finally he quotes the authority of Scripture.

> For in the Book of Numbers is it writ:
> When the man dies, let the inheritance
> Descend unto the daughter. (*H5*, 1.2.98)

Holofernes mildly ridicules Sir Nathaniel's habit of quoting texts.

Holofernes. I beseech your society.

Nathaniel. And thank you too; for society (saith the text) is the happiness of life.

Holofernes. And certes the text most infallibly concludes it. (*LLL*, 4.2.166)

Feste introduces this figure when he closes his brief apostrophe to wit with a quotation.

Wit, an't be thy will, put me into good fooling! Those wits that think they have thee do very oft prove fools; and I that am sure I lack thee may pass for a wise man. For what says Quinapulus? 'Better a witty fool than a foolish wit.' (*TN*, 1.5.35)

Epicrisis adds to the authority cited the opinion of the speaker, who may agree or disagree, or make exceptions, as Cassius does in his comment to Messala.

> You know that I held Epicurus strong
> And his opinion. Now I change my mind
> And partly credit things that do presage. (*JC*, 5.1.76)

He proceeds to tell of the ominous birds of prey that hover over their army, ravens, crows and kites, whose shadows seem a canopy most fatal.

Chria, a very short exposition of a deed or word, with the name of the author recited, furnishes Britain's queen with a spirited argument against Rome's renewed claim to British tribute.

> A kind of conquest
> Caesar made here; but made not here his brag
> Of 'came, and saw, and overcame.' With shame
> (The first that ever touch'd him) he was carried
> From off our coast, twice beaten. (*Cym.*, 3.1.22)

Armado sets much store by this argument from authority.

Armado. Comfort me, boy. What great men have been in love?

Moth. Hercules, master.

Armado. Most sweet Hercules! More authority, dear boy, name more . . .

Moth. Samson, master. (*LLL*, 1.2.67–73)

Oaths, vows, and pledges are forms of human testimony of which Shakespeare makes full use. Orcos, an oath affirming that one speaks the truth, adds weight to Hubert's declaration that he had no part in Arthur's death.

> If I in act, consent, or sin of thought
> Be guilty of the stealing that sweet breath

> Which was embounded in this beauteous clay,
> Let hell want pains enough to torture me! (*KJ*, 4.3.135)

Emilia with her last breath vouches for the truth of Desdemona's love and fidelity to Othello:

> So come my soul to bliss as I speak true.
> So speaking as I think, I die, I die. (5.2.250)

The lovely oaths of some of Shakespeare's women contrast with the often violent oaths of the men. Olivia avows:

> Cesario, by the roses of the spring,
> By maidhood, honour, truth, and everything,
> I love thee. (*TN*, 3.1.161)

Euche is a vow to keep a promise. A dramatically impressive instance of it is the oath which Hamlet, seconded by the ghost speaking from below, exacts from Horatio and Marcellus, when he demands that they solemnly swear on his sword never by word or look to reveal what they have seen and heard that night (1.5.145–81). Most vehement and intense vows of revenge against Cassio and Desdemona are uttered by Othello and Iago kneeling together (3.3.453–69). The Archbishop of York and his fellow leaders of revolt are so convinced by the sworn pledge of John of Lancaster that they dismiss the rebel army, not noting the loophole John has left for himself.

> *John.* I . . . swear here by the honour of my blood,
> My father's purposes have been mistook . . .
> My lord, these griefs shall be with speed redress'd;
> Upon my soul, they shall . . .
> *Archbishop.* I take your princely word for these redresses.
>   (*2H4*, 4.2.54–66)

Later, when John arrests the army-less leaders and orders their execution as traitors, he reminds them that he swore to redress the grievances of which they complained, and that he will keep his oath to do so. He did not promise amity to them; they merely assumed that he did.

Buckingham, led to execution, ironically recalls his violated vows.

> This is the day which in King Edward's time
> I wish'd might fall on me when I was found
> False to his children and his wive's allies.
> This is the day wherein I wish'd to fall

> By the false faith of him whom most I trusted . . .
> That high All-seer which I dallied with
> Hath turn'd my feigned prayer on my head
> And given in earnest what I begg'd in jest. (*R3*, 5.1.13–22)

Cleopatra is not convinced by Antony's oaths of fidelity to her.

> Why should I think you can be mine, and true,
> Though you in swearing shake the throned gods,
> Who have been false to Fulvia? Riotous madness,
> To be entangled with those mouth-made vows
> Which break themselves in swearing? (1.3.27)

Diana, too, is skeptical of the facile multiplication of oaths, although she has faith in the worth of a sincere vow.

> 'Tis not the many oaths that makes the truth,
> But the plain single vow that is vow'd true. (*AW*, 4.2.21)

Eustathia, a pledge of constancy, is Florizel's undismayed response when threatened with disinheritance of a kingdom, should he persist in loving Perdita.

> From my succession wipe me, father! . . .
> Not for Bohemia nor the pomp that may
> Be thereat glean'd, for all the sun sees or
> The close earth wombs or the profound sea hides
> In unknown fadoms, will I break my oath
> To this my fair belov'd. (*WT*, 4.4.491–503)

Coriolanus flaunts a perverse constancy in his disdain of the populace.

> Let them pull all about mine ears; present me
> Death on the wheel or at wild horses' heels;
> Or pile ten hills on the Tarpeian Rock,
> That the precipitation might down stretch
> Below the beam of sight—yet will I still
> Be thus to them. (3.2.1)

Asphalia, the offer of surety for another, strengthens Miranda's entreaty that her father be less severe toward Ferdinand.

> Sir, have pity.
> I'll be his surety. (*Tem.*, 1.2.474)

A memorable example of asphalia is Antonio's giving his bond as surety for Bassanio's loan from Shylock (*MV*, 3.1), for which he nearly paid the forfeit of his life. Yet at the end of the play, when Portia accuses Bassanio of breaking faith in parting with the ring she had given him, loyal Antonio again offers himself for his friend.

> *Antonio.*　　　I dare be bound again,
> My soul upon the forfeit, that your lord
> Will never more break faith advisedly.
> *Portia.* Then you shall be his surety. (*MV*, 5.1.251)

Three figures of testimony interpret revelations or events as good or evil. Euphemismus, the prognostication of good, characterizes the Roman soothsayer's interpretation of his dream in *Cymbeline*.

> Last night the very gods show'd me a vision . . .
> I saw Jove's bird, the Roman eagle, wing'd
> From the spongy South to this part of the West,
> There vanish'd in the sunbeams; which portends
> (Unless my sins abuse my divination)
> Success to th' Roman host. (4.2.346)

At the end of the play, when Cymbeline has voluntarily offered to resume paying tribute to Rome, the soothsayer declares that his vision is therein fully accomplished,

> 　　　　　　for the Roman eagle,
> From South to West on wing soaring aloft,
> Lessen'd herself and in the beams o' th' sun
> So vanish'd; which foreshow'd our princely eagle,
> Th' imperial Caesar, should again unite
> His favour with the radiant Cymbeline,
> Which shines here in the West. (5.5.470)

Paraenesis is a warning of impending evil, as when Margaret warns Buckingham against Richard.

> O Buckingham, take heed of yonder dog!
> Look, when he fawns he bites; and when he bites,
> His venom tooth will rankle to the death.
> Have not to do with him, beware of him. (*R3*, 1.3.289)

Ominatio is a prognostication of evil, as in Priam's plea to Hector.

> 　　　　　Come, Hector, come, go back.
> Thy wife hath dreamt; thy mother hath had visions;
> Cassandra doth foresee; and I myself
> Am like a prophet suddenly enrapt

> To tell thee that this day is ominous.
> Therefore come back. (*T & C*, 5.3.62)

Horatio, having seen the ghost, concludes:

> . . . in the gross and scope of my opinion,
> This bodes some strange eruption to our state. (*Ham.*, 1.1.68)

From a sign that is ominous to the boatswain Gonzalo professes to draw comfort for himself while the ship is threatened by the storm.

> *Gonzalo.* I have great comfort from this fellow. Methinks he hath no drowning mark upon him; his complexion is perfect gallows.[7] Stand fast, good Fate, to his hanging! . . . If he be not born to be hang'd, our case is miserable. (*Tem.*, 1.1.30)

In *Julius Caesar* the interpretation of a dream is crucial to the plot. Caesar tells Decius he will not go to the Capitol that day, the ides of March, because

> Calphurnia here, my wife, stays me at home.
> She dreamt to-night she saw my statue,
> Which, like a fountain with an hundred spouts,
> Did run pure blood; and many lusty Romans
> Came smiling and did bathe their hands in it.
> And these does she apply for warnings and portents
> And evils imminent, and on her knee
> Hath begg'd that I will stay at home to-day. (2.2.75)

Rejecting Calphurnia's prognostication of evil, the conspirator Decius interprets the dream as a favorable omen.

> This dream is all amiss interpreted;
> It was a vision fair and fortunate.
> Your statue spouting blood in many pipes,
> In which so many smiling Romans bath'd,
> Signifies that from you great Rome shall suck
> Reviving blood, and that great men shall press
> For tinctures, stains, relics, and cognizance.
> This by Calphurnia's dream is signified. (2.2.83)

Convinced by this argument, Caesar yields and goes to his death.

Inartificial arguments of witnesses heavenly, earthly, and infernal, important in many of Shakespeare's plays, are most impressive in *Mac-*

---

[7] See Peacham, p. 312, below, who in discussing ominatio speaks of gallows. Shakespeare may possibly owe something to him here.

beth, where the preternatural assumes a grander scale than in any other play, occupying the stage with lightning, thunder, the weird sisters, and the apparitions evoked by their evil incantations. In addition, other prodigies are reported. Lady Macbeth's reminder to her husband that he swore to murder Duncan is a weighty argument in her barrage against his hesitancy. The prophecies and their partial fulfillment beget in Macbeth an inordinate reliance on preternatural aid which saps his manliness. As a soldier he might have fought for power with human means. He is disposed toward an interpretation of prophecies which is favorable to his own designs; yet, ironically, he hedges himself with cruel safeguards of human canniness, such as the murder of Banquo, and the measures against Macduff. Almost to the last he retains his desperate trust in the deceitful prophecies, an optimism (euphemismus) which ruins him. Too late he seizes his sword and warlike shield and cries out to his adversary, "Lay on, Macduff!"

2. *Definition*

First in order among artificial arguments, those derived from a subject by the art of topical investigation, is definition, which explains the nature or essence of a subject in terms of its genus and difference. "Define, define, well-educated infant," demands Armado of his quick-witted page Moth (*LLL*, 1.2.99). Polonius with characteristic redundancy declares,

> to define true madness,
> What is't but to be nothing else but mad? (*Ham.*, 2.2.93)

In Sonnet CXVI Shakespeare defines love by telling what it is and what it is not: it is a marriage of true minds, an ever-fixed mark, which alters not when it finds alteration; it is not Time's fool, but perseveres even to the edge of doom. This and other definitions in Shakespeare represent, not the strict type of the logicians, but the less precise, more imaginative form of the rhetoricians called the figure horismus. Coriolanus defines democracy, or allowing the plebeians a voice, as government

> where gentry, title, wisdom
> Cannot conclude but by the yea and no
> Of general ignorance. (3.1.144)

Lady Macbeth explains how a feast should differ from eating at home.

> The feast is sold
> That is not often vouch'd, while 'tis a-making,

'Tis given with welcome. To feed were best at home.
From thence, the sauce to meat is ceremony. (3.4.33)

Touchstone offers a humorous definition, citing details, to prove that he has been a courtier.

I have trod a measure; I have flatt'red a lady; I have been politic with my friend, smooth with mine enemy; I have undone three tailors; I have had four quarrels, and like to have fought one. (*AYLI*, 5.4.45)

Systrophe is the heaping together of many definitions of one thing. An amusing instance is the series of definitions of love by Silvius, each followed ludicrously by a chorus of assent.

> *Phebe*. Good shepherd, tell this youth what 'tis to love.
> *Silvius*. It is to be all made of sighs and tears;
> And so am I for Phebe.
> *Phebe*. And I for Ganymede.
> *Orlando*. And I for Rosalind.
> *Rosalind*. And I for no woman.
> *Silvius*. It is to be all made of faith and service;
> And so am I for Phebe. (*AYLI*, 5.2.89)

The others chime in again. Silvius adds more definitions which are similarly confirmed, until at last Rosalind utters what is probably Shakespeare's own comment on the performance: "Pray you, no more of this: 'tis like the howling of Irish wolves against the moon" (118). Macbeth employs systrophe to heap together the benefits of sleep, appreciated most keenly when he realizes that he himself will no longer enjoy

> Sleep that knits up the ravell'd sleave of care,
> The death of each day's life, sore labour's bath,
> Balm of hurt minds, great nature's second course,
> Chief nourisher in life's feast. (2.2.37)

Shakspeare makes use of the more profound concepts which enter into logical definition, such as difference, property, essence. Mindful that rational judgment constitutes the specific difference between man and beasts, the king deplores the state of

> poor Ophelia
> Divided from herself and her fair judgment,
> Without the which we are pictures or mere beasts.
> (*Ham.*, 4.5.84)

On a lighter note, Beatrice remarks of Benedick:

In our last conflict four of his five wits went halting off, and now is the whole man govern'd with one; so that if he have wit enough to keep himself warm, let him bear it for a difference between himself and his horse; for it is all the wealth that he hath left to be known a reasonable creature. (*MA*, 1.1.65)

Property is not, like the specific difference, a part of the essence, but it is a distinguishing feature of the species.

> Sweet love, I see, changing his property,
> Turns to the sourest and most deadly hate. (*R2*, 3.2.135)

> His voice was propertied As all the tuned spheres. (*A & C*, 5.2.83)

> the property of rain is to wet and fire to burn. (*AYLI*, 3.2.27)

With profound poetic insight Shakespeare delves into the philosophical implications of essence in "The Phoenix and Turtle."

> So they lov'd as love in twain
> Had the essence but in one;
> Two distincts, division none:
> Number there in love was slain. . . .

> Property was thus appalled,
> That the self was not the same;
> Single nature's double name
> Neither two nor one was called. (25–40)

Related to essence is the contrast of shadow and substance which seems to have singularly interested Shakespeare, since he adverts to it nearly a score of times.

> Each substance of a grief hath twenty shadows. (*R2*, 2.2.14)

> But Henry now shall wear the English crown
> And be true king indeed, thou but the shadow. (*3H6*, 4.3.50)

> Grief has so wrought on him
> He takes false shadows for true substances. (*Tit.*, 3.2.79)

> the very substance of the ambitious is merely the shadow of a dream.
> (*Ham.*, 2.2.264)

> 'Tis but the shadow of a wife you see,
> The name and not the thing. (*AW*, 5.3.308)

> Ah me! how sweet is love itself possess'd,
> When but love's shadows are so rich in joy! (*R & J*, 5.1.10)

A consideration of essence as opposed to its accidental modifications becomes an important underlying theme in Shakespeare's historical plays: the distinction between kingship and kings, between the ideal and its embodiment in imperfect men, results in great reverence for kingship, despite the unworthiness of wicked kings. Richmond pointedly emphasizes this distinction when in his oration to his soldiers he speaks of Richard III as

> A base foul stone, made precious by the foil
> Of England's chair, where he is falsely set. (*R3*, 5.3.251)

Shakespeare and his contemporaries seem never to have lost sight of the essence of kingship, which is the root of its dignity and intrinsic honor, namely, that it is a principle of order, a delegation of divine authority made sacred by anointing. It was apparently their capacity to distinguish between the exalted essence of kingship and its perversion in frail men which enabled the Elizabethans to witness with equanimity the parade of former kings upon their stage—futile, pleasure-bent, devoted to ill-chosen favorites and not to the public good, arbitrary, dissolute, scheming, ruthless, tyrannical, even murderous—without weakening one whit in their faith and devotion to monarchy.

3. Division: Genus and Species, Whole and Parts

Logical division of a genus into its species, known to the rhetoricians as the figure diaeresis, is closely related to definition. The distinction which Jaques makes between his melancholy and other melancholies illustrates this relation, for while dividing he briefly characterizes and so in a measure defines each kind.

I have neither the scholar's melancholy, which is emulation; nor the musician's, which is fantastical; nor the courtier's, which is proud; nor the soldier's, which is ambitious; nor the lawyer's, which is politic; nor the lady's, which is nice; nor the lover's, which is all these: but it is a melancholy of mine own, compounded of many simples, extracted from many objects, and indeed the sundry contemplation of my travels, in which my often rumination wraps me in a most humorous sadness. (*AYLI*, 4.1.10)

Another example of diaeresis is Posthumus' division of vice into its kinds to express his bitter misogyny, brought on by Iachimo's plausible tale of Imogen's infidelity. The division intensifies the general statement with which he begins by making it in the strict logical sense specific.

> There's no motion
> That tends to vice in men but I affirm
> It is the woman's part. Be it lying, note it,
> The woman's; flattering, hers; deceiving, hers;
> Lust and rank thoughts, hers, hers; revenges, hers;
> Ambitions, covetings, change of prides, disdain,
> Nice longing, slanders, mutability—
> All faults that may be nam'd, nay, that hell knows,
> Why, hers, in part or all; but rather all! (*Cym.*, 2.5.20)

Malcolm employs logical division, or the figure diaeresis, when he lists the species of

> the king-becoming graces,
> As justice, verity, temp'rance, stableness,
> Bounty, perseverance, mercy, lowliness,
> Devotion, patience, courage, fortitude. (*Mac.*, 4.3.91)

Synecdoche is a trope which heightens meaning by substituting genus for species, species for genus, part for whole, whole for part.

> Pour down thy weather. (*KJ*, 4.2.109)

> Like to a pair of lions smear'd with prey. (*TNK*, 1.4.18)

> These are the ushers of Marcius. Before him he carries noise. (*Cor.*, 2.1.174)

> Two thousand souls and twenty thousand ducats
> Will not debate the question of this straw. (*Ham.*, 4.4.25)

> The locks between her chamber and his will. (*RL*, 302)

> till new-born chins Be rough and razorable. (*Tem.*, 2.1.249)

> To dance our ringlets to the whistling wind. (*MND*, 2.1.86)

> Yet, poor old heart, he holp the heavens to rain. (*Lear*, 3.7.62)

Differing from diaeresis, which divides a genus into its species, merismus, or partitio, divides a whole into its parts, as when Caliban, discussing Prospero's coming to the island, reminds him:

> then I lov'd thee
> And show'd thee all the qualities o' th' isle,
> The fresh springs, brine-pits, barren place and fertile.
> (*Tem.*, 1.2.336)

By singling out the marks of old age in every part of Falstaff's body the Lord Chief Justic shows how ridiculous it is for the fat knight to identify himself with youth.

Do you set down your name in the scroll of youth, that are written down old with all the characters of age? Have you not a moist eye, a dry hand, a yellow cheek, a white beard, a decreasing leg, an increasing belly? Is not your voice broken, your wind short, your chin double, your wit single, and every part about you blasted with antiquity? And will you yet call yourself young? (*2H4*, 1.2.201)

In *A Midsummer Night's Dream*, after Snout has explained that he will act the part of Wall in the ensuing interlude, one of the audience, punning on partitio,[8] comments:

It is the wittiest partition that ever I heard discourse, my lord. (5.1.168)

Eutrepismus is a figure of division which numbers and orders the parts under consideration. The Prince of Arragon, seeking Portia's hand, enumerates the parts of the contract he has sworn to abide by before making his choice of the caskets.

> I am enjoin'd by oath to observe three things:
> First, never to unfold to anyone
> Which casket 'twas I chose; next, if I fail
> Of the right casket, never in my life
> To woo a maid in way of marriage;
> Lastly,
> If I do fail in fortune of my choice,
> Immediately to leave you and be gone. (*MV*, 2.9.9)

Although the present study does not undertake to establish definite sources for Shakespeare's knowledge of the figures, one striking parallel may be noted. A comparison of Peacham's counsel against the misuse of merismus and eutrepismus and Dogberry's actual misuse of them in *Much Ado* reveals a resemblance so arresting that it argues Shakespeare's familiarity with the 1593 edition of *The Garden of Eloquence*— the only one of the works investigated by the present writer which offers any such parallel or which appends a caution against the misuse of the figures. Peacham warns against the misuse of merismus, which he calls partitio.

Also a grosse absurditie is committed when a partition is made by Synonymies, which he did, that divided his Oration into these foure partes: Why? where-

---

[8] T. W. Baldwin, in his *William Shakspere's Small Latine and Lesse Greeke*, remarks: "Apparently the pun grows directly out of Cicero's definition in *Topica*, when he used *parietem* as an illustration of something which exists, and therefore can be partitioned into parts." II, 110.

fore, for what cause, and to what end, this is called the division, or partition without a difference. (p. 124)

Discussing eutrepismus, he cautions against forgetfulness,

as he that promised to expound the twelve articles of the Creed, and after could remember but nine. (p. 130)

Dogberry's misuse of these two figures in precisely the ways against which Peacham warned is emphasized by Pedro's mocking echo and by Claudio's comment on the two errors in division.

> *Pedro.* Officers, what offence have these men done?
> *Dogberry.* Marry, sir, they have committed false report; moreover, they have spoken untruths; secondarily, they are slanders; sixth and lastly, they have belied a lady; thirdly, they have verified unjust things; and to conclude they are lying knaves.
> *Pedro.* First, I ask thee what they have done; thirdly, I ask thee what's their offence; sixth and lastly, why they are committed; and to conclude, what you lay to their charge.
> *Claudio.* Rightly reasoned, and in his own division; and by my troth there's one meaning well suited. (*MA*, 5.1.217)

Enumeratio employs the third kind of division, that of a subject into its adjuncts, a cause into its effects, an antecedent into its consequents. Holofernes anatomizes Armado by listing his adjuncts.

His humour is lofty, his discourse peremptory, his tongue filed, his eye ambitious, his gait majestical, and his general behaviour vain, ridiculous, and thrasonical. He is too picked, too spruce, too affected, too odd, as it were, too peregrinate. (*LLL*, 5.1.10)

Lear cries:

Let them anatomize Regan. See what breeds about her heart. (3.6.80)

Hamlet interrupts Osric's enumeration of the good qualities of Laertes, which threatens to be long drawn out, with

I know, to divide him inventorially would dozy th' arithmetic of memory. (5.2.118)

Portia exclaims to Bassanio:

> Beshrow your eyes!
> They have o'erlook'd me and divided me. (*MV*, 3.2.14)

Speaking to an apparently reluctant Cressida, Pandarus enumerates the merits of Troilus.

Pandarus. Have you any eyes? Do you know what a man is? Is not birth, beauty, good shape, discourse, manhood, learning, gentleness, virtue, youth, liberality, and such-like, the spice and salt that season a man?

Cressida. Ay, a minc'd man! (1.2.274)

Cressida recognizes her uncle's description as a figure of division and thereupon with quick wit caps his speech with the pert, completely apt pronouncement that Troilus is "a minced man." The naturalness and spontaneity of such comment, while it marks Shakespeare's awareness of the figure he is using, contrasts with the more obvious manner in which his contemporaries introduce references to the precepts of art. For example, in Sidney's pastoral interlude "The Lady of May," performed before Queen Elizabeth at Wanstead in 1578, the schoolmaster Rombus pedantically explains to the shepherds the principles of division.

Why you brute Nebulons have you had my *Corpusculum* so long among you, and cannot yet tell how to edifie an argument? . . . First you must divisionate your point, *quasi* you should cut a cheese into two particles, for thus must I uniforme my speech to your obtuse conceptions; for *Prius dividendum oratio antequam definiendum exemplum gratia,* either *Therion* must conquer this Dame *Maias* Nimphe, or *Espilus* must overthrow her, and that *secundum* their dignity, which must also be subdivisionated into three equall *species,* either according to the penetrancie of their singing, or the meliority of their functions, or lastly the superancy of their merits *De* singing *satis. Nunc* are you to argumentate of the qualifying of their estate first, and then whether hath more infernally, I meane deeply deserved.[9]

The figure propositio is a brief summary of what is to follow, as when the duke, disguised as Friar Lodowick, outlines the scheme he proposes to Isabel.

I do make myself believe that you may most uprightteously do a poor wronged lady a merited benefit; redeem your brother from the angry law; do no stain to your own gracious person; and much please the absent Duke. (*MM,* 3.1.205)

Restrictio is a figure whereby after making a general statement one excepts a part, as the senator does in discussing Timon.

> I love and honour him,
> But must not break my back to heal his finger. (*Tim.,* 2.1.23)

[9] Sidney, "The Lady of May," in *Complete Works,* ed. by A. Feuillerat, II, 335. This passage also exemplifies the vice cacozelia, or the affectation of fine language, and soraismus, the mingling of languages. Cf. pp. 72 and 65, above, and pp. 303 and 300, below.

Imogen, about to open a letter from Posthumus, exclaims:

> You good gods,
> Let what is here contain'd relish of love,
> Of my lord's health, of his content! yet not
> That we two are asunder; let that grieve him!
>   (*Cym.*, 3.2.29)

Florizel, undaunted by his father's angry threats, assures Perdita:

> I am but sorry, not afeard; delay'd
> But nothing alt'red. What I was, I am;
> More straining on for plucking back. (*WT*, 4.4.474)

Prolepsis is a general statement amplified by dividing it into parts, as in Arviragus' description of life in a cave with his brother and foster-father.

> We are beastly: subtle as the fox for prey,
> Like warlike as the wolf for what we eat.
> Our valour is to chase what flies; our cage
> We make a choir, as doth the prison'd bird,
> And sing our bondage freely. (*Cym.* 3.3.40)

Apemantus makes a significant general statement to Timon, then particularizes it, expressing the central theme of a play which anatomizes both flattery and misanthropy.

The middle of humanity thou never knewest, but the extremity of both ends. When thou wast in thy gilt and thy perfume, they mock'd thee for too much curiosity; in thy rags thou know'st none, but art despis'd for the contrary. (*Tim.*, 4.3.300)

Epanodos differs from prolepsis only in repeating the terms of the general proposition in the amplification which particularizes it, as in Sonnet XLVI.

> Mine eye and heart are at a mortal war
> How to divide the conquest of thy sight;
> Mine eye my heart thy picture's sight would bar,
> My heart mine eye the freedom of that right. . . .
> To 'cide this title is impanneled
> A quest of thoughts, all tenants to the heart,
> And by their verdict is determined
> The clear eye's moiety and the dear heart's part:
>   As thus—mine eye's due is thy outward part,
>   And my heart's right thy inward love of heart.

Synathroesmus, on the other hand, first gives details, then gathers them up in recapitulation, as when Scroop informs Richard II of the rebellion led by Bolingbroke.

> White-beards have arm'd their thin and hairless scalps
> Against thy majesty. Boys with women's voices
> Strive to speak big, and clap their female joints
> In stiff unwieldy arms against thy crown.
> The very beadsmen learn to bend their bows
> Of double-fatal yew against thy state.
> Yea, distaff-women manage rusty bills
> Against thy seat. Both young and old rebel,
> And all goes worse than I have power to tell. (*R2*, 3.2.112)

Synathroesmus in another sense, sometimes called congeries, merely heaps together words of different meaning, without recapitulation, as when Macbeth, having just announced that he has killed Duncan's grooms, gives this excuse for his impulsiveness:

> Who can be wise, amaz'd, temp'rate and furious,
> Loyal and neutral, in a moment? No man. (2.3.114)

Epiphonema, an epigrammatic summary, gathers into a pithy, sententious utterance what has preceded, as in the last lines of Blanche's exclamation of distress when on her wedding day war breaks out between France and England, the war which her marriage to the Dauphin was to avert.

> Husband I cannot pray that thou mayst win;
> Uncle, I needs must pray that thou mayst lose;
> Father, I may not wish the fortune thine;
> Grandam, I will not wish thy wishes thrive.
> Whoever wins, on that side shall I lose:
> Assured loss before the match be play'd! (*KJ*, 3.1.331)

Berowne, having stated the details of the agreement to live apart and study philosophy, to which he and his three companions have sworn, summarizes them, exclaiming:

> O these are barren tasks, too hard to keep—
> Not to see ladies, study, fast, not sleep! (*LLL*, 1.1.47)

After reporting in detail to a British lord the gallant stand of old Belarius and the two young princes, which won the victory over the Romans, Posthumus somewhat derisively proposes an epigram to sum up all that he has said.

> Will you rhyme upon't
> And vent it for a mock'ry? Here is one:
> 'Two boys, an old man (twice a boy), a lane
> Preserv'd the Britons, was the Romans' bane!' (*Cym.*, 5.3.55)

Of greater dramatic significance than the figures of division is the disjunctive proposition, which expresses alternatives that divide the pos-
sibilities contemplated. Shakespeare employs disjunction to characterize
a man of vigorous action, such as the bastard shows himself when he urges
immediate attack on the invading French.

> Straight let us seek, or straight we shall be sought. (*KJ*, 5.7.79)

Awakened to a new sense of responsibility, Prince Hal rides against the
rebels and cries:

> The land is burning; Percy stands on high;
> And either they or we must lower lie. (*1H4*, 3.3.226)

Antony, once a man of action, tries to rouse himself from the luxurious
lethargy into which Cleopatra has lulled him.

> These strong Egyptian fetters I must break
> Or lose myself in dotage. (*A & C*, 1.2.120)

A disjunction often poses a mental conflict, as in Hamlet's soliloquy where
he is trying to reach a decision on the question "To be or not to be"
(3.1.56). It expresses a decision already reached, a point of view serenely
held, in Brutus' answer to Antony who demands, as they stand by Caesar's
body,

> *Antony.*   reasons
> Why and wherein Caesar was dangerous.
> *Brutus.* Or else were this a savage spectacle. (*JC*, 3.1.221)

Othello, convinced of Desdemona's infidelity, contemplates the alternatives which in consequence rive his tortured soul.

> But there where I have garner'd up my heart,
> Where either I must live or bear no life,
> The fountain from the which my current runs
> Or else dries up—to be discarded thence,
> Or keep it as a cistern for foul toads
> To knot and gender in—(4.2.57)

Important distinctions, which are forms of division, profoundly affect
the moral quality of certain characters. For example, ravished Lucrece

in anguish of soul takes refuge in the essential distinction between a pure mind and a violated body.

> Immaculate and spotless is my mind;
> That was not forc'd; that never was inclin'd
>   To accessary yieldings, but still pure
>   Doth in her poison'd closet yet endure. (*RL*, 1656)

The distinction between the general and the particular, a concept dominant in Brutus' mind, confers nobility on his character and acts.

> I know no personal cause to spurn at him,
> But for the general. He would be crown'd. (*JC*, 2.1.11)

>   pity to the general wrong of Rome . . .
> Hath done this deed on Caesar. (3.1.170)

> Not that I lov'd Caesar less, but that I lov'd Rome more. (3.2.23)

It is upon this very principle of judgment that Antony at the end of the play sets Brutus apart from the other conspirators.

> This was the noblest Roman of them all. . . .
> He, only in a general honest thought
> And common good to all, made one of them. (5.5.68–72)

4. Subject and Adjuncts

Shakespeare reveals in his plays penetrating observations regarding the relation of subject and adjuncts. Horatio demands of the ghost, "What art thou that usurp'st . . . that fair and warlike form . . . the majesty of buried Denmark?" (1.1.46). The identity of the subject beneath the perceptible adjuncts becomes the central problem for Hamlet: is the ghost really his father's spirit, or is it an evil spirit in his habiliments? On this question hinges the play.

A man's real adjuncts do not depend on the thoughts and words of another person, as Malcolm assures Macduff.

> That which you are, my thoughts cannot transpose. (*Mac.*, 4.3.21)

And Rosalind retorts to her usurping uncle's charge:

> Yet your mistrust cannot make me a traitor. . . .
> Treason is not inherited, my lord. (*AYLI*, 1.3.58, 63)

There can, however, be a change in adjuncts so great as to constitute almost a new subject, a transformation that Oliver claims for himself as a result of his conversion.

> 'Twas I. But 'tis not I! I do not shame
> To tell you what I was, since my conversion
> So sweetly tastes, being the thing I am. (*AYLI*, 4.3.136)

A change of characteristics, the loss of some and the gaining of others, is important in *1* and *2 Henry IV*, where the king at first anxiously compares his son unfavorably with Hotspur, Northumberland's son,

> A son who is the theme of honour's tongue,
> Amongst a grove the very straightest plant;
> Who is sweet Fortune's minion and her pride;
> Whilst I, by looking on the praise of him,
> See riot and dishonour stain the brow
> Of my young Harry. O that it could be prov'd
> That some night-tripping fairy had exchang'd
> In cradle clothes our children where they lay,
> And call'd mine Percy, his Plantagenet!
> Then would I have his Harry, and he mine. (*1H4*, 1.1.81)

Hotspur later becomes a rebel, and King Henry sees Prince Hal manifest characteristics worthy of a monarch. The king tells the prince how he himself acquired certain adjuncts in order to win the good opinion of the people whose favor helped him to gain his crown.

> And then I stole all courtesy from heaven,
> And dress'd myself in such humility,
> That I did pluck allegiance from men's hearts,
> Loud shouts and salutations from their mouths
> Even in the presence of the crowned King. (*1H4*, 3.2.50)

Good qualities unused, however, are no credit to their possessor. Agamemnon rebukes Achilles because his virtues

> like fair fruit in an unwholesome dish
> Are like to rot untasted. (*T & C*, 2.3.129)

And he asserts that a stirring dwarf is better than a sleeping giant (146).

A delegation of authority may be regarded as a transfer of adjuncts from one subject to another; consequently after the duke commissioned Angelo and Escalus, they can truly say:

> The Duke's in us, and we will hear you speak. (*MM*, 5.1.297)

Habit, an adjunct which signifies clothing, weapons, and other accouterments, is a topic which furnishes Shakespeare with material for interesting effects both serious and comic. In reporting that new revolts against Macbeth break out every minute and that none obey him except through fear, Angus remarks how hollowly the external adjuncts of majesty rest upon him.

> Now does he feel his title
> Hang loose about him, like a giant's robe
> Upon a dwarfish thief. (5.2.20)

Afraid of a thunderstorm, Trinculo creeps under the garments of Caliban, who is lying on the ground to escape notice. Drunken Stephano coming upon the scene believes he sees a monster: "Four legs and two voices— a most delicate monster!" (*Tem.*, 2.2.93) That clothes do not make the man is the disillusioned judgment of a nobleman who had been deceived by the pretensions of Parolles.

I will never trust a man again for keeping his sword clean, nor believe he can have everything in him by wearing his apparel neatly. (*AW*, 4.3.165)

The contrary opinion, "Clothes make the man," is the theme which underlies the following:

> *Perdita.*   Sure this robe of mine
> Does change my disposition. (*WT*, 4.4.134)

Clown. [*to Autolycus*] You are well met, sir. You denied to fight with me this other day, because I was no gentleman born. See you these clothes? Say you see them not and think me still no gentleman born. You were best say these robes are not gentlemen born . . .
Autolycus. I know you are now, sir, a gentleman born.
Clown. Ay, and have been so any time these four hours. (*WT*, 5.2.140)

In Shakespeare's plays clothing is accepted as a perfect disguise. The operation of this dramatic convention is seen, to mention but a few instances, in the completely effective disguises of Polixenes, Autolycus, "Friar Lodowick," Viola, Imogen, Rosalind. When in the last act of *As You Like It* Rosalind, divested of her boy's attire, appears in her true dress, her identity is a complete surprise.

> *Duke Sr.* If there be truth in sight, you are my daughter.
> *Orlando.* If there be truth in shape, you are my Rosalind.
> *Phebe.*   If sight and shape be true,
> Why then, my love adieu! (5.4.124)

Peristasis, a figure of speech which amplifies by detailing the circumstances affecting a person or a thing, is employed in *Cymbeline* (1.1.28–

54) by a gentleman who sketches Posthumus' life, telling of his country, his parentage, his family's deeds of renown, his education, his own deeds and character. When Macbeth decides to proceed no further in the plan to murder Duncan, who has lately honored him, Lady Macbeth assails her husband with an argument from time and place, which are circumstances of a thing.

> What beast was't then
> That made you break this enterprise to me?
> . . . Nor time nor place
> Did then adhere, and yet you would make both.
> They have made themselves, and that their fitness now
> Does unmake you. (1.7.47–54)

In eager haste to be married to Juliet, Romeo assured Friar Lawrence:

> When, and where, and how
> We met, we woo'd, and made exchange of vow,
> I'll tell thee as we pass. (2.3.61)

Armado's letter to the king, accusing Costard of violating the royal edict, meticulously cites the circumstances.

I . . . betook myself to walk. The time When? About the sixth hour. . . . Now for the ground Which? . . . It is ycliped thy park. Then for the place Where? where, I mean, I did encounter that obscene and most prepost'rous event . . . It standeth north-north-east and by east from the west corner of thy curious knotted garden. There did I see that low-spirited swain, . . . (*LLL*, 1.1.236–52)

Apparently Armado had carefully conned a lesson in rhetoric similar in content to Thomas Wilson's summary in verse for ready memorizing as an aid to invention.[10]

> Who, what, and where, by what helpe, and by whose:
> Why, how, and when, doe many things disclose. (*AR*, p. 17)

Cymbeline, in his eagerness to know the circumstances of Imogen's adventures, demands:

> When shall I hear all through? This fierce abridgment
> Hath to it circumstantial branches, which

[10] T. W. Baldwin, *William Shakspere's Small Latine and Lesse Greeke*, II, 311, regards Armado's letter as a narration following the order prescribed by Aphthonius, who puts time before place. But Peacham also puts time before place in his caution against the misuse of peristasis (see p. 319, below).

Distinction should be rich in. Where? How liv'd you?
And when came you to serve our Roman captive?
How parted with your brothers? how first met them?
Why fled you from the court? and whither? These . . .
And all the other by-dependences . . .
Will serve our long inter'gatories. (*Cym.*, 5.5.382–92)

Encomium is high praise and commendation of a person or thing by
extolling the inherent qualities or adjuncts, as in Lafew's sincere praise
of Helena,

Whose beauty did astonish the survey
Of richest eyes; whose words all ears took captive;
Whose dear perfection hearts that scorn'd to serve
Humbly call'd mistress. (*AW*, 5.3.16)

Hamlet exclaims:

What a piece of work is a man! how noble in reason! how infinite in faculties!
in form and moving how express and admirable! in action how like an angel!
in apprehension how like a god! the beauty of the world, the paragon of ani-
mals! (2.2.315)

Taxis is a figure which distributes to every subject its proper adjunct.
Oppressed with Macbeth's tyranny, a lord speaks to Lennox of a time
he hopes for, when

we may again
Give to our tables meat, sleep to our nights,
Free from our feasts and banquets bloody knives,
Do faithful homage and receive free honours—
All which we pine for now. (3.6.33)

Asked whether he will marry, Touchstone replies, using this figure:

As the ox hath his bow, sir, the horse his curb, and the falcon her bells, so man
hath his desires; and as pigeons bill, so wedlock would be nibbling. (*AYLI*,
3.3.80)

In *The Winter's Tale* (4.4.73–129) is a lovely scene which acquires new
charm if it is regarded as an extension of the figure taxis to include not
only words but action. Perdita as hostess at the sheep-shearing distributes
to each his proper flower: to elderly disguised Polixenes and Camillo
rosemary and rue, lavender, mints, marjoram, flowers of winter and
middle life. She laments that she has not flowers of spring for Florizel
and for the girls upon whose virgin branches their maidenheads still are
growing, but she describes the flowers so vividly and so beautifully—

daffodils, violets, pale primroses, oxlips, lilies—that her words are preferable to the flowers themselves.

Epitheton attributes to a person or thing a quality by way of addition, as when Prospero remarks, "Why, that's my dainty Ariel" (*Tem.*, 5.1.95) and when Horatio asserts that the beard of Hamlet's father was, like the ghost's, "A sable silver'd" (1.2.242). Armado explains to his page Moth that he called him

tender juvenal as a congruent epitheton appertaining to thy young days, which we may nominate tender. (*LLL*, 1.2.14)

The compound epithet, although not mentioned by the Tudor rhetoricians in their treatment of epitheton,[11] was popular with Elizabethan writers and merits consideration here because Shakespeare used it more copiously and with greater freedom than his fellow dramatists,[12] and by means of it created language picturesque, sudden, and evocative.

I am bride-habited, But maiden-hearted. (*TNK*, 5.1.150)

Had I been thief-stolen As my two brothers, happy! (*Cym.*, 1.6.5)

their discipline (Now wing-led with their courages) (*Cym.*, 2.4.23)

Now from head to foot I am marble-constant. (*A & C*, 5.2.239)

thou mongrel beef-witted lord (*T & C*, 2.1.14)

the Thunderer, whose bolt, you know Sky-planted (*Cym.*, 5.4.95)

Jove's lightnings . . . more momentary And sight-outrunning were not. (*Tem.*, 1.2.201)

[11] Peacham treated the composition of two words, such as pickthank for flatterer, as a subdivision of onomatopoeia (p. 14).

[12] See Alfred Hart, *Shakespeare and the Homilies*, p. 234. Hart has made other interesting observations on Shakespeare's compounds. See also his "Vocabularies of Shakespeare's Plays," *Review of English Studies*, XIX (April, 1943), 128–40. Also Bernard Groom, "The Formation and Use of Compound Epithets from 1579," *Tract* 49. Society for Pure English.

Joseph Hall, in Satire VI, 1598, asserted that Sidney had of late introduced the compound epithet from France. But Rubel, in *Poetic Diction in the English Renaissance*, points out many illustrations of the compound epithet in Chaucer, traces its use continuously from Skelton through Spenser, and observes that the French Pléiade's sanction of it merely added impetus and prestige to the force of native example. Certainly it abounds in *Piers Ploughman* and in Old English literature. Sidney, "An Apologie for Poetrie" (Smith, *Elizabethan Critical Essays*, I, 204), Mulcaster, *Elementarie*, p. 117, and Ben Jonson, *English Grammar*, p. 76, remark upon the natural capacity of English, like Greek, for such compounding. It is employed frequently in Golding's translation of Ovid's *Metamorphoses*, 1561, in Sidney's *Arcadia* and in his poems, but most copiously in Du Bartas' *La Semaine* and in Joshua Sylvester's translation of it, the first part of which appeared in 1594.

I met her Deity Cutting the clouds towards Paphos, and her son Dove-drawn with her (*Tem.*, 4.1.92–4)

There stand, For you are spell-stopp'd (*Tem.*, 5.1.60)

Other examples of Shakespeare's compound epithets may be more briefly listed.

pity-pleading eyes, woe-wearied tongue, flower-soft hands, heart-struck injuries, cold-pale weakness, belly-pinched wolf, marrow-eating sickness, carry-tale Jealousy, wonder-wounded hearers, oak-cleaving thunderbolts, to-and-fro-conflicting wind and rain, world-without-end hour . . .

Antonomasia is of two forms. The first substitutes a descriptive phrase for a proper name, as when Rosalind, without naming Cupid, speaks of

that same wicked bastard of Venus that was begot of thought, conceiv'd of spleen, and born of madness, that blind rascally boy that abuses every one's eyes because his own are out. (*AYLI*, 4.1.216)

The second form, on the other hand, substitutes a proper name for a quality associated with it.

> *Valeria.* [*to Virgilia*] You would be another Penelope.
> (*Cor.*, 1.3.92)
> *Clown.* I am no great Nabuchadnezzar, sir;
> I have not much skill in grass. (*AW*, 4.5.21–22)

Periphrasis is the use of a descriptive phrase for a common name, often to give an air of solemnity or elevation or to avoid a harsh word.

> *Macduff.* Most sacrilegious murther hath broke ope
> The Lord's anointed temple and stole thence
> The life o' th' building! (*Mac.*, 2.3.72)

> *1 Queen.*   for our crowned heads we have no roof
> Save this, which is the lion's and the bear's,
> And vault to everything. (*TNK*, 1.1.52)

> *Puck.* I'll put a girdle round about the earth
> In forty minutes. (*MND*, 2.1.175)

> When that fell arrest
> Without all bail shall carry me away. (*Son. 74*)

> *Henry V.* [*to the traitors*] You have . . .
> Join'd with an enemy proclaim'd, and from his coffers
> Receiv'd the golden earnest of our death. (*H5*, 2.2.167)

The substitution of subject for adjunct, or adjunct for subject, is a form of metonymy.

> Their cheeks are paper (*H5*, 2.2.74)
>
> Conferring them on younger strengths (*Lear*, 1.1.41)
>
> and giddy censure Will then cry out (*Cor.*, 1.1.272)
>
> as doublet and hose ought to show itself courageous to petticoat. (*AYLI*, 2.4.6)
>
> [*of Duncan*] renown and grace is dead (*Mac.*, 2.3.99)
>
> Bell, book, and candle shall not drive me back (*KJ*, 3.3.12)

Hypotyposis, or enargia, was the generic name given to figures of lively description or counterfeit representation, indispensable to creating the illusion of reality essential to drama. The Elizabethans recognized many species, each with its own name signifying that it was a description of persons, manners, gestures, speech, events, places, or times, either real or imaginary.

Prosopographia was the name given to the lively description of a person, as when Pericles simultaneously describes his wife and Marina, who stands before him.

> My dearest wife was like this maid, and such a one
> My daughter might have been. My queen's square brows;
> Her stature to an inch; as wand-like straight;
> As silver-voic'd; her eyes as jewel-like,
> And cas'd as richly; in pace another Juno;
> Who starves the ears she feeds, and makes them hungry,
> The more she gives them speech. (*Per.*, 5.1.108)

He might have commented, as Boult did earlier in the play,

> I have drawn her picture with my voice. (4.2.101)

Prosopopoeia, the attribution of human qualities to dumb or inanimate creatures, wins mercy for young Arthur, whose eyes Hubert is about to put out with hot irons by order of King John.

> *Arthur.* There is no malice in this burning coal;
> The breath of heaven hath blown his spirit out
> And strew'd repentant ashes on his head.
> *Hubert.* But with my breath I can revive it, boy.
> *Arthur.* And if you do, you will but make it blush

> And glow with shame of your proceedings, Hubert. . . .
> All things that you should use to do me wrong
> Deny their office. Only you do lack
> That mercy which fierce fire and iron extends,
> Creatures of note for mercy-lacking uses. (*KJ*, 4.1.109–21)

Stung by defeat, Antony employs this figure to assert new spirit and resolution.

> The next time I do fight,
> I'll make Death love me; for I will contend
> Even with his pestilent scythe. (*A & C*, 3.13.192)

Characterismus is the description of the body or mind. In a series of six thumb-nail sketches (1.2.43–97) Portia characterizes her suitors. As a friend who knows him well, Menenius describes Coriolanus.

> His nature is too noble for the world.
> He would not flatter Neptune for his trident
> Or Jove for's power to thunder. His heart's his mouth;
> What his breast forges, that his tongue must vent,
> And being angry does forget that ever
> He heard the name of death. (*Cor.*, 3.1.255)

Ethopoeia is the description of natural propensities, manners and affections, such as seeking to win favor by flattery. In *The Tempest* Antonio urges Sebastian to kill Gonzalo while he himself dispatches Alonso. This will be safe, for all the others are mere time-servers.

> They'll take suggestion as a cat laps milk;
> They'll tell the clock to any business that
> We say befits the hour. (2.1.288)

Mimesis is the imitation of gesture, pronunciation, utterance. Ulysses complains that Patroclus entertains Achilles by derisive mimicry of the Greek leaders till Achilles cries:

> Excellent! 'Tis Agamemnon just.
> Now play me Nestor. Hem, and stroke thy beard,
> As he being dress'd to some oration. . . .
> 'Tis Nestor right. Now play him me, Patroclus,
> Arming to answer in a night alarm.' (*T & C*, 1.3.164)

Thersites, in order to make clear to Achilles the overweening conceit of Ajax at being chosen to fight against Hector, resorts to mimesis.

I will put on his presence. Let Patroclus make his demands to me, you shall see the pageant of Ajax. (*T & C*, 3.3.271–300)

Dialogismus, the framing of speech suitable to the person speaking, is essential to good drama, and is, of course, exemplified throughout Shakespeare's plays. A signal instance of it occurs in *The Winter's Tale* (2.1.21–32) where Hermione bids her little son Mamillius tell her a story. The talk of both mother and child in this brief dialogue, interrupted just when the boy has begun his story, is remarkable for its charm, ease, and life-like quality. In *King John* the bastard, newly knighted, gives vent in soliloquy to his exuberant spirits by feigning a conversation with a traveler in the catechetical manner of the ABC book [13] and giving it the technical name dialogue.

> Now your traveller,
> He and his toothpick at my worship's mess:
> And when my knightly stomach is suffic'd,
> Why, then I suck my teeth and catechize
> My picked man of countries. 'My dear sir,'
> Thus, leaning on mine elbow, I begin,
> 'I shall beseech you.' That is question now,
> And then comes answer like an Absey-book:
> 'O sir,' says answer, 'at your best command,
> At your employment, at your service, sir!'
> 'No, sir,' says question. 'I, sweet sir, at yours!'
> And so, ere answer knows what question would—
> Saving in dialogue of compliment,
> And talking of Alps and Apennines,
> The Pyrenean and the river Po—
> It draws toward supper in conclusion so.
> But this is worshipful society
> And fits the mounting spirit like myself. (1.1.189)

Pragmatographia is the vivid description of an action or event, as when Cominius tells how Coriolanus won the city Corioles single-handed.

> From face to foot
> He was a thing of blood, whose every motion
> Was tim'd with dying cries. (2.2.112)

Cleopatra so realistically pictures her place in Caesar's intended triumph that she gains the help of her women in ending her life and thus escapes humiliation (5.2.208–21). The vividness with which Belarius recounts

---

[13] See T. W. Baldwin, *William Shakspere's Small Latine and Lesse Greeke*, II, 233.

his deeds evokes a lively response in the two young princes, and first
in Guiderius.

> When on my three-foot stool I sit and tell
> The warlike feats I have done, his spirits fly out
> Into my story . . . he sweats,
> Strains his young nerves, and puts himself in posture
> That acts my words. The younger brother Cadwal,
> Once Arviragus, in as like a figure
> Strikes life into my speech and shows much more
> His own conceiving. (*Cym.*, 3.3.89–98)

Pragmatographia is of great value in drama to report events which occur
off-stage. The sergeant and Ross give Duncan a stirring account of Macbeth's and Banquo's bravery in the battle which won the victory (1.2.7–
58). Othello declares that his recital of the deeds that brought him honor
from the state won him Desdemona's love (1.3.128–69). Cornelius reports the death of the queen in *Cymbeline* and all her wicked plots which
she confessed (5.5.31–61). In *The Winter's Tale* (5.2.47–63) Shakespeare substitutes description for action that might well have been presented on the stage. Instead of witnessing the dramatic meeting between
Polixenes and Leontes and the discovery that Perdita is Leontes' lost
heir, the audience hears it described by three gentlemen. The description
is so vivid, however, that it constitutes an exciting denouement.

Chronographia is the description of times, as of dawn by Romeo.

> Look, love, what envious streaks
> Do lace the severing clouds in yonder East.
> Night's candles are burnt out, and jocund day
> Stands tiptoe on the misty mountain tops. (3.5.7)

Dusk is described in *Venus and Adonis* (529–34), and night in that lyric
passage where Lorenzo and Jessica recall other nights like this, when the
moon looked down on lovers of old, on Troilus, on Thisbe, on Dido, on
Medea (*MV*, 5.1.1–22).

Topographia is the description of places. The queen, urging Cymbeline
not to yield to Rome's demand for tribute, eloquently reminds him of
Britain's natural barriers against invasion.

> The natural bravery of your isle, which stands
> As Neptune's park, ribbed and paled in
> With rocks unscalable and roaring waters,
> With sands that will not bear your enemies' boats
> But suck them up to th' topmast. (3.1.18)

Topothesia is the description of imaginary places, such as the house of envy in Ovid's *Metamorphoses* or the bower of bliss in *The Faerie Queene*. Shakespeare describes no place such as these. His nearest approach is the fairyland where Oberon and Titania rule. Oberon speaks of a mermaid singing on a promontory (*MND*, 2.1.148–54) and of a bank where Titania sleeps among violets and musk-roses, over-canopied with woodbine (249–56). Although the details are familiar in the realm of earth, Titania tells Oberon: "I know When thou hast stolen away from fairyland" (64).

The relation of subject and adjuncts is of particular interest in *A Midsummer Night's Dream*. On this relation hinge the arguments, confusions, humor. The play opens with an argument about real adjuncts, whether Demetrius or Lysander has genuine love for Hermia; but most of it is concerned with adjuncts misplaced by magic. Puck explains to Oberon:

> Believe me, king of shadows, I mistook.
> Did not you tell me I should know the man
> By the Athenian garments he had on? (3.2.347)

Puck's excuse is that the adjuncts mentioned were insufficient to identify the proper subject. The mistaking of adjuncts helps to move the plot forward. Because Helena, whose love for Demetrius was unrequited, thinks she is being mocked when both Demetrius and Lysander profess love for her, every word spoken in sincerity is understood by her as scorn. The spirit of the play is expressed in the lines: "mark the unusual confusion Of hounds and echo in conjunction . . . so musical a discord" (4.1.113,121). Even the misplaced punctuation in Quince's prologue (5.1.108–17) is a misplaced adjunct contributing humor. Magic is employed to remove adjuncts and to restore them with equal suddenness. It is the very work of fantasy, of "imagination all compact . . . that gives to airy nothing a habitation and a name" (5.1.8,17), thus whimsically to transfer adjuncts from their subjects, creating an amusing confusion where there is "nothing impaired but all disordered" (126), and then at the last to restore all to better order and general delight.

5. Contraries and Contradictories

Contraries and contradictories are of special interest to the dramatist, concerned as he is with conflict and contrast. Shakespeare recognized the value of contraries as dramatic foils.

Hamlet. I'll be your foil, Laertes. In mine ignorance
Your skill shall, like a star i' th' darkest night,
Stick fiery off indeed. (5.2.266)

Benvolio. [*to Romeo of Rosaline*] Tut! you saw her fair, none else being
by. (*R & J*, 1.2.98)

Prince Hal. [*alone*] My reformation, glitt'ring o'er my fault,
Shall show more goodly and attract more eyes
Than that which hath no foil to set it off. (*1H4*, 1.2.237)

Justice. [*to Falstaff*] Your day's service at Shrewsbury hath a little gilded
over your night's exploit on Gadshill. (*2H4*, 1.2.168)

Unexpected contrast humorously barbs the retort in the following:

> *King.* Now at the latest minute of the hour
> Grant us your loves.
> *Princess.*   A time methinks too short
> To make a world-without-end bargain in. (*LLL*, 5.2.796)

In *The Tempest* is a lovely instance of the use of contrast to awaken
sudden and fresh wonder. Miranda, having grown up in the unpeopled
island where she had seen only her father and Caliban, exclaims at the
unwonted sight of the voyagers gathered before Prospero's cell:

> O wonder!
> How many goodly creatures are there here!
> How beauteous mankind is! O brave new world
> That has such people in't! (5.1.181)

Kent invokes the incompatibility of contraries to express with utmost
vehemence his abhorrence of Oswald.

> No contraries hold more antipathy
> Than I and such a knave. (*Lear*, 2.2.93)

Because contrary terms are mutually repugnant, they serve to represent mental conflict and confusion.

> *Isabel.* I am At war 'twixt will and will not. (*MM*, 2.2.32)
>
> *Malcolm.*   Why are you silent?
> *Macduff.* Such welcome and unwelcome things at once
> 'Tis hard to reconcile. (*Mac.*, 4.3.137)

By methods of mounting intensity Shakespeare depicts a hierarchy of
disorder and confusion. Physical disorder, eruptions, prodigies of nature

betoken disorder in the state, such as an attack on lawful authority. Civil disorder consequent on Caesar's assassination is prophesied by Antony. The disorder in proper family relations represented by a mother kneeling to her son so shocks Coriolanus that he can imagine no confusion in nature to match it.

> Your knees to me? to your corrected son?
> Then let the pebbles on the hungry beach
> Fillop the stars! Then let the mutinous winds
> Strike the proud cedars 'gainst the fiery sun,
> Murd'ring impossibility, to make
> What cannot be, slight work! (5.3.57)

Whenever Shakespeare wishes to represent the acme of disorder and confusion, he introduces logical confusion, that is, a mutually destructive merging of incompatibles by ignoring the opposition of contraries and contradictories. Timon, for example, utters a curse on mankind:

> Piety and fear
> Religion to the gods, peace, justice, truth,
> Domestic awe, night-rest and neighbourhood,
> Instruction, manners, mysteries and trades,
> Degrees, observances, customs and laws,
> Decline to your confounding contraries
> And let confusion live! (*Tim.*, 4.1.15)

The confusion of contradictory judgments produces in Othello intolerable mental suffering.

> [*To Iago*]   By the world,
> I think my wife be honest, and think she is not;
> I think that thou art just, and think thou art not.
> I'll have some proof. (3.3.383)

Troilus will not believe the testimony of his own eyes that have seen Cressida transfer her love from him to Diomed, nor of his ears that have heard her say, not knowing he was near, "Troilus, farewell!" In anguish of mind, he cries,

> O madness of discourse,
> That cause sets up with and against itself!
> Bifold authority! where reason can revolt
> Without perdition, and loss assume all reason
> Without revolt: this is, and is not, Cressid! (5.2.142)

Supreme logical disorder, the acceptance of a contradiction, expresses the height of the emotional confusion of Troilus and his bitter disillusionment.

Shakespeare is especially fond of negative terms,[14] which are the contradictories of the corresponding positive terms. By them he achieves vigor and freshness.

We will untread the steps of damned flight (*KJ*, 5.4.52)

Though you would seek t'unsphere the stars with oaths (*WT*, 1.2.48)

Here's such ado to make no stain a stain . . . (*WT*, 2.2.19)

lest her . . . beauty unprovide my mind again (*Oth.*, 4.1.217)

As if some planet had unwitted men (*Oth.*, 2.3.182)

No! First shall war unpeople this my realm (*3H6*, 1.1.126)

He is unqualitied with very shame (*A & C*, 3.11.44)

Unshout the noise that banish'd Marcius (*Cor.*, 5.5.4)

will he not . . . Untent his person and share the air with us? (*T & C*, 2.3.177)

We come unseasonably; but when could grief
Cull forth, as unpang'd judgment can, fitt'st time
For best solicitation? (*TNK*, 1.1.168)

have you any way then to unfool me again? (*MWW*, 4.2.119)

Unscissor'd shall this hair of mine remain (*Per.*, 3.3.29)

I do beseech You, . . . to unthink your speaking (*H8*, 2.4.103)

in his meed he's unfellowed (*Ham.*, 5.2.150)

a little to disquantity your train (*Lear*, 1.4.270)

but by the displanting of Cassio (*Oth.*, 2.1.284)

Dispropertied their freedoms (*Cor.*, 2.1.264)

like a star disorb'd (*T & C*, 2.2.46)

---

[14] Alfred Hart, "Shakespeare and the Vocabulary of *The Two Noble Kinsmen*," in *Shakespeare and the Homilies*, p. 253, asserts that words beginning with the prefix *un-* amount to nearly 4 percent of Shakespeare's vocabulary; about a fourth of these are "new" to literature, of Shakespeare's own coinage. They help us to differentiate his plays from those of his predecessors and contemporaries (p. 229). Shakespeare has coined thirty-two words beginning with *dis-*; such formations were rarely invented by his predecessors (p. 256).

Having usurped Prospero's dukedom, Antonio artfully uses a negative term to insinuate to Sebastian that now, since the heir Ferdinand is drowned, he may obtain his brother Alonso's kingdom.

> *Antonio.* 'Tis as impossible he's undrown'd
> As he that sleeps here swims.
> *Sebastian.* I have no hope That he's undrown'd.
> *Antonio.* O, out of that no hope What great hope have you!
> (*Tem.*, 2.1.237)

The ghost in *Hamlet* employs negative terms to emphasize the great wrong he suffered.

> Thus was I, sleeping, by a brother's hand
> Of life, of crown, of queen, at once dispatch'd;
> Cut off even in the blossoms of my sin,
> Unhous'led, disappointed, unanel'd. (1.5.74)

Shakespeare, like his contemporaries, appreciated the force of privative terms,[15] which express the absence or the loss of a characteristic that ought to be present.

> *Arthur.* I give you welcome with a powerless hand. (*KJ*, 2.1.15)

> *Miranda.* How features are abroad I am skilless of. (*Tem.*, 3.1.52)

> *Prospero.* And ye that on the sands with printless foot
> Do chase the ebbing Neptune. (*Tem.*, 5.1.34)

> *Fairy.* And bootless make the breathless housewife churn. (*MND*, 2.1.37)

> *Gloucester.*   you, my sovereign lady, . . .
> Causeless have laid disgraces on my head . . .
> And all to make away my guiltless life. (*2H6*, 3.1.161)

> To be imprison'd in the viewless winds
> And blown with restless violence round about (*MM*, 3.1.124)

> All form is formless, order orderless,
> Save what is opposite to England's love (*KJ*, 3.1.253)

> The dateless limit of thy dear exile.
> The hopeless word of 'never to return' (*R2*, 1.3.151)

---

[15] George Gordon, "Shakespeare's English," Society for Pure English, *Tract* 29, p. 273, remarks: "Shakespeare makes public love to a suffix in *1 Henry VI* (2.5.10–14), where he uses pithless, sapless, strengthless in lines 11–13, one in each of the three." Alfred Hart, "Shakespeare and the Vocabulary of the *Two Noble Kinsmen*," in *Shakespeare and the Homilies*, p. 255, notes that Shakespeare coined many such adjectives and that they abound in *3 Henry VI*.

Privative terms are used with taunting effect in the following rapid dialogue.

> *Cassio.*   Antony,
> The posture of your blows are yet unknown;
> But for your words, they rob the Hybla bees,
> And leave them honeyless.
> *Antony.*   Not stingless too.
> *Brutus.* O yes, and soundless too!
> For you have stol'n their buzzing, Antony,
> And very wisely threat before you sting. (*JC*, 5.1.32)

More explicit in its exposition of the logical doctrine on privative terms than any instance in Shakespeare is a sophistical argument in George Chapman's play *The Conspiracie of Charles Duke of Byron* (1608). When Byron declares that he will serve the lords in any office but disloyalty, Pycote answers him:

> The habite of a servile loyaltie,
> Is reckond now amongst privations,
> With blindnesse, dumbnesse, deafnesse, scilence, death,
> All which are neither natures by themselves
> Nor substances, but mere decayes of forme,
> And absolute decessions of nature,
> And so, 'tis nothing, what shall you then loose? (Act I, Sc. i)

Pycote argues speciously that servile loyalty is privation, privation is nothing, and therefore to give up servile loyalty is to give up nothing.

Litotes is a figure whereby, instead of affirming a predicate of a subject, one denies its contrary or its contradictory. It may be used to avoid an appearance of boasting or to veil a threat.

> *Flavius.* [*to Timon*]   I did endure
> Not seldom, nor no slight checks, when I have
> Prompted you in the ebb of your estate
> And your great flow of debts. (*Tim.*, 2.2.148)

> *Gloucester.* [*of Edgar*]   Let him fly far,
> Not in this land shall he remain uncaught. (*Lear*, 2.1.58)

Synoeciosis, a composition of contraries, stimulates attention by the seeming incompatibility of the terms it unites.

> *Pisanio.* Wherein I am false I am honest; not true to be true. (*Cym.*, 4.3.42)

Hamlet. They have a plentiful lack of wit. (2.2.201)

Hamlet. I must be cruel, only to be kind. (3.4.178)

Diomed. A juggling trick—to be secretly open. (*T & C*, 5.2,24)

Bottom. I'll speak in a monstrous little voice (*MND*, 1.2.54)

Flavius. [*of Timon*]   O monument
And wonder of good deeds evilly bestow'd! (4.3.466)

Claudio. To sue to live, I find I seek to die;
And seeking death, find life. Let it come on. (*MM*, 3.1.42)

Adam. [*to Orlando*] Your virtues, gentle master,
Are sanctified and holy traitors to you.
O, what a world is this, when what is comely
Envenoms him that bears it! (*AYLI*, 2.3.12)

Paradox, a figure which excites wonder, often involves apparent self
contradiction.

Senator. [*to Alcibiades*] You undergo too strict a paradox,
Striving to make an ugly deed look fair. (*Tim.*, 3.5.24)

Berowne. No face is fair that is not full so black.
King. O paradox! Black is the badge of hell,
The hue of dungeons, and the school of night . . .
Berowne. And therefore is she born to make black fair.
                 (*LLL*, 4.3.254–61)

Or paradox may express a view contrary to the opinion of most men.
Hamlet reveals his cynicism by avowing belief in an argument which
has been regarded as a paradox:

Ophelia. Could beauty, my lord, have better commerce than with honesty?
Hamlet. Ay, truly, for the power of beauty will sooner transform honesty
from what it is to a bawd than the force of honesty can translate beauty into
its likeness. This was sometime a paradox, but now the time gives it proof.
(3.1.109)

By urging the advantages of insanity Gloucester manifests the weight
of sorrow that oppresses him.

                   Better I were distract.
So should my thoughts be sever'd from my griefs,
And woes by wrong imaginations lose
The knowledge of themselves. (*Lear*, 4.6.288)

More forced and emotionally less convincing is the paradox maintained by Orleans in Thomas Dekker's *Old Fortunatus* (1600) in praise of deformity.

> Now Agripyne's not mine, I vow to be
> In love with nothing but deformity.
> O fair Deformity, I muse all eyes
> Are not enamoured of thee: thou didst never
> Murder men's hearts, or let them pine like wax,
> Melting against the sun of destiny;
> Thou art a faithful nurse to chastity;
> Thy beauty is not like to Agripyne's,
> For cares, and age, and sickness hers deface,
> But thine's eternal. O Deformity,
> Thy fairness is not like to Agripyne's,
> For, dead, her beauty will no beauty have,
> But thy face looks most lovely in the grave. (Act III, Sc. i)

Antithesis sets contraries in opposition to give greater perspicuity by contrast, as when Lord Rivers tries to comfort the widowed queen.

> Drown desperate sorrow in dead Edward's grave
> And plant your joys in living Edward's throne. (*R3*, 2.2.99)

Pisanio employs this figure with exceptional artistry in reporting the departure of Posthumus

> with glove or hat or handkerchief
> Still waving, as the fits and stirs of 's mind
> Could best express how slow his soul sail'd on,
> How swift his ship. (*Cym.*, 1.3.11)

Very similar is syncrisis which compares contrary things in contrasting clauses.

> *Caesar.* Cowards die many times before their deaths;
> The valiant never taste of death but once. (*JC*, 2.2.32)

> *Lear.* Through tatter'd clothes small vices do appear;
> Robes and furr'd gowns hide all. Plate sin with gold,
> And the strong lance of justice hurtless breaks;
> Arm it in rags, a pygmy's straw does pierce it. (4.6.168)

A conspirator uses this figure to further inflame Aufidius against Coriolanus:

> Your native town you enter'd like a post
> And had no welcome home; but he returns
> Splitting the air with noise. (*Cor.*, 5.6.49)

Antanagoge is the balancing of an unfavorable aspect with a favorable one, as in Phebe's comments on Ganymede.

> 'Tis but a peevish boy; yet he talks well.
> But what care I for words? Yet words do well
> When he that speaks them pleases those that hear. . . .
> But sure he's proud; and yet his pride becomes him.
> (*AYLI*, 3.5.110–14)

If this figures admits the reverse process, stating the unfavorable aspect last, it is one which Cleopatra reprehends when she excitedly interrupts a messenger who, having brought her good news, hedges with "But yet, madam."

> *Cleopatra.* I do not like 'but yet.' It does allay
> The good precedence. Fie upon 'but yet'!
> 'But yet' is as a jailer to bring forth
> Some monstrous malefactor. (*A & C*, 2.5.30)

The figure inter se pugnantia points out discrepancy between theory and practice.

> *Portia.* It is a good divine that follows his own instructions.
> I can easier teach twenty what were good to be done than be
> one of the twenty to follow mine own teaching. (*MV*, 1.2.15)

> *Ophelia.* [*to Laertes*] But, good my brother,
> Do not as some ungracious pastors do,
> Show me the steep and thorny way to heaven,
> Whiles, like a puff'd and reckless libertine,
> Himself the primrose path of dalliance treads
> And recks not his own rede. (*Ham.*, 1.3.46)

> *Claudius.* The harlot's cheek, beautied with plast'ring art,
> Is not more ugly to the thing that helps it
> Than is my deed to my most painted word.
> O heavy burthen! (*Ham.*, 3.1.51)

The remaining figures based on contraries are all forms of irony. Scheming to reach the throne, Richard, Duke of Gloucester, remarks to himself concerning his brother:

> Simple plain Clarence! I do love thee so
> That I will shortly send thy soul to heaven,
> If heaven will take the present at our hands. (*R3*, 1.1.118)

Irony permeates the speech of Lennox voicing his suspicions of Macbeth, who had expressed pity for murdered Duncan and denounced Duncan's sons who fled (3.6.1–20).

Antiphrasis, or the broad flout, is irony of one word, as in the lord's gibe to Bertram. Bertram's esteem of Parolles in spite of the adverse opinion of others is shaken when he hears derisive verses about himself.

> *Bertram.* He shall be whipp'd through the army with this rhyme in 's forehead.
> *Lord.* This is your devoted friend, sir. (*AW*, 4.3.262)

An outstanding instance of antiphrasis is the repetition of "honorable man," spoken at first with apparent sincerity in Antony's speech over Caesar, but growing in biting irony until it exerts no slight influence in inciting the plebeians against the conspirators (*JC*, 3.2.88–219).

Paralipsis is a figure which, while pretending to pass over a matter, tells it most effectively. Antony uses it with consummate skill to sway the crowd.

> Let but the commons hear this testament,
> Which (pardon me) I do not mean to read,
> And they would go and kiss dead Caesar's wounds . . .
> Have patience, gentle friends; I must not read it.
> It is not meet you know how Caesar lov'd you. . . . .
> 'Tis good you know not that you are his heirs. (3.2.136–51)

Similarly, Iago by feigning reluctance insinuates all the more effectively into Othello's mind rankling suspicions regarding Cassio and Desdemona (3.3.115–76). This figure is parodied in *Love's Labour's Lost* (5.1.100–119) where Armado keeps saying "but let that pass" while continuing to add brag to brag; and again in *The Taming of the Shrew* (4.1.74–86) where Grumio declares that he might have told, even while he does tell, what Katherina has had to endure from Petruchio.

Epitrope is an ironical permission, such as Cleopatra gives Antony when he is summoned to Rome by great affairs of state:

> *Antony.*   Most sweet queen—
> *Cleopatra.* Nay, pray you seek no colour for your going,
> But bid farewell, and go. When you su'd staying,

> Then was the time for words. No going then!
> Eternity was in our lips and eyes. (*A & C*, 1.3.31)

Richard II pre-eminently illustrates Shakespeare's skill in the use of contraries and contradictories. The negative terms are particularly arresting. Dying Gaunt entertains a hope that Richard, although hitherto misled by his favorites, may at last hearken to the earnest counsel of a dying man.

> My death's sad tale may yet undeaf his ear. (2.1.16)

Bolingbroke, having captured these same favorites and condemned them to death, charges:

> You have misled a prince, a royal king . . .
> By you unhappied and disfigured clean. (3.1.8–10)

Upon report that these friends have made peace with Bolingbroke, Richard curses them, but Scroop entreats:

> Again uncurse their souls. Their peace is made
> With heads, and not with hands. (3.2.137)

Compelled at last to abdicate, Richard exclaims:

> God save King Harry, unking'd Richard says. (4.1.220)

> Think that I am unking'd by Bolingbroke. (5.5.37)

Richard, ordered to prison, employs a striking negative term in taking leave of his wife.

> Let me unkiss the oath 'twixt me and thee. (5.1.74)

Contrariety and mutual repugnance underlie the confusions which pervade this play. Loyal York notes Richard's confusion of the true order of his duties in going far away to Ireland to safeguard his interests there, while leaving England open to an attack by Bolingbroke. In contrast to Richard, York himself under trying circumstances justly estimates the priority of duties. Although he feels strong sympathy for Bolingbroke, who had been wronged by Richard, York firmly holds his primary duty to be toward the king, for "To find out right with wrong—it may not be" (2.3.145). It is the Bishop of Carlisle, however, who sees most clearly the disorder, confusion, and disaster which will follow if subjects should do so foul a wrong as to depose the figure of God's majesty, a lawful and anointed king. One of his speeches epitomizes the central thesis not only of this play but also of the whole series of Shakespeare's historical plays by picturing the evils that will result if lawful authority is impugned.

> in this seat of peace tumultuous wars
> Shall kin with kin and kind with kind confound;
> Disorder, horror, fear, and mutiny
> Shall here inhabit. (4.1.140)

If we reflect that kind means species and that two or more species are repugnant terms mutually exclusive, these words leap into fiery poetry expressing the ultimate concept of disorder, disorder through logical confusion, the confounding of kind with kind. Richard pronounces himself a traitor for permitting himself to be deposed, and he depicts the resulting disorder by coupling contraries.

> I find myself a traitor with the rest;
> For I have given here my soul's consent
> To undeck the pompous body of a king;
> Made glory base, and sovereignty a slave,
> Proud majesty a subject, state a peasant. (4.1.248)

Both *Richard II* and *A Midsummer Night's Dream* stress disorder, the former through confusion of contraries, the latter through confusion of adjuncts; the one very seriously, the other playfully, exulting in free imagination that is delightful and diverting, not touching the heart of civil and personal order and integrity.

6. Similarity and Dissimilarity

Observing Lady Macbeth as she walks in her sleep and noting the words and gestures that divulge her guilt, the doctor reasons from the character of the effect to a similar character in the cause.

> Unnatural deeds Do breed unnatural troubles. (5.1.79)

Timon in his warped, bitter spirit encourages the banditti in their profession by arguing from example, a form of similitude.

> Do villany, do, since you protest to do't,
> Like workmen. I'll example you with thievery.
> The sun's a thief, and with his great attraction
> Robs the vast sea. The moon's an arrant thief,
> And her pale fire she snatches from the sun.
> The sea's a thief, whose liquid surge resolves
> The moon into salt tears. The earth's a thief,

> That feeds and breeds by a composture stol'n
> From gen'ral excrement. Each thing's a thief. (4.3.437)

Ravished Lucrece, mentally searching the earth in her misery, proceeds by induction from examples to a general conclusion which furnishes her a modicum of comfort.

> Why should the worm intrude the maiden bud?
> Or hateful cuckoos hatch in sparrows' nests?
> Or toads infect fair founts with venom mud?
> Or tyrant folly lurk in gentle breasts?
> Or kings be breakers of their own behests?
>   But no perfection is so absolute
>   That some impurity does not pollute. (*RL*, 848–54)

Touchstone provides a sprightly parody of inadequate induction or argument from example when he challenges Corin's generalization that the manners of the court are ridiculous in the country. Corin asserts, as an instance, that to kiss hands in saluting would be uncleanly among shepherds. Touchstone argues down this instance and others which Corin offers with

Shallow, shallow! A better instance, I say. Come . . . A more sounder instance, come. . . . Mend the instance, shepherd,

until at last Corin acknowledges defeat:

You have too courtly a wit for me. I'll rest. (*AYLI*, 3.2.53–72)

In *All's Well* Helena finds comfort in an argument from similitude which acquaints the audience not only with her love for Bertram but also with her nobility of mind.

>   'Twere all one
> That I should love a bright particular star
> And think to wed it, he is so above me.
> In his bright radiance and collateral light
> Must I be comforted, not in his sphere. (1.1.96)

A palpable argument from dissimilitude, on the other hand, is that of Hamlet when holding before his mother's eyes the pictures of his dead father and of Claudius he declares them as dissimilar as a wholesome and a mildewed ear of grain and demands, "what judgment Would step from this to this?" The answer, he assures her, can be only that her sense is apoplexed, or that the devil deceives her, or that reason panders will (3.4.53–88).

By using first a dissimilitude and then a similitude Othello emphasizes the irrevocability of the deed he contemplates, the killing of Desdemona. Entering the bedroom where she lies asleep, he reflects as he gazes on the light in his hand:

> If I quench thee, thou flaming minister,
> I can again thy former light restore,
> Should I repent me; but once put out thy light,
> Thou cunning'st pattern of excelling nature,
> I know not where is that Promethean heat
> That can thy light relume. When I have pluck'd the rose,
> I cannot give it vital growth again;
> It needs must wither. I'll smell it on the tree. [*He kisses her*] (5.2.8)

The Tudor rhetoricians called the general figure of similitude homoe-osis and distinguished as its species icon, parabola, paradigma, and fable. Icon is a figure which paints the likeness of a person by imagery. Richard II, who is characteristically weak when strong action is needed, dissipates his energy in making such comparisons. Even in prison he will hammer them out. Summoned by Bolingbroke, who is waiting in the court below, Richard describes himself through icon.

> Down, down I come, like glist'ring Phaeton,
> Wanting the manage of unruly jades. (*R2*, 3.3.178)

Parabola is a moral or mystical resemblance, such as the poet in *Timon* points out to the painter.

> Sir, I have upon a high and pleasant hill
> Feign'd Fortune to be thron'd. . . . Amongst them all
> Whose eyes are on this sovereign lady fix'd
> One do I personate of Lord Timon's frame,
> Whom Fortune with her ivory hand wafts to her. (1.1.63–70)

The poem shows that when Fortune spurns her late favorite, his flattering followers let him slip down and refuse him aid. Later, Timon himself relates the event in a sort of parable.

> *Alcibiades.* How came the noble Timon to this change?
> *Timon.* As the moon does, by wanting light to give.
> But then renew I could not, like the moon;
> There were no suns to borrow of. (4.3.66)

Paradigma, an argument from example judging the present from the past, is parodied in Fluellen's far-fetched analogy between Harry of Monmouth and Alexander of Macedon:

There is a river in Macedon, and there is also moreover a river at Monmouth.
. . . and there is salmons in both. If you mark Alexander's life well, Harry of Monmouth's life is come after it indifferent well; for there is figures in all things. . . . As Alexander kill'd his friend Cleitus, being in his ales and cups, so also Harry Monmouth, being in his right wits and good judgments, turn'd away the fat knight. (*H5*, 4.7.28–50)

Fable is another figure based on resemblance. To calm the anger of the plebeians against the patricians in *Coriolanus*, Menenius tells them a fable of how the body's members once rebelled against the belly (1.1.99–150).[16]

> 2. *Citizen.*   How apply you this?
> *Menenius.* The senators of Rome are this good belly,
> And you the mutinous members. . . .
> No public benefit which you receive
> But it proceeds or comes from them to you,
> And no way from yourselves. (151–58)

Simile, metaphor, and onomatopoeia are figures familiar to the modern reader. Lear, shouting in the storm, uses onomatopoeia.

> Blow, winds, and crack your cheeks! rage! blow!
> You cataracts and hurricanoes, spout . . .
>   And thou, all-shaking thunder,
> Strike flat the thick rotundity o' th' world,
> Crack Nature's moulds. (3.2.1–7)

A few similes may be noted.[17]

> *Imogen.*   comes in my father,
> And, like the tyrannous breathing of the North,
> Shakes all our buds from growing. (*Cym.*, 1.3.35)

---

[16] See Wilson's reference to this fable, p. 327, below. Shakespeare, of course, found it in his source, Plutarch.

[17] Spurgeon, in *Shakespeare's Imagery and What It Tells Us*, makes an exhaustive study of the content of Shakespeare's imagery. Tuve, in "Imagery and Logic: Ramus and Metaphysical Poetics," *Journal of the History of Ideas*, III (October, 1942), 365–400, shows how the topics of logic determined the character of imagery in the work of Elizabethan poets in terms of the function of poetry as they conceived it, namely, to teach, to move or persuade, and to delight.

Lucio. [*urging Isabel to plead less coldly*] If you should need a pin,
You could not with more tame a tongue desire it. (*MM*, 2.2.45)

to as much end As give a crutch to th' dead. (*H8*, 1.1.171)

Maria. [*of Malvolio*] He does smile his face into more lines than is in
the new map with the augmentation of the Indies. (*TN*, 3.2.84)

Ariel. [*to Prospero*] So I charm'd their ears
That calf-like they my lowing follow'd through
Tooth'd briers, sharp furzes, pricking goss, and thorns,
Which ent'red their frail shins. (*Tem.*, 4.1.178)

Many of Shakespeare's metaphors suggest the activity, aliveness, and freshness commended by Aristotle.

> Now strange words simply puzzle us; ordinary words convey only what we know already; it is from metaphor that we can best get hold of something fresh. . . . the metaphors must not be far-fetched, or they will be difficult to grasp, nor obvious, or they will have no effect. The words, too, ought to set the scene before our eyes; for events ought to be seen in progress rather than in prospect. (*Rhetoric*, 3.10, 1410 ^{b} 12, 32)

Antony. I, that . . . o'er green Neptune's back
With ships made cities. (*A & C*, 4.14.57–59)

Sebastian. [*of Gonzalo*] Look, he's winding up the watch of his wit;
by-and-by it will strike. (*Tem.*, 2.1.12)

Sicinius. [*of Coriolanus*] his soaring insolence
Shall touch the people . . . will be his fire
To kindle their dry stubble; and their blaze
Shall darken him forever. (*Cor.*, 2.1.270–75)

Lucio. Lord Angelo—a man whose blood Is very snow-broth. (*MM*, 1.4.57)

Hector. [*to Nestor*] Let me embrace thee, good old chronicle,
That hast so long walk'd hand in hand with time. (*T & C*, 4.5.202)

The figure allegory continues a metaphor through an entire speech, as when Iago observes:

Our bodies are our gardens, to the which our wills are gardeners; so that if we will plant nettles or sow lettuce, set hyssop and weed up thyme, supply it with one gender of herbs or distract it with many—either to have it sterile with idleness or manured with industry—why, the power and corrigible authority of this lies in our wills. (*Oth.*, 1.3.322)

An outstanding instance of this figure is Jaques' speech beginning, "All the world's a stage" (*AYLI*, 2.7.138–66).

Catachresis, a figure which we would call an implied metaphor, is the wrenching of a word, most often a verb or an adjective, from its proper application to another not proper, as when one says that the sword devours. This figure, like the use of nouns as verbs, and the formation of compounds and negatives, is in Shakepeare's hands a vital creative instrument with which he forges sudden concentrations of meaning, and secures the compression, energy, and intensity which characterize great poetry.

Lent him our terror, dress'd him with our love (*MM*, 1.1.20)

Your eye in Scotland Would create soldiers (*Mac.*, 4.3.186)

I have supp'd full with horrors (*Mac.*, 5.5.13)

supple knees Feed arrogance. (*T & C*, 3.3.48)

Mine eyes, ev'n sociable to the show of thine,
Fall fellowly drops. (*Tem.*, 5.1.63)

your ears . . . so fortified against our story (*Ham.*, 1.1.31)

If his occulted guilt Do not itself unkennel in one speech (*Ham.*, 3.2.85)

I will speak daggers to her, but use none. (*Ham.*, 3.2.414)

For we will fetters put upon this fear
Which goes too free-footed. (*Ham.*, 3.3.25)

a sponge . . . that soaks up the King's countenance (*Ham.*, 4.2.16)

We have kiss'd away Kingdoms and provinces. (*A & C*, 3.10.7)

And he will fill thy wishes to the brim
With principalities (*A & C*, 3.13.18)

Whose eye beck'd forth my wars and call'd them home (*A & C*, 4.12.26)

your fame Knolls in th' ear o' th' world (*TNK*, 1.1.133)

Methinks My favour here begins to warp (*WT*, 1.2.365)

But now my heavy conscience sinks my knee (*Cym.*, 5.5.413)

'Tis deepest winter in Lord Timon's purse (*Tim.*, 3.4.14)

Most rich in Timon's nod (*Tim.*, 1.1.62)

Rain sacrificial whisperings in his ear (*Tim.*, 1.1.81)

Measure his woe the length and breadth of mine (*MA*, 5.1.11)

7. Comparison: Greater, Equal, Less

Arguments from the greater, the equal, and the less are employed with force and frequency in Shakespeare's plays. When Cassius charges that Brutus has done him wrong, Brutus argues from the greater likelihood to the less.

> Judge me, you gods! wrong I mine enemies?
> And if not so, how should I wrong a brother? (*JC*, 4.2.38)

Beholding Ophelia bereft of reason, Laertes is pierced with an argument stronger than reason could utter.

> Hadst thou thy wits, and didst persuade revenge,
> It could not move me thus. (*Ham.*, 4.5.168)

Lear will not enter the hovel, but to escape from grief prefers to remain out in the raging storm.

> This tempest will not give me leave to ponder
> On things would hurt me more. (3.4.24)

When Menenius comes to tell Coriolanus that he must return to the tribunes and repent what he has so disdainfully spoken, Coriolanus protests:

> I cannot do it to the gods. Must I then do 't to them? (3.2.38)

A simple gardener comments on an important political fact in Britain, the influence of the English peers.

> But in the balance of great Bolingbroke,
> Besides himself, are all the English peers,
> And with that odds he weighs King Richard down. (*R2*, 3.4.88)

Belarius compares his free life in the mountains with life at court as he has known it.

> O, this life
> Is nobler than attending for a check,
> Richer than doing nothing for a bribe,
> Prouder than rustling in unpaid-for silk. (*Cym.*, 3.3.21)

Florizel defends his disguise as a swain when he comes to visit Perdita.

> The gods themselves,
> Humbling their deities to love, have taken
> The shapes of beasts upon them. Jupiter

> Became a bull, and bellow'd; the green Neptune
> A ram, and bleated; and the fire-rob'd god,
> Golden Apollo, a poor humble swain,
> As I seem now. (*WT*, 4.4.25)

Posthumus achieves the superlative in adverse self-appraisal when he declares:

> It is I
> That all the abhorred things o' the earth amend
> By being worse than they. (*Cym.*, 5.5.215)

Falstaff defends himself by contending that his temptation was greater than Adam's.

Dost thou hear, Hal? Thou knowest in the state of innocency Adam fell; and what should poor Jack Falstaff do in the days of villany? Thou seest I have more flesh than another man, and therefore more frailty. (*1H4*, 3.3.185)

The Archbishop of York justifies the rebellion against Henry IV by maintaining that it is the lesser of two evils.

> I have in equal balance justly weigh'd
> What wrongs our arms may do, what wrongs we suffer,
> And find our griefs heavier than our offences. (*2H4*, 4.1.66)

Macbeth argues from the less to the greater.

> I'll go no more.
> I am afraid to think what I have done;
> Look on't again I dare not. (2.2.50)

Suddenly he sees the bloody, ineradicable deed stain all his future.

> Will all great Neptune's ocean wash this blood
> Clean from my hand? No. This my hand will rather
> The multitudinous seas incarnadine,
> Making the green one red. (2.2.60)

Later, grown more desperate, he argues from equals.

> I am in blood
> Stepp'd in so far that, should I wade no more,
> Returning were as tedious as go o'er. (3.4.136)

An officer gives an excellent diagnosis of Coriolanus, balancing extremes equally bad.

Now to seem to affect the malice and displeasure of the people is as bad as that which he dislikes—to flatter them for their love. (2.2.24)

Through a comparison ostensibly of equals Thersites insults and debases Ajax.

Thou grumblest and railest every hour on Achilles; and thou art as full of envy at his greatness as Cerberus is at Proserpina's beauty—ay, that thou bark'st at him. (*T & C*, 2.1.35)

Imogen, while arguing from equals, rebukes Iachimo and praises Posthumus with superlative force.

> Thou wrong'st a gentleman who is as far
> From thy report as thou from honour. (*Cym.*, 1.6.145)

Maecenas tersely sums up Antony's character.

> His taints and honours Wag'd equal with him. (*A & C*, 5.1.30)

In *The Arte of Logick* Blundeville warns against a fallacy in reasoning from these topics of comparison.

You must beware that you take not the More for the Lesse, nor the Lesse for the More, for many times that which seemeth to be the More in number or quantitie, is the Lesse in purpose, and contrariwise. (p. 111)

Lear makes this mistake in estimating his daughters' statements of their love for him. Again, when Regan wants to cut down his hundred followers to twenty-five, he turns to Goneril.

> I'll go with thee.
> Thy fifty yet doth double five and twenty,
> And thou art twice her love. (2.4.261)

The hero of Chapman's play *The Conspiracie of Charles Duke of Byron* expresses an uncommon view when he declares:

> Happinesse
> Denies comparison, of lesse, or more,
> And not at most, is nothing. (Act I, Sc. i)

Auxesis is a figure which advances from less to greater by arranging words or clauses in a sequence of increasing force, as the Bishop of Carlisle does in order to impress upon the English lords the greatness of the wrong they would commit in judging Richard II.

> What subject can give sentence on his king?
> And who sits here that is not Richard's subject?
> Thieves are not judg'd but they are by to hear,
> Although apparent guilt be seen in them;
> And shall the figure of God's majesty,
> His captain, steward, deputy elect,
> Anointed, crown'd, planted many years,
> Be judg'd by subject and inferior breath,
> And he himself not present? (*R2*, 4.1.121)

Polonius enumerates the stages by which, he is confident, Hamlet became mad.

> And he, repulsed, a short tale to make,
> Fell into a sadness, then into a fast,
> Thence to a watch, thence into a weakness,
> Thence to a lightness, and, by this declension,
> Into the madness wherein now he raves. (2.2.146)

Florizel praises Perdita.

> Each your doing,
> So singular in each particular,
> Crowns what you are doing in the present deed,
> That all your acts are queens. (*WT*, 4.4.143)

This figure is travestied in *Love's Labour's Lost* where Armado asserts his devotion to Jaquenetta.

I do affect the very ground (which is base) where her shoe (which is baser) guided by her foot (which is basest) doth tread. (1.2.173)

And again, in *As You Like It*, where Touchstone explains each of the steps involved in a lie seven times removed: the Retort Courteous, the Quip Modest, the Reply Churlish, the Reproof Valiant, the Countercheck Quarrelsome, the Lie Circumstantial, and the Lie Direct. (5.4. 71–86).

Another form of auxesis amplifies by hyperbole, as when Prince Hal calls Falstaff "this horseback-breaker, this huge hill of flesh" (*1H4*, 2.4. 268), and Doll Tearsheet proclaims him "as valorous as Hector of Troy, worth five of Agamemnon, and ten times better than the Nine Worthies" (*2H4*, 2.4.237).

Augmentation through hyperbole gives to *Antony and Cleopatra* much of its surge and sweep.

> *Antony.* Let Rome in Tiber melt and the wide arch
> Of the rang'd empire fall! Here is my space. (1.1.33)

Enobarbus.   th' air, which, but for vacancy,
Had gone to gaze on Cleopatra too,
And made a gap in nature. (2.2.221)

Cleopatra. [*of Antony*] His face was as the heav'ns, and therein stuck
A sun and moon, which kept their course and lighted
The little O, the earth. . . .
His legs bestrid the ocean: his rear'd arm
Crested the world . . . Realms and islands were
As plates dropp'd from his pocket. (5.2.79–92)

Troilus epitomizes the beauty of Helen.

He brought a Grecian queen, whose youth and freshness
Wrinkles Apollo's and makes stale the morning. (*T & C*, 2.2.78)

Through hyperbole Ross vividly pictures the sufferings of Scotland.

Ross. Where sighs and groans, and shrieks that rent the air
Are made, not mark'd . . . The dead man's knell
Is there scarce ask'd for who . . .
Malcolm.   What's the newest grief?
Ross. That of an hour's age doth hiss the speaker;
Each minute teems a new one. (*Mac.*, 4.3.168–76)

In contrast to auxesis and hyperbole, meiosis belittles, as when the
bastard describes the Dauphin's army.

This apish and unmannerly approach,
This harness'd masque and unadvised revel,
This unhair'd sauciness and boyish troop,
The King doth smile at, and is well prepar'd
To whip this dwarfish war, these pygmy arms,
From out the circle of his territories. (*KJ*, 5.2.131)

Meiosis, often achieved through a trope of one word, may range from
bitter scorn to light derision.

Coriolanus. Go get you home, you fragments! . . .
The Volsces have much corn. Take these rats thither
To gnaw their garners. (*Cor.*, 1.1.226, 253)

Hotspur. What a frosty-spirited rogue . . . Zounds, an I were now by
this rascal, I could brain him with his lady's fan. (*1H4*, 2.3.22)

Hamlet. What should such fellows as I do, crawling between earth and
heaven? (*Ham.*, 3.1.131)

Prospero. [*to Antonio and Sebastian*] But you, my brace of lords . . . (*Tem.*, 5.1.126)

Celia. [*to Rosalind of Orlando*] I found him under a tree, like a dropp'd acorn. (*AYLI*, 3.2.247)

Rosalind. [*to Phebe*] What though you have no beauty—
As, by my faith, I see no more in you
Than without candle may go dark to bed! (*AYLI*, 3.5.37)

Antonio. [*of Gonzalo*] What impossible matter will he make easy next?
Sebastian. I think he will carry this island home in his pocket and give it his son for an apple. (*Tem.*, 2.1.88)

Paradiastole is a figure which extenuates in order to flatter or soothe. It is clearly referred to by Ajax when he speaks of Achilles.

Yes, lion-sick, sick of proud heart. You may call it melancholy, if you will favour the man; but, by my head, 'tis pride. (*T & C*, 2.3.93)

Isabel remarks on the disposition to color an act by giving it a more pleasing name when certain privileged persons do it.

> Great men may jest with saints. 'Tis wit in them,
> But in the less, foul profanation. . . .
> That in the captain's but a choleric word
> Which in the soldier is flat blasphemy. (*MM*, 2.2.127–31)

Charientismus is a figure through which one mollifies threatening words by answering them with a smooth and appeasing mock.

> *Coriolanus.* What's the matter, you dissentious rogues
> That, rubbing the poor itch of your opinion,
> Make yourselves scabs?
> *2. Citizen.* We have ever your good word. (1.1.168)

Catacosmesis is the ordering of words from greatest to least in dignity, an order which Antigonus observes when he warns Leontes not to proceed rashly against Hermione.

> Be certain what you do, sir, lest your justice
> Prove violence, in the which three great ones suffer,
> Yourself, your queen, your son. (*WT*, 2.1.127)

Dogberry, aware of this propriety, directs that it be observed in recording the replies of Borachio and Conrade to the constable's questions.

Write down that they hope they serve God; and write God first, for God defend but God should go before such villains. (*MA*, 4.2.20)

Epanorthosis, or correction, amends a first thought by altering it to make it stronger or more vehement.

> *Henry V.* A good heart, Kate, is the sun and the moon; or rather, the sun, and not the moon, for it shines bright and never changes, but keeps his course truly. (*H5*, 5.2.171)

> *Troilus.* And when fair Cressid comes into my thoughts—
> So, traitor? 'when she comes'? When is she thence? (*T & C*, 1.1.30)

> *Iago.* I see, sir, you are eaten up with passion.
> I do repent me that I put it to you.
> You would be satisfied?
> *Othello.*   Would? Nay, I will. (3.3.391)

> *Posthumus.* I speak not out of weak surmises, but from proof as strong as my grief and as certain as I expect my revenge. (*Cym.*, 3.4.23)

> *Adam.* [*to Orlando*] Your brother (no, no brother! yet the son—
> Yet not the son—I will not call him son
> Of him I was about to call his father)
> Hath heard your praises, and this night he means
> To burn the lodging where you use to lie
> And you within it. (*AYLI*, 2.3.19)

By the figure dirimens copulatio a point is added to balance or outweigh what has already been said, as when Falstaff, taking the part of King Henry IV, rebukes Prince Hal in the course of an elaborate parody of euphuism.

Harry, I do not only marvel where thou spendest thy time, but also how thou art accompanied. . . . For, Harry, now do I not speak to thee . . . in words only, but in woes also. (*1H4*, 2.4.439–59)

Emphasis is a figure which gives prominence to a quality or trait by conceiving it as constituting the very substance in which it inheres. Shakespeare apparently liked this figure, for he uses it frequently with swift and supple ease.

> *Cesario.* [*to Olivia*] Farewell, fair cruelty (*TN*, 1.5.307)

> *Troilus.* I am all patience (*T & C*, 5.2.64)

> *Prospero.* [*to Caliban*] Shrug'st thou, malice? (*Tem.*, 1.2.367)

> *Caliban.* [*of Prospero*] make him By inchmeal a disease! (*Tem.*, 2.2.2)

> *Prospero.* [*to Ariel*] Bravely, my diligence (*Tem.*, 5.1.241)

> *Escalus.* [*of Angelo*] but my brother justice have I found so severe that he hath forc'd me to tell him he is indeed Justice. (*MM*, 3.2.266)

Similar to the last of these is an example in Jonson's *Bartholomew Fair*.

> *Lanterne.* Sir, I present nothing, but what is licens'd by authority.
> *Busy.* Thou art all *license*, even licentiousnesse it selfe. (5.5.14)

Synonymia iterates the same thing in many words of the same meaning, to increase its force, as when Macbeth, informed that Fleance has escaped the murderers sent to kill him, realizes the significance of this news to himself.

> But now I am cabin'd, cribb'd, confin'd, bound in
> To saucy doubts and fears. (3.4.24)

Fluellen defends himself against the imputation of error by an appeal to this figure.

> *Fluellen.* What call you the town's name where Alexander the Pig was born?
> *Gower.* Alexander the Great.
> *Fluellen.* Why, I pray you, is not 'pig' great? The pig, or the great, or the mighty, or the huge, or the magnanimous are all one reckoning, save the phrase is a little variations. (*H5,* 4.7.13)

Exergasia, or expolitio, augments by repeating the same thought in many figures.

> *Florizel.* [*to Perdita*] I take thy hand—this hand,
> As soft as dove's down and as white as it,
> Or Ethiopian's tooth, or the fann'd snow that's bolted
> By th' northern blasts twice o'er.
> *Polixenes.*   What follows this?
> How prettily the young swain seems to wash
> The hand was fair before! (*WT,* 4.4.373)

Coriolanus, taking leave of his mother as he goes into exile, reminds her of her own counsels of fortitude efficaciously worded in various forms.

> Come, leave your tears. . . . Nay, mother,
> Where is your ancient courage? You were us'd
> To say extremity was the trier of spirits;
> That common chances common men could bear;
> That when the sea was calm, all boats alike
> Show'd mastership in floating; fortune's blows
> When most struck home, being gentle wounded craves
> A noble cunning. You were us'd to load me

> With precepts that would make invincible
> The heart that conn'd them. (4.1.1)

Rather loosely related to augmentation are three figures: an introductory narrative to open a speech, called paradiegesis; a digression; and
a return from digression. Titus Andronicus prefaces his plea to the tribunes and senators in behalf of his two sons, who are being led to execution, with a brief narrative reminding them of his deeds for Rome.

> Hear me, grave fathers—noble Tribunes, stay,
> For pity of mine age, whose youth was spent
> In dangerous wars whilst you securely slept.
> For all my blood in Rome's great quarrel shed,
> For all the frosty nights that I have watch'd,
> And for these bitter tears which now you see
> Filling the aged wrinkles in my cheeks,
> Be pitiful to my condemned sons. (*Tit.*, 3.1.1)

When Westmoreland, sent by John, Duke of Lancaster, comes to confer
with Mowbray and the Archbishop of York, he digresses from his errand
to discuss the ancient quarrel between Mowbray's father and Bolingbroke. Explicitly acknowledging the digression, he returns to the subject
of his mission.

> But this is mere digression from my purpose.
> Here come I from my princely general
> To know your griefs; to tell you from his Grace
> That he will give you audience. (*2H4*, 4.1.140)

In *Measure for Measure* there is ludicrous digression or meandering
from the point in Pompey's testimony. Speaking of two prunes in a dish,
he digresses to tell that it is a dish worth some three pence, not a China
dish, but very good; the judges have seen such dishes. And so throughout
his testimony, until the wearied judge cries, "This will last out a night
in Russia When nights are longest there" (2.1.91–139).

Among Shakespeare's plays the one which places strongest emphasis
on comparison of the less with the greater is *Titus Andronicus*. For Lavinia's wrong, which is greater than Philomel's, there shall be a revenge
greater than Progne's (5.2.195). Titus has one thousand times more cause
than Virginius had to slay his ravished daughter (5.3.51), and his wrongs
were greater than any living man could bear (127). Aaron the Moor,
about to suffer death for his villainy, wishes only that he had done more
evil (187).

8. Cause and Effect, Antecedent and Consequent

Cause and effect, antecedent and consequent are relations vital to dramatic structure. As a playwright keenly alive to this fact, Shakespeare draws arguments from the four causes—efficient, material, formal, and final—but most often from the last, since motives deeply affect both character and plot.

Caesar professes his own imperious will to be the adequate efficient cause for refusing to go to the capitol, as he had promised.

> The cause is in my will: I will not come. (*JC*, 2.2.71)

Inconstant Proteus tries to convince himself that Sylvia's beauty is an efficient cause so inherently efficacious that he must helplessly relinquish his pledged allegiance to Julia and his loyalty to his friend Valentine.

> the remembrance of my former love
> Is by a newer object quite forgotten. . . .
> Methinks my zeal to Valentine is cold . . .
> If I can check my erring love, I will;
> If not, to compass her I'll use my skill. (*TGV*, 2.4.194–214)

Helena reproaches herself as the ultimate efficient cause of her husband's death, should Bertram be killed in battle, since it was his disdain for her that impelled him to go away to war.

> Poor lord! is't I
> That chase thee from thy country and expose
> Those tender limbs of thine to the event
> Of the none-sparing war? . . . to be the mark
> Of smoky muskets? . . .
> Whoever shoots at him, I set him there;
> Whoever charges on his forward breast,
> I am the caitiff that do hold him to't,
> And though I kill him not, I am the cause
> His death was so effected. (*AW*, 3.2.105–19)

Morton figuratively represents Hotspur as having been until his death the formal and the material cause of transforming even peasants into courageous soldiers.

> his . . . spirit lent a fire
> Even to the dullest peasant in his camp . . .
> For from his metal was his party steel'd,
> Which once in him abated, all the rest

Turn'd on themselves, like dull and heavy lead.
(*2H4*, 1.1.112–18)

As Abraham Fraunce points out in *The Lawiers Logike*, practical judgments as to what is honest or useful generally rest upon a consideration of the final cause, which is the motive of the agent.

All the arguments that common Rhetoricians fetch from *Honestum* and *Utile*, are for the most part derived from the end or finall cause, sith for the cause of these two, most things are enterprised. In like maner, the gesses and conjectures of Judges are fet from the end, as, hee was most like to woorke the mischiefe, who might have any end or profit in practising of the same.

Whose use is good, that is good, but not contrarily, the thing is bad because it is abused.

The end doth not alwayes follow the efficient cause, eyther because the efficient could not accomplish the thing alone or els because hee would not. (*LL*, fol. 26ʳ)

The last remark is worth pondering in relation to Hamlet. And Falstaff's catechism of honor is an investigation of *honestum* and *utile*, in search of a motive, or rather, an excuse.

To know why the ghost comes is Hamlet's insistent demand in his first speech to the apparition (1.4.39–57) ending: "Say why is this? Wherefore?" In instructing the players Hamlet explains the final cause or purpose of Shakespeare's own art of writing and acting plays.

For anything . . . overdone is from the purpose of playing, whose end, both at the first and now, was and is, to hold, as 'twere, the mirror up to nature; to show virtue her own feature, scorn her own image, and the very age and body of the time his form and pressure. (3.2.22)

Sir Toby states the motives for the trick planned against Malvolio, to put him bound into a dark room.

We may carry it thus, for our pleasure and his penance, till our very pastime, tired out of breath, prompt us to have mercy on him. (*TN*, 3.4.150)

And Prospero tells why he has benignly wrought confusion of his enemies.

They being penitent,
The sole drift of my purpose doth extend
Not a frown further. (*Tem.*, 5.1.28)

The final cause is of paramount importance in portraying Brutus, for it

is the unswerving sincerity of his motives that shows him ever noble.
Years later, Pompey recognizes this fact.

> What was't . . .
> Made the all-honour'd honest Roman, Brutus,
> With the arm'd rest, . . .
> To drench the Capitol, but that they would
> Have one man but a man? (*A & C*, 2.6.14–19)

Troilus argues from the effects to the cause when he speaks of the
bloody war between the Greeks and the Trojans.

> Helen must needs be fair
> When with your blood you daily paint her thus! (*T & C*, 1.1.93)

Iago, competent soldier but evil poisoner of Othello's mind and heart,
bears out an observation made by Raphe Lever in *The Arte of Reason*
regarding the comparative value of effects wrought by mind and body.

The worke of the mind in good things is alwayes more excellente, then the
worke of the body: but in ill things it is farre worse. (p. 181)

Metonymy is a trope related to cause and effect as well as to subject
and adjunct. The substitution of an author's name for his work is
metonymy of the efficient cause, as when Tranio warns Lucio not to be
so devoted to philosophy,

> As Ovid be an outcast quite abjur'd. (*TS*, 1.1.33)

The following illustrate metonymy of the material cause.

> he tilts With piercing steel at bold Mercutio's breast. (*R & J*, 3.1.163)

> *Benedick.* [*of music being played*] Is it not strange that sheep's guts
> should hale souls out of men's bodies? (*MA*, 2.3.61)

Metonymy may also substitute the effect for the cause.

> I have made my way through more impediments
> Than twenty times your stop. (*Oth.*, 5.2.263)

> I think the honey guarded with a sting. (*RL*, 493)

> We see the ground whereon these woes do lie. (*R & J*, 5.3.179)

> All torment, trouble, wonder, and amazement
> Inhabits here. (*Tem.*, 5.1.104–5)

Metalepsis is a figure which attributes a present effect to a remote cause,
as when Isabel exclaims to Claudio:

> There spake my brother! There my father's grave
> Did utter forth a voice. (*MM*, 3.1.86)

This figure serves Hamlet's cast of thought as he watches the grave-diggers.

To what base uses we may return, Horatio! Why may not imagination trace the noble dust of Alexander till he find it stopping a bunghole? . . . Alexander died, Alexander was buried, Alexander returneth into dust; the dust is earth; of earth we make loam; and why of that loam (whereto he was converted) might they not stop a beer barrel? (5.1.223–35)

Closely akin to the relation of cause and effect is that of antecedent and consequent, which may be expressed in the form of a hypothetical proposition. Shakespeare often states in such a proposition an important problem of the plot.

> *Hamlet.* [*of Claudius*] If his occulted guilt
> Do not itself unkennel in one speech,
> It is a damned ghost that we have seen. (3.2.85)

> *Agamemnon.* [*of Hector*] If in his death the gods have us befriended,
> Great Troy is ours, and our sharp wars are ended. (*T & C*, 5.9.9)

> *Ford.* If I suspect without cause . . . let me be your jest. (*MWW*, 3.3.159)

> *Cesario.* [*to Olivia*] Lady, you are the cruell'st she alive
> If you will lead these graces to the grave,
> And leave the world no copy. (*TN*, 1.5.259)

> *Carlisle.* [*of Bolingbroke*] And if you crown him, let me prophesy,
> The blood of English shall manure the ground
> And future ages groan for this foul act. (*R2*, 4.1.136)

> *Macbeth.* If chance will have me King, why, chance may crown me,
> Without my stir. (1.3.143)

In *Coriolanus* a serving man enumerates the consequences of peace, as he sees them.

This peace is nothing but to rust iron, increase tailors, and breed ballad-makers. (4.5.234)

Iago pretends to hold back what he might say to Othello, in view of the consequent injury to both of them.

> It were not for your quiet nor your good,
> Nor for my manhood, honesty, or wisdom,
> To let you know my thoughts. (3.3.152)

Arguing from a supposed consequence, Othello justifies his decision to kill Desdemona.

> Yet she must die, else she'll betray more men. (5.2.6)

Shakespeare draws profound reflections from a consideration of antecedent and consequent.

> *Antony.* But when we in our viciousness grow hard
> (O misery on't!) the wise gods seel our eyes,
> In our own filth drop our clear judgments, make us
> Adore our errors, laugh at's while we strut
> To our confusion. (*A & C*, 3.13.111)

> *Flavius.* [*to Timon*] Ah, when the means are gone that buy this praise,
> The breath is gone whereof this praise is made.
> Feast-won, fast-lost. (*Tim.*, 2.2.178)

The relation between antecedent and consequent is either necessary or contingent. It is worthy of note that Brutus makes the crucial decision to kill his friend Caesar on grounds of contingency, on a consideration of what Caesar might do, not what he has done or must do.

> It must be by his death; . . . He would be crown'd.
> How that might change his nature, there's the question. . . .
> And then I grant we put a sting in him
> That at his will he may do danger with.
> Th' abuse of greatness is, when it disjoins
> Remorse from power . . . So Caesar may.
> Then lest he may, prevent. (*JC*, 2.1.9–27)

Caesar, on the other hand, arguing from necessity, shows the unreasonableness of fearing death.

> It seems to me most strange that men should fear,
> Seeing that death, a necessary end,
> Will come when it will come. (2.2.35)

Antisagoge is a figure, based on antecedent and consequent, which joins to a precept a promise of reward and to its violation, punishment. Thus, Leontes, having enjoined Camillo to poison Polixenes, admonishes him:

Do't, and thou hast the one half of my heart;
Do't not, thou splitt'st thine own. (*WT*, 1.2.348)

Leontes later commends Camillo for having disregarded his injunction and describes in the very terms of its definition the figure he himself had used.

the good mind of Camillo tardied
My swift command, though I with death and with
Reward did threaten and encourage him
Not doing it and being done. (*WT*, 3.2.163)

A travesty of this figure occurs in *Much Ado*, where Dogberry is instructing the watch. The humor depends on the inanity of the penalties.

Dogberry. You are to bid any man stand, in the Prince's name.
Watch. How if 'a will not stand?
Dogberry. Why then, take no note of him, but let him go, and presently call the rest of the watch together and thank God you are rid of a knave.
Verges. If he will not stand when he is bidden, he is none of the Prince's subjects.
Dogberry. True, and they are to meddle with none but the Prince's subjects. . . . you are to call at all the alehouses and bid those that are drunk get them to bed.
Watch. How if they will not?
Dogberry. Why then, let them alone till they are sober. If they make you not then the better answer, you may say they are not the men you took them for. (3.2.26–51)

Argument based on antecedent and consequent is especially significant in *Much Ado about Nothing*, where it marks important turns in the plot. The prince, planning with Claudio to make Benedick and Beatrice fall in love, thus epitomizes the consequence, should their scheme prove successful (as it does).

If we can do this, Cupid is no longer an archer; his glory shall be ours. (2.1.402)

In the more serious part of the story, Borachio enumerates for Don John the consequences of the deception by which he plans to slander Hero and thereby keep Claudio from marrying her.

Proof enough to misuse the Prince, to vex Claudio, to undo Hero, and kill Leonato. (2.2.28)

Led on by Don John, Claudio declares:

If I see anything tonight why I should not marry her tomorrow, in the congregation where I should wed, there will I shame her. (3.2.126)

He does so, and as a consequence Hero swoons and is thought dead. Friar Francis, confident of her innocence, has a plan the consequence of which will be to "change slander to remorse" (4.1.212). His plan succeeds and the play ends happily.

9. Notation and Conjugates

Since the ordinary purpose of words is to name things and their attributes and to convey ideas from mind to mind, words are usually like a transparent window through which we see, but of which we are unaware. Yet words may be regarded as words both in their relation to things and to each other.

Argument from conjugates, that is, from words having the same derivation, as *just, justice, justly,* was favored by Plato and Aristotle. It necessarily involves a figure which the rhetoricians called polyptoton, namely, the repetition of words differing only in termination. Shakespeare uses this topic and figure with cogency.

> *Antony.*   The noble Brutus
> Hath told you Caesar was ambitious.
> If it were so, it was a grievous fault
> And grievously hath Caesar answer'd it. (*JC*, 3.2.83)

> *Enobarbus.* The loyalty well held to fools does make
> Our faith mere folly. (*A & C*, 3.13.42)

> *Duke.* Spirits are not finely touch'd But to fine issues.
>   (*MM*, 1.1.36)

> *Aeneas.* How now, Prince Troilus? Wherefore not afield?
> *Troilus.* Because not there. This woman's answer sorts,
> For womanish it is to be from thence. (*T & C*, 1.1.108)

A notation or name may illuminate meaning through etymology, as in "An Apologie for Poetrie," where Sidney argues the excellence and dignity of the poet from the names that have been given him, *vates* by the Romans, *maker* by the English echoing the Greeks. The soothsayer in *Cymbeline* explains by etymology the enigmatic oracle given to Posthumus Leonatus.

> Thou, Leonatus, art the lion's whelp.
> The fit and apt construction of thy name,
> Being *Leo-natus,* doth import so much;

[*To Cymbeline*] The piece of tender air, thy virtuous daughter.
Which we call *mollis aer*, and *mollis aer*
We term it *mulier;* which *mulier* I divine
Is this most constant wife. (*Cym.*, 5.5.443)

At least three of Shakespeare's characters have names whose etymology
sheds light on them.

Hermione. [*to Antigonus, in a dream*] and, for the babe
Is counted lost for ever, Perdita
I prithee call't. (*WT*, 3.3.32)

Pericles. My gentle babe Marina—whom,
For she was born at sea, I have nam'd so—(3.3.12)

Ferdinand. Admir'd Miranda!
Indeed the top of admiration, worth
What's dearest to the world! (*Tem.*, 3.1.37)

Etymology is, however, only one aspect of argument from the name.
Another is the relation between the name and the thing. Perhaps the most
famous argument from a name is that of Juliet, protesting to Romeo:

'Tis but thy name that is my enemy. . . .
O, be some other name!
What's in a name? That which we call a rose
By any other name would smell as sweet. (*R & J*, 2.2.38–44)

Shakespeare himself argues from the name to the person bearing it.

Make but my name thy love, and love that still,
And then thou lovest me, for my name is Will. (*Son. 136*)

Argument from the name is important in *All's Well.* The shallow
cause of Bertram's disdain and rejection of Helena is that she is a poor
physician's daughter. Hence the king, whom she has cured, reasons:

'Tis only title thou disdain'st in her, the which
I can build up. . . . If she be
All that is virtuous—save what thou dislik'st,
A poor physician's daughter—thou dislik'st
Of virtue for the name. . . . Good alone
Is good without a name; vileness is so:
The property by what it is should go,
Not by the title. . . . The mere word's a slave . . .
If thou canst like this creature as a maid,

> I can create the rest. Virtue and she
> Is her own dower; honour and wealth from me. (2.3.124–51)

Bertram's mother turns against him because of his cruel antipathy toward his wife and assures Helena:

> He was my son;
> But I do wash his name out of my blood
> And thou art all my child. (3.2.69)

Argument from the name functions in the denouement when Helena, who has been thought dead, unexpectedly appears in court.

> *King.* Is't real that I see?
> *Helena.*   No, my good lord,
> 'Tis but the shadow of a wife you see,
> The name and not the thing.
> *Bertram.*   Both, both! O pardon! (5.3.307)

A third aspect of a word or notation is its ambiguity, its capacity to signify more than one meaning. The distinction between the various meanings of a word is included by Renaissance logicians among the forms of division. Therefore to play upon the various meanings of a word represented an intellectual exercise, a witty analysis commended and relished by Aristotle, practiced by Plato and by the great dramatists of Greece, esteemed and used by Cicero, employed by medieval and Renaissance preachers in their sermons, regarded as a rhetorical ornament by the Elizabethans, but frequently despised as false or degenerate wit from the eighteenth century to the present day. In *The Spectator*, No. 61, for May 10, 1711, Addison sketches the history of puns. Although he admits the high regard in which they were held by all rhetoricians and by both classical and Renaissance writers, and notes their frequency in the most serious works such as Bishop Andrews' sermons and Shakespeare's tragedies, he concludes that they are blemishes discovered in writers of genius by critics of a later age, who although they could not reach the beauties of the former could reprehend and avoid their imperfections. It must be acknowledged that when the word *pun* first came to be applied to verbal quibbling, about fifty years before Addison wrote, the excessive punning in political acrostics, anagrams, and facetious tales during the preceding years had brought the practice into the disrepute and contempt which remain attached to it today. Very different from this attitude was that of Shakespeare's contemporaries, as Frank P. Wilson notes:

To an Elizabethan the play upon words was not merely an elegance of style and a display of wit; it was also a means of emphasis and an instrument of persuasion. An argument might be conducted from step to step—and in the pamphleteers it often is—by a series of puns. The genius of the language encouraged them.[18]

Rightly to appreciate Shakespeare's puns, one should regard them as examples of four highly esteemed figures of Renaissance rhetoric—antanaclasis, syllepsis, paronomasia, and asteismus—which have their roots in the logical distinction between the various meanings of a word, and depend for their effect on the intellectual alertness necessary to perceive the ambiguity. These figures may be adapted to comic or to serious purposes. Rosaline said most truly:

> A jest's prosperity lies in the ear
> Of him that hears it, never in the tongue
> Of him that makes it. (*LLL*, 5.2.870)

Antanaclasis is a figure which in repeating a word shifts from one of its meanings to another.

Fabian. [*of Sir Andrew*] This is a dear manikin to you, Sir Toby.

Toby. I have been dear to him, lad—some two thousand strong, or so. (*TN*, 3.2.57)

1. Page. [*of singing*] We kept time, we lost not our time.

Touchstone. By my troth, yes! I count it but time lost to hear such a foolish song. (*AYLI*, 5.3.38)

Armado. By the North Pole, I do challenge thee.

Costard. I will not fight with a pole, like a Northern man. I'll slash; I'll do it by the sword. (*LLL*, 5.2.699)

Shallow. Use his men well, Davy; for they are arrant knaves and will backbite.

Davy. No worse than they are backbitten, sir; for they have marvail's foul linen.

Shallow. Well conceited, Davy. (*2H4*, 5.1.35)

Pistol. To England will I steal, ant there I'll steal. (*H5*, 5.1.92)

The Elizabethan pronunciation of *ea* permitted Falstaff to pun on reasons and raisins.

[18] Frank P. Wilson, "Shakespeare and the Diction of Common Life," *Proceedings of the British Academy*, XXVII (1941), 14.

Give you a reason on compulsion? If reasons were as plentiful as blackberries, I would give no man a reason upon compulsion, I. (*1H4*, 2.4.264)

Syllepsis is the use of a word having simultaneously two different meanings, although it is not repeated.

> *Falstaff.* [*to Pistol*] At a word, hang no more about me. I am no gibbet for you. (*MWW*, 2.2.16)

> *E. Dromio.* Am I so round with you, as you with me,
> That like a football you do spurn me thus? . . .
> If I last in this service, you must case me in leather. (*CE*, 2.1.82–85)

> *Rosalind.* [I dwell] here in the skirts of the forest, like fringe upon a petticoat. (*AYLI*, 3.2.354)

> *Beatrice.* If the Prince be too important, tell him there is measure in everything, and so dance out the answer. (*MA*, 2.1.73)

Paronomasia differs from antanaclasis in that the words repeated are nearly but not precisely alike in sound.

> *Touchstone.* [*to Audrey*] I am here with thee and thy goats, as the most capricious poet, honest Ovid, was among the Goths. (*AYLI*, 3.3.7)

> *Falstaff.* [*to Prince Hal*] Were it not here apparent that thou art heir apparent (*1H4*, 1.2.64)

> *Messenger.* [*of Benedick*] And a good soldier, too, lady.
> *Beatrice.* And a good soldier to a lady; but what is he to a lord? (*MA*, 1.1.53)

> *Cloten.* Out, sword, and to a sore purpose! (*Cym.*, 4.1.26)

> *Constance.* [*to Austria*] Thou little valiant, great in villany! (*KJ*, 3.1.116)

> *Richard.* We are the Queen's abjects, and must obey (*R3*, 1.1.106)

> *Arcite.*   Dear Cousin Palamon—
> *Palamon.* Cozener Arcite—give me language such
> As thou hast show'd me feat! (*TNK*, 3.1.43)

In *Cynthia's Revels* by Ben Jonson, Phantaste employs paronomasia in a ludicrous etymology offered in an exchange of wit.

> *Hedon.* But why Breeches, now?
> *Phantaste.* Breeches, *quasi* beare-riches; when a gallant beares all his riches in his breeches.
> *Amorphus.* Most fortunately *etymologyz'd*. (4.3.157)

Asteismus is a figure of reply in which the answerer catches a certain word and throws it back to the first speaker with an unexpected twist, an unlooked for meaning. It usually has a mocking or scoffing character, as when a lord catches up Cloten's remark concerning one to whom that braggart had given a blow.

Cloten. Would he had been one of my rank!
Lord. [*aside*] To have smell'd like a fool. (*Cym.*, 2.1.17)

Orlando gives a facetious answer to Jaques.

Jaques. By my troth, I was seeking for a fool when I found you.
Orlando. He is drown'd in the brook. Look but in and you shall see him. (*AYLI*, 3.2.303)

Rosalind is a merry scoffer.

Rosalind. Well, in her person, I say I will not have you.
Orlando. Then, in mine own person, I die.
Rosalind. No, faith, die by attorney. (*AYLI*, 4.1.92)

Apemantus exhibits a more bitter scoffing spirit in using this figure.

Timon. Whither art going?
Apemantus. To knock out an honest Athenian's brains.
Timon. That's a deed thou't die for.
Apemantus. Right, if doing nothing be death by th' law. (*Tim.*, 1.1.191)

1. Lord. What time o' day is't, Apemantus?
Apemantus. Time to be honest.
1. Lord. That time serves still.
Apemantus. The more accursed thou that still omit'st it. (1.1.265)

Varro's Servant. How dost, fool?
Apemantus. Dost dialogue with thy shadow?
Varro's Servant. I speak not to thee.
Apemantus. No 'tis to thyself. (2.2.51)

In the following passages a number of these figures of ambiguity are combined:

Falstaff. My honest lads, I will tell you what I am about.
Pistol. Two yards, and more.
Falstaff. No quips now, Pistol! Indeed I am in the waist two yards about; but I am now about no waste: I am about thrift. (*MWW*, 1.3.42)

Falstaff. [*refusing to lend money to Pistol*] Not a penny. . . . I have grated upon my friends for three reprieves for you and your coach-fellow

Nym; or else you had looked through the grate, like a geminy of baboons. (*MWW*, 2.2.5)

Polonius. I did enact Julius Caesar; I was kill'd i' th' Capitol; Brutus kill'd me.

Hamlet. It was a brute part of him to kill so capital a calf there. (*Ham.*, 3.2.108)

Shakespeare's use of these figures of ambiguity in serious, even in tragic, contexts brings home the difference between his attitude toward what we call puns and our own. He conceives them in the spirit of his age. We need only recall Donne's punning on his own name at the very climax of his solemnly serious and moving "Hymn to God the Father" to remind ourselves how much a play on words was then esteemed. There is a similar pun in *Richard II* when dying Gaunt vents his grief by playing upon his name in a speech concluding:

Gaunt am I for the grave, gaunt as a grave. (2.1.73–83)

Wounded to death, Mercutio says to his friends:

Ask for me tomorrow, and you shall find me a grave man. (*R & J*, 3.1.101)

Each of the four figures of ambiguity is used by Shakespeare in a serious manner. The following illustrate antanaclasis:

Antony. [*of dead Caesar*] O world, thou wast the forest to this hart;
And this indeed, O world, the heart of thee! (*JC*, 3.1.207)

Chief Watch. We see the ground whereon these woes do lie,
But the true ground of all these piteous woes
We cannot without circumstance descry. (*R & J*, 5.3.179)

Menenius. [*to the tribunes*] You have made fair hands,
You and your crafts! You have crafted fair. (*Cor.*, 4.6.117)

Angelo. [*of Isabel*]   She speaks, and 'tis
Such sense that my sense breeds with it. (*MM*, 2.2.141)

Nerissa. It is no mean happiness, therefore, to be seated in the mean. (*MV*, 1.2.7)

Hubert. And with hot irons must I burn them [your eyes] out.
Arthur. Ah, none but in this iron age would do it. (*KJ*, 4.1.59)

Gratiano. [*to Shylock, whetting his knife*] Not on thy sole, but on thy soul, harsh Jew, Thou mak'st thy knife keen. (*MV*, 4.1.123)

Syllepsis, most subtle of the figures of ambiguity, best manifests Shakespeare's peculiar genius with words, especially when it is employed in a serious context. Shakespeare apparently liked to contemplate the richness of language, to perceive simultaneously the multiple meanings of a word like the tones in a musical chord, to resolve them in a manner dictated by sudden impulse. Coleridge, with his usual insight, commented on this characteristic.

Shakspeare's intellectual action is wholly unlike that of Ben Jonson or Beaumont and Fletcher. The latter see the totality of a sentence or passage, and then project it entire. Shakspeare goes on creating, and evolving B out of A, and C out of B, and so on, just as a serpent moves, which makes a fulcrum of its own body, and seems forever twisting and untwisting its own strength. . . . In Shakspeare one sentence begets the next naturally; the meaning is all inwoven. He goes on kindling like a meteor through the dark atmosphere. (*Table Talk*, March 5, 1834, and April 7, 1833)

After citing these remarks of Coleridge, E. E. Kellett continues:

We can, indeed, almost watch him at the task of thinking, and see, as he would have expressed it, into "the quick forge and working-house of thought." . . . we are often permitted to see how one line gave birth to the next. Sometimes . . . it is a single word on which his mind dwells for an instant, passing in a flash from one association of the word to another. . . . very often we shall see that his thought has taken a double edge because the word was double. He lights upon it in one of its senses, and before we have time to turn round we behold him leaving it in another. . . . [as] in the speech of Metellus, (*Julius Caesar*, II.I.143) urging the inclusion of Cicero in the plot:

> O let us have him, for his *silver* hairs
> Will *purchase* us a good opinion . . .

[or] the sudden leap in Prospero's account to Miranda (Act I, Sc. 2) of the conduct of his treacherous brother, who

> Having both the *key*
> Of officer and office, set all hearts in the state
> To what tune pleased his ear.

As the thought of a key *entered* Prospero's mind, it was the idea simply of a key to unlock a door; but ere it *left*, it had become also the idea of a tuning key: and the change is made so naturally and quickly that we scarcely notice it.[19]

[19] Kellett, "Some Notes on a Feature of Shakspere's Style," in *Suggestions*, pp. 57–78, *passim*. Frank P. Wilson, "Shakespeare and the Diction of Common Life," points out that Walter Whiter (1794) anticipated Coleridge and Kellett in noting this characteristic of Shakespeare's style. Whiter interpreted it in terms of a new principle of criticism derived from Locke's doctrine of the association of ideas.

Kellett quotes a score of other examples, among them the following:

> *Jaques.* I am ambitious for a motley coat.
> *Duke S.* Thou shalt have one.
> *Jaques.*   It is my only suit,
> Provided that you weed your better judgments
> Of all opinion that grows rank in them
> That I am wise. (*AYLI*, 2.7.43)
>
> *Ross.* Thou seest the heavens, as troubled with man's act,
> Threaten his bloody stage. (*Mac.*, 2.4.5)

And Caroline Spurgeon notes: [20]

> *Henry IV.*   all the soil of the achievement goes
> With me into the earth. (*2H4*, 4.5.190)
>
> *Kent.* [*of Lear*] Vex not his ghost. O, let him pass! He hates him
> That would upon the rack of this tough world
> Stretch him out longer. (*Lear*, 5.3.313)

Here is impressive evidence that the figures of ambiguity can be instruments of power and pathos in an artist's hands. Paronomasia, too, is capable of serious use.

> *Cassius.* Now is it Rome indeed, and room enough,
> When there is in it but one only man! (*JC*, 1.2.156)
>
> *Camillo.* [*to Perdita*] I should leave grazing, were I of your flock
> And only live by gazing. (*WT*, 4.4.109)
>
> *Antony.* [*thinking Cleopatra dead*] now
> All length is torture. Since the torch is out,
> Lie down, and stray no further. (4.14.45)
>
> *Lady Macbeth.*   If he do bleed,
> I'll gild the faces of the grooms withal,
> For it must seem their guilt. (2.2.55)

Prince John employs paronomasia with argumentative force in a stinging rebuke to the Archbishop of York for having been a leader of the rebels against King Henry IV,

[20] Caroline F. E. Spurgeon, in "Imagery in the *Sir Thomas More* Fragment," *Review of English Studies*, VI, 263, discusses the same point as Kellett and comments: "This method of swift evolution by way of association and suggestion is a marked feature of Shakespeare's style in metaphor, and especially of his middle and later style, from about 1594 onwards, and it is one in which he differs from most, if not all of his contemporaries." Both Miss Spurgeon and R. W. Chambers, in "Shakespeare and the Play of *More*," *Man's Unconquerable Mind*, pp. 204–49, find in Shakespeare's peculiar use of this figure an argument, among others, for his authorship of the *More* fragment.

Turning the word to sword, and life to death. (*2H4*, 4.2.10)

Paronomasia serves to convey the fragile delicacy of Desdemona.

> I cannot say 'whore.'
> It doth abhor me now I speak the word. (*Oth.*, 4.2.161)

Asteismus is used with entire seriousness in *Macbeth*.

> *Doctor*. [*observing Lady Macbeth's sleepwalking*] Well, well, well.
> *Gentlewoman*. Pray God it be, sir. (5.1.63)

Distinction is a figure which removes ambiguities by explicitly adverting to the various meanings of a word, as when Portia remarks:

Let me give light, but let me not be light; for a light wife doth make a heavy husband. (*MV*, 5.1.129)

Although the ordinary function of words is to mirror thought, there are occasions when words are employed rather to veil meaning than to reveal it openly. Consequently the figures of deliberate obscurity, enigma, noema, and schematismus, depend on notation. The oracle delivered to Posthumus in his dream remained an enigma until the soothsayer interpreted it (*Cym.*, 5.5.435–58). A simpler example of enigma occurs in *Coriolanus*, where the figure is explicitly named.

> *1. Citizen*. You have deserved nobly of your country, and you have not deserved nobly.
> *Coriolanus*. Your enigma?
> *1. Citizen*. You have been a scourge to her enemies; you have been a rod to her friends. You have not indeed loved the common people. (2.3.94)

Noema is an obscure and subtle speech. Hamlet employs this figure, along with asteismus, in a veiled complaint and subtle threat to the king.

> *King*. How fares our cousin Hamlet?
> *Hamlet*. Excellent, i' faith; of the chameleon's dish. I eat the air, promise-cramm'd. You cannot feed capons so. (3.2.96)

Having bidden the poet and the painter to rid him of the villains with whom they company, Timon subtly replies to their question as to who the villains are.

> You that way, and you this—but two in company;
> Each man apart, all single and alone,
> Yet an arch-villain keeps him company.
> [*To Painter*] If, where thou art, two villains shall not be,

> Come not near him.—[*To Poet*] If thou wouldst not reside
> But where one villain is, then him abandon. (*Tim.*, 5.1.109)

Alcibiades uses schematismus, or circuitous speech, in addressing the senators of Athens, for he covertly reprehends their tyranny toward Timon by praising the contrary virtue.

> I am an humble suitor to your virtues;
> For pity is the virtue of the law,
> And none but tyrants use it cruelly.
> . . . O my lords,
> As you are great, be pitifully good. (*Tim.*, 3.5.7–52)

King Henry V assures the French ambassador that he need not resort to this figure in delivering his message.

> *Ambassador.* May't please your Majesty to give us leave
> Freely to render what we have in charge;
> Or shall we sparingly show you far off
> The Dauphin's meaning, and our embassy?
> *King.* We are no tyrant, but a Christian king,
> Unto whose grace our passion is as subject
> As are our wretches fett'red in our prisons.
> Therefore with frank and with uncurbed plainness
> Tell us the Dauphin's mind. (1.2.237)

Regarding invention in the contemporary and traditional sense of a systematic process for finding something to say, Shakespeare drew matter for his plays and poems from all the topics of invention including inartificial arguments, which were given an important place by the logicians and rhetoricians of his time. He employed all the rhetorical figures related to the several logical topics, sometimes adding comments which constitute a virtual definition of the figure. The characters in his plays manifest a knowledge and practice of logical and rhetorical theory, lively, concrete, specific, displayed in parody as well as in serious application, which were expected to win a commensurate response from an audience similarly disciplined and practiced in the arts of logic and rhetoric. The pedant Holofernes' question "What is the figure?" echoes the English schoolmaster's insistent and familiar *"Per quam figuram?"* There is contemporary evidence of the attention paid the figures by readers and listeners, such as the marginal notes in *The Epitaffe of the Most Noble and Valyaunt Jasper Late Duke of Beddeforde* (1495),[21] and in Sir

---

[21] At one time attributed wrongly, in Dyce's opinion, to Skelton.

Thomas More's *Of Comfort against Tribulacion* in the 1555–57 edition of his works.[22] In his gloss to Spenser's *Shepheardes Calender* E. K. frequently directed attention to the New Poet's use of the figures.

. . . a prety Epanorthosis in these two verses, and withall a Paronomasia or playing with the word . . . Hoarie lockes) metaphorically for withered leaves . . . Stouping Phaebus) is a Periphrasis of the sunne setting . . . A figure called Fictio. Which useth to attribute reasonable actions and speaches to unreasonable creatures. . . . A patheticall parenthesis, to encrease a carefull Hyperbaton . . . an Epiphonema, or rather the morall of the whole tale . . . a pretie allegory . . . Dan) One trybe is put for the whole nation per Synecdochen. . . . Tom Piper) An Ironicall Sarcasmus, spoken in derision of these rude wits, . . . a gallant exclamation moralized with great wisedom and passionate wyth great affection. . . . a lively Icon, or representation as if he saw her in heaven present . . . (*passim*)

In Ben Jonson's *The Alchemist* Subtle expostulates with Kastril.

> O, this's no true Grammar,
> And as ill *Logick!* You must render causes, child,
> Your first, and second *Intentions,* know your *canons,*
> And your *divisions, moodes, degrees,* and *differences,*
> Your *praedicaments, substance,* and *accident,*
> *Series externe,* and *interne,* with their *causes*
> *Efficient, materiall, formall, finall,*
> And ha' your *elements* perfect. (4.2.21)

Jonson and his fellow dramatists obviously expected a goodly number of the audience to have their elements perfect.

[22] See Crane, *Wit and Rhetoric in the Renaissance,* p. 210.

CHAPTER IV

LOGOS: ARGUMENTATION

ALTHOUGH interest in the clash of ideas is perennial, it was an outstanding characteristic of Elizabethan literature. Whether the contention was that of man against man in debate or of thought against thought within a man, Shakespeare and his fellow dramatists made full use of logical argumentation to develop conflict, which lies at the very heart of drama.

When the Bishop of Carlisle has concluded his speech defending the right of Richard II against the usurper Bolingbroke, Northumberland exclaims:

> Well have you argued, sir; and for your pains
> Of capital treason we arrest you here. (*R2*, 4.1.150)

In *1 Henry VI* a lawyer declares to Somerset, who maintains the right of Lancaster to the throne:

> Unless my study and my books be false,
> The argument you held was wrong in you, (*1H6*, 2.4.56)

and thereupon he espouses the cause of York. King Henry VI admits:

> Full well hath Clifford play'd the orator,
> Inferring arguments of mighty force. (*3H6*, 2.2.43)

In *The Merry Wives* Ford devises a plan to provide his desires "instance and argument to commend themselves" (2.2.256). In matters of great or slight import, of seriousness or of jest, Shakespeare displays an easy command of the forms and processes of argument.[1]

The simplest arguable relations of propositions are contradiction, contrariety, and conjunction. Since the first two have been touched on in Chapter III, only the third will be discussed here. A mere conjunction of propositions may occasion doubt or disagreement. For example, Moth, not satisfied with Armado's comment, wants to know his exact meaning.

---

[1] Hardin Craig, in "Shakespeare and Formal Logic," *Studies in English Philology: a Miscellany in Honor of Frederick Klaeber*, pp. 380–96, illustrates Shakespeare's familiarity with the terms of formal logic.

Armado. Pretty and apt.

Moth. How mean you, sir? I pretty, and my saying apt? or I apt, and my saying pretty? (*LLL*, 1.2.19)

Adrian incorrectly denies a conjunction of propositions which Gonzalo reasserts as true.

Adrian. Tunis was never grac'd before with such a paragon to their queen.
Gonzalo. Not since widow Dido's time. . . .
Adrian. 'Widow Dido' said you? . . . She was of Carthage, not of Tunis.
Gonzalo. This Tunis, sir, was Carthage. (*Tem.*, 2.1.74–84)

A conjunction of propositions is true only if all of its parts are true. It is false if any part is false. Thus, when Cymbeline calls Belarius a banished traitor, Belarius denies the conjunction: "Indeed a banish'd man; I know not how a traitor" (5.5.319). Leontes denies the conjunction asserted by Camillo, for in his jealous frenzy he will not allow that Hermione is good.

> *Leontes*. [*of Polixenes*] How came't, Camillo,
> That he did stay?
> *Camillo*. At the good Queen's entreaty.
> *Leontes*. 'At the Queen's' be't. 'Good' should be pertinent;
> But so it is, it is not. (*WT*, 1.2.219)

When Camillo affirms that affliction alters love's fresh complexion and its heart, Perdita will not agree that both propositions are true.

> One of these is true.
> I think affliction may subdue the cheek,
> But not take in the mind. (*WT*, 4.4.586)

Through conjunction Shakespeare skillfully and succinctly delineates both situation and character when Camillo conveys a warning to Polixenes, who is wondering what has so changed Leontes' attitude toward him.

Camillo. I dare not know, my lord.
Polixenes. How? dare not? do not? Do you know, and dare not
Be intelligent to me? (*WT*, 1.2.376)

And again, when Norfolk counsels Buckingham regarding Wolsey:

> I advise you . . . that you read
> The Cardinal's malice and his potency
> Together. (*H8*, 1.1.102–6)

Argumentation is, however, usually concerned with syllogistic reasoning. This involves a conjunction of propositions related not merely materially but formally as premises from which a conclusion spontaneously follows. If the premises are true, valid syllogistic reasoning yields true conclusions. Fallacious reasoning, which has only the appearance of validity, may draw false conclusions even from true premises. Reasoning may be exercised either in a single line by way of exposition or in opposing lines by way of disputation. Shakespeare's use of the various types of valid syllogistic reasoning will be considered first, then his use of fallacious reasoning, and lastly his use of either or both in disputation.

1. Syllogistic Reasoning

Shakespeare's characters are easily at home with the syllogism and its parts. After presenting an argument in his own defense, Feste remarks to Olivia:

If that this simple syllogism will serve, so; if it will not, what remedy? (*TN*, 1.5.55)

In *Henry VIII* Buckingham, convicted of treason, protests his innocence but declares:

> The law I bear no malice for my death:
> 'T has done, upon the premises, but justice. (2.1.62)

Falstaff flings at Prince Hal, who has just called him a natural coward without instinct:

> I deny your major. (*1H4*, 2.4.544)

Don Pedro caps an interchange of remarks about Benedick with:

> Conclude, conclude, he is in love. (*MA*, 3.2.64)

In *Love's Labour's Lost* (1.2.1–129) there is a lively exercise in logic and rhetoric which somewhat parallels the lesson in grammar in *The Merry Wives* (4.1), although it is more subtle and sophisticated. Armado praises Moth for his apt and quick answers. Lightly and swiftly they touch on salient points: distinctions of words, demonstration, definition, argument from authority. Brief comments mark their progress: "I am answered . . . True . . . He speaks the mere contrary . . . A congruent epitheton . . . A most fine figure! To prove you a cipher." This drama is a playground not only of the new language but also of the traditional arts of logic and rhetoric.

Although the syllogism underlies all reasoning, it seldom appears in discourse in full, explicit form. Shakespeare has a few fully stated syllogisms, for example, Timon's answer to his faithful steward Flavius expressing his complete misanthropy.

> *Flavius.* Have you forgot me, sir?
> *Timon.* Why dost ask that? I have forgot all men;
> Then, if thou grant'st th'art a man, I have forgot thee. (4.3.479)

Apemantus refers to all of Timon's guests as knaves.

> *Timon.* Why dost thou call them knaves? Thou know'st them not.
> *Apemantus.* Are they not Athenians?
> *Timon.* Yes.
> *Apemantus.* Then I repent not. (1.1.181)

Falstaff, accused of declaring that Prince Hal owes him a thousand pounds, increases the amount and then exonerates himself by means of a syllogism.

> *Prince.* Sirrah, do I owe you a thousand pound?
> *Falstaff.* A thousand pound, Hal? A million! Thy love is worth a million; thou owest me thy love. (*1H4*, 3.3.153)

Viola, as Cesario, proves syllogistically that she is Olivia's servant.

> *Cesario.* Cesario is your servant's name, fair princess.
> *Olivia.* My servant, sir? . . .
> Y'are servant to the Count Orsino, youth.
> *Cesario.* And he is yours, and his must needs be yours.
> Your servant's servant is your servant, madam. (*TN*, 3.1.108)

In *The Winter's Tale* the clown tries to hearten his shepherd father, who is fearful of incurring a share of the king's wrath directed against Prince Florizel and Perdita, by urging him to tell the king that Perdita is not his daughter, but an abandoned babe whom he has reared. This syllogism should free him from blame:

She being none of your flesh and blood, your flesh and blood has not offended the King, and so your flesh and blood is not to be punish'd by him. (4.4.709)

Usually only two of the three propositions of a syllogism are expressed, while one is merely implicit. Such an abridged syllogism is called an enthymeme. Malvolio, reading the letter which Maria has written in Olivia's hand in order to gull him, quotes a proposition, supplies a minor premise, and infers the hoped-for conclusion.

'I may command where I adore.' Why, she may command me: I serve her; she is my lady. Why, this is evident to any formal capacity. (*TN*, 2.5.126)

The conclusion, I am the one she adores, following from these premises is easily evident to Malvolio who smugly prides himself on his capacity for formal logic. In that form of enthymeme in which one of the premises is omitted there is a strong tendency to accept the conclusion without scrutinizing the missing premise on which the argument rests. For example, the plebeians, swayed by Antony speaking of Caesar, readily take for granted the conclusion he desires:

> 4. *Plebeian*. Mark'd ye his words? He would not take the crown.
> Therefore 'tis certain he was not ambitious. (*JC*, 3.2.118)

They do not question the implicit major premise, A man who refuses a crown is not ambitious. They regard the conclusion as certain. King Henry VIII deems Cranmer's tears sufficient evidence for the inference that he is honest and loyal.

> Look, the good man weeps!
> He's honest, on mine honour! God's blest Mother!
> I swear he is true-hearted, . . . (*H8*, 5.1.152)

Portia's enthymeme, "God made him, and therefore let him pass for a man" (*MV*, 1.2.60), is a good one dramatically, though the implicit major premise will hardly pass muster.

In Sidney's pastoral interlude "The Lady of May" the schoolmaster Rombus pompously pronounces judgment on an argument of the shepherd Dorcas.

> Thus he sayth, that sheepe are good, *ergo* the shepheard is good, An *Enthimeme a loco contingentibus*, as my finger and my thumbe are *Contingentes*: againe he sayth, who liveth well is likewise good, but shepheards live well, *Ergo* they are good; a *Sillogisme* in *Darius* king of *Persia* a *Conjugatis*; as you would say, a man coupled to his wife, two bodies but one soule: but do you but acquiescate to my exhortation, and you shall extinguish him. Tell him his major is a knave, his minor is a foole, and his conclusion both.[2]

The most usual form of the enthymeme or abridged syllogism is that which states the conclusion first, supported by the major or the minor premise. Rhetoricians called this the figure aetiologia, a reason given for a sentence uttered, as when Hamlet, in directing that the players be well

---

[2] Sidney, *The Complete Works*, ed. by Feuillerat, II, 336.

provided for, gives a reason which expresses Shakespeare's esteem of his own profession.

Let them be well us'd; for they are the abstract and brief chronicles of the time. (2.2.547)

Renaissance rhetoricians defined the figure enthymeme as a reason given to things contrary, thus limiting it to a particular kind of enthymeme, whereas the logicians conceived the term more broadly. Because the figure enthymeme combines antithesis with inference and works out two opposing arguments in a small space it is particularly effective.

> *Brutus.* Had you rather Caesar were living, and die all slaves, than that Caesar were dead, to live all freemen? (*JC*, 3.2.24)
>
> *Coriolanus.* Wouldst thou have laugh'd had I come coffin'd home That weep'st to see me triumph? (2.1.193)
>
> *Ulysses.* The amity that wisdom knits not, folly may easily untie. (*T & C*, 2.3.110)
>
> *Falstaff.* If to be fat be to be hated, then Pharoah's lean kine are to be loved. (*1H4*, 2.4.520)
>
> *Ferdinand.* [*of Miranda*]   O she is Ten time more gentle than her father's crabbed; And he's composed of harshness! (*Tem.*, 3.1.7)
>
> *Arcite.* [*to Palamon*]   'Tis your passion That thus mistakes; the which, to you being enemy, Cannot to me be kind. (*TNK*, 3.1.48)

The figure syllogismus, even more abridged in form, presents a single vivid suggestion, from which the mind leaps to the desired inference without adverting to the process of reasoning which underlies it. Expansion into a full syllogism reveals in detail the mental process, just as a slow motion picture reveals the technique of any rapid operation. For example, when the fool in *Lear* admonishes Kent,

> Sirrah, you were best take my coxcomb,

the full implication is: You are a fool. A fool wears a coxcomb. Therefore you should wear a coxcomb. Kent understands this, for he asks:

> *Kent.* Why, fool?
> *Fool.* Why? For taking one's part that's out of favour.
>   (1.4.109–12)

The following examples of syllogismus are vivid and clear in implication and all the more stimulating for their brevity:

Falstaff. Eight yards of uneven ground is threescore and ten miles afoot with me, and the stony-hearted villains know it well enough. (*1H4,* 2.2.25)

Clown. But I am not to say it is a sea, for it is now the sky; betwixt the firmament and it you cannot thrust a bodkin's point. (*WT,* 3.3.85)

Volumnia. [*of Coriolanus*] He had rather see the swords and hear a drum than look upon his schoolmaster. (*Cor.,* 1.3.60)

A sorites is a chain of reasoning, a series of abridged syllogisms or enthymemes. A sorites normally involves repetition of the last word of each sentence or clause at the beginning of the next, a figure which the rhetoricians called climax or gradation, because it marks the degrees or steps in the argument. Using sorites with climax, Rosalind refers to the figure almost in terms of its definition.

[*To Orlando*] For your brother and my sister no sooner met but they look'd; no sooner look'd but they lov'd; no sooner lov'd but they sigh'd; no sooner sigh'd but they ask'd one another the reason; no sooner knew the reason but they sought the remedy: and in these degrees have they made a pair of stairs to marriage. (*AYLI,* 5.2.35)

Referring to the degrees or steps of this "climbing figure" as a pair of stairs, Shakespeare manifests his conscious use of gradation without directly naming it as Ben Jonson does in *Bartholomew Fair,* where Justice Overdo laments:

To see what bad events may peepe out o' the taile of good purposes! the care I had of that civil yong man, I tooke a fancy to this morning, (and have not left it yet) drew me to that exhortation, which drew the company, indeede, which drew the cut-purse; which drew the money; which drew my brother *Cokes* his losse; which drew on *Wasp's* anger; which drew on my beating: a pretty gradation! (3.3.13)

Sir Philip Sidney gracefully employs climax in his first sonnet, which Abraham Fraunce quotes to illustrate this figure in *The Arcadian Rhetorike* (sig. C 8 ʳ).

> Loving in truth, and faine in verse my love to show,
> That the deare she might take some pleasure of my pain,
> Pleasure might cause her read, reading might make her know,
> Knowledge might pity win, & pity grace obtain.

Climax emphasizes the forthright character of King Henry V, who in wooing Katherine tells her that he is a fellow of plain and uncoined constancy.

If thou would have such a one, take me; and take me, take a soldier; take a soldier, take a king. And what say'st thou then to my love? (*H5*, 5.2.173)

Richard II warns Northumberland that Bolingbroke, whom he has helped to usurp the throne, will later distrust him, for

> The love of wicked men converts to fear;
> That fear to hate, and hate turns one or both
> To worthy danger or deserved death. (*R2*, 5.1.66)

Richard III, in a moment of honest introspection, asserts:

> My conscience hath a thousand several tongues,
> And every tongue brings in a several tale,
> And every tale condemns me for a villain. (*R3*, 5.3.194)

Othello scouts the idea that he might become a prey to jealousy. Desdemona chose him with her eyes open. He will act with reason. He will not even harbor suspicion.

> I'll see before I doubt; when I doubt, prove;
> And on the proof there is no more but this—
> Away at once with love or jealousy! (3.3.190)

Occasionally the thought moves along syllogistically in a sorites without the repetition of words, which is an essential characteristic of the figure climax. For example, the tribune Brutus is quite sure that he and his colleague can count on Coriolanus to ruin himself, as they desire.

> Put him to choler straight. . . .
>   Being once chaf'd . . . he speaks
> What's in his heart, and that is there which looks
> With us to break his neck. (*Cor.*, 3.3.25–30)

A chain of reasoning underlies the words which Lear speaks to Cordelia when he returns to consciousness after his exposure to the storm and sees the daughter whom he has wronged.

> If you have poison for me, I will drink it.
> I know you do not love me; for your sisters
> Have, as I do remember, done me wrong.
> You have some cause, they have not. (4.7.72)

When Brabantio, indignant and grief-stricken because Desdemona has married Othello, asks her where she owes most obedience, she answers with the utmost respect and courtesy, yet with reason and firmness that convince even her father:

> My noble father,
> I do perceive here a divided duty.
> To you I am bound for life and education;
> My life and education both do learn me
> How to respect you: you are the lord of duty;
> I am hitherto your daughter. But here's my husband;
> And so much duty as my mother show'd
> To you, preferring you before her father,
> So much I challenge that I may profess
> Due to the Moor my lord. (1.3.180)

Three examples of sustained and closely knit syllogistic reasoning in Shakespeare's plays may be cited here. Each of the first two begins with a sententious proposition supported by the minor premise of an enthymeme which is itself confirmed by many arguments, the whole being gathered into a final conclusion.[3] In both passages the speaker prefaces his argument, "Reason thus." In the first example, from *Measure for Measure*, the duke, disguised as Friar Lodowick, comes to Claudio who is condemned to die, to persuade him that death ought not to be dreaded.

	Claudio. I have hope to live, and am prepar'd to die.
Proposition	*Duke*. Be absolute for death. Either death or life
	Shall thereby be the sweeter. Reason thus with life:
Minor	If I do lose thee, I do lose a thing
Minor is proved	That none but fools would keep. (1) A breath thou art,
	Servile to all the skyey influences
	That do this habitation where thou keep'st
	Hourly afflict. (2) Merely thou art death's fool;
	For him thou labour'st by thy flight to shun,
	And yet runn'st toward him still. (3) Thou art not noble;
	For all th' accommodations that thou bear'st

---

[3] T. W. Baldwin (*William Shakspere's Small Latine and Lesse Greeke*, II, 84, 88) presents these two arguments as examples of a form of reasoning set forth in *Ad Herennium*, and he remarks that they also conform to the rules for developing a *sententia* prescribed by Aphthonius. As for the thought, Baldwin points out (II, 601–4) that *MM* 3.1.17–19 (and also *Ham.*, 3.1.60–65) are derived through Cicero's *Tusculan Disputations* ultimately from Plato's *Apology*. In Baldwin's opinion, Erasmus' *De conscribendis*, based mainly on Cicero's *De inventione*, is the specific guide for the third argument, from *King John* (II, 277). See p. 364, below, for contemporary illustrations of both forms.

Are nurs'd by baseness. (4) Thou'rt by no means valiant;
For thou dost fear the soft and tender fork
Of a poor worm. Thy best of rest is sleep,
And that thou oft provok'st; yet grossly fear'st
Thy death, which is no more. (5) Thou art not thyself;
For thou exist'st on many a thousand grains
That issue out of dust. (6) Happy thou art not;
For what thou hast not, still thou striv'st to get,
And what thou hast, forget'st. (7) Thou art not certain;
For thy complexion shifts to strange effects,
After the moon. (8) If thou art rich, thou'rt poor;
For, like an ass whose back with ingots bows,
Thou bear'st thy heavy riches but a journey,
And death unloads thee. (9) Friend hast thou none;
For thine own bowels which do call thee sire,
The mere effusion of thy proper loins,
Do curse the gout, serpigo, and the rheum
For ending thee no sooner. (10) Thou hast nor youth nor age,
But as it were an after-dinner's sleep,
Dreaming on both; for all thy blessed youth
Becomes as aged, and doth beg the alms
Of palsied eld; and when thou art old and rich,
Thou hast neither heat, affection, limb, nor beauty
To make thy riches pleasant. What's yet in this
That bears the name of life? (11) Yet in this life
Lie hid moe thousand deaths; yet death we fear,
That makes these odds all even.
    Claudio.   I humbly thank you.

Conclusion   To sue to live, I find I seek to die;
And seeking death, find life: let it come on. (3.1.3–43)

In the second example, from *Richard II*, Gaunt follows the same method of reasoning in an attempt to console his son who has been exiled.

Proposition   All places that the eye of heaven visits
Are to a wise man ports and happy havens.
Teach thy necessity to reason thus:
Minor   There is no virtue like necessity.
Minor is proved (1) Think not the King did banish thee,
But thou the King. Woe doth the heavier sit
Where it perceives it is but faintly borne.
Go, say I sent thee forth to purchase honour,
And not, the King exil'd thee; (2) or suppose

> Devouring pestilence hangs in our air
> And thou art flying to a fresher clime.
> (3) Look, what thy soul holds dear, imagine it
> To lie that way thou goest, not whence thou com'st:
> Suppose the singing birds musicians,
> The grass whereon thou treads't the presence strow'd,
> The flowers fair ladies, and thy steps no more
> Than a delightful measure or a dance;

Conclusion
> For gnarling sorrow hath less power to bite
> The man that mocks at it and sets it light. (1.3.275–93)

The third example, from *King John*, is in complete syllogistic form, with full proof of the minor.[4] Cardinal Pandulph is urging the King of France to set aside his recent oath of amity toward King John. His first argument is based on the conflict of this oath with an earlier oath he had taken to be the champion of the church.

Proposition
> So mak'st thou faith an enemy to faith
> And like a civil war set'st oath to oath,
> Thy tongue against thy tongue.

Major
>   O let thy vow
> First made to heaven, first be to heaven perform'd,
> That is, to be the champion of our Church!

Minor   What since thou swor'st is sworn against thyself

Conclusion   And may not be performed by thyself;

Minor is proved For that which thou hast sworn to do amiss

   Major   Is not amiss when it is truly done;

   Minor   And being not done where doing tends to ill,

  Conclusion   The truth is then most done, not doing it. (3.1.263–73)

The second argument maintains that the second oath is contrary to the nature of a valid oath.

Major   It is religion that doth make vows kept;

Minor   But thou hast sworn against religion,
> By what thou swear'st against the thing thou swear'st,

 Explanation And mak'st an oath the surety for thy truth

 of minor   Against an oath.

Minor is proved   The truth thou art unsure
> To swear, swears only not to be forsworn;

  Major   Else what a mockery should it be to swear!

---

[4] The following analysis of Pandulph's speech is taken from Gerard M. Greenewald, O.M.Cap., *Shakespeare's Attitude towards the Catholic Church in "King John,"* p. 137.

Minor	But thou dost swear, only to be forsworn,
	And most forsworn to keep what thou dost swear.
Conclusion	Therefore thy later vows against thy first
	Is in thyself rebellion to thyself. (279–99)

Similarly, Constance argues (3.1.98–129) that France and Austria are forsworn, because their new oath to John conflicts with their earlier oath to support Arthur's cause.

Besides the simple syllogism, simple even when continued in a series or sorites, there are the compound forms: the hypothetical syllogism, the disjunctive syllogism, and the dilemma.

The hypothetical syllogism is one that has for its major premise a hypothetical proposition. An interesting dramatic use of the hypothetical syllogism occurs in *As You Like It.*

> *Rosalind.* But if you do refuse to marry me,
> You'll give yourself to this most faithful shepherd?
> *Phebe.* So is the bargain. (5.4.13)

Thinking the bargain a safe one, Phebe readily accepts the major premise. In the denouement, however, Rosalind appears, not as the youth Ganymede, whom Phebe loved, but as a woman. Therefore Phebe perforce supplies the minor premise by refusing to marry Rosalind and, abiding by her bargain, accepts the conclusion by agreeing to marry the shepherd whom she had disdained. Touchstone's comment on the hypothetical syllogism applies well to this situation: "Your If is the only peacemaker. Much virtue in If" (5.4.107). A citizen ably summarizes in a hypothetical syllogism the situation which forced Coriolanus to ask for the votes of the people.

> 'I would be consul,' says he. 'Aged custom
> But by your voices will not so permit me.
> Your voices therefore!' (*Cor.*, 2.3.176)

Epilogus is a figure related to the hypothetical syllogism, whereby after a brief argumentation of those things that have before been spoken or done one infers what will follow. The tribune Brutus infers from the past enmity of Coriolanus toward the people the greater harm they will suffer if through their voices he becomes consul:

> When he had no power
> But was a petty servant to the state,
> He was your enemy; ever spake against

Your liberties and the charters that you bear
I' th' body of the weal; and now, arriving
A place of potency and sway o' th' state,
If he should still malignantly remain
Fast foe to th' plebeii, your voices might
Be curses to yourselves. . . . Did you perceive
He did solicit you in free contempt
When he did need your loves, and do you think
That his contempt shall not be bruising to you
When he hath power to crush? (2.3.185–210)

A disjunctive syllogism has for its major premise a disjunctive proposition expressing alternatives, one of which the minor premise affirms or denies, while the conclusion in consequence affirms or denies the other. With a great show of learning, Touchstone employs the disjunctive syllogism as an impressive climax in convincing the unlearned country fellow William that he, not William, will marry Audrey.[5]

Touchstone. You do love this maid?
William. I do, sir.
Touchstone. Give me your hand. Art thou learned?
William. No, sir.
Touchstone. Then learn this of me: to have is to have; for it is a figure in rhetoric that drink, being pour'd out of a cup into a glass, by filling the one doth empty the other; for all your writers do consent that *ipse* is he. Now, you are not *ipse*, for I am he.
William. Which he, sir?
Touchstone. He, sir, that must marry this woman. (*AYLI*, 5.1.40)

The disjunctive syllogism is important in *Hamlet*. The prince must know whether the ghost is "a spirit of health or goblin damn'd" (1.4.40). Hamlet later puts the issue more concretely: either the king will unkennel his guilt, or the ghost is a damned spirit (3.2.85). The king does unkennel his guilt by his agitation at the play, thus supplying the minor premise. Hamlet thereupon concludes that the ghost is not evil:

O good Horatio, I'll take the ghost's word for a thousand pound! Didst perceive . . . Upon the talk of the poisoning? (3.2.297–300)

[5] T. W. Baldwin (*op. cit.*, II, 117) notes that this argument exemplifies the sixth dialectical mode explained in Cicero's *Topica* and restates it thus: "Ipse is not both this Touchstone and that William: but it is this Touchstone, not therefore that William. So the same drink cannot be in both the cup and the glass at the same time. As much as goes into the cup cannot remain in the glass."

The king, profoundly affected, confronts his conscience with the alternatives of a deep-reaching disjunction.

> And what's in prayer but this two-fold force,
> To be forestalled ere we come to fall,
> Or pardon'd being down? . . . But, O, what form of prayer
> Can serve my turn? 'Forgive me my foul murther'?
> That cannot be; since I am still possess'd
> Of those effects for which I did the murther—
> My crown, mine own ambition, and my queen.
> May one be pardon'd and retain th' offence? (3.3.48)

The last question poses his fundamental problem. He cannot bring himself to give up what he has foully won, even to gain pardon and peace for his guilty soul. He acknowledges that he cannot repent, that his bosom is black as death, that his soul, like a limed bird, becomes more entangled in struggling to be free. The irony is that Hamlet, coming in at that moment determined to kill the king now that he is assured of his guilt, is deterred by seeing him on his knees.

> And now I'll do't. And so he goes to heaven.
> And so am I reveng'd. That would be scann'd.
> A villain kills my father; and for that,
> I, his sole son, do this same villain send
> To heaven.
> Why this is hire and salary, not revenge! (74)

Hamlet's assumption in this hypothetical syllogism is false: If I kill him now, he will go to heaven. Therefore his conclusion, To kill the king now would bring me no revenge, is false. And his action on that conclusion, the sheathing of his drawn sword, is extremely ironical to the audience, who know that Hamlet has wrongly inferred from the king's posture of prayer, an external adjunct, that he is repentant and restored to God's friendship. The preceding soliloquy of the king showed that he is not, but that in desperation he had tried by the outward act of kneeling to induce an inward receptiveness to grace. That he has failed is evident when he rises from his knees after Hamlet's departure, saying:

> My words fly up, my thoughts remain below.
> Words without thoughts never to heaven go. (97)

Practically identical with the disjunctive syllogism is the figure which the rhetoricians called apophasis, whereby all alternatives are rejected except one. In a major premise the tribune Sicinius considers three courses of action for dealing with Coriolanus, who has just incensed the people by his contemptuous remarks to them. Sicinius rejects two and concludes to the third:

> For we are peremptory to dispatch
> This viperous traitor. To eject him hence
> Were but our danger, and to keep him here
> Our certain death. Therefore it is decreed
> He dies tonight. (3.1.286)

In contrast to apophasis, the figure prosapodosis rejects none of the alternatives, but supports each with a reason. Prospero tells Miranda that he had been Duke of Milan before he came to the island where they now live.

> *Miranda.* What foul play had we that we came from thence?
> Or blessed was't we did?
> *Prospero.*   Both, both, my girl!
> By foul play, as thou say'st, were we heav'd thence,
> But blessedly holp hither. (*Tem.,* 1.2.60)

Having stirred up Roderigo against Cassio, Iago concludes with satisfaction:

> Now whether he kill Cassio,
> Or Cassio him, or each do kill the other,
> Every way makes my game. (*Oth.,* 5.1.12)

The most complex form of reasoning is the dilemma, a compound syllogism having for its major premise a compound hypothetical proposition and for its minor premise a disjunctive proposition. An abridged form with only the major premise stated and the rest implied was named by the rhetoricians the figure dialysis or dilemma. King Henry V chides his lords for wishing they had more men at Agincourt to fight the French who outnumber them five to one. He rallies their spirits by presenting the stakes of the battle in a dilemma.

> If we are mark'd to die, we are enow
> To do our country loss; and if to live,
> The fewer men, the greater share of honour.
> God's will! I pray thee wish not one man more. (*H5,* 4.3.20)

In *The Winter's Tale* Camillo, clearly realizing the dilemma that confronts him, resolves to escape between the horns; he will flee.

> What case stand I in? I must be the poisoner
> Of good Polixenes; and my ground to do't
> Is the obedience to a master . . .
> Promotion follows. If I could find example
> Of thousands that had struck anointed kings
> And flourish'd after, I'ld not do't. But since
> Nor brass nor stone nor parchment bears not one,
> Let villany itself forswear't. I must
> Forsake the court. To do't, or no, is certain
> To me a break-neck. (1.2.352–63)

In the source of this play, Greene's *Pandosto*, the shepherd Porrus, who has just discovered the babe set adrift in a boat with jewels and a rich purse, faces a dilemma.

Necessitie wisht him at the least, to retaine the Golde, though he would not keepe the childe: the simplicity of his conscience feared him from such deceiptfull briberie. Thus was the poore manne perplexed with a doubtfull *Dilemma*, until at last the covetousnesse of the coyne overcame him. . . . So that he was resolved in himselfe to foster the child, and with the summe to relieve his want.[6]

In *Coriolanus* Volumnia poses one dilemma after another in her earnest effort to turn her son from his revengeful purpose to destroy Rome. She speaks for his wife and child as well as for herself.

> Thou barr'st us
> Our prayers to the gods, which is a comfort
> That all but we enjoy. For how can we,
> Alas, how can we for our country pray,
> Whereto we are bound, together with thy victory,
> Whereto we are bound? . . . We must find
> An evident calamity, though we had
> Our wish, which side would win; for either thou
> Must as a foreign recreant be led
> With manacles through our streets, or else
> Triumphantly tread on thy country's ruin
> And bear the palm for having bravely shed
> Thy wife and children's blood. (5.3.104–18)

She denies that he has but two alternatives, to destroy Rome and thereby keep his word to the Volsces, or to save Rome and thereby betray the Volsces. She shows a happy way of escape between the horns of this

---

[6] Greene, *The Life and Complete Works*, ed. by Grosart, IV, 266.

dilemma, a third course, namely, to make peace between the Romans and the Volsces and so be blessed by both sides instead of cursed. In a final dilemma she challenges his honesty.

> Say my request's unjust,
> And spurn me back. But if it be not so,
> Thou art not honest, and the gods will plague thee
> That thou restrain'st from me the duty which
> To a mother's part belongs. (164)

Shakespeare not only had at his command the terms of formal logic and the forms of syllogistic reasoning, together with the associated figures, but he used them with dramatic power, variety, and fitness. They enter into the very texture of his thought and permeate his work.

2. Fallacious Reasoning

The sophist employs the outward forms of logic to hide the fallacy in his specious reasoning. The resultant incongruity between the pretension and the reality is a frequent occasion of humor,[7] as Elizabethan dramatists fully recognized.[8] The Prologue in Gascoigne's *Supposes* hints, as a means to arouse interest,

Some percase will suppose we meane to occupie your eares with sophisticall handling of subtill Suppositions.

Shakespeare's clowns are adept in using sophistical devices to entrap their victims in their lively verbal bouts. As the princess remarks to Rosaline in *Love's Labour's Lost*,

> Folly, in wisdom hatch'd,
> Hath wisdom's warrant, and the help of school,
> And wit's own grace to grace a learned fool. (5.2.70)

Antipholus of Syracuse, puzzled at being called husband by Adriana, whom he has never seen before, resolves:

[7] Francis P. Donnelly, S.J., has an interesting chapter on "Humor: a Denatured Fallacy," in his *Literature, the Leading Educator*.

[8] Allan H. Gilbert in "Logic in the Elizabethan Drama," *Studies in Philology*, XXXII, 544 f. remarks: "The comic writer evidently counted on sufficient knowledge in his audience to furnish an immediate response to jests involving logical terms or knowledge . . . the fallacious syllogism allows an instructed auditor that glory of superiority that Hobbes finds in the comic; even the uninstructed hearer realizes enough of absurdity to get some share of superior feeling. Logic also offers opportunity for incongruity when the supposedly truth-bringing and dignified process with its technical verbiage is exercised on a trifle or an absurdity."

> Until I know this sure uncertainty,
> I'll entertain the offer'd fallacy. (*CE*, 2.2.188)

Fallacious argument may, however, have consequences of utmost seriousness. Henry VI, who has been deposed, reflects that even while he speaks Warwick in France

> smooths the wrong,
> Inferreth arguments of mighty strength (*3H6*, 3.1.49)

in behalf of Edward IV.

Fallacies are either formal or material. Formal fallacies are those which violate the rules of the syllogism and therefore yield no valid conclusion, even when the premises are true. The most common formal fallacy is that which ignores the necessity of using the middle term in its full extension in at least one of the premises, as when Portia remarks of one of her suitors, the bibulous German:

I will do anything, Nerissa, ere I will be married to a sponge. (*MV*, 1.2.107)

The implied syllogism is: A sponge drinks. He drinks. Therefore he is a sponge. Portia's metaphor is the more piquant because of the fallacy. This fallacy occurs also in two successive syllogisms of Berowne, who soliloquizes:

Well, 'set thee down, sorrow!' for so they say the fool said, and so say I, and I the fool. Well proved, wit. By the Lord, this love is as mad as Ajax: it kills sheep; it kills me—I a sheep. Well proved again. (*LLL*, 4.3.4)

The first syllogism is: The fool said this. I say this. Therefore I am a fool. The second is similar.

Material fallacies are those which have their root in the matter, that is, in the terms of a syllogism which appears to be formally correct. Logicians distinguish thirteen material fallacies, six occasioned by the ambiguity of language and seven by a false assumption hidden in the thought. Ambiguity of language easily introduces into a syllogism a fourth term which destroys coherence and validity.

Most common of material fallacies is equivocation, the use of the middle term in two different senses. Equivocation therefore involves one of the figures of ambiguity, usually antanaclasis, and provides lively repartee.

Desdemona. Do you know, sirrah, where Lieutenant Cassio lies?
Clown. I dare not say he lies anywhere.

Desdemona. Why, man?

Clown. He's a soldier; and for one to say a soldier lies is stabbing. (*Oth.*, 3.4.1)

Alexander. [*of Ajax*] They say he is a very man per se
And stands alone.

Cressida. So do all men, unless they are drunk, sick, or have no legs.
(*T & C*, 1.2.15)

Cesario. Save thee, friend, and thy music! Dost thou live by thy tabor?

Feste. No, sir, I live by the church.

Cesario. Art thou a churchman?

Feste. No such matter, sir. I do live by the church; for I do live at my house, and my house doth stand by the church. (*TN*, 3.1.1)

Provost. Come hither, sirrah. Can you cut off a man's head?

Pompey. If the man be a bachelor, sir, I can; but if he be a married man, he's his wive's head, and I can never cut off a woman's head. (*MM*, 4.2.1)

Speed. What news then in your paper?

Launce. The black'st news that ever thou heard'st.

Speed. Why, man? how black?

Launce. Why, as black as ink. (*TGV*, 3.1.284)

1. Clown. There is no ancient gentlemen but gard'ners, ditchers, and gravemakers. They hold up Adam's profession.

2. Clown. Was he a gentleman?

1. Clown. 'A was the first that ever bore arms.

2. Clown. Why, he had none.

1. Clown. What, art a heathen? How dost thou understand the Scripture? The Scripture says Adam digg'd. Could he dig without arms? (*Ham.*, 5.1.33)

In Greene's *Tritameron* Panthia declares:

fancie is *Vox equivoca*, which either may be taken for honest love, or fond affection, for fancie ofttimes commeth of wealth or beautie, but perfect love ever springeth from vertue and honestie. (*Works*, III, 60)

Love, too, is an equivocal term, as Ismena warns in Greene's *Penelope's Web*.

Take heede quoth *Ismena* . . . that in this word love, you deceive not your-selfe: for there is an Amphibologicall Equivocation in it, which drowneth the hearers oft in a laberinth of perplexed conceipts. As how quoth *Penelope* let us heare you make this distinction? *Ismena* that was young and very quicke-witted, willing to content her Ladies humour by beguyling the night with prattle, applying as well her fingers to the web as her tongue to the tale, went forward thus in her description . . . (*Ibid.*, V, 154)

In the fallacy of amphibology the ambiguity lies, not in a word, but in the grammatical construction. An amusing instance occurs in *The Winter's Tale*, where the clown tells Autolycus:

But I was a gentleman born before my father; for the King's son took me by the hand and call'd me brother; and then the two kings call'd my father brother. (5.2.150)

In the passage preceding this, *gentleman born* has been used repeatedly as a phrase meaning *born a gentleman*, but here *born* links itself to *before*, making the remark ludicrous. The fallacy of amphibology, often present in oracles, permits them to be interpreted in more than one way, so that they may be accounted true, whatever the result. The spirits invoked by the conjurers in *2 Henry VI* utter just such an ambiguous prophecy.

The Duke yet lives that Henry shall depose. (1.4.33)

The prophecies of the witches in Macbeth, however, involve more than amphibology and more than the equivocation of one word. Their ambiguity lies in the application of words to unexpected acts and facts throughout the whole of a speech. When Malcolm's army marches toward Dunsinane, each soldier bearing a bough cut from Birnam wood, and a messenger reports to Macbeth that as he watched, the wood began to move, Macbeth suddenly realizes that he has relied on the prophecies in vain.

I pull in resolution, and begin
To doubt th' equivocation of the fiend,
That lies like truth. 'Fear not till Birnam wood
Do come to Dunsinane!' and now a wood
Comes toward Dunsinane. (5.5.42)

And when he hears in what sense Macduff is not born of woman, he finds his last prop removed and fully understands the witches' deceit.

And be these juggling fiends no more believ'd,
That palter with us in a double sense,
That keep the word of promise to our ear
And break it to our hope! (5.8.19)

The four other fallacies rooted in ambiguity occur less frequently. The fallacy of composition assumes that what is applicable to individual members of a group is applicable to the group. This fallacy seems to underlie Malvolio's attitude in wanting to bind his Puritanical ideas on all. Sir Toby objects:

Dost thou think, because thou art virtuous, there shall be no more cakes and ale? (*TN*, 2.3.123)

The fallacy of division is just the reverse of composition. No instance of Shakespeare's use of it has been observed by the present writer.

The fallacy of form of speech often arises from ambiguity in a verb phrase. Something of this kind appears in the following where *would*, meaning *wish* in Pisanio's remark, is in Imogen's retort construed as a mere auxiliary.

> *Pisanio.* I thought you would not back again.
> *Imogen.*   Most like,
> Bringing me here to kill me. (*Cym.*, 3.4.119)

The fallacy of accent appears when the true significance of a word is altered by pronunciation, and a wrong conclusion drawn, as in the scene where Pistol demands ransom of the French soldier he has taken on the battlefield.

> *French.* O, prenez miséricorde! ayez pitié de moi!
> *Pistol.* Moy shall not serve. I will have forty moys;
> Or I will fetch thy rim out at thy throat
> In drops of crimson blood.
> *French.* Est-il impossible d'eschapper la force de ton bras?
> *Pistol.* Brass, cur? . . . Offer'st me brass? (*H5*, 4.4.12–21)

In addition to the six fallacies arising from ambiguity of language, seven fallacies have their source outside the language in a hidden assumption. The fallacy of accident results from the false assumption that something which belongs only to a substance may be attributed to an accident or adjunct of that substance, or contrariwise. For example, when two countrymen discover Henry VI, who has been deposed, and arrest him as an enemy of King Edward IV, to whom they have sworn allegiance, Henry asks them whether they have not broken their oaths to be true subjects to him. One answers:

> *Sinklo.* No; for we were subjects but while you were king.
> *Henry.* Why, am I dead? Do I not breathe a man? (*3H6*, 3.1.80)

Here the question is whether the oath of allegiance attaches to the substance, the man who still lives, or to an accident, the quality of kingship. Differing in their answers to this question, each thinks the other guilty of the fallacy of accident. The distinction between substance and accident furnishes Falstaff with a specious excuse when challenged to keep his word to cudgel Prince Hal.

Prince. Darest thou be as good as thy word now?

Falstaff. Why, Hal, thou knowest, as thou art but man, I dare; but as thou art Prince, I fear thee as I fear the roaring of the lion's whelp. (*1H4*, 3.3.163)

Most common of the fallacies of false assumption is the confusion of absolute and qualified statement, called *secundum quid*, which assumes that what is true in some respect is true absolutely, or contrariwise. Thus, when Hamlet asks whose grave the clown is digging, the clown takes Hamlet's question in the absolute sense.

Hamlet. What man dost thou dig it for?

Clown. For no man, sir.

Hamlet. What woman then?

Clown. For none neither.

Hamlet. Who is to be buried in't?

Clown. One that was a woman, sir; but, rest her soul, she's dead.

Hamlet. How absolute the knave is! We must speak by the card, or equivocation will undo us. (5.1.141)

Hamlet recognizes the knave's persistence in taking in an absolute sense a word uttered in a qualified sense. In his remark on equivocation Hamlet seems to employ the word in a broad sense including any form of shifting meaning. The assertions made in an absolute sense by Jack Cade in *2 Henry VI* are mockingly admitted in a distinctly qualified and deflated sense by the butcher and the weaver.

Cade. I am able to endure much.

Butcher. [*aside*] No question of that; for I have seen him whipp'd three market days together.

Cade. I fear neither sword nor fire.

Weaver. [*aside*] He need not fear the sword, for his coat is of proof.

Butcher. [*aside*] But methinks he should stand in fear of fire, being burnt i' th' hand for stealing of sheep. (4.2.60)

After striking Pistol to avenge an insult, Fluellen contemptuously brushes aside that braggart's threat by turning it from a qualified to an absolute statement.

Pistol. Base Troyan, thou shalt die!

Fluellen. You say very true, scauld knave, when God's will is.

(*H5*, 5.1.32)

Realizing that he will be laughed at when he who had so railed against marriage begins to court a wife, Benedick, in soliloquy, facetiously argues away his own former attitude.

But doth not the appetite alter? A man loves the meat in his youth that he cannot endure in his age. Shall quips and sentences and these paper bullets of the
brain awe a man from the career of his humour? No, the world must be peo-
pled. When I said I would die a bachelor, I did not think I should live till I
were married. (*MA*, 2.3.246)

In *The Arte of Logick* Thomas Blundeville quotes as a common jest
a sorites vitiated by taking in an absolute sense what is true only in respect
to a particular time.

> Whoso drinketh well, sleepeth well,
> Whoso sleepeth well, sinneth not,
> Whoso sinneth not, shall be blessed:
> *Ergo*, Whoso drinketh well, shall be blessed. (p. 177)

Shakespeare may have become acquainted with this sorites in Melanchthon's *Erotemata dialectices*,[9] where it is pointed out that although a man
sins not while he sleeps he may sin before or after. Two of Shakespeare's
characters employ this specious reasoning. In his scurrilous description
of Captain Dumain, Parolles asserts:

Drunkenness is his best virtue, for he will be swine-drunk, and in his sleep he
does little harm. (*AW*, 4.3.285)

Among the hard conditions imposed by the oath which he and his companions have sworn to observe, Berowne lists the curtailment of sleep,
a time in which he had been accustomed to "think no harm" and commit
no sin.

> And then to sleep but three hours in the night
> And not be seen to wink of all the day
> (When I was wont to think no harm all night
> And make a dark night too of half the day) (*LLL*, 1.1.42)

Sir Toby tries to put a better color on their late roistering by assuring
Sir Andrew:

Not to be abed after midnight is to be up betimes; . . . To be up after midnight, and to go to bed then, is early; so that to go to bed after midnight is to
go to bed betimes. (*TN*, 2.3.1–9)

The time after midnight is early in respect to the clock hours, but it is
late in respect to the period of night itself. That clever logician Touch-

---

[9] Melanchthon, "Erotemata dialectices," *Opera, Corpus reformatorum*, XIII, 625. Wilson,
in *The Rule of Reason*, also quotes this sorites. T. W. Baldwin, *Shakspere's Small Latine
and Lesse Greeke*, II, 131, notes Shakespeare's use of this argument.

stone ostentatiously avoids the fallacy of *secundum quid,* although he introduces others, when he answers Corin's question as to how he likes the shepherd's life.

Truly, shepherd, in respect of itself, it is a good life; but in respect that it is a shepherd's life, it is naught. In respect that it is solitary, I like it very well; but in respect that it is private, it is a very vile life. Now in respect it is in the fields, it pleaseth me well; but in respect it is not in the court, it is tedious. As it is a spare life, look you, it fits my humour well; but as there is no plenty in it, it goes much against my stomach. (*AYLI,* 3.2.13)

The fallacy of ignorance of the elench is very like that of *secundum quid.* One is deceived by ignorance of the elench, which is a syllogism gathering a conclusion contrary to the assertion of the respondent, if the argument involves a change in some respect which passes unnoticed. When Celia asks Touchstone where he learned to swear by his honour, he answers:

Of a certain knight that swore by his honour they were good pancakes, and swore by his honour the mustard was naught. Now I'll stand to it, the pancakes were naught, and the mustard was good, and yet was not the knight forsworn. (1.2.66)

He then explains to Celia and Rosalind the sophistry by which this is concluded.

Touchstone. Stand you both forth now. Stroke your chins, and swear by your beards that I am a knave.
Celia. By our beards (if we had them), thou art.
Touchstone. By my knavery (if I had it), then I were. But if you swear by that that is not, you are not forsworn. No more was this knight, swearing by his honour, for he never had any; or if he had, he had sworn it away before ever he saw those pancakes or that mustard. (75)

The fallacy of consequent arises from the assumption that a proposition is convertible simply when it is not. Touchstone asks the shepherd Corin if he has ever been at court. When he replies that he has not, Touchstone declares him on that account damned, and offers this proof:

Why, if thou never wast at court, thou never saw'st good manners; if thou never saw'st good manners, then thy manners must be wicked; and wickedness is sin, and sin is damnation. Thou art in a parlous state, shepherd. (3.2.41)

It is falsely assumed that the proposition, Those at the court have good manners, is convertible to All those who have good manners are at the court. The second proposition is false; and there is a shift in the meaning of *good* and *wicked*, which further invalidates the sorites. In another instance Celia points out the fallacy of consequent in Rosalind's reasoning by showing what would follow from the like assumption in her own case.

Celia. Is it possible on such a sudden you should fall into so strong a liking with old Sir Rowland's youngest son?
Rosalind. The Duke my father lov'd his father dearly.
Celia. Doth it therefore ensue that you should love his son dearly? By this kind of chase, I should hate him, for my father hated his father dearly; yet I hate not Orlando. (1.3.27)

The fallacy of false cause consists in putting for a cause that which is not a cause, as Michael Williams does when he speaks to the disguised King Henry V of the soldiers who will die in battle. The king points out the fallacy in his reasoning.

Will. Now if these men do not die well, it will be a black matter for the King that led them to it . . .
King. So . . . by your rule . . . if a servant, under his master's command transporting a sum of money, be assailed by robbers and die in many irreconcil'd iniquities, you may call the business of the master the author of the servant's damnation. But this is not so. The King is not bound to answer the particular endings of his soldiers . . . nor the master of his servant; for they purpose not their death when they purpose their services. Besides, there is no king, be his cause never so spotless, if it come to the arbitrement of swords, can try it out with all unspotted soldiers. . . . Then if they die unprovided, no more is the King guilty of their damnation than he was before guilty of those impieties for the which they are now visited. Every subject's duty is the King's, but every subject's soul is his own. (*H5*, 4.1.150–86)

The fallacy of begging the question is present when the conclusion, or question to be proved, stated in the same or in equivalent words, is used in the proof and stands as one of the premises.

Fool. The reason why the seven stars are no moe than seven is a pretty reason.
Lear. Because they are not eight?
Fool. Yes indeed. Thou wouldst make a good fool. (1.5.38)

Begging the question is said to be an especial failing of women,[10] as Lucetta admits even while she offers it as her reason for thinking Proteus best among Julia's suitors.

[10] See Wilson's remarks, p. 372, below.

> *Julia.* Your reason?
> *Lucetta.* I have no other but a woman's reason;
> I think him so because I think him so. (*TGV*, 1.2.22)

Troilus also commits this fallacy and admits the implication of so doing.

> *Aeneas.* How now, Prince Troilus? Wherefore not afield?
> *Troilus.* Because not there. This woman's answer sorts,
> For womanish it is to be from thence. (*T & C*, 1.1.108)

The fallacy of many questions consists in demanding a simple answer to a complex question. Thus, Somerset asks questions of Richard Plantagenet so couched as to demand the answer yes. To answer either yes or no would involve Richard in difficulties. He answers by making distinctions and thereby avoids the snare.

> *Somerset.* Was not thy father, Richard Earl of Cambridge,
> For treason executed in our late king's days?
> And by his treason stand'st not thou attainted,
> Corrupted, and exempt from ancient gentry? . . .
> *Richard.* My father was attached, not attainted;
> Condemn'd to die for treason, but no traitor. (*1H6*, 2.4.90–97)

Parolles, too, avoids this trap, for when he is brought blindfolded before his inquisitors and asked many questions in a heap, he replies:

I beseech you let me answer to the particular of the inter'gatories. Demand them singly. (*AW*, 4.3.206)

In Greene's *Tritameron* Lacena shows her wariness of logical deceit by separating the complex question which Silvestro put to her into its parts.

Your question maketh a double demand in telling his name whome I love best: it craftely maketh inquisition whether I love or no, so that in granting this, I returne your demand with usurie: well, because you shall not thinke I live out of charitie, I confesse I love, and this is his name. (*Works*, III, 124)

In addition to these thirteen material fallacies distinguished by Aristotle seven captious arguments are treated by Wilson and Blundeville. Six of the seven may be illustrated from Shakespeare,[11] at least in their general spirit and effect.

Antistrephon is a captious argument which turns that which serves the opponent's purpose to one's own. Wilson cites as an example an incident

---

[11] No example has been noticed of utis, an argument in which the proof is as uncertain as the thing to be proved.

from Aristophanes,[12] which Lodge and Greene seem to have imitated in the following passage in *A Looking Glasse for London and England:*

Clowne. Why suppose maister, I have offended you, it is lawfull for the maister to beate the servant for all offences?

Smith. I marry is it knave.

Clowne. Then maister wil I prove by lodgick, that seeing all sinnes are to receive correction, the maister is to bee corrected of the man, and sir I pray you, what greater sinne is then jealousie? . . . I will beswinge jealousie out of you, as you shall love me the better while you live.

Smith. What beate thy maister knave?

Clowne. What beat thy man knave? and I maister, and double beate you, because you are a man of credit. (Sig. F 2 [v-r])

Sempronius resorts to antistrephon in *Timon of Athens.* When Timon's servant comes to him asking financial aid for his master, Sempronius complains because he is the first to be asked, as he thinks:

> Must he needs trouble me in't? Hum! 'Bove all others?
> He might have tried Lord Lucius or Lucullus;
> And now Ventidius is wealthy too,
> Whom he redeem'd from prison. (*Tim.,* 3.3.1)

But when Sempronius learns that all these men have refused Timon, he captiously turns this answer to his own advantage and complains because he is asked last.

> Must I be his last refuge? . . . I see no sense for't,
> But his occasions might have woo'd me first;
> For, in my conscience, I was the first man
> That e'er received gift from him;
> And does he think so backwardly of me now
> That I'll requite it last? No.
> So it may prove an argument of laughter
> To th' rest, and I 'mongst lords be thought a fool. (11–21)

And with this trumped-up reason for taking offense he justifies his refusal:

> Who bates mine honour shall not know my coin. (26)

Cacosistaton is an argument which serves as well for the one side as for the other. The gravediggers discuss the decision granting Christian burial

---

[12] See p. 373, below.

to Ophelia, who has drowned herself. The argument which won leniency is the very one of which they, with a touch of the grotesque, complain.

> *2. Clown.* Will you ha' the truth an't? If this had not been a gentlewoman, she should have been buried out o' Christian burial.
> *1. Clown.* Why, there thou say'st! And the more pity that great folk should have count'nance in this world to drown or hang themselves more than their even-Christen. (*Ham.*, 5.1.26) [13]

Touchstone puts Audrey into a quandary by speciously arguing against the desirability of honesty in her, whether she is beautiful or not.

> *Audrey.* Would you not have me honest?
> *Touchstone.* No, truly, unless thou wert hard-favour'd; for honesty coupled to beauty is to have honey a sauce to sugar. . . .
> *Audrey.* Well, I am not fair; and therefore I pray the gods make me honest.
> *Touchstone.* Truly, and to cast away honesty upon a foul slut were to put good meat into an unclean dish. (*AYLI*, 3.3.28–37)

To put another into such a position that whatever he says must needs be said amiss was called pseudomenos, as to ask whether a Cretan should be believed when he says, All Cretans are liars. Mercutio does this when he seeks to forestall credence in Romeo's dream before Romeo has had an opportunity to tell it:

> *Romeo.* I dreamt a dream tonight.
> *Mercutio.*   And so did I.
> *Romeo.* Well, what was yours?
> *Mercutio.*   That dreamers often lie.
>   (*R & J*, 1.4.50)

Assistaton is a kind of caviling, as to remark of one who has just said he holds his peace, He that holds his peace speaks. In this manner Sebastian mocks Gonzalo:

> *Antonio.* Fie, what a spendthrift he is of his tongue!
> *Alonso.* I prithee spare.
> *Gonzalo.* Well, I have done. But yet—
> *Sebastian.* He will be talking. (*Tem.*, 2.1.23)

Ceratin, or the horned argument, puts a matter in such terms that the propounder will win his point either way, as in Abhorson's argument.

---

[13] Compare Wilson's example of cacosistaton, p. 374, below. There also the argument is concerned with class distinction.

Every true man's apparel fits your thief. If it be too little for your thief, your true man thinks it big enough. If it be too big for your thief, your thief thinks it little enough. So every true man's apparel fits your thief. (*MM*, 4.2.46)

The crocodile's argument is one that harms the opponent either way. Falstaff's future state is thus direly represented by his friends.

Prince. Sir John stands to his word, the devil shall have his bargain; for he was never yet a breaker of proverbs. He will give the devil his due.

Poins. [*to Falstaff*] Then art thou damn'd for keeping thy word with the devil.

Prince. Else he had been damn'd for cozening the devil. (*1H4*, 1.2.130)

Thersites finds sardonic delight in contemplating either outcome of the combat between Ajax and Hector.

The man's undone for ever; for if Hector break not his neck i' th' combat, he'll break it himself in vainglory. (*T & C*, 3.3.258)

This, too, is the spirit of Timon speaking to Alcibiades.

Promise me friendship, but perform none. If thou wilt not promise, the gods plague thee, for thou art a man! if thou dost perform, confound thee, for thou art a man! (4.3.72)

Similarly, the fool in *Lear* explains that he is sure to be whipped whichever course he chooses.

Fool. Prithee, nuncle, keep a schoolmaster that can teach thy fool to lie. I would fain learn to lie.

Lear. An you lie, sirrah, we'll have you whipp'd.

Fool. I marvel what kin thou and thy daughters are. They'll have me whipp'd for speaking true; thou'lt have me whipp'd for lying; and sometimes I am whipp'd for holding my peace. (1.4.195)

Sophistic reasoning in Shakespeare ranges from the intention to deceive another to deliberate self-deception. Berowne is recognized as a clever sophist by his fellows who call upon him for some specious argument to furnish a pretext for escape from the contract they have sworn to, to study three years, to see no woman, not to love.

King. Then leave this chat; and, good Berowne, now prove
Our loving lawful and our faith not torn.

Dumain. Ay marry, there, some flattery for this evil!

Longaville. O, some authority how to proceed!

Some tricks, some quillets, how to cheat the devil!
Dumain. Some salve for perjury. (4.3.284)

In a long speech of sustained and conscious sophistic, Berowne supplies what they ask. Another sophist is Proteus, who tries to convince himself that he has some justification for his intended treachery toward Valentine and Julia.

> Love bade me swear, and Love bids me forswear.
> O sweet-suggesting Love, if thou hast sinn'd,
> Teach me, thy tempted subject, to excuse it! . . .
> Unheedful vows may heedfully be broken,
> And he wants wit that wants resolved will
> To learn his wit t' exchange the bad for better. . . .
> I to myself am dearer than a friend,
> For love is still most precious in itself;
> And Sylvia (witness heaven, that made her fair!)
> Shows Julia but a swarthy Ethiope.
> I will forget that Julia is alive,
> Rememb'ring that my love to her is dead;
> And Valentine I'll hold an enemy,
> Aiming at Sylvia as a sweeter friend.
> I cannot now prove constant to myself
> Without some treachery us'd to Valentine. (*TGV*, 2.6.6–32)

3. Disputation

Shakespeare fully shared the Elizabethan delight in building up both sides of an argument, a delight which Thomas Lodge, for example, manifests in "A Defence of Poetry" when he tells his opponent Stephen Gosson:

It pities me to consider the weaknes of your cause; I wyll therefore make your strongest reason more strong, and, after I have builded it up, destroy it agayn. (Smith, I, 73)

Before considering Shakespeare's use of disputation, it will be instructive to glance at its use in the work of his predecessors and contemporaries. The relish of disputation is a trait not Elizabethan merely but Renaissance, with a medieval heritage.

In the medieval debates, as in that between the body and the soul or between the owl and the nightingale, interest hinged on seeing what good arguments could be put forward on both sides. Disputation constituted the main attraction in the morality plays and in the interludes. A sort of dialectic repartee enlivens Erasmus' colloquy of the maid and the wooer, which might be compared in this respect with passages in *Romeo and Juliet*. Disputation as a form of refined pastime among ladies and gentlemen appears as an established practice in Castiglione's *Il cortegiano*. In *The Adventures of Master F. J.* by Gascoigne, the Lady Pergo proposes and leads such disputation as a form of entertainment. Disputation also constitutes no small part of Lyly's *Euphues and His England*. We catch something of the spirit of it in these snatches from Greene's *Morando: the Tritameron of Love:*

The case . . . which we have to discusse, is a maxim holden as true as a holie Oracle: but the doubt is, whether it is to be averred in men, or verified in women . . . What moves you (quoth *Morando*) to pop forth so sodainelie this darke probleme? . . . if it please my mother to give me leave, I will prove that the worst course of life is to love . . . You reason first of the definition of love . . . conclude not so readilie before the premises be graunted. . . . You men (quoth *Lacena*) . . . are so cunning in your sophistrie, that womens wits are halfe dazled with your contrarie fallacions . . . *Silvestre* hath so cunninglie confuted my daughters reasons . . . *Lacena* perceyving how pleasant *Silvestre* had beene in his problemes, meant to conclude in the same mood and figure . . . I will prove my premisses with most approved instances . . . *Morando* hearing how cunningly *Lacena* had resisted *Peratios* reasons, began to be halfe blanck, because *Panthia* pulling him by the sleeve saide. Sir (quoth she) although my daughter hath concluded in an imperfect *Moode*, yet it is hard to reduce it but *per impossible* . . . (Works, III, *passim*.)

Argument on both sides of a question is frequently presented as the reverie of a character in *Euphues*, *Arcadia*, Greene's *Pandosto*, and also in poems such as *The Rape of Lucrece*. Interest in building up opposite sides of a question characterizes Montaigne in his essays. As according to his own account he likes to walk for the mere exercise of walking, not with the intent to get anywhere, so, one feels, he likes to think for the mere exercise of thinking, not to arrive at any conclusion. He delights to gather from the ancients conflicting views and to see-saw between them. In *Pantagruel*, by Rabelais, there is the almost endless discussion as to whether Panurge should marry or not, with specious arguments in support of contrary opinions on the subject. In constructing such humorous surprises as Panurge's argument extolling the joys of being a debtor, Rabelais is engaged in the fascinating sport of paradox in the Renaissance sense of the word, namely, to maintain an opinion contrary to that of most men and contrary sometimes even to good sense.

The insistent movement of drama provides just those conditions of stress which Aristotle describes as constituting the particular problems of disputation, giving it a quality of excitement.

It is not the same thing to take an argument in one's hand and then to see and solve its faults, as it is to be able to meet it quickly while being subjected to questions: for what we know, we often do not know in a different context. Moreover . . . we are often too late for the right moment. (*De sophisticis elenchis*, Ch. 16, 175 ^{a} 20)

A good illustration of the technique of disputation occurs in *Gentylnes and Nobylyte: an Enterlude* which Kenneth Walter Cameron shows good reason to ascribe to John Heywood. The plowman first gets the knight and the merchant to grant certain points. They do this readily. On these admissions the plowman builds his argument that he is the noblest of them all.

> *Plowman.* Is not that the noblest thyng, indede,
> That of all other thyngis hath lest nede
> As God which reynith etern in blysse?
> Is not he the noblest thyng that is?
> *Knyght.* Yes, Mary, no man in reason can that deny.
> *Plowman.* Well, than there is no reason thereof why
> But because he is the thyng omnipotent
> And is in himself so suffycyent
> And nedyth the helpe of no nothyr thyng
> To the helpe of hys gloryous beyng,
> But every other thyng hath nede of his ayde.
> *Marchaunt.* Mary, that is very trough and well sayde. . . .
> *Plowman.* Ye be but caytyffes and wrechis both two!
> And by the same reason prove I shall
> That I am the noblyst man of us all,
> For I have nede of no maner thyng
> That ye can do to help of my lyffing,
> For every thyng whereby ye do lyf
> I noryssh it and to you both do gyf.
> . . . therefore I sey playn:
> I am more noble than other of you twayn. (lines 280–339)

As Cameron observes,

The author of the interlude makes it perfectly clear by his intended inconsistencies that he is attempting to produce laughter at the expense of the back-to-
nature school of thought. If one does not see the inconsistencies or detect the
trick of logic, one misses the genius of the play and the quality for which the
fun-loving, debate-loving court held it in esteem. The material is commonplace; only the clever logic and ridiculous emphases make it delightful entertainment.[14]

To prove a paradox offered a cherished opportunity to display clever-
ness in logic. Thus Shadow, in Dekker's *Old Fortunatus*, undertakes to
prove by a sorites that hunger preserves life.

Hunger was the first that ever opened a cook-shop, cooks the first that ever
made sauce, sauce being liquorish, licks up good meat; good meat preserves life:
hunger therefore preserves life. (Act II, Sc. ii)

In *Satiromastix*, also by Dekker, Blunt tells why such argument is
delightful.

> To proove that best, by strong and armed reason,
> Whose part reason feares to take, cannot but proove,
> Your wit's fine temper, and from these win love.
>   (lines 1809–11)

With this encouragement from Blunt, Crispinus goes on to praise bald-
ness (lines 1814–65) in order to outdo Horace who had earlier (lines
1454–91) praised hair. A page in Massinger's *The Unnatural Combat*
supports a paradox with an interesting argument that contains more than
a grain of truth.

> *Page.*   Ere I was
> Sworn to the pantofle, I have heard my tutor
> Prove it by logic, that a servant's life
> Was better than his master's; and by that
> I learn'd from him, if that my memory fail not,
> I'll make it good.
> *Usher.* Proceed, my little wit
> *In decimo sexto.*
> *Page.* Thus then: from the king
> To the beggar, by gradation, all are servants,
> And you must grant, the slavery is less
> To study to please one, than many.
> *Usher.* True.
> *Page.* Well then; and first to you, sir. You complain

---

[14] Cameron, *Authorship and Sources of "Gentleness and Nobility,"* p. 35.

You serve one lord, but your lord serves a thousand,
Besides his passions, that are his worst masters;
You must humour him, and he is bound to sooth
Every grim sir above him: . . .
Nay, more: that high disposer of all such
That are subordinate to him, serves and fears
The fury of the many-headed monster,
The giddy multitude: and as a horse
Is still a horse, for all his golden trappings,
So your men of purchased titles, at their best, are
But serving-men in rich liveries.
Usher. Most rare infant!
Where learnd'st thou this morality?
Page. Why, thou dull pate,
As I told thee, of my tutor. (Act III, sc. ii)

In Lyly's *Sapho and Phao* is an example of sophistic disputation in rapid dialogue beginning with paradox.

Molus. Cálipho, I will prove thee to bee the divell.
Calypho. Then will I sweare thee to bee a God.
Molus. The divell is black.
Calypho. What care I?
Molus. Thou art black.
Calypho. What care you?
Molus. Therefore thou art the divell.
Calypho. I denie that.
Molus. It is the conclusion, thou must not denie it.
Calypho. In spite of all conclusions, I will denie it. (2.3.49–58)

Molus is guilty of a formal fallacy. The middle term is not used in its full extension in either of the premises of his syllogism: The divell is black. Thou art black. Therefore thou art the divell. Calypho, not smart enough to recognize this fallacy, merely repeats his denial, offering no reason. His answer is like the Cuckoes Song, as Wilson named the fallacy of begging the question. Even in attack Calypho seems able to construct an argument only by begging the question with mere repetitious babbling.

Calypho. Thou art a Smith: therefore thou art a smith. The conclusion, you say, must not bee denyed: & therfore it is true, thou art a smith.
Molus. I, but I denie your Antecedent.
Calypho. I, but you shal not. Have I not toucht him, Cryticus?

Criticus. You have both done learnedly: for as sure as he is a smith, thou art a divell. (2.3.83–89)

In Dekker's *If It Be Not Good, the Devil Is in It,* the technique of the schools is vaunted in sophistic disputation which appears to convince all but the subprior.[15]

Shackle-soule. He that eats not good meate is dambd: *Sic Disputo.* If he that feedes well hath a good soule, then *e Contra.* No, he that feedes ill, hath a bad and a poore soule.

Scumbroth. Thats wee.

Shackle-soule. And so consequently is dambd, for who regards poore soules? and if they be not regarded they are cast foorth, and if cast foorth, then they are dambde.

Subprior. I deny your minor, he that feedes well hath a good soule.

Shackle-soule. Sic probo: the soule followes the temperature of the body, hee that feedes well hath a good temperature of body, *Ergo,* hee that feedes well hath a good soule.

Prior. A ful and edifying argument.

Omnes. Hum, hum, hum.

Subprior. I deny that the soule followes the temperature of the body.

Shackle-soule. Anima sequitur temperaturam Corpori[s], It is a principle, *& contra principia non est disputandum.* All wee.

Prior. Its most apparent.

Scumbroth. O most learned *Rush!*

Subprior. A shallow Sophister, heare me farder.

Prior. Subprior, weele heare the rest disputed at our leisure: you take too much upon you. (Act III, Sc. ii)

The love of disputation is obvious in Ben Jonson's *The Alchemist,* where Subtle offers to teach Kastril how to quarrel.

> I'll ha' you to my chamber of *demonstrations,*
> Where I'll shew you both the *Grammar,* and *Logick*
> And *Rhetorick* of quarrelling; my whole method,
> Drawne out in tables. (4.2.63)

Shakespeare's use of logic and rhetoric is less obvious and more artistic than that of his contemporaries because it is more thoroughly assimilated into his work and adapted to each character and circumstance. In lighter moods argument in his plays is regarded as a mettlesome game. Clowns

---

[15] Allan H. Gilbert, *op. cit.,* directed the attention of the present writer to the illustration from Dekker which follows, the one from Massinger above, and a few others quoted earlier in this book.

are particularly adept in such encounters. Feste challenges his mistress Olivia to a contest of wit and easily wins by employing a well recognized method of dialectic; he gets from his opponent through question and provocation a statement by which to prove his allegation out of her own mouth.

Feste. Good madonna, give me leave to prove you a fool.
Olivia. Can you do it?
Feste. Dexteriously, good madonna.
Olivia. Make your proof.
Feste. I must catechize you for it . . . Good madonna, why mourn'st thou?
Olivia. Good fool, for my brother's death.
Feste. I think his soul is in hell, madonna.
Olivia. I know his soul is in heaven, fool.
Feste. The more fool, madonna, to mourn for your brother's soul, being in heaven. Take away the fool, gentlemen. (*TN*, 1.5.64–78)

Cesario comments on Feste.

> This fellow is wise enough to play the fool,
> And to do that well craves a kind of wit.
>   . . . This is a practice
> As full of labour as a wise man's art. (3.1.67–73)

In a duel of wits opponents zestfully prove contradictory propositions. Proteus has asserted that Speed is a sheep.

Speed. Nay, that I can deny by a circumstance.
Proteus. It shall go hard but I'll prove it by another.
Speed. The shepherd seeks the sheep, and not the sheep the shepherd; but I seek my master, and my master seeks not me. Therefore I am no sheep.
Proteus. The sheep for fodder follow the shepherd; the shepherd for food follows not the sheep. Thou for wages followest thy master; thy master for wages follows not thee. Therefore thou art a sheep.
Speed. Such another proof will make me cry 'baa.' (*TGV*, 1.1.84)

The gravediggers in *Hamlet* are rustic clowns, skilled disputants, their gruesome occupation no bar but rather a stimulus to their grim bantering.

1. Clown. What is he that builds stronger than either the mason, the shipwright, or the carpenter?
2. Clown. The gallows-maker, for that frame outlives a thousand tenants.
1. Clown. I like thy wit well, in good faith. The gallows does well. But how

does it well? It does well to those that do ill. Now, thou dost ill to say the gallows is built stronger than the church. Argal, the gallows may do well to thee. To't again, come!

    2. Clown. Who builds stronger than a mason, a shipwright, or a carpenter? . . .

    1. Clown. Cudgel thy brains no more about it. . . . say 'a grave-maker.' The houses he makes lasts till doomsday. (5.1.46–67)

Delight in intellectual fencing is manifested in Shakespeare's plays not only by clowns but also by men and women of all classes of society. The princess in *Love's Labour's Lost* exclaims after a combat of words between Katherine and Rosaline:

> Well bandied both! a set of wit well play'd. (5.2.29)

Mercutio compliments Romeo on his art displayed in a lively sparring of wits:

Why, is not this better now than groaning for love? Now art thou sociable, now art thou Romeo; now art thou what thou art by art as well as by nature. (2.4.92)

Leonato remarks of his niece Beatrice:

There is a kind of merry war betwixt Signior Benedick and her. They never meet but there's a skirmish of wit between them. (*MA,* 1.1.62)

Sometimes the argument is on a mere notational level, an altercation of words, not ideas.

> *Benedick.* Sweet Beatrice, wouldst thou come when I call'd thee?
> *Beatrice.* Yea, signior, and depart when you bid me.
> *Benedick.* O, stay but till then!
> *Beatrice.* 'Then' is spoken. Fare you well now. (*MA,* 5.2.42)

Such, too, is this duello between Pandarus and a servant.

> *Pandarus.* What music is this?
> *Servant.* I do but partly know, sir. It is music in parts.
> *Pandarus.* Know you the musicians?
> *Servant.* Wholly, sir.
> *Pandarus.* Who play they to?
> *Servant.* To the hearers, sir.
> *Pandarus.* At whose pleasure, friend?
> *Servant.* At mine, sir, and theirs that love music.
> *Pandarus.* Command, I mean, friend.
> *Servant.* Who shall I command, sir?

Pandarus. Friend, we understand not one another. I am too courtly, and thou art too cunning. At whose request do these men play? (*T & C*, 3.1.17)

In *Love's Labour's Lost* Armado enthusiastically commends Moth's quick wit displayed in bandying less than a word, mere single letters, with Holofernes who teaches boys their letters from the hornbook.[16]

Moth. What is a, b, spell'd backward and with the horn on his head?
Holofernes. Ba, pueritia, with a horn added.
Moth. Ba, most seely sheep, with a horn!—You hear his learning.
Holofernes. Quis, quis, thou consonant?
Moth. The last of the five vowels, if You repeat them; or the fifth, if I.
Holofernes. I will repeat them:—a, e, I—
Moth. The sheep: the other two concludes it—O, U.
Armado. Now by the salt wave of the Mediterranean, a sweet touch, a quick venew of wit! Snip, snap, quick and home! It rejoiceth my intellect. True wit! (5.1.50)

Juliet's father chides her for choplogic in her reply to his indignant question as to whether she is not thankful and proud because of the match he has arranged for her with Paris.

Juliet. Not proud you have, but thankful that you have.
Proud can I never be of what I hate,
But thankful even for hate that is meant love.
Capulet. How, how, how, how, choplogic? What is this?
'Proud'—and 'I thank you'—and 'I thank you not'—
And yet 'not proud'? (*R & J*, 3.5.147)

A clever play on contingency and necessity marks Juliet's interchange of words with Paris.

Paris. Happily met, my lady and my wife!
Juliet. That may be, sir, when I may be a wife.
Paris. That may be must be, love, on Thursday next.
Juliet. What must be shall be.
Paris.   That's a certain text. (4.1.18)

[16] O. J. Campbell, *Satire in Shakespeare*, p. 34, points out that this dialogue is based on a colloquy in a work by the Spanish educator Juan Luis Vives, *Linguae Latinae exercitatio*, devised to teach little boys the five vowels, all of which are found in the Spanish word *oveia*, meaning *sheep*. Moth, having contrived to get Holofernes to say *Ba*, interrupts him when he says *I*, to call him sheep, and drives home the gibe with O U [sheep]. Thus Shakespeare pokes fun at a foolishly ingenious method of teaching a simple matter. In doing so he employs verbal equivocation.

Cressida is one of Shakespeare's capable logicians, but there is in her banter a marked quality of pertness. In replying to Pandarus, who says that Helen praised Troilus' complexion above that of Paris, Cressida makes *above*, which qualified in respect to beauty of color, qualify in respect to intensity of color, thus spicing her rejoinder with a form of the fallacy of *secundum quid*.

> *Cressida*. Why Paris hath colour enough.
> *Pandarus*. So he has.
> *Cressida*. Then Troilus should have too much. If she prais'd him above, his complexion is higher than his. He having colour enough, and the other higher, is too flaming a praise for a good complexion. (1.2.108)

Apemantus is a sardonic disputant who never misses an opportunity to scoff, as when he gibes at a merchant:

> *Apemantus*. Art not thou a merchant?
> *Merchant*. Ay, Apemantus.
> *Apemantus*. Traffic confound thee, if the gods will not!
> *Merchant*. If traffic do it, the gods do it.
> *Apemantus*. Traffic's thy god; and thy god confound thee. (*Tim.*, 1.1.242)

Here the ball is deftly tossed back and forth: Apemantus states a disjunction; the merchant denies it by affirming that the alternatives are identical; Apemantus catches up the identification, betters it, and hurls it back, making his last statement stronger than his first by virtue of the cue which his opponent has unintentionally given him. When Thersites calls Agamemnon, Achilles, Patroclus, and himself fool, his companions eagerly demand a reason.

> *Achilles*. Derive this, come.
> *Thersites*. Agamemnon is a fool to offer to command Achilles; Achilles is a fool to be commanded of Agamemnon; Thersites is a fool to serve such a fool; and Patroclus is a fool positive.
> *Patroclus*. Why am I a fool?
> *Thersites*. Make that demand to the Creator. It suffices me thou art. (*T & C*, 2.3.66)

Fluellen, too, likes disputation, but his is in a different spirit.

Captain Macmorris, I beseech you now, will you voutsafe me, look you, a few disputations with you, as partly touching or concerning the disciplines of the war, the Roman wars? In the way of argument, look you, and friendly communication. (*H5*, 3.2.100)

Among Shakespeare's characters Falstaff outdoes all others in employing certain devices of sophistry in defense.

Falstaff. But, as the devil would have it, three misbegotten knaves in Kendal green came at my back, and let drive at me; for it was so dark, Hal, that thou couldst not see thy hand. (*1H4*, 2.4.245)

In his ready and voluble fictionizing Falstaff has overreached himself. Prince Hal seizes the opportunity to confute his story out of his own mouth.

. . *Prince.* Why, how couldst thou know these men in Kendal green when it was so dark thou couldst not see thy hand? Come, tell us your reason. What sayest thou to this?

Poins. Come, your reason, Jack, your reason.

Falstaff. What, upon compulsion? Zounds, an I were at the strappado or all the racks in the world, I would not tell you on compulsion. Give you a reason on compulsion? If reasons were as plentiful as blackberries, I would give no man a reason upon compulsion, I. (256)

Falstaff having thus tried to divert attention from his discomfiture by taking umbrage at the very idea of compulsion, which he himself trumps up, Prince Hal confronts him with the truth: he and Poins were the men who set upon Falstaff and his three companions and seized their booty while they ignominiously fled.

Prince. What a slave art thou to hack thy sword as thou hast done, and then say it was in fight! What trick, what device, what starting hole canst thou now find out to hide thee from this open and apparent shame? (288)

Unabashed and nimble in excuse, Falstaff readily finds a starting hole,[17] taking his cue from the Prince's word, *apparent.*

Falstaff. By the Lord, I knew ye as well as he that made thee. Why, hear you, masters. Was it for me to kill the heir apparent? Should I turn upon the true prince? Why, thou knowest I am as valiant as Hercules; but beware instinct. The lion will not touch the true prince. Instinct is a great matter. I was now a coward on instinct. I shall think the better of myself, and thee, during my life—I for a valiant lion, and thou for a true prince. (295)

Having thus wrested valor out of cowardice, Falstaff, glad that the booty is safe, in great good fellowship proposes a merry celebration.

Before turning to Shakespeare's use of disputation in serious matters

---

[17] Both Wilson and Fraunce (see pp. 376, 378, below) warn that the answerer will seek starting holes to escape meeting an argument directly.

it will be convenient to consider his use of the rhetorical figures which parallel logical disputation and show the importance accorded to argumentation in all forms of Renaissance theory dealing with composition. These figures are concerned with every form of arguing both sides of a question whether with oneself or with an opponent.

The figure aporia is a doubting or deliberating with oneself. Having contrived by murder to clear his path to the throne, and having prearranged that Buckingham should offer him the crown, Richard III employs this figure when he poses as the reluctant candidate and addresses the people for whom this scene is staged.

> I cannot tell if to depart in silence,
> Or bitterly to speak in your reproof,
> Best fitteth my degree or your condition. (*R3*, 3.7.141)

In the soliloquies there are many examples of aporia, where Shakespeare's characters consider reasons for and against a course of action. King Henry V, desiring his lords to leave, informs them:

> I and my bosom must debate awhile,
> And then I would no other company. (*H5*, 4.1.31)

When Macbeth is told that he will not be slain by any man of woman born, he debates with himself, arguing both sides:

> Then live, Macduff. What need I fear of thee?
> But yet I'll make assurance double sure
> And take a bond of fate. Thou shalt not live! (4.1.82)

Pondering whether it is better to be or not to be, Hamlet weighs reasons.

> To die—to sleep—
> No more; and by a sleep to say we end
> The heartache, and the thousand natural shocks
> That flesh is heir to. 'Tis a consummation
> Devoutly to be wish'd. . . . Who would these fardels bear,
> To grunt and sweat under a weary life,
> But that the dread of something after death—
> The undiscover'd country, from whose bourn
> No traveller returns—puzzles the will,
> And makes us rather bear those ills we have
> Than fly to others that we know not of? (3.1.60–82)

Anthypophora is a reasoning with self, asking questions and answering them oneself, as Falstaff does in his catechism of honor.

Honour pricks me on. Yea, but how if honour prick me off when I come on? How then? Can honour set to a leg? No. . . . Or an arm? No. Or take away the grief of a wound? No. What is honour? A word. What is that word honour? Air. A trim reckoning! Who hath it? He that died a Wednesday. Doth he feel it? No. Doth he hear it? No. 'Tis insensible then? Yea, to the dead. But will it not live with the living? No. Why? Detraction will not suffer it. Therefore I'll none of it. Honour is a mere scutcheon—and so ends my catechism. (*1H4*, 5.1.131)

Iago uses this figure to inflame Roderigo against Cassio, effectively supplying the answers to his own questions as to whether Desdemona will tire of Othello and turn to another (2.1.223–53).

By the figure anacoenosis the speaker asks counsel of his hearers, as when Brutus demands of the Romans:

Brutus. Who is here so base that would be a bondman? If any, speak; for him have I offended. Who is here so rude that would not be a Roman? If any, speak; for him have I offended. Who is here so vile that will not love his country? If any, speak; for him have I offended. I pause for a reply.
All. None, Brutus, none!
Brutus. Then none have I offended. (*JC*, 3.2.31)

In like manner Hermione deliberates with Leontes, who is both her accuser and her judge.

Now, my liege,
Tell me what blessings I have here alive
That I should fear to die. (*WT*, 3.2.107)

Synchoresis is a figure whereby the speaker, trusting strongly in his own cause, freely gives his questioner leave to judge him, as the steward Flavius does when he invites his master, Timon,

If you suspect my husbandry or falsehood,
Call me before th' exactest auditors
And set me on the proof. (*Tim.*, 2.2.164)

Brutus is so confident of rectitude in the killing of Caesar that he will let the adversary judge the cause.

Our reasons are so full of good regard
That were you, Antony, the son of Caesar,
You should be satisfied. (*JC*, 3.1.224)

By the figure procatalepsis a speaker confutes the objection which his opponent is likely to make, even before he has uttered it, as Volumnia

does when she forestalls Coriolanus' strongest objection against acceding
to her plea by showing that he reasons from a fallacious dilemma. He has
not considered all the alternatives. He need not choose between two evils.
There is a third course, an escape between the horns of his dilemma, which
will bring blessing on him from both sides, instead of a curse.

> If it were so that our request did tend
> To save the Romans, thereby to destroy
> The Volsces whom you serve, you might condemn us
> As poisonous of your honour. No! our suit
> Is that you reconcile them while the Volsces
> May say 'This mercy we have show'd,' the Romans,
> 'This we receiv'd,' and each in either side
> Give the all-hail to thee and cry 'Be blest
> For making up this peace!' (*Cor.*, 5.3.132)

Paromologia is a figure whereby one admits something unfavorable
to his own position and then brings in a point which overthrows what was
granted. Thus Menenius admits in part the charge of Sicinius against
Coriolanus, but overthrows his conclusion, that Coriolanus ought therefore to be put to death.

> *Sicinius.* He's a disease that must be cut away.
> *Menenius.* O, he's a limb that has but a disease:
> Mortal, to cut it off; to cure it easy. (3.1.295)

Concessio is a figure whereby the speaker grants a point which hurts
the adversary to whom it is granted, as in the reply of the Lord Chief
Justice to Falstaff whom he has sent for.

> *Falstaff.* Boy, tell him I am deaf.
> *Page.* You must speak louder. My master is deaf.
> *Justice.* I am sure he is, to the hearing of anything good. (*2H4*, 1.2.77)

This figure is used with outstanding dramatic effect in *The Merchant
of Venice*. Portia as judge finally grants to Shylock, who has resisted all
appeals of mercy, his insistent plea, the literal application of the terms
of the bond forfeit by Antonio. This point is then turned against him
to whom it is granted, with sudden vengeance.

> *Shylock.*   I stay here on my bond. . . .
> *Portia.* [*to Antonio*] Therefore lay bare your bosom.
> *Shylock.*   Ay, his breast—
> So says the bond; doth it not, noble judge?

Nearest his heart. Those are the very words.
Portia. It is so. . . .
A pound of that same merchant's flesh is thine . . .
And you must cut this flesh from off his breast.
The law allows it, and the court awards it.
Shylock. Most learned judge! A sentence! Come, prepare!
Portia. Tarry a little; there is something else.
This bond doth give thee here no jot of blood;
The words expressly are 'a pound of flesh.'
Take then thy bond, take thou thy pound of flesh;
But in the cutting it if thou dost shed
One drop of Christian blood, thy lands and goods
Are, by the laws of Venice, confiscate
Unto the state of Venice. . . .
Shylock. Is that the law?
Portia.   Thyself shalt see the act;
For, as thou urgest justice, be assur'd
Thou shalt have justice more than thou desir'st.

(MV, 4.1.242–316)

Similar to concessio is metastasis, the turning back of an objection against him who made it. Thus King Henry V, unmasking the traitors, answers their plea for mercy by turning back upon them their own protest uttered only a few moments before against his leniency in pardoning a man who had been guilty of a minor infraction:

The mercy that was quick in us but late,
By your own counsel is suppress'd and kill'd.
You must not dare (for shame) to talk of mercy;
For your own reasons turn into your bosoms
As dogs upon their masters, worrying you. (*H5*, 2.2.79)

When Lear, in a rage, pronounces banishment on Kent for having dared to remonstrate against his unjust and arbitrary exercise of power, Kent turns the sentence back upon the king.

Fare thee well, King. Since thus thou wilt appear,
Freedom lives hence, and banishment is here. (1.1.183)

Adam, befriending Orlando, turns back upon Oliver his own reproach.

Oliver. Get you with him, you old dog!
Adam. Is 'old dog' my reward? Most true, I have lost my teeth in your service. (*AYLI*, 1.1.85)

Moth knows how to turn an offense to his own favor. In the pageant of the Nine Worthies, he is to be young Hercules and to strangle a snake. With foresight he exclaims to Holofernes:

An excellent device! So, if any of the audience hiss, you may cry 'Well done, Hercules! Now thou crushest the snake!' That is the way to make an offence gracious, though few have the grace to do it. (*LLL*, 5.1.144)

By the figure apodioxis one rejects the argument of an opponent, as Alcibiades does in answering the senator who holds that "To revenge is no valour but to bear."

> Why do fond men expose themselves to battle
> And not endure all threats? sleep upon't,
> And let the foes quietly cut their throats
> Without repugnancy? If there be
> Such valour in the bearing, what make we
> Abroad? Why then, women are more valiant
> That stay at home, if bearing carry it;
> And the ass more captain than the lion; the felon
> Loaden with irons wiser than the judge,
> If wisdom be in suffering. (*Tim.*, 3.5.42)

Diasyrmus is a figure whereby an opponent's argument is depraved or made ridiculous through base similitude. Prince Hal would rout Falstaff out of this refuge.

When thou hast tired thyself in base comparisons, hear me speak. (*1H4*, 2.4.276)

Diasyrmus is a characteristic weapon of Thersites. Nestor and Ulysses complain of his buffoonery.

> *Nestor.* Ajax, . . . sets Thersites,
> A slave whose gall coins slanders like a mint,
> To match us in comparisons with dirt,
> To weaken and discredit our exposure,
> How rank soever rounded in with danger.
> *Ulysses.* They tax our policy and call it cowardice,
> Count wisdom as no member of the war,
> Forestall prescience, and esteem no act
> But that of hand. The still and mental parts, . . .
> Why, this hath not a finger's dignity!
> They call this bedwork, mapp'ry, closet war.
> (*T & C*, 1.3.188–205)

In this fashion Thersites epitomizes the Trojan war.

All the argument is a whore and a cuckold—a good quarrel to draw emulous factions and bleed to death upon. (2.3.78)

Aufidius successfully employs diasyrmus to wreak his vengeance on Coriolanus, who has just been welcomed with trumpets on his return to Corioles and has explained to the citizens the honorable and advantageous terms of peace he concluded with Rome. Aufidius calls him a traitor and retells the incident in terms that deprave it.

> *Aufidius.* He has betray'd your business and given up,
> For certain drops of salt, your city Rome
> (I say 'your city') to his wife and mother;
> Breaking his oath and resolution like
> A twist of rotten silk; never admitting
> Counsel o' th' war; but at his nurse's tears
> He whin'd and roar'd away your victory . . .
> *Coriolanus.*   Hear'st thou, Mars?
> *Aufidius.* Name not the god, thou boy of tears! . . .
> *Coriolanus.* Measureless liar, thou hast made my heart
> Too great for what contains it. Boy? . . . False hound!
> If you have writ your annals true, 'tis there,
> That, like an eagle in a dovecote, I
> Flutter'd your Volscians in Corioles.
> Alone I did it. Boy? (5.6.91–116)

Having thus craftily provoked in Coriolanus this ill-timed boast of the harm he has wrought on these very citizens of Corioles, Aufidius easily rouses them on the instant to kill him.

By the figure antirrhesis one rejects an opponent's argument or opinion because of its error or wickedness. Thus Imogen indignantly rejects Iachimo and his fabricated testimony against Posthumus when he urges her to revenge herself by admitting him to her affections.

> Away! I do condemn mine ears that have
> So long attended thee. If thou wert honourable,
> Thou wouldst have told this tale for virtue, not
> For such an end thou seek'st, as base as strange.
> Thou wrong'st a gentleman who is as far
> From thy report as thou from honour, and
> Solicit'st here a lady that disdains
> Thee and the devil alike. (*Cym.*, 1.6.141)

Aphorismus is a figure which reprehends by raising a question about the proper application of a word, as when Hermione declares:

> if I shall be condemn'd
> Upon surmises . . . I tell you,
> 'Tis rigour, and not law. (*WT*, 3.2.112–15)

There is contempt as well as reprehension in Lafew's comment on Parolles.

> I saw the man today, if man he be. (*AW*, 5.3.203)

Commoratio is a figure whereby one seeks to win an argument by continually coming back to one's strongest point, as Shylock does when he keeps insisting that Antonio pay the penalty and forfeit of the bond (*MV*, 4.1.36–242).

Similar to commoratio, and often joined to it, is epimone, the repetition of the same point in the same words, somewhat in the manner of a refrain, as when Othello in a jealous frenzy repeatedly demands the handkerchief.

> *Desdemona.* Pray you let Cassio be receiv'd again.
> *Othello.* Fetch me the handkerchief! My mind misgives.
> *Desdemona.* Come, come!
> You'll never meet a more sufficient man.
> *Othello.* The handkerchief!
> *Desdemona.*   I pray talk me of Cassio.
> *Othello.* The handkerchief!
> *Desdemona.*   A man that all his time
> Hath founded his good fortunes on your love,
> Shar'd dangers with you—
> *Othello.* The handkerchief!
> *Desdemona.* In sooth, you are to blame.
> *Othello.* Away! (3.4.89)

In Cloten's mind Imogen's taunt that she values him less than Posthumus' meanest garment so rankles that he keeps repeating "His meanest garment" (*Cym.*, 2.3.138–61) until the gibe is so burned into his consciousness that later he plans a revenge in which the garments of Posthumus play a significant part. Because of its insistent repetition of an idea in the same words, epimone is an effective figure in swaying the opinions of a crowd. Thus Antony repeats over and over at intervals, but with changing significance, that Brutus and his fellow conspirators are honorable men. And Sicinius proclaims that Coriolanus shall be banished from

Rome, never to return, on penalty of being hurled from the Tarpeian Rock. Skillfully the tribune sounds the keynote which the inflamed mob repeats in the manner of a refrain.

> *Sicinius.* I' th' people's name,
> I say it shall be so.
> *All.* [*Plebeians*] It shall be so! it shall be so! Let him away!
> He's banish'd, and it shall be so! (3.3.104)

Cominius attempts to plead in Coriolanus' behalf, but he is cut off by another "It shall be so" of the tribune Brutus, echoed again by the people (117–19).

Apoplanesis is a figure of disputation whereby one seeks to evade the issue by digressing to another matter. It is a characteristic dodge of Falstaff, who habitually seeks escape in starting holes of evasion when he finds himself unable or unwilling to meet an issue squarely, as has been observed in the illustration quoted above (p. 213). Falstaff resorts to this figure again when the Lord Chief Justice says he wishes to have a word with him.

> *Justice.* Sir John, I sent for you before your expedition to Shrewsbury.
> *Falstaff.* An't please your lordship, I hear his Majesty is return'd with some discomfort from Wales.
> *Justice.* I talk not of his Majesty. You would not come when I sent for you.
> *Falstaff.* And I hear, moreover, his Highness is fall'n into this same whoreson apoplexy. (*2H4*, 1.2.115)

One who cannot meet the issue in argument, nor evade it, may seek refuge in excuse. There are three figures of excuse. By proecthesis one defends what he has said or done and gives a reason why he ought not to be blamed, as Cymbeline does when he learns of the queen's deathbed confession of her wicked scheming; though she proved false, he had reason to love and trust her.

> Mine eyes
> Were not in fault, for she was beautiful;
> Mine ears that heard her flattery; nor my heart,
> That thought her like her seeming. It had been vicious
> To have mistrusted her. Yet (O my daughter!)
> That it was folly in me thou mayst say,
> And prove it in thy feeling. Heaven mend all! (5.5.62)

By dicaeologia, or anangeon, one excuses his word or action by necessity. This is Antony's plea to Cleopatra.

> Hear me, Queen,
> The strong necessity of time commands
> Our services awhile. . . . Our Italy
> Shines o'er with civil swords. (*A & C,* 1.3.41–45)

By pareuresis one offers an excuse of such might as to vanquish all objections. Such is Hamlet's excuse to Laertes for having killed his father, and Laertes accepts it.

> If Hamlet from himself be ta'en away,
> And when he's not himself does wrong Laertes,
> Then Hamlet does it not, Hamlet denies it.
> Who does it, then? His madness. If 't be so,
> Hamlet is of the faction that is wrong'd;
> His madness is poor Hamlet's enemy. (5.2.245)

Pysma is a figure which asks many questions requiring diverse answers, in order to gain attention, to provoke, to confirm, or to confute. With many pointed questions Queen Margaret confirms her prophecy that sorrow would befall the queen of Edward IV.

> Where is thy husband now? Where be thy brothers?
> Where be thy two sons? Wherein dost thou joy?
> Who sues and kneels and says 'God save the Queen'?
> Where be the bending peers that flattered thee?
> Where be the thronging troops that followed thee?
> Decline all this, and see what now thou art. (*R3,* 4.4.92)

If this figure is carried too far or used for deceit, it becomes the fallacy of many questions. Thus, when Regan begins to pour out questions on Gloucester, who sits bound and accused of treason for sending Lear to Dover, Cornwall interrupts and checks her vehement impetuosity.

> *Regan.* Wherefore to Dover? Wast thou not charg'd at peril—
> *Cornwall.* Wherefore to Dover? Let him first answer that.
> (*Lear,* 3.7.52)

With no such veering toward fallacy, Imogen hurls at Pisanio questions laying bare the difficulties which she objects against his plan merely to pretend that he has obeyed Posthumus' command to kill her.

> Why, good fellow,
> What shall I do the while? where bide? how live?
> Or in my life what comfort, when I am
> Dead to my husband? (*Cym.,* 3.4.130)

The general figures of dissuasion and persuasion, dehortation and protrope, combine many figures to achieve their effect. Andromache, Cassandra, and Priam vainly employ dehortation in their efforts to keep Hector from going out to fight on the day that proved fatal. (*T & C*, 5.3.1–25; 59–90). Menenius successfully uses dehortation to dissaude the citizens from hurling Coriolanus down from the Tarpeian Rock, as the tribunes had incited them to do. Coriolanus, he says, has spilt his blood in his country's service. Let not Rome, like an unnatural mother, eat up her own. Let them proceed according to law, for evils resulting from violence are too late discerned and end one knows not where. (3.1.290–326).

Protrope is a figure which persuades by joining promises, threats, and commands with mighty reasons to move the mind to the course desired. So Marcius animates the soldiers to follow him into Corioles (*Cor.*, 1.4.23–42). Later, blood-smeared, he impels them to follow up the victory (1.6.67–80). Perhaps the most urgent persuasion in Shakespeare's plays is that of Volumnia, first when she beseeches Coriolanus to go back to the people humbly, to speak mildly and win their favor (3.2.15–110), and again when she appeals with aching insistence to both his reason and his feeling to induce him to spare Rome (5.3.87–182). She succeeds both times against her extremely stubborn son. In *The Two Noble Kinsmen* (1.1.25–186) the three queens persistently and vehemently implore Theseus' help against Creon, who is letting their husbands' bodies rot unburied on the battlefield. So eloquent are they that Hippolyta and Emilia join in supplication, and Theseus yields to the combined entreaties of the women. Hamlet so forcefully represents to his mother the wickedness of her course that she protests he turns her eyes into her very soul. He exhorts her then:

> Confess yourself to heaven;
> Repent what's past; avoid what is to come;
> And do not spread the compost on the weeds
> To make them ranker. (3.4.149)

In haranguing the people Jack Cade stirs up rebellion by employing protrope in an evil manner, joining promises, threats, and commands. He promises his followers penny loaves and land in common when he is king (*2H6*, 4.2.69–76). His main argument is based on a premise which in an aside he admits to be false, namely, that he is the grandson of Edmund Mortimer, and heir to the crown (144–63). He threatens the lives of all nobles and gentlemen (194). He orders his men to kill and to parley with none (4.8.1–5). He berates the crowd for listening to Clifford, wins them, loses them again to Clifford, and at last, deserted by his inconstant followers, he ignominiously flees (20–67).

Shakespeare's attitude toward disputation is evidenced particularly in his serious work, both in the space allotted to it and in the increasing mastery with which it is used. In *The Rape of Lucrece* disputation occupies more than one-third of the poem. Three passages are noteworthy: Tarquin argues with his conscience, reason contending with passion, and passion wins (190–280); Lucrece argues with him in close-fencing dialectic, but in vain (470–667); violated Lucrece rails at Night, Opportunity, Time, "Holds disputation with each thing she views" . . . "Thus cavils she with everything she sees" or hears—the sun, the birds—finally resolving on death (747–1211).

An outstanding instance of Shakespeare's dramatic use of earnest and weighty disputation occurs in the opening scene of *3 Henry VI* (1.1.70–205). When King Henry and his lords enter the Parliament House, they see York seated on the throne, surrounded by his followers. Henry forbids his men to draw the sword in that place of state and invokes reason to settle the dispute in which all vehemently join.

K. Henry. Cousin of Exeter, frowns, words, and threats
Shall be the war that Henry means to use.
Thou factious Duke of York, descend my throne
And kneel for grace and mercy at my feet.
I am thy sovereign.
York.   Thou art deceiv'd. I am thine.
Exeter. For shame! come down. He made thee Duke of York.
York. It was my inheritance, as the earldom was.
Exeter. Thy father was a traitor to the crown.
Warwick. Exeter, thou art a traitor to the crown
In following this usurping Henry.
Clifford. Whom should he follow but his natural king?
Warwick. True, Clifford; and that's Richard Duke of York.
K. Henry. And shall I stand, and thou sit in my throne?
York. It must and shall be so. Content thyself. . . .
Will you we show our title to the crown?
If not, our swords shall plead it in the field.
K. Henry. What title hast thou, traitor, to the crown?
Thy father was, as thou art, Duke of York; . . .

I am the son of Henry the Fifth . . .
Montague. [*to York*] Good brother, as thou lov'st and honourest arms,
Let's fight it out and not stand cavilling thus. . . .
Warwick. Plantagenet shall speak first. Hear him, lords . . .
K. Henry. My title's good, and better far than his.
Warwick. Prove it, Henry, and thou shalt be King.
Henry. Henry the Fourth by conquest got the crown.
York. 'Twas by rebellion against his king.
K. Henry. [*aside*] I know not what to say; my title's weak.—
Tell me, may not a king adopt an heir? . . .
An if he may, then am I lawful king;
For Richard, in the view of many lords,
Resign'd the crown to Henry the Fourth,
Whose heir my father was, and I am his. . . .
Exeter. No; for he could not so resign his crown
But that the next heir should succeed and reign.
K. Henry. Art thou against us, Duke of Exeter?
Exeter. His is the right, and therefore pardon me. . . .
My conscience tells me he is lawful king. . . .
Northumberland. Plantagenet, for all the claim thou lay'st,
Think not that Henry shall be so depos'd.
Warwick. Depos'd he shall be, in despite of all. . . .
Clifford. King Henry, be thy title right or wrong,
Lord Clifford vows to fight in thy defence.
May that ground gape and swallow me alive
Where I shall kneel to him that slew my father!
K. Henry. O Clifford, how thy words revive my heart!

(*3H6*, 1.1.72–163)

Clifford breaks off the disputation, dismisses reasoning, right or wrong,
and invokes the arbitrament of arms, as Montague had tried to do a little
earlier. Henry, who in the beginning had insisted on settling the dispute
by reason, now approves with his heart, if not his head, Clifford's recourse
to the sword. Through the parley of words which he himself invited he
has lost the support of Exeter, who is convinced by reason that York's
claim is just. Warwick follows up the argument by demanding that
Henry do York justice and yield the crown. The whole concludes with
a political compromise: Henry shall reign during his lifetime, but York
shall be his heir, the very arrangement that has just been denounced as
unlawful in the case of Richard II. Westmoreland indignantly leaves
weak King Henry and goes to Queen Margaret with the news that Henry
has disinherited his son. He is accompanied by Clifford and Northum-

berland, both of whom hate York because he has slain their fathers. Exeter, who has followed reason, characterizes the others:

> They seek revenge and therefore will not yield. (190)

Yet, when he sees Margaret coming, he wants to steal away from her anger (212).

Soon, however, one of Shakespeare's cleverest dialecticians disrupts this settlement. York's young son Richard, a master of sophistic, declares that his father is not bound by his oath to let Henry reign quietly during his lifetime, and maintains that he can prove it.

> *Richard.* An oath is of no moment, being not took
> Before a true and lawful magistrate
> That hath authority over him that swears.
> Henry had none, but did usurp the place.
> Then seeing 'twas he that made you to depose,
> Your oath, my lord, is vain and frivolous.
> Therefore to arms. . . .
> *York.* Richard, enough. I will be King or die!
>
> $\qquad$ (*3H6*, 1.2.22–35)

Richard pays no regard to the substance of the oath or to the integrity of him who made it, but only to an accidental circumstance, the authority of him before whom it was made. Richard's speech galvanizes York into action. He gives orders to assemble armed forces.

Later, Richard, as Duke of Gloucester, woos Lady Anne, who is following the corpse of Henry VI to burial. She curses him for having killed this good Henry and also his son Edward, her husband. Richard's most adroit maneuver is to concede her charges, even while he cleverly turns her arguments in his own favor. He asserts it was her beauty that set him on.

> *Anne.* Villain, thou know'st no law of God nor man.
> No beast so fierce but knows some touch of pity.
> *Richard.* But I know none, and therefore am no beast.
> *Anne.* O wonderful, when devils tell the truth!
> *Richard.* More wonderful, when angels are so angry. . . .
> *Anne.* Didst thou not kill this king?
> *Richard.* $\qquad$ I grant ye.
> *Anne.* Dost grant me, hedgehog? . . .
> O, he was gentle, mild, and virtuous.
> *Richard.* The better for the King of Heaven, that hath him . . .

Let him thank me that holp to send him thither. . . .
                    But, gentle Lady Anne,
To leave this keen encounter of our wits
And fall something into a slower method—
Is not the causer of the timeless deaths
Of these Plantagenets, Henry and Edward,
As blameful as the executioner?
Anne. Thou wast the cause and most accurs'd effect.
Richard. Your beauty was the cause of that effect— . . .
Anne. Black night o'ershade thy day, and death thy life!
Richard. Curse not thyself, fair creature! Thou art both . . .
He that bereft thee, lady, of thy husband,
Did it to help thee to a better husband. (*R3,* 1.2.70–139)

He gives her his sword, kneels, bares his breast, and asks her to kill him.
Instead, she accepts his ring. Richard exultingly comments to himself on
winning her by such strange wooing:

> And I no friends to back my suit withal
> But the plain devil and dissembling looks? (235)

There is another striking example of Richard's sheer effrontery and
resourcefulness in argument, characteristics which add not a little to the
quality of his villainy. He is now king. His train has been stopped by his
mother and by Edward IV's queen, that they may curse him. Not denying
that he killed her young sons, Richard tells the queen he loves her
daughter Elizabeth and seeks the mother's aid in wooing her. The queen
recites his crimes. She scorns his plea that he committed all these wrongs
for her daughter's sake. He tries another argument; he says that he repents, but since he cannot mend the past, he will mend the future.

> *Richard.* If I did take the kingdom from your sons,
> To make amends I'll give it to your daughter. . . .
> Your children were vexation to your youth,
> But mine shall be a comfort to your age.
> The loss you have is but a son being king,
> And by that loss your daughter is made queen. . . .
> Again shall you be mother to a king . . .
> Go then, my mother; to thy daughter go . . .
> Prepare her ears to hear a wooer's tale . . .
> Tell her the King, that may command, entreats.
> *Queen.* That at her hands which the King's King forbids.
>   (*R3,* 4.4.294–346)

She challenges him to swear by something that he has not wronged. He has wronged the world, his father's death, himself, God, the time to come, and so she will not let him swear by any of these. At last he calls upon his present good intention to repent and invoking evil upon himself if he does not truly love her daughter, he declares that the marriage will prevent ruin to the realm which cannot be otherwise avoided. He begs her to woo for him:

> Plead what I will be, not what I have been. (414)

The queen at last consents and goes her way, while Richard reflects:

> Relenting fool, and shallow, changing woman! (431)

Richard's hired assassins discuss the situation before they murder Clarence, who is asleep. Thought of the judgment day, when Clarence will awake if they kill him now, breeds remorse in the second murderer.

> *1. Murderer.* What? Art thou afraid?
> *2. Murderer.* Not to kill him, having a warrant; but to be damn'd for killing him, from the which no warrant can defend me.
> *1. Murderer.* I thought thou hadst been resolute.
> *2. Murderer.* So I am, to let him live. . . .
> *1. Murderer.* Remember our reward when the deed's done.
> *2. Murderer.* Zounds, he dies! I had forgot the reward.
> *1. Murderer.* Where's thy conscience now?
> *2. Murderer.* O, in the Duke of Gloucester's purse. . . . I'll not meddle with it; it makes a man a coward. A man cannot steal but it accuses him; a man cannot swear but it checks him . . . It made me once restore a purse of gold that (by chance) I found. It beggars a man that keeps it. (*R3*, 1.4.111–45)

Clarence awakes and sees the murderers.

> *Clarence.* In God's name, what art thou?
> *1. Murderer.* A man, as you are.
> *Clarence.* But not as I am, royal.
> *1. Murderer.* Nor you as we are, loyal. (168)

They admit that they have come to murder him, and say it is at the command of King Edward IV. Clarence pleads for his life, setting before them a greater command.

> *Clarence.* Erroneous vassals! the great King of Kings
> Hath in the table of his law commanded

> That thou shalt do no murther. Will you then
> Spurn at his edict, and fulfil a man's? (200)

Finally they tell him it is his brother Gloucester who has sent them to murder him. He cannot believe it.

> *Clarence.* It cannot be, for he bewept my fortune,
> And hugg'd me in his arms, and swore with sobs
> That he would labour my delivery.
> *1. Murderer.* Why, so he doth when he delivers you
> From this earth's thraldom to the joys of heaven. (249)

It is evident that Richard's minion well understands the sophistic of his master, which depends in this instance on a confusion of absolute and qualified statement, *secundum quid*.

In the same play Buckingham speciously argues that young York cannot claim sanctuary and that therefore it will be no violation to pluck him from it.

> Weigh it but with the grossness of his age,
> You break not sanctuary in seizing him.
> The benefit thereof is always granted
> To those whose dealings have deserv'd the place
> And those who have the wit to claim the place.
> This prince hath neither claim'd it nor deserv'd it,
> And therefore, in mine opinion, cannot have it.
> Then, taking him from thence that is not there,
> You break no privilege nor charter there.
> Oft have I heard of sanctuary men,
> But sanctuary children ne'er till now. (*R3*, 3.1.46)

Buckingham is guilty of the fallacy of accident; he would allow sanctuary only to persons of a certain age or condition. Also that of *secundum quid*; according to his warped interpretation, the young prince is not in the place of sanctuary in a legal sense, even though he is there bodily and really. His sophistry, however, succeeds in overruling the scruples of the cardinal, who thereupon goes with Hastings to remove the prince from his place of refuge.

In *Richard II* there is earnest argument on a question important to the theme of all Shakespeare's historical plays. York protests vigorously against Richard's seizing the inheritance of Henry Bolingbroke, Duke of Hereford, and shows by clear reasoning that the principle he would thereby violate is that on which his own right rests.

> Take Hereford's rights away, and take from Time
> His charters and his customary rights;
> Let not tomorrow then ensue today;
> Be not thyself—for how art thou a king
> But by fair sequence and succession? . . .
> If you do wrongfully seize Hereford's rights, . . .
> You pluck a thousand dangers on your head,
> You lose a thousand well-disposed hearts,
> And prick my tender patience to those thoughts
> Which honour and allegiance cannot think. (R2, 2.1.195–208)

Nevertheless, York rebuffs his nephew Bolingbroke and charges him with treason for returning to England before the period of his exile has expired and for leading armed forces against the lawful king. Bolingbroke replies:

> As I was banish'd, I was banish'd Hereford;
> But as I come, I come for Lancaster. (2.3.113)

This argument rests on the fallacy of accident, for Bolingbroke was banished in his own person, not in his quality as Duke of Hereford. He proceeds to state his case more fully.

> What would you have me do? I am a subject,
> And I challenge law. Attorneys are denied me,
> And therefore personally I lay my claim
> To my inheritance of free descent. (133)

York, however, will not entertain this view and addresses the lords who have joined Bolingbroke:

> My lords of England, let me tell you this:
> I have had feeling of my cousin's wrongs,
> And labour'd all I could to do him right;
> But in this kind to come, in braving arms,
> Be his own carver and cut out his way
> To find out right with wrong—it may not be;
> And you that do abet him in this kind
> Cherish rebellion and are rebels all. (140)

Yet because he is unable to oppose the rebels by force, York declares himself neutral and welcomes them as neither friends nor foes.

Richard II upbraids Northumberland, when he comes with a message from Bolingbroke, for not greeting him as king and confronts him with this dilemma.

And if we be, how dare thy joints forget
To pay their awful duty to our presence?
If we be not, show us the hand of God
That hath dismiss'd us from our stewardship;
For well we know no hand of blood and bone
Can gripe the sacred handle of our sceptre,
Unless he do profane, steal, or usurp. (3.3.75)

In this play Shakespeare demonstrates his grasp of the function peculiar to dialectic and rhetoric alone, the capacity to generate arguments on both sides of a question. He makes the audience see, like York, the good and the wrong on both sides of the controversy.

In *King John* also there is question who is the lawful king of England. The King of France denies John's claim to the throne and upholds Arthur's.

That Geffrey was thy elder brother born,
And this his son. England was Geffrey's right,
And this is Geffrey's. In the name of God,
How comes it then that thou art call'd a king . . . ? (2.1.104)

A citizen of Angiers admits that he and his fellow citizens are England's subjects. This is the major premise in his argument. He declares, however, that the gates of Angiers shall be closed to both contending parties as long as there is doubt about the minor premise, the answer to the question Who is the lawful king? Thereupon John engages in battle to establish this point, "In dreadful trial of our kingdom's king" (286).

Later in the same play Constance, hearing Cardinal Pandulph pronounce Rome's curse upon King John, begs the cardinal to cry amen to her own vehement curse against John for wronging Arthur.

Pandulph. There's law and warrant, lady, for my curse.
Constance. And for mine too! When law can do no right,
Let it be lawful that law bar no wrong.
Law cannot give my child his kingdom here,
For he that holds his kingdom holds the law.
Therefore, since law itself is perfect wrong,
How can the law forbid my tongue to curse? (3.1.184)

The ambiguity of *law*, which renders this argument fallacious through equivocation, is not so readily apparent as to rob it of all strength. Constance argues as if the law of England, misheld by John and by him made perfect wrong, is identical with the law of God forbidding individuals to curse. Shakespeare is never at a loss to fashion arguments for his characters, whether sophistic or valid, to serve their turn or their need and at the same time reveal their intellectual, moral, and emotional caliber.

One of Shakespeare's finest logicians is Isabel, of whom her brother Claudio remarks truly:

> she hath prosperous art
> When she will play with reason and discourse,
> And well she can persuade. (*MM*, 1.2.189)

In her interviews with Angelo she manifests proficiency in close reasoning on matters of grave import. Angelo rejects her one prepared plea for Claudio's life.

> *Angelo*. Condemn the fault, and not the actor of it?
> Why, every fault's condemn'd ere it be done.
> Mine were the very cipher of a function,
> To fine the faults whose fine stands in record,
> And let go by the actor.
> *Isabel*.   O just but severe law!
> I had a brother then.—Heaven keep your honour! (2.2.37)

She is about to go. But spurred by Lucio she enters a second plea. Neither heaven nor man would grieve if he pardoned Claudio. It is not too late. She can call back a word, and so can he. Nothing so becomes king, deputy, or judge as mercy. Angelo is unmoved.

> *Angelo*. Your brother is a forfeit of the law,
> And you but waste your words. . . .
> *Isabel*. Why, all the souls that were were forfeit once,
> And he that might the vantage best have took
> Found out the remedy. How would you be
> If he which is the top of judgment should
> But judge you as you are? O, think on that!
> And mercy then will breathe within your lips. (71)

This third plea to Angelo, to judge as he would be judged, fails, for he declares that her brother must die tomorrow. This sudden announcement of the imminency of Claudio's execution shocks her, and she enters her fourth plea, begging more time so that her brother may prepare for death. Her fifth plea is that others have been guilty of that for which Claudio is condemned. Angelo answers:

> *Angelo.* Those many had not dar'd to do that evil
> If that the first that did th' edict infringe
> Had answer'd for his deed. . . .
> *Isabel.* Yet show some pity.
> *Angelo.* I show it most of all when I show justice;
> For then I pity those I do not know,
> Which a dismiss'd offence would after gall,
> And do him right that, answering one foul wrong,
> Lives not to act another. Be satisfied.
> Your brother dies tomorrow. Be content. (91–105)

Isabel follows his objection to her sixth plea, for pity, with her seventh, a rebuke to him for exercising his power just because he has it.

> *Isabel.* O it is excellent
> To have a giant's strength; but it is tyrannous
> To use it like a giant. (107)

The tyrannous exercise of power by proud man dressed in a little brief authority, she continues, makes the angels weep. Her eighth and last plea has an effect unlooked for.

> *Isabel.* Go to your bosom,
> Knock there, and ask your heart what it doth know
> That's like my brother's fault. If it confess
> A natural guiltiness such as is his,
> Let it not sound a thought upon your tongue
> Against my brother's life.
> *Angelo.* [*aside*] She speaks, and 'tis
> Such sense that my sense breeds with it. (136)

Looking into his own bosom, Angelo suddenly realizes his own temptation toward her. When she says she will bribe him with prayers, he thinks of another bribe and asks her to return tomorrow.

In her second interview with Angelo the dramatic tension increases. Isabel is mainly on the defensive, for Angelo leads the argument in the direction he desires. He remarks that fornication is as wicked as murder, and craftily catches up her answer.

> *Isabel.* 'Tis set down so in heaven but not in earth.
> *Angelo.* Say you so? Then I shall pose you quickly. (2.4.50)

Isabel answers unhesitatingly that she would not save Claudio, nor would she save her own life, at the price of virtue.

> *Isabel.* Better it were a brother died at once
> Than that a sister, by redeeming him,
> Should die for ever.
> *Angelo.* Were not you then as cruel as the sentence
> That you have slander'd so?
> *Isabel.* Ignomy in ransom and free pardon
> Are of two houses. Lawful mercy
> Is nothing kin to foul redemption. (106)

She will proclaim Angelo for what he is, one who would himself be guilty
of that which in another he has so rigorously condemned. He rests unper-
turbed in his unspotted reputation:

> *Angelo.* Who will believe thee, Isabel?
> My unsoil'd name, th' austereness of my life,
> My vouch against you, and my place i' th' state
> Will so your accusation overweigh
> That you shall stifle in your own report
> And smell of calumny . . .
> Say what you can; my false outweighs your true. (154–70)

Iago is another of Shakespeare's characters who is an accomplished
dialectician, as well as a master of innuendo and suggestion. His smooth
and plausible reasoning serves the important dramatic purpose of showing
how an upright man like Othello could be completely deceived. Iago
knows each of his victims, works upon the weak or the good points of
each, and plays one against the other to his own evil advantage. He convinces Roderigo that Desdemona loves Cassio and that it will be to his
advantage to provoke Cassio to a quarrel and so displant him (2.1.220–
90). The resultant brawl brings Cassio into disgrace with Othello. Iago
convinces Cassio that he should ask Desdemona to intercede for him with
Othello (2.3.318–38). Thereupon in soliloquy Iago discloses his evil
plot.

> And what's he then that says I play the villain,
> When this advice is free I give and honest. . . .
>   How am I then a villain
> To counsel Cassio to this parallel course,
> Directly to his good? Divinity of hell!
> When devils will the blackest sins put on,
> They do suggest at first with heavenly shows,
> As I do now. For whiles this honest fool
> Plies Desdemona to repair his fortunes,

> And she for him pleads strongly to the Moor,
> I'll pour this pestilence into his ear—
> That she repeals him for her body's lust;
> And by how much she strives to do him good,
> She shall undo her credit with the Moor.
> So will I turn her virtue into pitch,
> And out of her own goodness make the net
> That shall enmesh them all. (2.3.342–68)

Seeming reluctant and thereby more convincing, philosophizing nobly on the value of a good name, on jealousy, on contentment, Iago so plants suspicion in Othello that Desdemona's pleading in Cassio's favor takes on a sinister color (3.3.41–256). By subtle devices Iago convinces Othello simultaneously of his own honesty and of Desdemona's guilt.

> *Othello.* If thou dost slander her and torture me,
> Never pray more; abandon all remorse . . .
> *Iago.* God b' wi' you! take mine office. O wretched fool,
> That liv'st to make thine honesty a vice!
> O monstrous world! Take note, take note, O world.
> To be direct and honest is not safe.
> I thank you for this profit; and from hence
> I'll love no friend, sith love breeds such offence.
> *Othello.* Nay, stay. Thou shouldst be honest.
> *Iago.* I should be wise; for honesty's a fool
> And loses that it works for. . . .
> *Othello.* Give me a living reason she's disloyal.
> *Iago.* I do not like the office.
> But sith I am enter'd in this cause so far,
> Prick'd to't by foolish honesty and love,
> I will go on. (3.3.368–413)

Shakespeare achieves here a fusion of thought and feeling, of logic and psychology, of dianoia, character, and plot in supreme poetic. To give Othello the proof he demands, Iago now resorts to lying, though up to this point he has relied on insinuation and deceit. He inflames Othello by telling him that he heard Cassio in his sleep disclose his illicit love for Desdemona (413–26). Iago pours further lies and insinuations into Othello's mind (4.1.1–45), gives him the ocular proof of the handkerchief in Cassio's hand, and misconstrues Cassio's words to Bianca, which he has arranged that Othello shall overhear (153–226). It is enough. An unfaithful wife, Othello holds, should be punished by death. This is his major premise. Iago has convinced him that Desdemona is unfaithful—the minor premise. With swift resolve Othello moves to the conclusion of this relentless syllogism: She shall die. Fitly he will strangle her in her bed.

Lady Macbeth has some of Iago's ability to whip up passion through argument. Macbeth has debated with himself the killing of Duncan, arguing both sides. He apprehends clearly all that faith and courtesy advise, the virtues of his victim, the immediate and remote effects of the deed. He craves a motive but finds only ambition to spur him on, not passion. His will is cold. Lady Macbeth enters as a goad. She argues so forcefully and vehemently that Macbeth exclaims in admiration, "Bring forth men-children only," and declares that he is now resolved to "bend up Each corporal agent to this terrible feat" (1.7).

King Lear will hold a contest to determine which of his daughters loves him most, that he may bestow meet awards. He holds out to them material gain to induce them to speak so as to satisfy his vanity.

> Which of you shall we say doth love us most?
> That we our largest bounty may extend
> Where nature doth with merit challenge. (1.1.52)

And when Cordelia's turn comes, he fondly repeats:

> what can you say to draw
> A third more opulent than your sisters? Speak. (87)

She answers, "Nothing, my lord." Again, as an enticement, he reminds her of the tangible reward.

> Nothing can come of nothing. Speak again. (92)

She says she cannot heave her heart into her mouth. A fourth time he warns:

> How, how, Cordelia? Mend your speech a little,
> Lest it may mar your fortunes. (96)

Then follows the argument between an honest daughter and an obtuse father.

> *Cordelia.*   Good my lord,
> You have begot me, bred me, lov'd me; I
> Return those duties back as are right fit,
> Obey you, love you, and most honour you.
> Why have my sisters husbands, if they say

They love you all? Haply, when I shall wed,
That lord whose hand must take my plight shall carry
Half my love with him, half my care and duty.
Sure I shall never marry like my sisters,
To love my father all.
Lear. But goes thy heart with this?
Cordelia.   Ay, good my lord.
Lear. So young, and so untender?
Cordelia. So young, my lord, and true. (1.1.97)

In a rage Lear solemnly swears that he disclaims Cordelia forever. Kent protests the wrong, characterizing Cordelia and, by implication, her two sisters.

Thy youngest daughter does not love thee least,
Nor are those empty-hearted whose low sound
Reverbs no hollowness. (154)

He speaks in vain. Lear banishes Kent and later learns the bitter folly of his unreasoning trust in words.

In *Troilus and Cressida* the clash of opinion in debate determines action in matters of momentous importance in both the Greek and Trojan councils of war. The Greeks deliberate on the question why, after seven years of siege, Troy's walls stand. Agamemnon asserts that these delays and checks are wrongly called shames. Rather they are the protractive trials of Jove, who not in Fortune's love, but in the wind and tempest of her frown finds out the constancy of men. Nestor accepts Agamemnon's thesis and states it anew with a clear call to sustained valor:

In the reproof of chance
Lies the true proof of men. (1.3.33)

On a smooth sea, he continues, boats large and small sail with equal ease. But let a storm rage, and the strong-ribbed bark cuts through liquid mountains while the shallow bauble boat either flees to harbor or is lost.

Even so,
Doth valour's show and valour's worth divide
In storms of fortune. (45)

Ulysses goes deeper. His appeal is intellectual rather than emotional. The specialty of rule has been neglected. When degree is shaken, enterprise is sick, discord follows, right and wrong lose their names, power is lost in will and will in appetite.

> This chaos, when degree is suffocate,
> Follows the choking. . . . The general's disdain'd
> By him one step below, he by the next;
> That next by him beneath. . . .
> And 'tis this fever that keeps Troy on foot,
> Not her own sinews. To end a tale of length,
> Troy in our weakness stands, not in her strength. (125–37)

Nestor and Agamemnon agree to Ulysses' diagnosis of the nature of the sickness. What is the remedy? Ulysses answers with more specific charges against Achilles and Patroclus. Nestor adds that others are infected by these two. The problem becomes immediate when Hector's challenge to single combat is proclaimed among the Greeks. Who shall meet Hector? Ulysses states the dilemma showing that they are bound to lose either way, if Achilles is permitted to answer Hector. Should he win, his already insufferable insolence will become even worse; should he lose the Greeks will suffer the taint and loss of their best warrior. Therefore Ulysses proposes that a man be chosen by lot so devised that Ajax shall draw it. This will pose a new dilemma, according to which they are sure to win either way: if Ajax wins against Hector, he plucks down Achilles' plumes; if he loses, the Greeks can still say that they have better men in reserve.

In the council of war among the Trojans the question is: shall they accept the Greek offer to make peace provided the Trojans deliver Helen to her countrymen? Hector answers yes, for Helen is not theirs and is not worth the dearer lives of so many men which she has cost. Troilus answers no, and reasons against reason which, he says, makes "livers pale and lustihood deject." He accounts the subjective the measure of worth:

> What is aught but as 'tis valu'd?

To which Hector replies:

> But value dwells not in particular will. (2.2.52)

There are in the argument of Troilus two palpable instances of the fallacy of consequent, which involves illicit conversion. First, when he asserts:

> If you'll avouch 'twas wisdom Paris went
> (As you must needs, for you all cried 'Go, go!') (2.2.84)

the valid argument, It is wise; therefore we will do it, is fallaciously converted to We did it; therefore it is wise. The second instance is the reply of Troilus when Cassandra enters and prophesies the alternatives, "Troy burns, or else let Helen go" (112):

> Cassandra's mad. Her brainsick raptures
> Cannot distaste the goodness of a quarrel
> Which hath our several honours all engag'd
> To make it gracious. (122)

Here what would be a true major premise, A quarrel that is gracious and good should engage our honors, is wrongly converted to A quarrel that engages our honors is gracious and good. Furthermore, although Troilus acknowledges that Helen was stolen, he would regard it as shameful to restore her.

> O theft most base,
> That we have stol'n what we do fear to keep! (92)

Paris declares that he would never retract what he has done. To this Priam retorts:

> You have the honey still but these the gall. (144)

Hector reasons cogently that not to return Helen is to persist in wrong and make it much more heavy. Yet he casts away reason and yields to his brothers' will to keep Helen.

> For 'tis a cause that hath no mean dependence
> Upon our joint and several dignities. (192)

And with this decision the deliberation ends.

Achilles is stung when the Greek leaders coached by Ulysses pass him by as if he were forgotten. Ulysses comes reading a book, and as he hopes, Achilles questions him. The discussion turns on worth and its recognition, and Ulysses seizes the opportunity to rebuke Achilles for having ceased to take part in the war against Troy:

> no man is the lord of anything . . .
> Till he communicate his parts to others . . .
> Perseverance, dear my lord,
> Keeps honour bright. To have done is to hang
> Quite out of fashion, like a rusty mail
> In monumental mock'ry . . . Keep then the path,
> For emulation hath a thousand sons
> That one by one pursue. If you give way,
> Or hedge aside from the direct forthright,

Like to an ent'red tide they all rush by
And leave you hindmost . . .
     Then what they do in present,
Though less than yours in past, must o'ertop yours . . .
      Let not virtue seek
Remuneration for the thing it was . . .
The present eye praises the present object. . . .
    things in motion sooner catch the eye
Than what not stirs. (3.3.115–84)

Equipped as every educated man of his time was with a thorough knowledge of the terms, the forms, and the processes of argumentation, Shakespeare skillfully adapts these devices to every conceivable dramatic purpose. Often the skirmish of wits is light and playful, as in *Twelfth Night*, *As You Like It*, *Much Ado*, *Love's Labour's Lost*, *The Two Gentlemen of Verona*, *Romeo and Juliet*, displayed sometimes in a bandying of words, sometimes of ideas. An Elizabethan audience could be relied upon to follow the turns and twists of an argument, to note the skill, the adroitness, the fumbles, as readily as a modern crowd notes these points in a football game. Touchstone, Feste, and the other clowns, Rosalind, Beatrice, Benedick, Romeo, Juliet, Cressida are skillful fencers with words, adept at the quick retort, the pert reply. The gravediggers in *Hamlet* match Touchstone and Feste in light sophistic, even though the subject of their banter is grim. Richard III and Iago reason fallaciously, even falsely, in pursuit of deepest villainy. Despite his personal feeling and sympathies, York in *Richard II* upholds what reason tells him is the right. Desdemona and Hermione argue with dignity and cogency before judges at a public trial. Isabel contends with superb skill and honesty against the craft and deceit of Angelo, the reputed saint. Portia eloquently pleads that mercy temper justice; yet, upholding the literal application of the law, with consummate cunning she turns the tables on revenge-bent Shylock. Logic contributes much to the interest of *All's Well* and *Julius Caesar*. It is vital in the soliloquies of Hamlet.

In impregnating dramatic scenes of human urgency with the tension of genuine debate Shakespeare easily excels his contemporaries. Combining intellectual power with imaginative and emotional persuasion, he successfully blends logic, rhetoric, and poetic. He so fuses character and plot, thought and feeling, that they become almost indistinguishable and thereby more intense, more convincing, moving both mind and heart.

This is particularly true of his great tragedies, *Othello*, *Macbeth*, *Hamlet*, *Lear*, *Coriolanus*, *Antony and Cleopatra*, and of the dark comedy *Troilus and Cressida*. In these he mirrors the whole of man's composite but integrated nature.

CHAPTER V

PATHOS AND ETHOS

1. Pathos

Pathos is that form of persuasion by which one endeavors to put the auditor into whatever frame of mind is favorable to one's purpose. Marlowe uses the word pathetical in this technical sense when he shows Theridamas converted from foe to ally by the speech of Tamburlaine inviting him to share his destined empire and glory.

> *Theridamas.* Not *Hermes* Prolocutor to the Gods,
> Could use perswasions more patheticall. (Part I, lines 405–6)

Sidney rests his strongest claim for the excellence of poetry on its power to move the hearer or reader, and he maintains that in this respect it surpasses history and even philosophy.

> For suppose it be granted (that which I suppose with great reason may be denied) that the Philosopher, in respect of his methodical proceeding, doth teach more perfectly then the Poet, yet do I thinke that no man is so much *Philophilosophos* as to compare the Philosopher, in mooving, with the Poet.
> And that mooving is of a higher degree then teaching, it may by this appeare, that it is wel nigh the cause and the effect of teaching. For who will be taught, if he bee not mooved with desire to be taught? and what so much good doth that teaching bring forth (I speak still of morall doctrine) as that it mooveth one to doe that which it dooth teach? for, as *Aristotle* sayth, it is not *Gnosis* but *Praxis* must be the fruit. And howe *Praxis* cannot be, without being mooved to practise, it is no hard matter to consider. (Smith, I, 171)

The practical measure of a speech or a play is its effect on the hearer, as Hamlet appreciates.

> The play's the thing
> Wherein I'll catch the conscience of the King. (2.2.632)

Hamlet understands, too, the means to arouse a desired response.[1]

---

[1] T. W. Baldwin, *William Shakspere's Small Latine and Lesse Greeke*, (II, 204), points out that these views are derived from Quintilian 6.2.34.

Is it not monstrous that this player here,
But in a fiction, in a dream of passion,
Could force his soul so to his own conceit
That from her working, all his visage wann'd,
Tears in his eyes, distraction in's aspect,
A broken voice, and his whole function suiting
With forms to his conceit? And all for nothing!
For Hecuba! . . .　　　What would he do,
Had he the motive and the cue for passion
That I have? He would drown the stage with tears
And cleave the general ear with horrid speech;
Make mad the guilty, and appal the free,
Confound the ignorant, and amaze indeed
The very faculties of eyes and ears. (2.2.577–92)

Iago is one who understands the value of *pathos* in argument, and he knows well that passion colors judgment. Having wrought Othello to a pitch of jealous frenzy, he realizes that a mere show of tangible evidence will serve his turn, for

Trifles light as air
Are to the jealous confirmations strong
As proofs of holy writ. (3.3.322)

King Henry VIII urges Cranmer to defend himself with vehemence against his enemies, who will not hesitate to charge him falsely.

The best persuasions to the contrary
Fail not to use, and with what vehemency
Th' occasion shall instruct you. (*H8*, 5.1.147)

In considering *pathos* in drama it must be remembered that there are two groups of hearers: the other characters in the play, who are the persons immediately addressed, and the audience attending the play, who are the ones ultimately addressed. Good drama must be poetic, that is, must cause the members of an audience to identify themselves with the characters, to share in their thoughts and feelings and so to enter vicariously into the play. Consequently *pathos*, which is, strictly speaking, the temper of mind induced in the hearers by the speaker, includes in drama even more than in oratory the feelings of the speaker himself. It is precisely by means of this identification of the feelings of the audience with those of the characters in the play that the catharsis of their emotions is effected, the purging through pity and fear in tragedy, through laughter in comedy. It follows from this identification that to analyze the emotions of the speakers with whom the audience is in sympathy is equivalent to analyzing the *pathos* of the play.

To move to laughter is one way of disposing hearers favorably toward the cause one has in hand. In drama, however, humor is likely to be introduced for entertainment rather than, as in oratory, for winning an audience to a certain proposal urged by the speaker. Of Shakespeare's characters, perhaps the fool in *Lear* comes nearest to using foolery as a means of persuasion to something deeper, although his wit is barbed and is seldom the kind to provoke a laugh.

> *Fool.* Give me an egg, nuncle, and I'll give thee two crowns.
> *Lear.* What two crowns shall they be?
> *Fool.* Why, after I have cut the egg i' th' middle and eat up the meat, the two crowns of the egg. When thou clovest thy crown i' th' middle and gav'st away both parts, thou bor'st thine ass on thy back o'er the dirt. Thou hadst little wit in thy bald crown when thou gav'st thy golden one away. (1.4.170)

> *Fool.* Canst tell how an oyster makes his shell?
> *Lear.* No.
> *Fool.* Nor I neither; but I can tell why a snail has a house.
> *Lear.* Why?
> *Fool.* Why, to put's head in; not to give it away to his daughters, and leave his horns without a case. (1.5.26)

Pathos in drama is effected less often by humor than by indignation, scorn, hate, sorrow, pity, desire, wonder, joy—powerful in persuasion. Shakespeare sweeps through the orbit of these emotions, intensifying *logos* with *pathos*. He employs all the figures of vehemence distinguished by the Tudor rhetoricians.

By the figure exuscitatio one deeply moved by emotion shows it in his utterance and stirs his hearers to the like feeling. Thus York's last passionate speech against Queen Margaret, who hands him a napkin stained with the blood of his young son Rutland, moves even his enemy Northumberland to tears.

> O tiger's heart wrapp'd in a woman's hide!
> How couldst thou drain the lifeblood of the child,
> To bid the father wipe his eyes withal,
> And yet be seen to bear a woman's face? . . .
> This cloth thou dipp'dst in blood of my sweet boy,
> And I with tears do wash the blood away. (*3H6*, 1.4.137–58)

In a number of figures the very form of the language reveals emotion. Aposiopesis is the sudden breaking off of speech, as when Lear, beside himself with rage because Goneril and Regan deny his need of even one retainer, exclaims:

> I will have revenges on you both
> That all the world shall—I will do such things—
> What they are yet, I know not; but they shall be
> The terrors of the earth! (2.4.282)

This figure, used with fine dramatic effect, marks a turning point in the character of Richard III. After Ratcliff has announced that Richmond aided by Buckingham is coming against the king, fear loosens reason's habitual strong hold on Richard and causes him to lose control of the situation. With erratic nervous energy he issues swift commands, ineffectual because they are incomplete.

> *Richard.* Some light-foot friend post to the Duke of Norfolk.
> Ratcliff, thyself—or Catesby—where is he?
> *Catesby.* Here, my good lord.
> *Richard.*   Catesby, fly to the Duke.
> *Catesby.* I will, my lord, with all convenient haste.
> *Richard.* Ratcliff, come hither. Post to Salisbury.
> When thou com'st thither—[*To Catesby*] Dull unmindful villain,
> Why stay'st thou here and go'st not to the Duke?
> *Catesby.* First, mighty liege, tell me your Highness' pleasure,
> What from your Grace I shall deliver to him. (*R3*, 4.4.440)

Ecphonesis is exclamation, the most widely used figure of vehemence and one expressing every species of emotion. Cleopatra, seeing Antony brought to her dying, cries out:

> O sun,
> Burn the great sphere thou mov'st in! Darkling stand
> The varying shore o' th' world! O Antony,
> Antony, Antony! (*A & C*, 4.15.9)

Thaumasmus is the particular name given to an exclamation of wonder. Coming upon his former master, Timon, in the woods, the faithful steward Flavius exclaims:

> O you gods!
> Is yond despis'd and ruinous man my lord?
> Full of decay and failing? O monument
> And wonder of good deeds evilly bestow'd! (*Tim.*, 4.3.464)

This figure is sometimes used to express wonder at the negligence of men. Posthumus, disguised as a peasant, has been asked by an English lord for details of the battle against the Romans. He exclaims with scorn, irony, and wonder, as the lord walks away:

> This is a lord! O noble misery,
> To be i' th' field, and ask 'What news?' of me!
> To-day how many would have given their honours
> To have sav'd their carcasses! took heel to do't
> And yet died too! (*Cym.*, 5.3.64)

By erotema, or rhetorical question, one may affirm or deny an assertion as clearly as by mere statement, and in a more lively and stirring manner combining emotion with thought. Laertes, for example, already distraught with news of his father's death, sees that Ophelia is mad and cries out:

> O heavens! is't possible a young maid's wits
> Should be as mortal as an old man's life? (*Ham.*, 4.5.159)

The questions put to King Richard II by his queen constitute an argument against his yielding to defeat.

> What, is my Richard both in shape and mind
> Transform'd and weakened? Hath Bolingbroke depos'd
> Thine intellect? Hath he been in thy heart? (*R2*, 5.1.26)

When Macbeth has determined to proceed no further against Duncan, Lady Macbeth lashes him with questions more effective than statement.

> Was the hope drunk
> Wherein you dress'd yourself? Hath it slept since?
> And wakes it now to look so green and pale
> At what it did so freely? From this time
> Such I account thy love. Art thou afeard
> To be the same in thine own act and valour
> As thou art in desire? (1.7.35)

Apostrophe is literally a turning of speech from the persons previously addressed to another, sometimes to a thing or an abstraction personified. So Iachimo, having been introduced to Imogen, speaks first to himself.

> All of her that is out of door most rich!
> If she be furnish'd with a mind so rare,
> She is alone th' Arabian bird, and I

> Have lost the wager. Boldness be my friend!
> Arm me, audacity, from head to foot! (*Cym.*, 1.6.15)

Mark Antony turns aside from his talk to the assassins and speaks to Caesar's corpse.

> That I did love thee, Caesar, O, 'tis true!
> If then thy spirit look upon us now,
> Shall it not grieve thee dearer than thy death
> To see thy Antony making his peace,
> Shaking the bloody fingers of thy foes,
> Most noble! in the presence of thy corse? (*JC*, 3.1.194)

Most bitter and cynical is Timon's apostrophe to gold, which proved his undoing both when he had it and when he lacked it. Now in the forest where he eats roots, he has found gold worthless except to attract men, whom he hates. He dwells on the near-contradictories which make gold almost a deity.

> O thou sweet king-killer, and dear divorce
> 'Twixt natural son and sire! . . . thou visible god,
> That sold'rest close impossibilities
> And mak'st them kiss! that speak'st with every tongue
> To every purpose! O thou touch of hearts . . .
> Set them into confounding odds, that beasts
> May have the world in empire! (*Tim.*, 4.3.382–93)

Apostrophe, which is usually combined with other figures, such as exclamation, interrogation, and personification, is an effective means to heighten feeling. In an apostrophe to ceremony King Henry V calls it an idol that plays subtilely with a king's repose while peasants soundly sleep (*H5*, 4.1.257–301). Lear's crying out to the elements expresses intense vehemence (3.2). Macbeth asks the earth not to hear his steps and the stones not to prate of his whereabouts as he goes to murder Duncan (2.1.56). Planning to quell his fears by Banquo's murder, he longs for night.

> Come, seeling night,
> Scarf up the tender eye of pitiful day,
> And with thy bloody and invisible hand
> Cancel and tear to pieces that great bond
> Which keeps me pale! (3.2.46)

In contrast to apostrophe, which by direct address conveys the immediacy of the present, anamnesis is a recital of matters past, most often of woes or injuries. Margaret joins the old Duchess of York and Edward IV's queen, inviting them to a chorus of woe emphasized by figures of repetition, which begins thus:

> Tell o'er your woes again by viewing mine.
> I had an Edward, till a Richard kill'd him;
> I had a Harry, till a Richard kill'd him:
> Thou hadst an Edward, till a Richard kill'd him;
> Thou hadst a Richard, till a Richard kill'd him. (*R3*, 4.4.39)

This figure serves an important dramatic purpose when it is used to narrate what happened before the play begins. Thus Prospero recites to Miranda the wrongs he suffered from his usurping brother (*Tem.*, 1.2.66–151). In contentious dialogue Prospero and Caliban (332–62) rehearse the story of Caliban's past, of Prospero's early kindness to him, and the reason for his present harshness. And at the moment when he freely abjures magic, Prospero recounts the deeds he has wrought by it.

> I have bedimm'd
> The noontide sun, call'd forth the mutinous winds,
> And 'twixt the green sea and the azur'd vault
> Set roaring war; to the dread rattling thunder
> Have I given fire and rifted Jove's stout oak
> With his own bolt; the strong-bas'd promontory
> Have I made shake and by the spurs pluck'd up
> The pine and cedar; graves at my command
> Have wak'd their sleepers, op'd, and let 'em forth
> By my so potent art. (*Tem.*, 5.1.41)

Anamnesis is parodied by that master of parody, Touchstone. Silvius tells him that if he remembers not the slightest folly that he did for love, he has not loved. Thereupon Touchstone, not to be outdone, makes recital of the silly things he did when in love.

I remember, when I was in love I broke my sword upon a stone and bid him take that for coming a-night to Jane Smile; and I remember the kissing of her batlet, and the cow's dugs that her pretty chopt hands had milk'd; and I remember the wooing of a peas-cod instead of her, from whom I took two cods, and giving her them again, said with weeping tears, 'Wear these for my sake.' (*AYLI*, 2.4.44)

Most of the figures of vehemence depend primarily, not on the manner of utterance, but on the emotion expressed. Thus threnos is a lament.

Shakespeare was unquestionably familiar with this figure, for in "The Phoenix and Turtle" he affirms that Reason

> made this threne
> To the phoenix and the dove,
> Co-supremes and stars of love,
> As chorus to their tragic scene.

And the word threnos stands as title to the five stanzas of lament that follow and conclude the poem. *Richard III* abounds in murders, and consequently in lamentation. Lady Anne, following the corpse of King Henry VI, invokes his ghost

> To hear the lamentations of poor Anne,
> Wife to thy Edward, to thy slaught'red son
> Stabb'd by the selfsame hand that made these wounds!
> Lo, in these windows that let forth thy life
> I pour the helpless balm of my poor eyes. (*R3*, 1.2.9)

Clarence's children mourn the murder of their father; Queen Elizabeth bewails Edward IV and later her two sons. The old Duchess of York laments all these, who are her sons and grandsons, and asserts that her grief is therefore greatest of all. Threnos is also prominent in *Titus Andronicus*, another bloody play.

Apocarteresis is the casting away of all hope in one direction and turning to another for aid, as when Hermione, seeing that Leontes is preconvinced of her guilt, turns her hope to the gods.

> It shall scarce boot me
> To say 'Not guilty.' Mine integrity,
> Being counted falsehood, shall, as I express it,
> Be so receiv'd. But thus:—if pow'rs divine
> Behold our human actions (as they do)
> I doubt not then but innocence shall make
> False accusation blush and tyranny
> Tremble at patience. (*WT*, 3.2.26)

Optatio is an ardent wish or prayer. Perhaps the best-known instance of it in Shakespeare is the cry of Richard III, "A horse! a horse! my kingdom for a horse!" (*R3*, 5.4.7), uttered on the battlefield when he is eager to find Richmond and slay him. This figure varies much with the occasion and the character of the speaker. Octavia, fearful of impending war between Antony and her brother, prays against this very evil that her marriage to Antony was designed to prevent.

> The Jove of power make me most weak, most weak,
> Your reconciler! Wars 'twixt you twain would be
> As if the world should cleave, and that slain men
> Should solder up the rift. (*A & C*, 3.4.29)

Lear, in the storm, moved by the primal strength of the elements, which searches hearts, calls on wickedness to disclose itself.

> Let the great gods,
> That keep this dreadful pudder o'er our heads,
> Find out their enemies now. Tremble, thou wretch,
> That hast within thee undivulged crimes
> Unwhipp'd of justice. Hide thee, thou bloody hand;
> Thou perjur'd, and thou simular man of virtue
> That art incestuous. Caitiff, in pieces shake
> That under covert and convenient seeming
> Hast practis'd on man's life. Close pent-up guilts,
> Rive your concealing continents, and cry
> These dreadful summoners grace. (3.2.49)

Convinced of Desdemona's guilt, Othello pours out the desires surging from his outraged heart.

> O that the slave had forty thousand lives!
> One is too poor, too weak for my revenge. . . .
> Arise, black vengeance, from the hollow hell!
> Yield up, O love, thy crown and hearted throne
> To tyrannous hate! Swell, bosom, with thy fraught,
> For 'tis of aspics' tongues! (3.3.442–50)

Emilia desires that heaven punish the knave who has abused Othello and wrought him to unfounded jealousy.

> O heaven, that such companions thou'dst unfold,
> And put in every honest hand a whip
> To lash the rascals naked through the world
> Even from the East to th' West! (4.2.141)

Closely akin to optatio is vehement supplication, called deesis, or obtestatio. It is used when the Duchess of York and Aumerle on their knees before King Henry IV supplicate for Aumerle's life, despite his admitted treason, while his indignant father pleads as earnestly for his punishment (*R2*, 5.3.30–135). So, also, Rutland (*3H6*, 1.3) and Clarence (*R3*, 1.4) beg for life, but in vain. Arthur beseeches Hubert not to blind him, and

wins his petition (*KJ*, 4.1). In *Titus Andronicus* Tamora entreats in vain
for the life of her son (1.1.104–20), Lavinia for her virtue (2.3.136–78),
and Titus for the lives of his two sons (3.1.1–26). In *The Two Noble
Kinsmen* there are three supplications of extreme earnestness, intensity,
and beauty, beginning with praise and ending with petition, and rich with
many figures: Arcite's to Mars (5.1.49–66), Palamon's to Venus (77–97;
126–35), and Emilia's to Diana (137–72). In *Lear* Cordelia implores
the gods to restore her father's mind and health.

> O you kind gods,
> Cure this great breach in his abused nature!
> Th' untun'd and jarring senses, O, wind up
> Of this child-changed father! (4.7.14)

Macduff has one fervent petition to heaven when he hears that his wife
and children have been murdered by Macbeth.

> But, gentle heavens,
> Cut short all intermission. Front to front
> Bring thou this fiend of Scotland and myself.
> Within my sword's length set him. (4.3.231)

Macbeth, a prey to growing fears, revisits the witches and beseeches them
to answer his questions though they untie the winds (4.1.50). Probably
the most fearful supplication in all of Shakespeare is Lady Macbeth's
invocation of the spirits of evil, which appears to be nothing less than a
plea to be possessed by demons.

> Come, you spirits
> That tend on mortal thoughts, unsex me here,
> And fill me, from the crown to the toe, top-full
> Of direst cruelty! Make thick my blood;
> Stop up th' access and passage to remorse,
> That no compunctious visitings of nature
> Shake my fell purpose nor keep peace between
> Th' effect and it! Come to my woman's breasts
> And take my milk for gall, you murth'ring ministers,
> Wherever in your sightless substances
> You wait on nature's mischief! (1.5.41)

Not far removed from supplication is mempsis, a complaint against
injuries and a craving for redress. Thus the Archbishop of York complains of wrongs and griefs so great that their redress even through revolt
is justified, since peaceful access to the king has been denied.

> [We] have the summary of all our griefs,
> When time shall serve, to show in articles,
> Which long ere this we offer'd to the King
> And might by no suit gain our audience.
> When we are wrong'd and would unfold our griefs
> We are denied access unto his person
> Even by those men that most have done us wrong. . . .
> Then take, my Lord of Westmoreland, this schedule,
> For this maintains our general grievances.
> Each several article herein redress'd . . .
> We come within our awful banks again
> And knit our powers to the arm of peace. (*2H4*, 4.1.72–177)

Alcibiades complains to the senate that they have wronged him in reject-ing his plea for Timon, for he has deserved from them a more gracious hearing.

> I cannot think but your age has forgot me. .
> It could not else be I should prove so base
> To sue, and be denied such common grace.
> My wounds ache at you. (*Tim.*, 3.5.93)

Far from winning redress, this remonstrance only enrages the senators, who instantly banish Alcibiades. Indignant at this new injury he com-plains bitterly:

> I have kept back their foes
> While they have told their money and let out
> Their coin upon large interest, I myself
> Rich only in large hurts. All those for this?
> Is this the balsam that the usuring Senate
> Pours into captains' wounds? Banishment! (106)

If wrongs or sorrows cannot be averted, they may be placated or as-suaged. Of the three figures concerned with their alleviation, the first is paramythia, which seeks to console or to diminish sorrow. Francisco tries to comfort Alonso, who is grieving because he believes Ferdinand is drowned.

> Sir, he may live.
> I saw him beat the surges under him
> And ride upon their backs. He trod the water,
> Whose enmity he flung aside, and breasted
> The surge most swol'n that met him. . . . I not doubt
> He came alive to land. (*Tem.*, 2.1.113–32)

Titus Andronicus assures his son Lucius that he ought to rejoice rather than grieve at his banishment from Rome.

> Why, foolish Lucius, dost thou not perceive
> That Rome is but a wilderness of tigers?
> Tigers must prey, and Rome affords no prey
> But me and mine. How happy art thou then
> From these devourers to be banished! (*Tit.*, 3.1.53)

Medela is a figure which seeks to palliate by conciliatory words the offenses of a friend when they can neither be defended nor denied. Thus Alcibiades admits but extenuates Timon's faults.

> To kill, I grant, is sin's extremest gust;
> But, in defence, by mercy, 'tis most just.
> To be in anger is impiety;
> But who is man that is not angry?
> Weigh but the crime with this. (3.5.54)

Menenius endeavors to mollify the people's wrath against Coriolanus by reminding them that his faults are in some measure occasioned by his services to them.

> Consider this: he has been bred i' th' wars
> Since 'a could draw a sword, and is ill-school'd
> In bolted language; meal and bran together
> He throws without distinction. (3.1.320)

Philophronesis seeks to mitigate by gentle speech and humble submission the anger of an adversary whose might is too great to be overcome. Mark Antony resorts to this figure immediately on learning of Caesar's murder, in order to gain a safe interview with the assassins. He sends his servant with this message to Brutus:

> *Servant.* Thus, Brutus, did my master bid me kneel;
> Thus did Mark Antony bid me fall down;
> And being prostrate thus he bade me say:
> Brutus is noble, wise, valiant, and honest;
> Caesar was mighty, bold, royal, and loving.
> Say I love Brutus and I honour him;
> Say I fear'd Caesar, honour'd him and lov'd him.
> If Brutus will vouchsafe that Antony
> May safely come to him and be resolv'd
> How Caesar hath deserv'd to lie in death,

> Mark Antony shall not love Caesar dead
> So well as Brutus living; but will follow
> The fortunes and affairs of noble Brutus
> Thorough the hazards of this untrod state
> With all true faith. So says my master Antony. (*JC*, 3.1.123)

Cleopatra kneels before Octavius Caesar, military victor over her own and Antony's forces.

> My master and my lord
> I must obey. . . . Sole sir o' th' world . . .
>   'Tis yours, and we,
> Your scutcheons and your signs of conquest, shall
> Hang in what place you please! (*A & C*, 5.2.116–36)

In contrast to figures that seek to placate are those that mock and taunt.[2] Mycterismus is a scornful mock, sometimes accompanied by facial gesture, as drawing the lip awry. The tribunes remark how Coriolanus mocked them in precisely this manner.

> *Sicinius*. When we were chosen tribunes for the people—
> *Brutus*. Mark'd you his lip and eyes?
> *Sicinius*.   Nay, but his taunts!
> *Brutus*. Being mov'd, he will not spare to gird the gods.
> *Sicinius*. Bemock the modest moon. (*Cor.*, 1.1.258)

When it is conveyed by words without facial gesture, mycterismus is a subtle rather than an open mock. Antony notes it in Cleopatra's rejoinder to his remark on Octavius' swift approach.

> *Cleopatra*. Celerity is never more admir'd
> Than by the negligent.
> *Antony*.   A good rebuke,
> Which might have well becom'd the best of men
> To taunt at slackness. (*A & C*, 3.7.25)

Hamlet comments scornfully on his mother's hasty marriage.

> The funeral bak'd meats
> Did coldly furnish forth the marriage tables. (1.2.180)

Mycterismus is characteristic of Apemantus.

---

[2] Shakespeare often refers to them. For instance: "bitter taunts" (*3H6*, 2.6.66), "bitter scoffs" (*R3*, 1.3.104), "biting jest" (*R3*, 2.4.30), "bitter jest" (*LLL*, 4.3.174), "sharp mocks" (*LLL*, 5.2.251), "bitter mock" (*H5*, 2.4.122), "He [Falstaff] was full of jests, and gipes, and knaveries, and mocks" (*H5*, 4.7.51).

Apemantus. Canst not read?
Page. No.
Apemantus. There will little learning die, then, that day thou art hang'd.
(*Tim.*, 2.2.84)

Timon, however, outdoes him at his own game.

Apemantus. There is no leprosy but what thou speak'st.
Timon. If I name thee. (4.3.367)

The tennis balls and the message sent to King Henry V by the Dauphin constitute a mock at Henry's reveling youth, and are so received by him. Henry sends back an answer which turns the derisive gift of tennis balls to his own advantage.

> When we have match'd our rackets to these balls,
> We will in France (by God's grace) play a set
> Shall strike his father's crown into the hazard.
> . . . tell the pleasant Prince this mock of his
> Hath turn'd his balls to gunstones . . . (*H5*, 1.2.261–82)

Sarcasmus is a more bitter taunt than mycterismus, a more open mock. An instance excellent for its very hideousness occurs in *Titus Andronicus*, where Demetrius and Chiron mock Lavinia after they have maimed and ravished her.

> *Demetrius.* So, now go tell, and if thy tongue can speak,
> Who 'twas that cut thy tongue and ravish'd thee.
> *Chiron.* Write down thy mind, bewray thy meaning so,
> An if thy stumps will let thee play the scribe.
> *Demetrius.* See how with signs and tokens she can scrowl. . . .
> *Chiron.* An 'twere my cause, I should go hang myself.
> *Demetrius.* If thou hadst hands to help thee knit the cord.
> (2.4.1–10)

The bastard mercilessly taunts the Duke of Austria, deriding him as an arrant coward wearing a lion's hide. He keeps repeating the gibe he caught up from Constance:

> And hang a calve's-skin on those recreant limbs. (*KJ*, 3.1.128–299)

Antony seizes an opportunity to scoff at Brutus.

> *Brutus.* Good words are better than bad strokes, Octavius.
> *Antony.* In your bad strokes, Brutus, you give good words;
> Witness the hole you made in Caesar's heart,
> Crying 'Long live! Hail, Caesar!' (*JC*, 5.1.29)

With impudent sarcasm the watchmen twit Menenius with his own words
uttered in protest a few moments before when they had attempted to deny
him access to Coriolanus, who has just rebuffed him.

> *1. Watch.* Now, sir, is your name Menenius?
> *2. Watch.* 'Tis a spell, you see, of much power. You know the way home
> again. . . . What cause do you think I have to swoond? (5.2.101)

Not far removed from mocks and taunts are accusations and reprehen-
sions. By the figure epiplexis, or percontatio, one asks questions, not in
order to know, but to chide or reprehend. Thus with scathing questions
Coriolanus denounces the tribunes for having incensed the people against
him after he had begged and obtained their voices for the consulship.

> Are these your herd?
> Must these have voices, that can yield them now
> And straight disclaim their tongues? What are your offices?
> You being their mouths, why rule you not their teeth?
> Have you not set them on? (3.1.33)

Upbraiding another for ingratitude or impiety constitutes onedismus,
a figure which Shakespeare uses with intense vehemence. Suffering from
Goneril's ingratitude, Lear wishes her to have no child, or else one that
will

> Turn all her mother's pains and benefits
> To laughter and contempt, that she may feel
> How sharper than a serpent's tooth it is
> To have a thankless child! (1.4.308)

King Henry V bitterly reproaches Lord Scroop who, having borne the
key of all his counsels and known the very bottom of his soul, has nonetheless connived to betray him for foreign gold. This treason is so odious
that it has got the voice in hell for excellence and is like another fall of
man (*H5*, 2.2.94–142). The bastard excoriates the English lords who
joined the Dauphin against King John.

> And you degenerate, you ingrate revolts,
> You bloody Neroes, ripping up the womb
> Of your dear Mother England, blush for shame! (*KJ*, 5.2.151)

Coriolanus upbraids the plebeians for their inconstancy.

> He that trusts to you,
> Where he should find you lions, finds you hares;

Where foxes, geese. You are no surer, no,
Than is the coal of fire upon the ice
Or hailstone in the sun. . . . He that depends
Upon your favours swims with fins of lead
And hews down oaks with rushes. Hang ye! Trust ye?
With every minute you do change a mind
And call him noble that was now your hate,
Him vile that was your garland. (*Cor.*, 1.1.174–88)

By categoria one lays open the secret wickedness of another before his face, as Hamlet does when he accuses his mother of

Such an act
That blurs the grace and blush of modesty;
Calls virtue hypocrite; takes off the rose
From the fair forehead of an innocent love,
And sets a blister there; makes marriage vows
As false as dicer's oaths. (3.4.40)

Octavius charges Antony:

I wrote to you
When rioting in Alexandria. You
Did pocket up my letters, and with taunts
Did gibe my missive out of audience. (*A & C*, 2.2.71)

Proclees is a figure whereby one provokes an adversary to the conflict by a vehement accusation or by a confident offer of justification. Bolingbroke goads Mowbray to combat by sharply accusing him of appropriating to his own uses the soldiers' pay, of plotting Gloucester's death, and of having a hand in many treasons (*R2*, 1.1.88–103). The tribunes quite deliberately use this figure to provoke Coriolanus to his own ruin, knowing how easily and to what uncontrolled passion he can be aroused. When he comes back to the people, resolved to speak mildly, Sicinius demands that he answer their charge.

We charge you that you have contriv'd to take
From Rome all season'd office and to wind
Yourself into a power tyrannical,
For which you are a traitor to the people. (*Cor.*, 3.3.63)

The provocation works as planned. Mildness forgotten, Coriolanus answers in unrestrained fury, caring not that he courts death in so doing. Later Aufidius easily gains his revenge by the same device, calling Coriolanus "thou boy of tears" (5.6.100), provoking him thereby so to vent his spleen that the people cry, "Tear him to pieces!" and the conspirators kill him. An instance of the second kind of proclees, the confident offer of justification, is Duke Humphrey's challenge to the lords who have arrested him for treason:

> A heart unspotted is not easily daunted.
> The purest spring is not so free from mud
> As I am clear of treason to my sovereign.
> Who can accuse me? Wherein am I guilty? (*2H6*, 3.1.100)

Bdelygmia is a figure whereby one expresses hate or abhorrence, usually in a few words, as Lear does when he exclaims to Oswald, Goneril's steward,

> Out, varlet, from my sight! (2.4.190)

At greater length Coriolanus voices his abhorrence of the common soldiers who retreated instead of following him.

> You shames of Rome! you herd of— Biles and plagues
> Plaster you o'er, that you may be abhorr'd
> Farther than seen . . . You souls of geese
> That bear the shapes of men, how have you run
> From slaves that apes would beat! Pluto and hell!
> All hurt behind! backs red, and faces pale
> With flight and agued fear! (1.4.31–8)

Troilus uses this figure to express his scorn for the counsel of Hector, who would conclude a negotiated peace with the Greeks by restoring Helen to them, as Nestor demands.

> Fie, fie my brother!
> Weigh you the worth and honour of a king
> So great as our dread father in a scale
> Of common ounces? Will you with counters sum
> The past-proportion of his infinite?
> And buckle in a waist most fathomless
> With spans and inches so diminutive
> As fears and reasons? Fie, for godly shame! (*T & C*, 2.2.25)

Answering Troilus, Helenus estimates his argument for what it is, an impassioned appeal to feeling, empty of reason.

Threats and curses abound in Shakespeare's works. By the figure cataplexis one threatens plagues or punishments, as when Richard II declares to the rebels:

> Yet know, my master, God omnipotent,
> Is mustering in his clouds on our behalf
> Armies of pestilence, and they shall strike
> Your children yet unborn and unbegot
> That lift your vassal hands against my head
> And threat the glory of my precious crown. (*R2*, 3.3.85)

Richard's veneration of the sacredness of an anointed king and his faith in God's sanction of his rights confer on his character, despite his faults, a dignity which gives his fall the quality of tragedy. His use of cataplexis has in consequence an elevation of tone quite lacking in Cleopatra's use of the same figure to threaten the messenger who brings her news of Antony's marriage to Octavia.

> Hence,
> Horrible villain! or I'll spurn thine eyes
> Like balls from me. I'll unhair thy head!
> Thou shalt be whipp'd with wire and stew'd in brine,
> Smarting in ling'ring pickle. (*A & C*, 2.5.62)

Prospero answers Caliban's greeting, which is a curse, with the assurance that he shall be punished for it.

> For this, be sure, to-night thou shalt have cramps,
> Side-stitches that shall pen thy breath up; urchins
> Shall, for that vast of night that they may work,
> All exercise on thee; thou shalt be pinch'd
> As thick as honeycomb, each pinch more stinging
> Than bees that made 'em. (*Tem.*, 1.2.325)

In the use of the figure ara, or cursing, Shakespeare rivals the writers of the imprecatory psalms in both variety and vehemence. Lucrece calls upon Time to curse Tarquin in every moment of his day and night (*RL*, 968–99). When Imogen awakens from the drug which Pisanio had given her and sees a headless body dressed in familiar garments, she thinks it is the body of her husband Posthumus killed by Pisanio and cries out:

> Pisanio,
> All curses madded Hecuba gave the Greeks,
> And mine to boot, be darted on thee! (*Cym.*, 4.2.312)

Curses are numerous and vehement in *Richard III*. Margaret execrates all her enemies (1.3.195–303). Later she is asked by one of them, Edward IV's queen, whose wrongs from Richard are now piled high,

to teach her how to curse; and Richard's mother, too, joins in the imprecation (4.4). Caliban's characteristic response to Prospero is a malediction,
and it is chiefly by this means that he manifests his evil nature. Cursing
attains its peak, however, in *Timon*. Flaminius, Timon's loyal servant,
fitly reprobates Lucullus by wishing that molten gold, the gold which
he has refused to lend Timon, may scald him and that the meat which
he has eaten at Timon's cost may engender disease in him (3.1.54–66).
Alcibiades invokes a withering imprecation on the senators who have rejected his plea for Timon.

> Now the gods keep you old enough that you may live
> Only in bone, that none may look on you! (3.5.104)

In Timon himself, the man who was once the ultra-beneficent lover of
men and has now become the ultra-bitter misanthrope, hating even himself, cursing appears as a settled trait, all-inclusive in its scope and venom.

> O blessed breeding sun, draw from the earth
> Rotten humidity; below thy sister's orb
> Infect the air! . . . be abhorr'd
> All feasts, societies, and throngs of men! . . .
> Destruction fang mankind! (4.3.1–23)

When Alcibiades declares that he is on his way to attack Athens, Timon
answers:

> The gods confound them all in thy conquest,
> And thee after, when thou hast conquered! . . .
> Be as a planetary plague when Jove
> Will o'er some high-vic'd city hang his poison
> In the sick air. (103–10)

Not even death stops Timon's cursing, for on his gravestone is the epitaph
which he himself devised:

> A plague consume you wicked caitiffs left. (5.4.71)

A man may execrate himself, as Othello does when, having killed Desdemona, he learns of her innocence (5.2.276–80). There is special irony,
however, when a man unwittingly invokes a curse upon himself, as Macbeth does in imprecating the weird sisters.

> Infected be the air whereon they ride,
> And damn'd all those that trust them! (4.1.138)

Lady Anne unwittingly pronounces a malediction on herself in cursing

Richard's wife, if ever he have one (*R3*, 1.2.26). And so does Cressida,
when she exclaims:

> O you gods divine,
> Make Cressid's name the very crown of falsehood
> If ever she leave Troilus! (4.2.105)

The figure eulogia pronounces a blessing. Juno and Ceres sing songs
blessing Ferdinand and Miranda (*Tem.*, 4.1.106–17). An old man invokes a blessing on Ross and Macduff as they bid farewell to him.

> God's benison go with you, and with those
> That would make good of bad, and friends of foes!
>   (*Mac.*, 2.4.40)

Blinded Gloucester, seeing more clearly than with fleshly eyes the goodness of the son he has wronged, beseeches the gods:

> If Edgar live, O, bless him! (*Lear*, 4.6.40)

And when Edgar, whom he does not recognize, offers to lead him to a
place to dwell, he gives thanks and fervently blesses him.

> Hearty thanks.
> The bounty and the benison of heaven
> To boot, and boot! (228)

Restoring to Cymbeline the two sons whom he has fostered, Belarius invokes on them a blessing.

> The benediction of these covering heavens
> Fall on their heads like dew! for they are worthy
> To inlay heaven with stars. (*Cym.*, 5.5.350)

Paeanismus expresses exuberance of joy. Portia's joy when Bassanio
chooses the right casket is so great that she can hardly contain it.

> O love, be moderate; allay thy ecstasy;
> In measure rain thy joy; scant this excess!
> I feel too much thy blessing. Make it less
> For fear I surfeit! (*MV*, 3.2.111)

Pericles is so overcome with joy to find his lost daughter Marina that he
begs Helicanus:

> Give me a gash, put me to present pain,
> Lest this great sea of joys rushing upon me

> O'erbear the shores of my mortality
> And drown me with their sweetness. (*Per.*, 5.2.193)

Young Richard conceives the joy of wearing the crown with such lyric intensity that he moves his father York to take up arms to gain it.

> And, father, do but think
> How sweet a thing it is to wear a crown,
> Within whose circuit is Elysium
> And all that poets feign of bliss and joy. (*3H6*, 1.2.28)

Later he himself wades through blood to achieve it.

In their meticulous textbook analyses the figurists seem to have listed all variations in the scale of emotion, but one is impressed by their inadequacy to compass the range of Shakespeare, especially in his later tragedies. The poet in *Timon* confesses his inability to depict in words the wrongs Timon has suffered.

> I am rapt, and cannot cover
> The monstrous bulk of this ingratitude
> With any size of words. (5.1.67)

Unlike this poet, Shakespeare seems able to express the monstrous bulk of any passion with words that seem at times almost to split the powers of language in their mounting intensity. His growth in the capacity to express vehemence is one mark of his increasing control over the medium of his art. It is instructive to trace chronologically by means of the following selected passages his development in portraying *pathos*.

The vehemence of Margaret in *3 Henry VI* and in *Richard III* is less artistically delineated than the vehemence of Constance in *King John*. Both women have recourse to curses and figures of repetition; but Margaret's lamentations in the recital of her woes are rhetorical in the Senecan style, more formal, less varied, less human than Constance's effusion of grief—and this in spite of the fact that Margaret's losses were greater. Constance cannot believe the news that there is peace between Philip and John, peace that spells the utter frustration of her hopes and the invasion of clutching fears. Questions, exclamations, and the coupling of contraries mark her emotional excitement and confusion (*KJ*, 3.1.1–37). When Arthur is taken to England as a prisoner, she tears her hair, addresses death in vivid apostrophe, fears that canker-sorrow will so rob Arthur of his native beauty that she will not know him in heaven. She wishes to be maddened and thereby made less sensible of grief, for, she complains,

> Grief fills the room up of my absent child:
> Lies in his bed, walks up and down with me,
> Puts on his pretty looks, repeats his words,
> Remembers me of all his gracious parts,
> Stuffs out his vacant garments with his form. (*KJ*, 3.4.93)

A much greater advance in expressing vehemence appears in Hamlet's first and second soliloquies, where feeling predominates over thought.

> O that this too too solid flesh would melt . . .
> Or that the Everlasting had not fix'd
> His canon 'gainst self-slaughter! (1.2.120–32)

Exclamation, wishing, contempt conveyed through meiosis carry the burden: the world is an unweeded garden, the shoes his mother wore to his father's funeral were not old before she married his uncle. Although Hamlet pours out his emotion to relieve himself, the audience shares it, enters into it, and is moved by it, for here surely Shakespeare has achieved true poetic, in which the audience identifies itself with the character and participates in his experiences. The second soliloquy is remarkable in that Hamlet himself is moved by the *pathos* of the player's counterfeit passion to real passion at his own lack of vigor in punishing his father's murderer.

> O, what a rogue and peasant slave am I! . . .
> What's Hecuba to him or he to Hecuba,
> That he should weep for her? What would he do,
> Had he the motive and the cue for passion
> That I have? He would drown the stage with tears . . .
> But I am pigeon-liver'd and lack gall
> To make oppression bitter, or ere this
> I should have fatted all the region kites,
> With this slave's offal. Bloody, bawdy villain! (2.2.576–607)

Suddenly Hamlet sees this very pouring out of feeling to be a futile thing, cries "Fie upon't! foh! About, my brain!" (616), turns from *pathos* to *logos* and devises the plan to test both the ghost's veracity and the king's guilt by means of a play.

Shakespeare achieves in *Othello* an argument of *pathos* as remarkable for its convincingness as for its complexity. Coming to kill Desdemona asleep on her bed, the Moor repeats:

> It is the cause, it is the cause, my soul. (5.2.1)

Shakespeare somehow invests the strange, dread scene that follows with dignity, elevation, and deepest pathos. Somehow he causes us to accept

Othello at his own rating, as a sort of private priest sacrificing to justice what he most loves. Although we know he is deceived, there is convincing genuineness in his feelings whose subtle complexity he perfectly expresses. He kisses Desdemona.

> *Othello.* O balmy breath, that doth almost persuade
> Justice to break her sword! One more, one more!
> Be thus when thou art dead, and I will kill thee,
> And love thee after. One more, and this the last!
> So sweet was ne'er so fatal. I must weep,
> But they are cruel tears. This sorrow's heavenly;
> It strikes where it doth love. She wakes.
> *Desdemona.* Who's there? Othello?
> *Othello.*   Ay, Desdemona. . . .
> If you bethink yourself of any crime
> Unreconcil'd as yet to heaven and grace,
> Solicit for it straight. . . . I will walk by.
> I would not kill thy unprepared spirit.
> No, heaven forfend! I would not kill thy soul.
> *Desdemona.* Talk you of killing?
> *Othello.*   Ay, I do.
> *Desdemona.*   Then heaven
> Have mercy on me!
> *Othello.*   Amen, with all my heart! (5.2.16–34)

Surely, thus to give us Desdemona and Othello with equal and perfect sympathy, to present a deed of death and vengeance with equal attention to heaven and prayer on the part of slayer and slain, strangely to invest the whole at one stroke with nobility and darkest tragedy, is perfect dramatic art. We enter with heart and mind into each character—think, feel, suffer with each.

The *pathos* of Lear is rooted in his imperious sense of the power and force of his will, which can make and unmake, can confer worth or remove it arbitrarily. For instance, he addresses Burgundy regarding Cordelia:

> Will you, with these infirmities she owes,
> Unfriended, new adopted to our hate,
> Dow'r'd with our curse, and stranger'd with our oath,
> Take her, or leave her? (1.1.205)

Burgundy will not take her dowerless. But her other suitor, the King of France, comments on the unreason, the blind passion of Lear.

> This is most strange,
> That she that even but now was your best object,
> The argument of your praise, balm of your age,
> Most best, most dearest, should in this trice of time
> Commit a thing so monstrous to dismantle
> So many folds of favour. (216)

France recognizes that Cordelia is herself a dowry and, praising her in coupled contraries, joyfully chooses her for his queen.

> Fairest Cordelia, that art most rich, being poor;
> Most choice, forsaken; and most lov'd, despis'd . . .
> Thy dow'rless daughter, King, thrown to my chance,
> Is queen of us, of ours, and our fair France. (253–60)

The amazement of Lear when Goneril rebukes him for the conduct of his retainers, and even his own, is so overwhelming, so great a shock to his accustomed sense of sovereignty, that it causes him to question his identity.

> Doth any here know me? This is not Lear. . . .
> Who is it that can tell me who I am? (1.4.246–50)

In a rage he curses Goneril, orders his horses saddled, and goes to Regan. He finds that she and Cornwall have contemptuously put his messenger Kent into the stocks. Regan outdoes Goneril by denying that her father needs even one retainer. Flouted by both his daughters, Lear leaves them both, exclaiming:

> I have full cause of weeping, but this heart
> Shall break into a hundred thousand flaws
> Or ere I'll weep. O fool, I shall go mad! (2.4.287)

He goes out into the storm and to the roaring elements unburdens his grief.

> I tax not you, you elements, with unkindness.
> I never gave you kingdom, call'd you children,
> You owe me no subscription. Then let fall
> Your horrible pleasure. Here I stand your slave,
> A poor, infirm, weak, and despis'd old man.
> But yet I call you servile ministers,
> That will with two pernicious daughters join
> Your high-engender'd battles 'gainst a head
> So old and white as this! O! O! 'tis foul! (3.2.16)

Shakespeare has indeed traveled a long way from the chorus of woes in *Richard III*. In *Lear* he depicts with dramatic intensity and power an anguished heart, a tottering brain, magnified into a world of woe against the cosmic background of a raging storm on a barren heath. To Kent, who would have him seek shelter, Lear explains:

> Thou think'st 'tis much that this contentious storm
> Invades us to the skin. So 'tis to thee;
> But where the greater malady is fix'd,
> The lesser is scarce felt. . . .
>   The tempest in my mind
> Doth from my senses take all feeling else
> Save what beats there. Filial ingratitude!
> Is it not as this mouth should tear this hand
> For lifting food to't? But I will punish home!
> No, I will weep no more. In such a night
> To shut me out! Pour on; I will endure.
> In such a night as this! O Regan, Goneril!
> Your old kind father, whose frank heart gave all!
> O, that way madness lies; let me shun that!
> No more of that. (3.4.6–21)

When Gloucester is brought bound before Regan and Cornwall, he reprehends their cruelty in shutting their doors on Lear.

> The sea, with such a storm as his bare head
> In hell-black night endur'd, would have buoy'd up
> And quench'd the stelled fires.
> Yet, poor old heart, he holp the heavens to rain.
> If wolves had at thy gate howl'd that stern time,
> Thou shouldst have said, 'Good porter, turn the key.' (3.7.59)

Their answer is to gouge out Gloucester's eyes and thrust him out of their gates. At the end, Lear, his mind partly restored by Cordelia's kindness, forgiveness, and love, is happy to go to prison with her, where they "two alone will sing like birds i' th' cage" (5.3.9). But he cannot endure the loss of this true love so hardly found, and when he comes upon the stage bearing in his arms her dead body whose breath will come now no more—never, never, never—he dies of grief.

Passion, both evil and good, is portrayed in *Macbeth* with clarity, swiftness, immediacy. Malcolm tries to console Macduff, who has just learned that his wife, children, and servants are all killed.

> *Malcolm.*   Be comforted.
> Let's make us med'cines of our great revenge
> To cure this deadly grief.

Macduff. He has no children. All my pretty ones?
Did you say all? O hell-kite! All? . . .
Malcolm. Dispute it like a man.
Macduff.   I shall do so;
But I must also feel it as a man. . . .
                        Did heaven look on
And would not take their part? (4.3.213–24)

In *Hamlet, Othello, Lear,* and *Macbeth* Shakespeare achieves a perfect balance and proportioning of thought and feeling, of *logos* and *pathos*, of dianoia, character, and plot. In the tragedies that follow, *Antony and Cleopatra, Coriolanus,* and *Timon,* emotion becomes increasingly preponderant, even excessive, although its expression remains poetic.

Cleopatra's frenzy at the news that Antony has married Octavia contrasts strongly with Margaret's frenzies and is a measure of Shakespeare's increased skill in expressing vehemence. Margaret's was Senecan declamation. This is rapid, lively dialogue, showing an imperious woman's petulant rage driving the messenger away with his story half told, calling him back, fearing to know, fearful not to know. Her emotional confusion expresses itself fitly in contradictories.

> Let him for ever go!—let him not!—Charmian,
> Though he be painted one way like a Gorgon,
> The other way's a Mars. (*A & C,* 2.5.115)

Antony in short space runs the gamut of emotion. Shamed by his flight from Caesar, he dismisses his men and upbraids Cleopatra.

> *Antony.* O whither hast thou led me, Egypt? See
> How I convey my shame out of thine eyes
> By looking back what I have left behind
> Stroy'd in dishonour.
> *Cleopatra.*   O my lord, my lord,
> Forgive my fearful sails! I little thought
> You would have followed.
> *Antony.*   Egypt, thou knew'st too well
> My heart was to thy rudder tied by th' strings,
> And thou shouldst tow me after. O'er my spirit
> Thy full supremacy thou knew'st, and that
> Thy beck might from the bidding of the gods
> Command me. (3.11.51)

Her contrition is enough, for even one of her tears is worth all that he has won and lost. Repaid with a kiss, he is no longer depressed. Will and

affection have so blinded his judgment that he writes a challenge to
Caesar to meet him in single combat. As Enobarbus remarks scornfully:

> Yes, like enough high-battled Caesar will
> Unstate his happiness and be stag'd to th' show
> Against a sworder . . . That he should dream,
> Knowing all measures, that full Caesar will
> Answer his emptiness! (3.13.29–36)

In a rage at seeing Caesar's ambassador kiss Cleopatra's hand, Antony
orders him whipped. Assured again of Cleopatra's love, his heart is renewed for the fight against Caesar. He will be treble-sinewed, will contend with death. Enobarbus comments:

> A diminution in our captain's brain
> Restores his heart. When valour preys on reason,
> It eats the sword it fights with. (198)

Cleopatra, who has been disarmed of her dagger by Proculeius, vehemently declares that she will not grace Caesar's triumph.

> 　　　　　　　　　Know, sir, that I
> Will not wait pinion'd at your master's court
> Nor once be chastis'd with the sober eye
> Of dull Octavia. Shall they hoist me up
> And show me to the shouting varlotry
> Of censuring Rome? Rather a ditch in Egypt
> Be gentle grave unto me! Rather on Nilus' mud
> Lay me stark-nak'd and let the waterflies
> Blow me into abhorring! Rather make
> My country's high pyramides my gibbet
> And hang me up in chains! (5.2.52)

When she sees Antony die, Cleopatra utters her conception of his un-
bounded greatness.

> The crown o' th' earth doth melt. . . . The odds is gone,
> And there is nothing left remarkable
> Beneath the visiting moon. . . . It were for me
> To throw my sceptre at the injurious gods,
> To tell them that this world did equal theirs
> Till they had stol'n our jewel. (4.15.63–78)

Coriolanus' bitter disdain and contempt of the people is the outstanding
passion of the play in which he appears. It is also the dominating theme

and motivating force in the plot, and the trait persistently perverting and poisoning the character of the hero. His military virtue, great as it is, cannot cover this defect. We first meet him answering a citizen:

> He that will give good words to thee will flatter
> Beneath abhorring. What would you have, you curs,
> That like nor peace nor war? The one affrights you,
> The other makes you proud. (1.1.171)

Importuned by his friends, but most of all impelled by his mother's strenuous arguments, Coriolanus consents to return to the people and speak gently to them in order to win their favor. But so repugnant is this to his proud nature that he invokes a harlot's spirit to possess him, reminding us of Lady Macbeth's invocation of the spirits of evil.

> Away, my disposition, and possess me
> Some harlot's spirit! My throat of war be turn'd,
> Which quier'd with my drum, into a pipe
> Small as an eunuch or the virgin voice
> That babies lulls asleep! The smiles of knaves
> Tent in my cheeks, and schoolboys' tears take up
> The glasses of my sight! A beggar's tongue
> Make motion through my lips, and my arm'd knees,
> Who bow'd but in my stirrup, bend like his
> That hath receiv'd an alms! . . . I'll mountebank their loves,
> Cog their hearts from them, and come home belov'd
> Of all the trades in Rome. . . . I'll return consul,
> Or never trust to what my tongue can do
> I' th' way of flattery further. (3.2.111–37)

The tribunes, however, know their man. Sicinius charges him with being a traitor to the people, and thereby applies the spark which instantly burns up his resolution to speak mildly.

> The fires i' th' lowest hell fold-in the people!
> Call me their traitor, thou injurious tribune?
> Within thine eyes sat twenty thousand deaths,
> In thy hands clutch'd as many millions, in
> Thy lying tongue both numbers, I would say
> 'Thou liest' unto thee with a voice as free
> As I do pray the gods. . . .
> Let them pronounce the steep Tarpeian death,
> Vagabond exile, flaying, pent to linger

> But with a grain a day—I would not buy
> Their mercy at the price of one fair word,
> Nor check my courage for what they can give,
> To hav't with saying 'Good morrow.' (3.3.68–93)

Saved from immediate violent death only by Menenius' intervention, Coriolanus is banished. In proud, unbending disdain, he flings at the people his answer to the sentence.

> You common cry of curs, whose breath I hate
> As reek o' th' rotten fens, whose loves I prize
> As the dead carcasses of unburied men
> That do corrupt my air, I banish you! . . .
> Let every feeble rumour shake your hearts!
> Your enemies with nodding of their plumes
> Fan you into despair! Have the power still
> To banish your defenders, till at length
> Your ignorance . . . deliver you, as most
> Abated captives, to some nation
> That won you without blows! Despising
> For you the city, I turn my back.
> There is a world elsewhere. (120–35)

Yet in this play all is not hate. Joy and blessing have a place. Lartius prays a blessing on Coriolanus as he goes to seek Aufidius on the battlefield.

> Now the fair goddess Fortune
> Fall deep in love with thee, and her great charms
> Misguide thy opposers' swords! Bold gentleman,
> Prosperity be thy page! (1.5.21)

And when he has won the victory, Coriolanus joyfully exclaims to his general, Cominius:

> O, let me clip ye
> In arms as sound as when I woo'd, in heart
> As merry as when our nuptial day was done . . . (1.6.29)

Some of the citizens, giving him their vote as consul, wish him well.

The gods give him joy and make him good friend to the people! (2.3.141)

And Coriolanus, a soldier, pronounces on his little son the blessing he most values.

> The god of soldiers,
> With the consent of supreme Jove, inform
> Thy thoughts with nobleness, that thou mayst prove

> To shame unvulnerable, and stick i' th' wars
> Like a great seamark, standing every flaw
> And saving those that eye thee! (5.3.70)

In Timon's misanthropy, bitter vehemence reaches the nadir of intensity, for here it has no lift, as in *Coriolanus*, where it achieves elevation both through a fundamental nobility in the hero's character and motives and through its soaring expression. Coriolanus abhors flattery, but Timon in his munificence is its complete pawn; in his want, a cynic thinking no man free of it. He is as undiscriminating in one extreme as in the other, and therefore as little admirable. His unalloyed bitterness, unreachable by reason, makes even Apemantus seem by contrast mild and sweet. Timon has rendered himself impenetrable to reason by besmirching all testimony, even all reasoning, at the root. If all Cretans are liars, no Cretan can be believed. Timon goes further than this, disbelieving, not one nation, but all mankind, for he declares every man a flatterer.

> Who dares, who dares
> In purity of manhood stand upright
> And say 'This man's a flatterer'? If one be,
> So are they all. (4.3.13)

It is the undiscriminating inclusiveness of Timon's bitterness which gives it its special character. Leaving Athens, he pours out his curses.

> Let me look back upon thee. O thou wall
> That girdles in those wolves, dive in the earth
> And fence not Athens! Matrons, turn incontinent!
> Obedience fail in children! Slaves and fools,
> Pluck the grave wrinkled Senate from the bench
> And minister in their steads! . . . Bankrupts, hold fast!
> Rather than render back, out with your knives
> And cut your trusters' throats! Bound servants, steal!
>   . . . Plagues incident to men,
> Your potent and infectious fevers heap
> On Athens, ripe for stroke! . . . Lust and liberty
> Creep in the minds and marrows of our youth,
> That 'gainst the stream of virtue they may strive
> And drown themselves in riot! . . . Breath infect breath,
> That their society (as their friendship) may
> Be merely poison! (4.1.1–32)

After this there is but one glimmer of light in the blackness of Timon's

life, and this is wrought by *pathos*, not by *logos*. Timon is finally touched
by the true grief of his faithful servant Flavius over his present condition.

> What, dost thou weep? Come nearer. Then I love thee
> Because thou art a woman and disclaim'st
> Flinty mankind, . . . Had I a steward
> So true, so just, and now so comfortable?
> It almost turns my dangerous nature mild.
> Let me behold thy face. Surely, this man
> Was born of woman. (4.3.489–501)

Immediately this evidence of genuine *pathos* is converted to *ethos*, to
confidence in this one man, when he distrusts and hates all others.

> Forgive my general and exceptless rashness,
> You perpetual-sober gods! I do proclaim
> One honest man. Mistake me not—but one!
> No more, I pray—and he's a steward,
> How fain would I have hated all mankind,
> And thou redeem'st thyself! But all save thee
> I fell with curses. (502)

2. *Ethos*

Ethos is the persuasion exerted upon the minds and hearts of the audience by the personal character of the speaker, causing them to believe in
his sincerity, his truth, his ability, his good will toward them. Both *logos*
and *pathos* promote *ethos*, for people more readily believe and trust a
speaker who reasons clearly and cogently and who creates in them a
friendly and sympathetic attitude toward himself and what he has to say.
Spontaneous and genuine feeling in him begets a like feeling in them and
convinces them of his sincerity. There is in *Macbeth* a good example of
pathos thus engendering *ethos*. To test Macduff, Malcolm tells him a
false story of his own wickedness. This arouses Macduff to such passion
that Malcolm, fully convinced of his integrity, truth, and honor, entrusts
to him his cause.

> Macduff, this noble passion,
> Child of integrity, hath from my soul
> Wip'd the black scruples, reconcil'd my thoughts
> To thy good truth and honour. Devilish Macbeth
> By many of these trains hath sought to win me
> Into his power; and modest wisdom plucks me
> From over-credulous haste; but God above

> Deal between thee and me! for even now
> I put myself to thy direction and
> Unspeak mine own detraction, here abjure
> The taints and blames I laid upon myself
> For strangers to my nature. (4.3.114)

There are four figures that promote *ethos* by revealing the sincerity and good will of the speaker.

By means of the figure comprobatio a man commends the good he sees in the judges whose confidence he wishes to win. Alcibiades, for example, prefaces his remarks to the senators of Athens on Timon's behalf with praise of their virtue and an expression of humility.

> Honour, health, and compassion to the Senate! . . .
> I am an humble suitor to your virtues;
> For pity is the virtue of the law . . .
> O my lords,
> As you are great, be pitifully good. (*Tim.*, 3.5.5–52)

By parrhesia one is humbly respectful or, if necessity demands, courageously outspoken in addressing those whom he ought to reverence or fear on a matter which concerns them or those near to them. Thus Paulina respectfully but fearlessly comes before Leontes to speak of his conduct toward his queen.

> Good my liege, I come;
> And I beseech you hear me, who professes
> Myself your loyal servant, your physician,
> Your most obedient counsellor; yet that dares
> Less appear so, in comforting your evils,
> Than such as most seem yours. I say, I come
> From your good queen. (*WT*, 2.3.52)

Savagely he rejects her and her plea, yet she persists.

> I'll not call you tyrant;
> But this most cruel usage of your queen
> (Not able to produce more accusation
> Than your own weak-hing'd fancy) something savours
> Of tyranny, and will ignoble make you,
> Yea, scandalous to the world. (115)

Although neither Alcibiades nor Paulina is successful in winning over the persons immediately addressed, their courage and honest intentions procure for each of them the good will of the audience attending the play.

By eucharistia one gives thanks for benefits received. Taking leave of
Cleon, Pericles expresses heartfelt thanks for both the hospitality ex-
tended to himself after a storm at sea and the promise to foster his babe
Marina.

> Most honour'd Cleon . . . You and your lady
> Take from my heart all thankfulness! The gods
> Make up the rest upon you! (*Per.*, 3.3.1–5)

Thaisa thanks Cerimon for saving her life.

> My recompense is thanks, that's all;
> Yet my good will is great, though the gift be small.
> (*Per.*, 3.4.17)

By syngnome one expresses forgiveness of injuries. An excellent example is Posthumus' forgiveness of Iachimo, who did him and Imogen
such grievous and malicious wrong.

> Kneel not to me.
> The pow'r that I have on you is to spare you;
> The malice towards you to forgive you. Live
> And deal with others better. (*Cym.*, 5.5.417)

In the *Rhetoric* Aristotle explains *ethos* as the confidence which the
personal goodness of the speaker inspires in the hearers, their belief in
his good sense, good moral character, and good will. And in the *Poetics*
he defines *ethos* or character as that element in a play which reveals the
moral purpose of the agents, the sort of thing they seek or avoid.[3] From
these two observations it seems fair to judge that the persuasion of *ethos*
in drama may be understood as the confidence and regard inspired in the
hearers by those characters who evince a good moral purpose. The characters in a play exercise this persuasion in two ways, rhetorically and
poetically. Because drama is poetic and because it posits two groups of
hearers, namely, the other characters in the play and the audience attending the play, *ethos* in drama presents certain complexities. It functions
rhetorically and directly when a character wins the confidence of other
characters by revealing, or appearing to reveal, a personal goodness which
is a factor in persuading them to do as he proposes. It functions poetically
and indirectly when the audience (whose office is to think, to judge, to
feel, but not to act) is persuaded of the goodness of a character, whether
the other characters in the play recognize that goodness or not and

---

[3] See p. 394, below.

whether they accept or reject what he proposes; in fact, the sympathy and admiration of the audience and the identification of themselves with the character tend to increase if he is rejected by his fellows. On the other hand, when the audience sees the other characters in the play deceived and led astray by the seeming goodness of a villain, the play acquires the note of dramatic irony.

Among the characters in Shakespeare's plays whose goodness and nobility win the admiration and high regard of the audience, we may single out for great personal integrity and adherence to principle York and the Bishop of Carlisle in *Richard II* and Banquo in *Macbeth*; for courage in opposing wrath and wrongdoing in a sovereign at risk to oneself, Kent, Camillo, Antigonus, and Paulina; for forgiveness of injuries and devotedness to him who wronged them, Kent, Cordelia, and Edgar; for loyalty and fidelity as a servant, Kent and Flavius; for limitless constancy and devotion to a friend, Antonio in *The Merchant of Venice;* for king-becoming and man-becoming graces, King Henry V.

So impressed is King Henry IV by the loyalty of York in reporting the treasonous plot to which York's own son Aumerle subscribed that he cries out in admiration:

> O loyal father of a treacherous son!
> Thou sheer, immaculate, and silver fountain,
> From whence this stream through muddy passages
> Hath held his current and defil'd himself! (*R2,* 5.3.60)

When the Bishop of Carlisle is brought to him as a prisoner, Henry pronounces a mild doom and high praise out of regard for the bishop's noble integrity evidenced in his speech championing Richard II (4.1.114–49), a fearless integrity respected even by the usurper whom Carlisle openly opposed.

> Carlisle, this is your doom:
> Choose out some secret place, some reverend room,
> More than thou hast, and with it joy thy life.
> So, as thou liv'st in peace, die free from strife;
> For though mine enemy thou hast ever been,
> High sparks of honour in thee have I seen. (5.6.24)

These two instances reveal interlinked *ethos,* for while the audience shares with King Henry the high regard for York and Carlisle evoked by the rectitude of their words and deeds, it accords to him its own esteem evoked by his generous praise of York and even more by his magnanimity displayed toward Carlisle.

Banquo had much the same external temptation as Macbeth. The witches told him he would be the father of kings, lesser than Macbeth and greater. Immediately recognizing the moral danger of accepting their prophecies as premises, he warns Macbeth:

> *Macbeth.* Do you not hope your children shall be kings,
> When those that gave the Thane of Cawdor to me
> Promis'd no less to them?
> *Banquo.*   That, trusted home,
> Might yet enkindle you unto the crown,
> Besides the Thane of Cawdor. But 'tis strange! (1.3.118)

There is not in Banquo's bosom, as in Macbeth's, a ready disposition to co-operate with evil; yet he is not cold or unhuman. Temptation kindles in him when reason is at rest, but he energetically resists it by rising from sleep and praying for help in the struggle.

> A heavy summons lies like lead upon me,
> And yet I would not sleep. Merciful powers,
> Restrain in me the cursed thoughts that nature
> Gives way to in repose! (2.1.6)

He meets Macbeth, who wants to discuss the weird sisters with him at some convenient time.

> *Macbeth.* It shall make honour for you.
> *Banquo.*   So I lose none
> In seeking to augment it but still keep
> My bosom franchis'd and allegiance clear,
> I shall be counsell'd. (2.1.26)

Macbeth recognizes all too well his friend's royalty of nature and the dauntless temper of his mind. In Banquo's integrity Macbeth's fears stick deep, and he hires murderers to dispatch him and his son Fleance in order to flout the prophecy that Banquo's children will be kings, and to relieve himself from fear (3.1).

Kent's respectful protest to Lear in Cordelia's behalf, an instance of the figure parrhesia, wins from the king only sudden and violent enmity and banishment, but it convinces the audience of Kent's uprightness and boundless honesty.

> *Kent.*   Royal Lear,
> Whom I have ever honour'd as my king,

Lov'd as my father, as my master follow'd,
As my great patron thought on in my prayers—
Lear. The bow is bent and drawn; make from the shaft.
Kent. Let it fall rather, though the fork invade
The region of my heart! Be Kent unmannerly
When Lear is mad. What wouldst thou do, old man?
Think'st thou that duty shall have dread to speak
When power to flattery bows? To plainness honour's bound
When majesty falls to folly. Reverse thy doom,
And in thy best consideration check
This hideous rashness. . . .
Lear. Kent, on thy life, no more!
Kent. My life I never held but as a pawn
To wage against thine enemies; nor fear to lose it,
Thy safety being the motive. . . .
Lear. O vassal! miscreant!
[*Lays his hand on his sword*] . . .
Kent. Do!
Kill thy physician, and the fee bestow
Upon the foul disease. Revoke thy gift,
Or, whilst I can vent clamour from my throat,
I'll tell thee thou dost evil. (1.1.141–69)

Kent's nobility of character is such that nothing can thwart it, for it converts all seeming-evil to good. Death has no fears for him, because he values more than his life the true good of his king who threatens it. Banishment he converts to an opportunity to cherish and safeguard as a servant the willful old man who rejected him as counsellor and friend. His forgiveness is in action, not in words, and his love extends far beyond mere forgiveness to devoted, self-sacrificing service and unquenchable constancy. When Lear dies of grief, Kent expresses relief that his racked life is at an end, and, faithful beyond death, he tells Albany that he himself will soon follow.

> I have a journey, sir, shortly to go.
> My master calls me; I must not say no. (5.3.321)

King Henry V exemplifies to an eminent degree the king-becoming graces listed by Malcolm (*Mac.*, 4.3.91–94), particularly justice, verity, mercy, lowliness, devotion, patience, and courage. To these are added faith and trust in God. Henry solemnly charges the two bishops justly and religiously to unfold his claim to France without wresting truth or miscreating titles, for it would be a dreadful wrong if lives should be spent in war for any but a just cause (*H5*, 1.2.9–32). He orders Exeter to free from prison a man who in excess of wine had railed against the king. Scroop, Grey, and Cambridge urge severity instead, that others may learn to fear. This counsel against mercy Henry turns upon their own heads when he reveals that their plot against his life has been discovered; to them he metes out justice (2.2.39–181: *cf*. Matt. 18:23–35).

Particularly before the Battle of Agincourt, Henry reveals his lowliness, patience, devotion, courage, and leadership. In disguise he mingles with his men the night before the battle, a soldier among soldiers. He endeavors to imbue them with his own conviction of the justice of their cause.

Methinks I could not die anywhere so contented as in the King's company, his cause being just and his quarrel honourable. (4.1.131)

He finds himself not too well thought of. Michael Williams doubts that the king will refuse to be ransomed, doubts his verity.

Ay, he said so, to make us fight cheerfully; but when our throats are cut, he may be ransom'd, and we ne'er the wiser. (204)

To bear this calumny requires patience, for Henry has indignantly rejected French overtures to negotiate a peace by ransom, and later he does so again. He remarks to the soldiers that the king is a man like themselves with like feelings, like fears; but that he may not show his fears, lest he dishearten his army. The soldiers reply that upon the king's conscience rests all responsibility for the lives to be lost, wives widowed, children orphaned. Their obedience frees them. Henry is struck anew by the burden of majesty, and when his subjects have gone, he pours out his heart.

> Upon the King! Let us our lives, our souls,
> Our debts, our careful wives,
> Our children, and our sins, lay on the King!
> We must bear all. O hard condition,
> Twin-born with greatness. . . . What infinite heart's ease
> Must kings neglect that private men enjoy!
> And what have kings that privates have not too,
> Save ceremony, save general ceremony?
> And what art thou, thou idol Ceremony? (247–57)

He reflects that not all the pomp of gorgeous ceremony,

> laid in bed majestical,
> Can sleep so soundly as the wretched slave,
> Who . . . like a lackey, from the rise to set,
> Sweats in the eye of Phoebus, and all night
> Sleeps in Elysium. (284–91)

He had foreseen this burden of majesty when as prince he addressed his dying father's crown (*2H4*, 4.5.23–31), but now he feels its weight greater than ever. He utters a heartfelt prayer:

> O God of battles, steel my soldiers' hearts,
> Possess them not with fear! Take from them now
> The sense of reck'ning, if th' opposed numbers
> Pluck their hearts from them. (306)

He beseeches God not to hold against them and him the fault his father committed in compassing the crown. He has tried to make amends by interring Richard's body worthily and having holy men continually offer prayers for his soul. He will do more. Next morning in a rousing speech he inspires his men with his own valiant courage and invincible leadership. The French outnumber them, but he points out that the fewer the men on the English side, the greater the honor if they win. He would not wish one man more.

> Rather proclaim it, Westmoreland, through my host,
> That he which hath no stomach to this fight,
> Let him depart; his passport shall be made,
> And crowns for convoy put into his purse.
> We would not die in that man's company
> That fears his fellowship to die with us. . . .
> For he to-day that sheds his blood with me
> Shall be my brother. Be he ne'er so vile,
> This day shall gentle his condition . . .
> All things are ready if our minds be so. (4.3.34–71)

Confident in the overwhelming superiority of their numbers, the French again offer to negotiate peace by ransom, warning Henry that his overthrow is sure. Undaunted, he replies:

> I pray thee bear my former answer back:
> Bid them achieve me and then sell my bones. . . .
> The man that once did sell the lion's skin
> While the beast liv'd, was kill'd with hunting him. . . .

> Our gayness and our gilt are all besmirch'd
> With rainy marching in the painful field. . . .
> But by the mass, our hearts are in the trim. (90–115)

The English win the Battle of Agincourt, as Henry assured them they would, with God going before their arms. To God the king ascribes the victory.

> O God, thy arm was here!
> And not to us, but to thy arm alone,
> Ascribe we all! When, without stratagem,
> But in plain shock and even play of battle,
> Was ever known so great and little loss
> On one part and on th' other? Take it, God,
> For it is only thine! . . .
> Let there be sung 'Non nobis' and 'Te Deum.' (4.8.111–28)

Although King Henry V has abjured the frivolity of his youth, he is not all seriousness. Young Prince Hal's love of a jest and of fellowship with ordinary men reappears in King Henry's ruse to provoke Michael Williams to challenge the glove which the king has induced Fluellen to wear in his cap. Reasoning cogently from a sound major premise, Williams respectfully defends himself before Henry and is rewarded, not punished.

> *King.* 'Twas I indeed thou promised'st to strike; . . . How canst thou make me satisfaction?
> *Williams.* All offences, my lord, come from the heart. Never came any from mine that might offend your Majesty.
> *King.* It was ourself thou didst abuse.
> *Williams.* Your Majesty came not like yourself. You appear'd to me but as a common man; witness the night, your garments, your lowliness. And what your Highness suffer'd under that shape, I beseech you take it for your own fault, and not mine; for had you been as I took you for, I made no offence. Therefore I beseech your Highness pardon me.
> *King.* Here, uncle Exeter, fill this glove with crowns
> And give it to this fellow. Keep it, fellow,
> And wear it for an honour in thy cap
> Till I do challenge it. (4.8.43–64)

Henry is a kingly king, even though in wooing Katherine he tells her he is so plain that he might be thought to have sold his farm to buy his crown (5.2.127). It is chiefly his plainness and lowliness which make him lovable and help to make him great.

Antony, in whom good and evil contend for mastery, does not, like Kent and the other characters just considered, exert a persuasion of *ethos* which elicits from his fellows or from the audience sustained admiration. Yet at least one of Antony's acts is a powerful argument of *ethos* which wins back the esteem of Enobarbus and fills him with shame. When Antony hears that Enobarbus has deserted him and gone over to Caesar's camp leaving his chests and treasure behind, he gives orders.

> Go, Eros, send his treasure after. Do it;
> Detain no jot, I charge thee. Write to him
> (I will subscribe) gentle adieus and greetings.
> Say that I wish he never find more cause
> To change a master. O, my fortunes have
> Corrupted honest men! Dispatch. Enobarbus!
>   (*A & C*, 4.5.12)

When the laden mules arrive, Enobarbus, overwhelmed at this evidence of Antony's Jove-like spirit, testifies to its force by decrying his own baseness in deserting such a leader.

> I am alone the villain of the earth,
> And feel I am so most. O Antony,
> Thou mine of bounty, how wouldst thou have paid
> My better service, when my turpitude
> Thou dost so crown with gold! This blows my heart.
> If swift thought break it not, a swifter mean
> Shall outstrike thought; but thought will do't, I feel.
> I fight against thee? No! I will go seek
> Some ditch wherein to die; the foul'st best fits
> My latter part of life. (4.6.30)

Enobarbus is resolved not to fight on Caesar's side against Antony, but he is ashamed to return to his master. He dies despising himself for having been unfaithful to one whose magnanimity is an ethical persuasion all the more poignant because the follower is not humble enough to accept an assured forgiveness.

>   O Antony,
> Nobler than my revolt is infamous,
> Forgive me in thine own particular,
> But let the world rank me in register
> A master-leaver and a fugitive!
> O Antony! O Antony! (4.9.18)

A play in which *ethos* shifts suddenly and frequently is *Titus Andronicus*. Tamora impresses the audience very favorably by her first speech, begging Titus to spare her son whom his son Lucius has demanded as a sacrifice to the shades of his dead brothers.

> Stay, Roman brethren! Gracious conqueror,
> Victorious Titus, rue the tears I shed,
> A mother's tears in passion for her son;
> And if thy sons were ever dear to thee,
> O, think my son to be as dear to me!
> Sufficeth not that we are brought to Rome
> To beautify thy triumphs, and return
> Captive to thee and to thy Roman yoke;
> But must my sons be slaughtered in the streets
> For valiant doings in their country's cause?
> O, if to fight for king and commonweal
> Were piety in thine, it is in these!
> Andronicus, stain not thy tomb with blood.
> Wilt thou draw near the nature of the gods?
> Draw near them then in being merciful.
> Sweet mercy is nobility's true badge.
> Thrice-noble Titus, spare my first-born son! (1.1.104)

This speech, foreshadowing Portia's on mercy, admirably combines *logos*, *pathos*, *ethos*, and is dramatically important because when it fails to elicit mercy it sets the motivating force of the plot in action: revenge demands revenge. The initial esteem of the audience for Tamora wanes, however, when it becomes clear that she publicly intercedes for Titus but privately reveals her dissembling craft and her plans for revenge (428–58). It turns to active dislike when Aaron the Moor discloses that he has long held her fettered in amorous chains (2.1.15), and the dislike increases as her deceits, cruelty, and crimes unfold. On the other hand, Bassianus, not liked at first, gains favor. At the end, Marcus appeals through *ethos* when he asks the Romans to believe him because of his white hairs and experience, and even more to believe Lucius, Rome's young captain and dear friend (5.3.67–95).

Iago represents the most remarkable instance in Shakespeare of ironical dramatic *ethos*, for by the very same words and acts he causes the other persons in the play to think well of him and the audience to think ill. His plots against others are known only to Roderigo, who nonetheless regards him as a friend he can trust. The audience, too, would think Iago a man of exceptional honesty if the scenes with Roderigo, the asides, and the soliloquies were removed. It is by means of these techniques that Shakespeare discloses consummate villainy at work and yet preserves the intellectual caliber of the other characters by showing how credible Iago appears to them and how inevitably they were deceived by this smoothest master of insinuation and intrigue. His starts, his hesitancies, his reluctances are his subtlest and most poisonous weapons of deceit. Othello declares:

> And, for I know thou'rt full of love and honesty
> And weigh'st thy words before thou giv'st them breath,
> Therefore these stops of thine fright me the more;
> For such things in a false disloyal knave
> Are tricks of custom; but in a man that's just
> They are close dilations, working from the heart
> That passion cannot rule. (3.3.118)

The audience sees irony in Othello's unquestioning acceptance of the major premise, for that which he takes for granted, namely, Iago's love and honesty, an argument essentially of *ethos*, is precisely what they know to be blackly false. When Emilia denies his charge against Desdemona, Othello answers as though his reply must perforce dissipate all doubt.

> *Emilia.* My husband say that she was false?
> *Othello.*   He, woman. . . .
> My friend, thy husband; honest, honest Iago. (5.2.152–54)

The tragedy is increased when one reflects that Othello invokes a good principle but misapplies it. It is only another indication of his unseeing goodness.

In his oration over Caesar, Antony combines *logos, pathos,* and *ethos* in an expert manipulation of the minds and feelings of the crowd whereby he diverts their approbation from Brutus toward himself. He takes up and at first seems to accept the thesis of Brutus' speech which has just preceded his, namely, that Caesar was ambitious. If this is true, he points out, Caesar has grievously paid for it. Antony presents this proposition first as an argument from authority, as testimony: it must be true, because Brutus says it, and Brutus is an honorable man. Here the accent is on *ethos.* Antony then begins to undermine the thesis, deftly, with questions, showing a contrast between what Brutus says and what Caesar was and did.

> He hath brought many captives home to Rome,
> Whose ransoms did the general coffers fill.
> Did this in Caesar seem ambitious?
> When that the poor have cried, Caesar hath wept;
> Ambition should be made of sterner stuff.
> Yet Brutus says he was ambitious;
> And Brutus is an honourable man.
> You all did see that on the Lupercal
> I thrice presented him a kingly crown,
> Which he did thrice refuse. Was this ambition?
> Yet Brutus says he was ambitious;
> And sure he is an honourable man.
> I speak not to disprove what Brutus spoke,
> But here I am to speak what I do know.
> You all did love him once, not without cause.
> What cause withholds you then to mourn for him? (*JC*, 3.2.94)

Thus far *logos* predominates. Swiftly Antony turns to *pathos*, using the figures exclamatio and exuscitatio.

> O judgment, thou art fled to brutish beasts,
> And men have lost their reason! Bear with me.
> My heart is in the coffin there with Caesar,
> And I must pause till it come back to me. (110)

The comments of the listeners, interposed while Antony weeps, provide evidence of the effectiveness of his threefold appeal.

> *1. Plebeian.* Methinks there is much reason in his sayings . . . [*logos*]
> *2. Plebeian.* Poor soul! his eyes are red as fire with weeping. [*pathos*]
> *3. Plebeian.* There's not a nobler man in Rome than Antony. [*ethos*]
> (114–122)

Antony then adroitly employs that same inciting hesitancy and seeming reluctance of which Iago also is master.

> O masters! If I were dispos'd to stir
> Your hearts and minds to mutiny and rage,
> I should do Brutus wrong and Cassius wrong,
> Who, you all know, are honourable men.
> I will not do them wrong. I rather choose
> To wrong the dead, to wrong myself and you,
> Than I will wrong such honourable men. (127)

He combines paralipsis, the figure whereby in seeming to withhold, one tells all, with an appeal to personal gain on the part of the plebeians, an argument of *ethos* convincing them of his regard for their interests and his good will toward them.

> But here's a parchment with the seal of Caesar.
> I found it in his closet; 'tis his will.
> Let but the commons hear this testament,
> Which (pardon me) I do not mean to read,
> And they would go and kiss dead Caesar's wounds
> And dip their napkins in his sacred blood . . .
> Have patience, gentle friends; I must not read it.
> It is not meet you know how Caesar lov'd you.
> You are not wood, you are not stones, but men;
> And being men, hearing the will of Caesar,
> It will inflame you, it will make you mad.
> 'Tis good you know not that you are his heirs;
> For if you should, O, what would come of it? (134–52)

As he had hoped, they demand to hear the will. It is the precise moment to turn the crowd from Brutus to himself.

> *4. Plebeian.* Read the will! We'll hear it, Antony!
> You shall read us the will, Caesar's will!
> *Antony.* Will you be patient? Will you stay awhile?
> I have o'ershot myself to tell you of it.
> I fear I wrong the honourable men
> Whose daggers have stabb'd Caesar; I do fear it.
> *4. Plebeian.* They were traitors. Honourable men!
> *All.* The will! the testament!
> *2. Plebeian.* They were villains, murderers! The will! Read the will!
> *Antony.* You will compel me then to read the will? (153)

He does not, however, read the will at once. His appeal now becomes primarily that of *pathos*, to rouse pity and anger. He shows them Caesar's mantle, points out where each conspirator's dagger entered, especially that of Brutus, which gave "the most unkindest cut of all." It was Brutus' ingratitude that vanquished Caesar, that burst his mighty heart. This argument of *pathos* proves potent.

> *Antony.* O, now you weep, and I perceive you feel
> The dint of pity. These are gracious drops.

> Kind souls, what weep you when you but behold
> Our Caesar's vesture wounded? Look you here!
> Here is himself, marr'd as you see with traitors.
> *1. Plebeian.* O piteous spectacle!
> *2. Plebeian.* O noble Caesar! . . .
> *4. Plebeian.* O traitors, villains! . . .
> *All.* Revenge! About! Seek! Burn! Fire!
> Kill! Slay! Let not a traitor live! (198–210)

The argument of *ethos* is also effective. Antony has won their complete confidence and belief.

> *1. Plebeian.* Peace there! Hear the noble Antony.
> *2. Plebeian.* We'll hear him, we'll follow him, we'll die with him!
> (212)

Antony pretends to try to quell them. Those who have done this deed no doubt have their reasons. He would not steal away their hearts; he is no orator like Brutus, but a plain blunt man who loves his friend Caesar. He tells them only what they know, shows them sweet Caesar's wounds, dumb mouths that speak for him. But were Brutus in his position, he would put a tongue in every wound of Caesar that should move the very stones of Rome to rise and mutiny. This is enough. With difficulty he restrains them, eager for revenge, to listen to his last inciting point, the details of Caesar's will. Roused to the highest pitch, they rush away to burn and destroy. Antony exclaims with satisfaction at the perfect success of his speech:

> Now let it work. Mischief, thou art afoot,
> Take thou what course thou wilt. (265)

This oration is simultaneously excellent rhetoric and excellent poetic, for it unquestionably persuades, and it is so woven into the plot as to constitute a twofold dramatic peripety: Antony's fortunes begin to rise, Brutus' to fall. Antony's speech was efficacious mainly because it rested on a better insight into the value of *pathos* in persuasion. Brutus failed to understand that assent to the truth of an argument is no guarantee of action.

3. Conclusion

Shakespeare knew the complete doctrine and method of composition regularly taught in the grammar schools of his day from a combination of Latin textbooks. He employed in his work the techniques prescribed in Cicero's *Topica*, the *Ad Herennium*, Susenbrotus' *Epitome troporum ac schematum*, Erasmus' *Copia* and *Modus conscribendi*, Aphthonius' *Progymnasmata*, Quintilian's *Institutio oratoria*, and a work on logic, perhaps Melanchthon's.[4] These techniques, comprising the core of grammar school discipline, were applied to both composition and the reading of classical Latin literature in a manner which formed the Renaissance creating and responding mind.

The Renaissance grammar school discipline justified itself by its results. Logic and rhetoric were, indeed, used too baldly in Gascoigne's works, Lyly's *Euphues*, Sidney's *Arcadia*, and Greene's *Tritameron*, which reveal apprenticeship to art rather than achievement; and logic was employed in a too-obvious, even though interesting, way in the interludes of John Heywood and in the plays of Lyly, Jonson, Dekker, Chapman, and Massinger. Nevertheless, it is the work of the apprentice rather than that of the finished artist which shows most clearly the currents of the time, and one has only to remember Ben Jonson's "To Celia" to realize how an impression of creative spontaneity and ease can be wrested from borrowed material by one trained as the Elizabethans were in imitative synthesis.

Many of the great passages in Shakespeare similarly transfigured materials that were borrowed from the Latin literature studied in grammar school, for Shakespeare also pressed his school learning into service and his early work discloses his own apprenticeship to art. There is some evidence of his continued interest as an adult in theoretical works [5] and of his acquaintance with a number of the English works on rhetoric and logic that have furnished the selections in Part III of the present study, which sets forth the Renaissance theory of composition. This theory was a penetrating and comprehensive analysis of thought and its expression, and there can be no doubt that formal training in it contributed vitally to the development of Shakespeare's genius. An intensive and thorough investigation of his use of any or all the features of this theory might prove as instructive and rewarding as a study of his blank verse, for verse was just one of many instruments of style carefully cultivated by Renaissance writers and brought to unprecedented perfection by Shakespeare. Verse was, in fact, a part of the theory, insofar as a study of prosody and the composition of verse were important features of Tudor grammar school training.

[4] See T. W. Baldwin, *William Shakspere's Small Latine and Lesse Greeke*, 1944.
[5] See p. 44, above.

Even though Shakespeare parodied the extremely narrow and artificial style of *Euphues,* his own early work was marked by a schematic use of the most obvious rhetorical and logical devices. Like many of his contemporaries, he too seems often to have been occupied in a pursuit of words rather than of ideas. In his mature work he continues to use these devices and many more, but with a delicate dramatic fitness and subtle inwardness adapted to minds and moods of a range unmatched by any other dramatist. Each point of view is fully entered into. Each person speaks in his own idiom, be it that of king, scholar, pedant, or rogue. With equally authentic accent Shakespeare speaks the language appropriate to the garrulous, the shallow, the ignorant, the grave. Mainly by a skillful use of the vices of language, he travesties the verbal affectation of Osric, the ineptitude of Dogberry, the misapprehension and confusion of Bottom and Mistress Quickly, the scurrility of Thersites. By means of fallacious and captious argument he creates the light sophistic of Feste and Touchstone, the dodges and nimble wit of Falstaff, the chicanery of Richard III, the cynical mockery of Apemantus, the barbed shafts of the fool in *Lear.* Through complete mastery of *logos, pathos,* and *ethos,* characters whom he has endowed with natural eloquence full of personal and vivid touches engage both the intellect and the feelings of the audience, whether they voice with experienced tongue the cogent application of analytic thought to grave affairs in public debate or in soliloquy unburden the heart of poignant doubt or fear or grief. Thought and image commensurate with the genuine stress of a compelling problem or passion forge language which by appealing simultaneously to the reason and the imagination confers beauty as well as vision. The style echoes the mood with sureness, though it shifts from unruffled deliberation to hysterical excitement, or from stern self-control to unbridled emotion in the movement of living drama. Shakespeare's creative art illustrates most fully the variety and compass of the Renaissance theory of composition.

The formal training which Shakespeare received contributed not only to the breadth and stature of his thought but also to the richness of the gorgeous panoply with which he invested it. His language, fresh, vibrant, exuberant, and free, makes use of the schemes of words as well as the schemes of construction. He effects sudden and vivid concentrations of meaning by a poetically superb and daring use of anthimeria (nouns as verbs), catachresis (verbs and adjectives employed in a transferred sense), hypallage (the transferred epithet), the compound epithet, metaphor, metonymy, syllepsis of the sense, negative and privative terms.[6] He secures swiftness of movement, compactness, and emphasis through anastrophe (inverted word order), parenthesis, zeugma (one verb serving two or more subjects), brachylogia and asyndeton (omission of conjunctions).[7]

With figures of repetition, Shakespeare weaves a haunting harmony of sound; through the schemes of grammar he achieves such control over movement and rhythm that like a figure skater he may dart, poise, turn, plunge, go where he will, his words fraught with penetrating thought and deep feeling—and all this but an art subservient to the larger art of the builder, to plot construction, character creation, and profound insight into human nature and its problems. Yet this myriad-minded man has time for fun and nonsense, for parody and foolery, for mere gleeful bandying of words.

One may read Shakespeare's plays, or see them produced, with attention to any or all these facets of his art. They give pleasure at many levels, as great music does. One who recognizes in the intricate web of harmonic and melodic progressions the chord structures and rhythmic design, and notes the fine gradation and coloring, experiences a deeper and keener delight in music than one who does not perceive these things; he enjoys not only what the untrained listener enjoys but also a detailed intellectual perception of the relation of parts to parts and to the whole. Similarly, to cultivate the alert attentiveness to patterns of sound and movement and the expert analysis of thought-relations habitual to educated Elizabethans quickens the responsiveness requisite to a full appreciation of Shakespeare's plays.

[6] See above, pp. 62, 146, 56, 124, 145, 126, and 158, 168, 133, 134.
[7] See above, pp. 54, 57, 58, 59.

The following pages present a selection from the sixteenth-century English works on logic and rhetoric of what seemed to the compiler the best treatment of each item arranged under grammar, *logos*, *pathos*, and *ethos*—functions basic to Aristotle's conception of rhetoric. A few items from Aristotle are included because his work influenced Renaissance theory both directly and indirectly.

The essentially complete general theory of composition and reading thus set forth was universal in European countries during the Renaissance.

CHAPTER VI

Schemes of Grammar, Vices of Language, and Figures of Repetition

THE SCHEMES of grammar represent deviations from ordinary expression to achieve swiftness, emphasis, rhythm, or some similar grace of style. If the deviation is excessive, lacking judgment or good taste, the language is faulty or vicious. When the repetition of words accentuates structure and rhythm, as it often does, the figures of repetition are seen to be related to those of grammatical construction, as Aristotle recognized in his discussion of style.

1. The Schemes of Grammar

The schemes of grammar are either of words or of construction.

a. Schemes of Words.—The orthographical schemes of words are devices for adapting words to meter and rhyme. The schemes may represent a choice among current forms of words or a variation introduced by the poet. After summarizing the types of variation Puttenham remarks:

These many wayes may our maker alter his wordes, and sometimes it is done for pleasure to give a better sound, sometimes upon necessitie, and to make up the rime. But our maker must take heed that he be not to bold . . . for unlesse usual speach and custome allow it, it is a fault and no figure . . . (p. 162)

Words may be varied by the addition, omission, or exchange of a syllable or letter. Butler and Susenbrotus illustrate the schemes of words from Latin literature. Wilson, Sherry, Peacham, and Puttenham explain them and give examples in English from which those in the following synopsis are selected.

Prosthesis is the addition of a syllable at the beginning of a word, as *embolden* for *bolden*, *berattle* for *rattle*, *ymade* for *made*, *adown* for *down*.

Epenthesis is the addition of a syllable or letter in the middle of a word, as *meeterly* for *meetly*, *goldylocks* for *goldlocks*, *relligion* for *religion*.

Proparalepsis, or paragoge, is the addition of a syllable at the end of a word, as *slacken* for *slack*, *spoken* for *spoke*, *hasten* for *haste*.

Aphaeresis is the omission of a syllable from the beginning of a word, as *'twixt* for *betwixt*.

Syncope is the omission of a letter or syllable from the middle of a word, as *tane* for *taken*, *idolatry* for *idololatry*, *prosprous* for *prosperous*.

Synaloepha is the omission or elision of one of two vowels coming together at the juncture of two words, as *thone* for *the one*, *t'attain* for *to attain*.

Apocope is the omission of the last syllable of a word, as *bet* for *better*, *morne* for *morning*.

Diastole, or eciasis, is the lengthening of a short syllable, or the stressing of an unstressed syllable, as to stress the first syllable of *endure*, the second of *possible*, or the third of *commendable*.

Systole is the shortening of a long syllable or the removal of stress from a stressed syllable as from *ve* in *perseverance*.

Metathesis is the exchange of letters in a word, as *brust* for *burst*.

Antisthecon is the exchange of one sound for another for the sake of rhyme, as *wrang* for *wrong*.

Tasis, though not strictly a figure, is mentioned by Sherry and Puttenham in close connection with the figures. Sherry describes it as

a swete and pleasaunte modulacion or tunableness . . . of the voyce in pleasaunte pronunciation. (Sig. C iii ʳ)

b. Schemes of Construction.—Puttenham remarks of the schemes of grammatical construction:

As your single words may be many waies transfigured to make the meetre or verse more tunable and melodious, so also may your whole and entire clauses be in such sort contrived by the order of their construction as the eare may receive a certaine recreation, although the mind for any noveltie of sence be little or nothing affected. And therefore al your figures of *grammaticall* construction, I accompt them but merely *auricular* in that they reach no furder then the eare. (p. 163)

Puttenham discusses schemes of grammatical construction that work by disorder, by defect, by surplusage, and by exchange.[1]

Hyperbaton is the genus of the syntactical figures that work by disorder. The species include anastrophe, tmesis, hysterologia, hysteron proteron, hypallage, parenthesis, and epergesis. Anastrophe is a departure from the normal word order, often to secure a desired emphasis, as when we say,

faults, no man liveth without, when order requireth we should say, No man liveth without faults. (Day, p. 362)

---

[1] Puttenham includes some, however, which do not fit into these four groups.

Tmesis is the interjection of a phrase between the parts of a compound word, thus:

Hys saying was true, as here shal appere after, for hereafter. (Sherry, sig. B viii ʳ)

When a phrase is interposed between a preposition and its object and the preposition is thereby joined rather to the verb that precedes it, the scheme is called hysterologia.

I ran after with as much speede as I coulde, the theefe that had undone me. (Peacham, 1577, sig. F iiii ʳ) [2]

Hysteron proteron is a disorder of time,

where that which ought to bee in the first place is put in the second, as thus, After he had given saile to the wind, and taken the seas, for after he had taken the seas, and given saile to the wind. (Day, p. 362) [3]

Hypallage, or the changeling, as Puttenham calls it, perverts the sense by shifting the application of words,

as, he that should say, for . . . *come dine with me and stay not, come stay with me and dine not.* . . . A certaine piteous lover to move his mistres to compassion, wrote among other amorous verses, this one.
Madame, I set your eyes before mine woes.
For, mine woes before your eyes, spoken to th' intent to winne favour in her sight. (p. 171)

Hypallage need not, however, be so strange and far-fetched. Day gives as an example (adding the comment, "The use hereof in *Poesie* is rife"),

the wicked wound thus given, for having thus wickedly wounded him. (p. 363)

Parenthesis interrupts a sentence by interposing words. Peacham quotes Saint Paul.

They are the ministers of Christ (I speake as a foole) I am more, &c. (p. 198)

Epergesis interrupts by interposing a word in apposition as an added interpretation.

[2] No example of this scheme has been noted in Shakespeare.

[3] Puttenham makes hysteron proteron a shift in time order when he discusses it as a figure (p. 170); a shift in word order, apparently the same as anastrophe, which he nowhere names, when he discusses it as a tolerable vice (p. 255). The latter is the only meaning entertained by Veré L. Rubel, who states that the former is not considered in her study, *Poetic Diction in the English Renaissance,* p. 285.

I know that in me, that is to say, in my flesh, dwelleth no good thing. Rom. 7:18. (Peacham, p. 191)

Grammatical figures that work by defect and so represent short-cuts in expression include eclipsis, zeugma, syllepsis, scesis onomaton, and diazeugma. Eclipsis, or ellipsis, is the omission of a word easily supplied by ordinary understanding, as

You are not to answere or compare with him, for you are not meet, sufficient, or able, to answere or compare with him. (Day, p. 359)

Zeugma is the use of a word, usually a verb, to serve two or more others. If the verb is expressed in the first clause and understood in the others, the figure is called prozeugma.

> *Her beautie perst mine eye, her speach mine wofull hart:*
> *Her presence all the powers of my discourse.* (Puttenham, p. 164)

If it is expressed in the middle clause it is called mesozeugma; if in the last clause, hypozeugma. Syllepsis differs from zeugma in that the word which serves two or more others agrees grammatically with only the nearest.

> *Judge ye lovers, if it be strange or no:*
> *My Ladie laughs for joy, and I for wo.* (*Ibid.*, p. 165)

If a verb is altogether lacking, and a saying is made up of only substantives and adjectives, the scheme is called scesis onomaton.[4]

A mayd in conversation chast, in speeche mylde, in countenaunce cheerefull, in behavioure modest, in bewty singuler, in heart humble and meeke, in honest myrth, merie with measure, in serving of God dilligent, to her parents obedient. (Peacham, 1577, sig. G iiii ᵛ)

Hypozeuxis is the contrary of zeugma, remarks Peacham, in that every clause has its own verb. To this characteristic Puttenham adds the iteration of the noun, thus:

> *My Ladie gave me, my Lady wist not what,*
> *Geving me leave to be her Soveraine . . .*

Here [*my Ladie gave*] and [*my Ladie wist*] be supplies with iteration, by vertue of this figure. (p. 166)

Also in contrast to zeugma, is diazeugma whereby one noun serves many verbs.

---

[4] No example of this scheme has been noted in Shakespeare.

The people of Rome destroyed Numance, overthrew Cartage, cast downe Corinth, and raced Fregels. (Sherry, sig. B vii ᵛ)

The rhythm of language and its tempo are affected by the use of brachylogia, asyndeton, polysyndeton, isocolon, homoioteleuton, and hirmus. Brachylogia, or articulus, omits the conjunction between single words, often imparting celerity and vehemence through brevity.

By sharpnes, voyce, countenaunce, thou madeste thyne enemyes afrayd. (Sherry, sig. D v ʳ)

Asyndeton, or brachiepia, omits conjunctions between clauses, with like effect.

The like brevitie *Simo* useth in *Terence:* The corps (saith he) goeth before, we follow after, we come to the grave, it is put into the fire, a lamentation is made. (Peacham, p. 182)

Polysyndeton, on the contrary, employs many conjunctions, producing a slow, deliberate, impressive effect.

Ye observe dayes, and moneths, and times, and yeares. Gal. 4. (Peacham, p. 53)

Isocolon is directly concerned with rhythm.

Compar, of the Grecians called *Isocolon* and *Parison,* is a figure . . . which maketh the members of an oration to be almost of a just number of sillables, yet the equalitie of those members or parts, are not to be measured upon our fingers as if they were verses, but to bee tried by a secret sence of the eare: . . . First, when the former parts of a sentence, or of an oration be answered by the later, and that by proper words respecting the former . . . See that equitie flow as the water, and righteousnesse as a mightie streame. Amos 5

Also it coupleth contraries, thus: An innocent, although hee be accused, he may be acquited, but the guiltie except he be accused he cannot be condemned.

Also by this figure effects may be made to answer their efficients, consequents their antecedents, habite privation: also contrariwise, and that by a very pleasant forme and proportion. This ornament is very often used of *Solomon* in his Proverbs and of *Esay* in his Prophesies. (*Ibid.,* p. 58) ⁵

⁵ Notice that Peacham shows how this figure can be used to emphasize the topics of logic. The Tudor rhetoricians do not make the distinction between isocolon and parison, explained by Morris Croll, in Croll and Clemens, *Euphues: the Anatomy of Wit* and *Euphues and His England.* London, 1916, Introduction, p. xvi. Peacham gives both these names for the same figure. The definitions of parison by Puttenham and Day make it identical with isocolon. This figure was in great favor among the Elizabethans as is seen from its schematic use not only in *Euphues,* but in the work of Lyly's imitators.

Homoioteleuton, combined with isocolon and with alliteration (as in *Euphues*) accentuates the rhythm of the equal members by its own similar endings.[6] As Puttenham remarks, of all the figures of the ancients homoioteleuton approaches nearest to rhyme, which became important as a structural factor in English verse. In illustrating homoioteleuton Peacham incidentally expresses his own, and the traditional, conception of the functions of rhetoric.

He is esteemed eloquent which can invent wittily, remember perfectly, dispose orderly, figure diversly, pronounce aptly, confirme strongly, and conclude directly. (p. 54)

Hirmus, the periodic sentence, is a figure whereby "the whole sence . . . is suspended till ye come to the last . . . which finisheth . . . with a full and perfit sence" (Puttenham, p. 176). Day offers this example:

God in the beginning made heaven, earth, sea, firmament, sunne, moone, starres, and all things in them contained. (p. 364)

Metabasis is a figure of grammatical transition whereby the speaker

in a few words sheweth what hath bene alreadie said, and also what shalbe said next, and that divers waies. From the equall: The matters which you have alreadie heard, were wonderfull, and those that you shall heare are no lesse marvellous . . . From consequents: You have bene told how he promised, and now I will tell you, how he performed. (Peacham, p. 175)

The figures that work by exchange include enallage, hendiadys, Graecismus, and anthimeria. Concerning enallage Puttenham remarks:

Your figures that worke *auricularly* by exchange, were more observable to the Greekes and Latines . . . for the multiplicitie of their Grammaticall accidents, . . . that is to say, their divers cases, moodes, tenses, genders, with variable terminations, by reason whereof, they changed not the very word, but kept the word, and changed the shape of him onely, using one case for another, or tense, or person, or gender, or number, or moode. We, having no such varietie of accidents, have little or no use of this figure. They called it *Enallage*. (p. 171) [7]

[6] Since English is little varied by cases, the ancient distinction between homoioptoton, similar case endings, and homoioteleuton, similar endings of uninflected words, practically disappears in English. Although this figure could with justice be placed among the figures of repetition, it seems preferable to treat it with isocolon because its outstanding use in Elizabethan literature was to mark off rhythmic units.

[7] Veré L. Rubel, throughout her *Poetic Diction in the English Renaissance*, employs the word enallage to mean the exchange of parts of speech; this meaning is properly attached to anthimeria. Miss Rubel avowedly bases her terminology on Puttenham and on Warren Tay-

Puttenham offers no illustration, but Peacham gives this example of enallage of number:

Thus, *Plinie* in *Africke,* the greater part of wylde beastes doe not drink in Som-
mer for want of showres, here the plurall is put for the singuler, for the greater
parte is the singuler number, and therefore so should the verbe be singuler also.
(1577 ed., sig. H iii ᵛ)

Hendiadys substitutes two nouns for a noun modified by an adjective.

> *Not you coy dame your lowrs nor your lookes*
For [*your lowring lookes.*]   (Puttenham, p. 177)

Graecismus employs in another language a construction proper to the
Greek. Butler quotes as not inelegant an example from Spenser's *Faerie
Queene.*

> For not to have beene dipt in Lethe Lake,
> Could save the sonne of Thetis from to die. *Vid.* c. 13.[8]

Anthimeria is the substitution of one part of speech for another.

he spake very hote you all can tell, for, he spoke very hotely you all can tell,
a nown [adjective] for an adverbe. (Peacham, 1577, sig., H iiii ᵛ)

2. *Vices of Language*

The line between the figures and the vices of language is sometimes
not easy to draw, for blemishes of style result from excess or misuse of
those very devices which, if used with taste and judgment, adorn it. Puttenham explains that

by ignorance of the maker a good figure may become a vice, and by his good
discretion, a vicious speach go for a vertue in the Poeticall science. This saying
is to be explaned and qualified, for some maner of speaches are alwayes intoller-
able and such as cannot be used with any decencie, but are ever undecent,
namely barbarousnesse, incongruitie, ill disposition, fond affectation, rusticitie,
and all extreme darknesse, such as it is not possible for a man to understand the
matter without an interpretour . . . I see not but the rest of the common
faultes may be borne with sometimes, or passe without any great reproofe, not
being used overmuch or out of season . . . so as every surplusage or prepos-
terous placing or undue iteration or darke word, or doubtfull speach are not

lor's "Dictionary of the Tudor Figures of Rhetoric," part of an unpublished dissertation
presented to the University of Chicago in 1937, published and distributed by the University
of Chicago Libraries. No justification for Miss Rubel's usage is to be found in either of
them.

[8] Butler, *Rhetoricae libri duo,* I, 34.

so narrowly to be looked upon in a large poeme, nor specially in the pretie
Poesies and devises of Ladies . . . whom we would not have too precise Poets
least with their shrewd wits, when they were maried they might become a little
too phantasticall wives, neverthelesse because we seem to promise an arte, which
doth not justly admit any wilful errour in the teacher . . . I will speake somewhat touching these viciosities of language . . . (p. 249)

Solecismus, the most obvious vice of language, is related to the figure
enallage, for it is the ignorant misuse of cases, genders, tenses. As Puttenham remarks, "every poore scholler knowes the fault, & cals it the
breaking of *Priscians* head, for he was among the Latines a principall
Grammarian" (p. 251). He gives no illustration.

Barbarismus, or foreign speech, is that

pronounced with straunge and ill-shapen accents, or written by wrong ortog-
raphie, as he that would say with us in England, a dousand for a thousand,
isterday, for yesterday, as commonly the Dutch and French people do . . .
(Puttenham, p. 250)

Soraismus, or the mingle-mangle, which Puttenham places among what
he terms the intolerable vices,[9] consists in making

our speach or writinges of sundry languages using some Italian word, or
French, or Spanish, or Dutch, or Scottish, not for the nonce or for any purpose
(which were in part excusable) but ignorantly and affectedly as one that said
using this French word *Roy*, to make ryme with another verse, thus,
>   *O mightie Lord of love, dame Venus onely joy,*
>   *Whose Princely power exceedes each other heavenly roy.*
The verse is good but the terme peevishly affected. (p. 252)

Heterogenium is a vice which consists in answering irrelevantly. Fenner explains it as a device of sophism.

Impertinent or not to the purpose is when any thing is brought for a proof,
which is nothing neere to the matter in hand, whereunto the common proverb
giveth answere: *I aske you of cheese, you answere mee of chauke.* (Sig. E 2 ᵛ)

Puttenham lists amphibologia, the ambiguous, among tolerable vices.

Then have ye one other vicious speach . . . and is when we speake or write
doubtfully and that the sence may be taken two wayes . . . Thus said a gen-

---

[9] Puttenham's treatment of the vices, and Sherry's also, is similar to Quintilian's (8.3.44–
61). A number of illustrations are identical. Puttenham's division of the vices into tolerable and intolerable seems, however, to be his own contribution to rhetorical theory.

tleman in our vulgar pretily notwithstanding because he did it not ignorantly, but for the nonce.

> *I sat by my Lady soundly sleeping,*
> *My mistresse lay by me bitterly weeping.*

No man can tell by this, whether the mistresse or the man, slept or wept: these doubtfull speaches were used much in the old times . . . by the Oracles of *Delphos* . . . and in effect all our old Brittish and Saxon prophesies be of the same sort, that turne them on which side ye will, the matter of them may be verified, neverthelesse carryeth generally such force in the heades of fonde people, that by the comfort of those blind prophecies many insurrections and rebellions have bene stirred up in this Realme, as that of *Jacke Straw,* & *Jacke Cade* in *Richard* the seconds time . . . which might be constred two or three wayes as well as that one whereunto the rebelles applied it . . . (p. 260)

Tapinosis is a vice whereby

the dignitie or majestie of a high matter is much defaced by the basenesse of a word, as to call . . . the Thames a brooke . . . great wisedome prettie witte . . . (Peacham, p. 168)

Puttenham cites the instance of a certain

Serjeant Bendlowes, when in a progresse time comming to salute the Queene . . . he said to her Cochman, stay thy cart good fellow, stay thy cart, that I may speake to the Queene, whereat her Majestie laughed . . . and all the rest of the company . . . (p. 259)

Puttenham attaches two meanings to cacemphaton, which he lists as a tolerable vice. The first meaning, the same as that which Sherry gives for aischrologia, is foul speech, often ambiguous, but permissible at times, thinks Puttenham, to move laughter, as do the jests of a buffoon or railing companion, whom the Latins called *Scurra* (p. 254). The second meaning of cacemphaton, according to Puttenham, is that of an unpleasant combination of sounds, as in rhyming too many like sounding words together, or as Sherry says, in using too many r's or t's, which cause a roughness or stammering (1555, fol. x^r), or as Peacham puts it, in

a contynuall jarring upon one string, thus . . . your strength is not to strive, or stryke agaynste the streame so strong . . . (1577, sig. G iii ^{r})

Puttenham alone gives the name tautology to such overuse of alliteration.

Cacosyntheton, a vice related to the scheme anastrophe, is an intolerable departure from acceptable word order. It occurs especially, explains Puttenham, when an adjective is placed after a substantive,

as one that said ridiculously. In my yeares lustie, many a deed doughtie did I.
(p. 253)

The vices of verbosity include tautologia, perissologia or macrologia,
parelcon, pleonasmus, homiologia, and periergia. Tautologia is the wearisome repetition of the same thing in different words or in the same words.

If you have a friend, keepe your friend, for an old friend is to be preferred before a new friend, this I say to you as your friend. (Peacham, p. 49)

Perissologia or macrologia is the addition of a superfluous clause which
adds nothing to the sense, thus:

Men of so high and excellent vertue, let them ever live and never die. (Day,
p. 362)

Puttenham accounts this a tolerable vice and cites Turberville's use of it

to shew the great annoy and difficultie of those warres of Troy, caused for
Helenas sake.

> *Nor Menelaus was unwise,*
> *Or troupe of Trojans mad,*
> *When he with them and they with him,*
> *For her such combat had . . .*

Menelaus fighting with the Trojans, the Trojans must of necessitie fight with
him. (p. 257)

Parelcon is the addition of a superfluous word such as *that* in the following:

when that I call, I pray yee be ready. (Peacham, 1577, sig. F iii ʳ)

Pleonasmus is redundancy,

where, with words seeming, wee doe increase our reasons, as thus, *with these
eares I heard him speake it.* Or, with mine eyes I beheld him sorrowing, where
wee well know, that, without eares or eyes, we cannot well heare, or see, yet
carrieth this kind of speech, a *vehemency inforcing* the matter . . . (Day,
p. 361)

Homiologia offends by a monotony unpleasing to both mind and ear,

when the whole matter is all alyke, and hath no varietie to avoyde tediousnes,
as: He came thither to the bath, yet he saide afterwardes. Here one servaunt bet
me. Afterwardes he sayde unto hym: I wyll consider. Afterwardes he chyd
hym, & cryed more and more when manye were presente. Suche a folyshe tell-
yng of a tale shall you heare in many simple & halfe folyshe persons. (Sherry,
sig. C i ʳ)

Periergia, a vice related to the figure periphrasis, is superfluity resulting from overlabor to seem fine and eloquent by expressing oneself curiously. Quintilian remarks that such overlabor differs "from judicious care, just as a fidgety man differs from an industrious one." [10] Puttenham quotes Gascoigne in illustration, and comments:

His intent was to declare how upon the tenth day of March he crossed the river of Thames, to walke in Saint *Georges* field, the matter was not great as ye may suppose.

> *The tenth of March when Aries received*
> *Dan Phoebus raies into his horned head,*
> *And I my selfe by learned lore perceived*
> *That Ver approcht and frosty winter fled*
> *I crost the Thames to take the cheerefull aire,*
> *In open fields, the weather was so faire.*

First, the whole matter is not worth all this solemne circumstance to describe the tenth day of March, but if he had left at the two first verses, it had bene inough. But when he comes with two other verses to enlarge his description, it is not only more than needes, but also very ridiculous, for he makes wise, as if he had not bene a man learned in some of the mathematickes (by learned lore) that he could not have told that the x. of March had fallen in the spring of the yeare: which every carter, and also every child knoweth without any learning. (p. 258)

There is inflation of both words and matter in the vice bomphiologia,

when trifling matters be set out with semblaunt and blasing wordes, used of none but of such as be eyther smell feastes, and Parasites, which mayntayne their good cheere with counterfayted prayses, or of great bosters and craking Souldyours, as of *Thraso* in *Terence*, and such lyke persons in Comodyes . . . Sometyme beggers use this figure, when the Constable is having of them to the stockes, they thincke then the beste waye for them is, to speake fayre, and to lift up the Constable to a hygh dignitie . . . evermore when words be as unmeete for the matter, as a chayne of Golde for an Ape, and a silver saddle for a Sowe, then may it be called *Bomphilogia*. And also when by Eloquence, glorious persons would have there cunning blased abroade, in makyng trifles, treasures, cottages, castles, thistles, mightie Oakes, and peeble stones, precious pearles. (Peacham, 1577, sig. G ii [r])

Cacozelia or fond affectation, according to Puttenham, is the coining of fine words out of Latin, and the use of newfangled speeches in order to appear learned (p. 252). Peacham accepts this meaning, but shows that

[10] . . . supervacua, ut sic dixerim, operositas, ut a diligenti curiosus et a religione superstitio distat (8.3.55), tr. by Watson, Bohn edition, II, 100.

such affectation on the part of the ignorant may deteriorate into that misapplication of words which we call malapropism.

Cacozelon, an ill imitation or affection, that is, when words be used over-
thwartly, or contrarily for want of judgement, used of foolish folk, who covet-
ing to tell an eloquent tale, doe deface that which they would fainest beautifie,
men not being content to speake plaine english, doe desire to use wordes bor-
owed of the latine tongue, imitatyng learned men, when they know no more
their signification, then a Goose, and therefore many tymes they apply them
so contrarily, that wyse men are enforced to laugh at their folly, and absurditie . . . A man comming through a Gentlemans pastures, and seeing there
a great number of Sheepe (as Mayster Wylson telleth the tale) and after speaking with the Gentleman, Syr, sayd he, your worship have goodly audience of
sheepe, whereby the Gentleman perceyved that he was more fyt to talke
amonge sheepe, then speake among men. On a time one was arrayned for stealing a Weather, and one of his neighboures, that was his friend, tooke upon him
to intreate for him to the Judge . . . I beseech your Lordship, quoth he, be
good Lord to my neighbour, for excessity distrainde him to steale, or else he
would never have done it, and he that accuse, is an unrude fellow, and very
contagious among his neighboures, and if he could conclare anye more, he
would I am sure, . . . now if his wordes had bene such, as he himselfe had
understood, he might have told a wyser tale, and have bene much lesse laughed
at. (1577, sig. G ii ᵛ) [11]

Acyron or impropriety is the use of a word opposite and utterly repugnant to what we would express, as to say,

I hope I shall be hanged tomorrow. For [I *feare me*] *I shall be hanged,* . . .
(Puttenham, p. 256)

or

you shall have sixe stripes whiche you long for: when thei long for them not
one whit. (Sherry, 1555, fol. vi ᵛ)

Aschematiston is the lack of figures, and this is no small fault, says
Sherry, echoing Quintilian.[12]

---

[11] Peacham places malapropism also under cacosyntheton, which he defines as including not
only words ill placed, as the other rhetoricians define it, but also words ill applied, thus:
"there is (quoth one) small adversity betweene your Mare and mine, for deversity" (sig.
G iiii ʳ). He remarks, however, that this misapplication is "much like to Cacozelon."

[12] Quintilian, 9.1.13, quoted on p. 32, above. Sherry, sig. C ii ʳ. This vice has not been
observed in Shakespeare's work.

3. Figures of Repetition

Alliteration, or paroemion, is the only one of the figures of repetition concerned with the repetition of letters only. As Peacham remarks, this figure is used more in poetry than in prose. Yet it gives

a pleasant facilitie in a Proverbe . . . as, to hold with the hare, and hunt with the hound: soone ripe, soone rotten. (p. 49)

All the other figures of repetition involve the repetition of words. In a series of clauses or sentences, the repetition of a word at the beginning of each is anaphora; at the end, epistrophe; the combination of these is symploce. Peacham gives as an example of anaphora:

The Lord sitteth above the water floods. The Lord remaineth a king for ever. The Lord shall give strength unto his people. The Lord shall give his people the blessing of peace. Psalm 29. . . .

The use hereof is chiefly to repeate a word of importance, and effectuall signification, as to repeate the cause before his singular effects, or contrariwise the effect before his severall causes, or any other word of principall accompt. It serveth also pleasantly to the eare, both in the respects of the repetition, and also of the varietie of the new clause. (p. 41)

Peacham clearly subordinates sound to sense; he would have the repetition enforce the meaning, and he conceives the latter in the familiar terms of the topics of logic. Similarly, he adds to his example of epistrophe a comment which stresses the function of the repetition.

When I was a child, I spake as a child, I understood as a child, I imagined as a child. 1 Cor. 13. . . . it serveth to leave a word of importance in the ende of a sentence, that it may the longer hold the sound in the mind of the hearer. (p. 43)

Symploce combines the two preceding figures.

Him would you pardon and acquite by your sentence, whom the Senate hath condemned, whom the people of Rome have condemned, whom all men have condemned. (Peacham, p. 43)

Epanalepsis is the repetition at the end of a sentence of the word or words with which it begins. Fraunce quotes an example from Sidney's Sonnet 34.

They love indeed, who quake to say, they love. (*AR*, sig. D 3 ᵛ)

Antimetabole is akin to logical conversion in that it repeats words in converse order, often thereby sharpening their sense.

We wish not peace to maintaine cruell warre,
But we make warre to maintaine us in peace.
(Puttenham, p. 208)

The repetition of the word ending one clause or sentence at the beginning of the next is called anadiplosis. Hoskyns quotes this example from Sidney's *Arcadia:*

why lived I alas? alas which loved I!

And Hoskyns adds: "as noe man is sicke in thought uppon one thinge, but for some vehemency or distress, Soe in speech there is noe repeticion without importance" (p. 126).

The same kind of repetition continued through three or more clauses or sentences is called climax, or gradatio.

Knowing that tribulations bring pacience, pacience bringeth experience, experience bringeth hope. Rom 5. (Peacham, p. 133)

The repetition of words which are derived from the same root, but have different endings or forms, is called polyptoton. This figure was a special favorite with Sidney, whom Fraunce quotes:

Thou art of blood, joy not to make things bleed:
Thou fearest death, thinke they are loth to dye. (*AR*, sig. D 6 ᵛ)

Puttenham calls polyptoton the tranlacer, "when ye turne and tranlace a word into many sundry shapes as the Tailor doth his garment, and after that sort do play with him in your dittie" (p. 203).

Diaphora is the repetition of a common name, used first in extension to designate, second in comprehension to qualify, thus:

What man is there living but will pitie such a case: if he be a man, in the repetition man signifieth humanity, or compassion proper to mans nature. (Peacham, p. 45)

Similar to diaphora is ploce, which Peacham and Day define as the repetition of a proper name with a different signification.

Cicero continued *Cicero* unto the day of his death, meaning a lover of his countrey, and a most faithfull patrone of the commonwealth. (Peacham, p. 44)

Puttenham, however, gives the name ploce to the speedy iteration of one word at frequent intervals. He offers this illustration from Sir Walter Raleigh.

Yet when I sawe my selfe to you was true,
I loved my selfe, bycause my selfe loved you. (p. 201)

Other rhetoricians call this epanodos or traductio. Peacham quotes this example:

To the weake I became as weake, to win the weake. 1 Cor. 9 (p. 49)

Diacope and epizeuxis express vehemence. Diacope is the repetition of a word with one or few between.

My heart is fixed, O God, my heart is fixed. Ps. 57 (Peacham, p. 48)

Epizeuxis is the repetition of words with none between.

Awake, awake and stand by O Jerusalem. Esay 46. (Peacham, p. 47)

In censuring the overuse of the figures of repetition, which were almost the sole stock in trade of certain versifiers of his day, Puttenham expresses his own theory regarding them.

These repetitions be not figurative but phantastical, for a figure is ever used to a purpose, either of beautie or of efficacie: and these last recited be to no purpose, for neither can ye say that it urges affection, nor that it beautifieth or enforceth the sence, nor hath any other subtiltie in it, and therefore is a very foolish impertinency of speech, and not a figure. (p. 202)

As Peacham most often points out, the figures of repetition in addition to pleasing the ear have the functional value of emphasizing ideas and the movement of thought, as, for instance, by accentuating parallel or antithetical structure. In an age when books like the *Arcadia* were read aloud in groups, the figures of repetition were especially valued. And, conversely, the use by Fraunce and Hoskyns of the exceedingly popular and highly regarded *Arcadia* to illustrate the figures quite naturally increased their vogue.

CHAPTER VII

Logos: The Topics of Invention

IN THE RENAISSANCE, as in earlier times, educated men amplified a subject by drawing it as a matter of course through the topics of invention.[1] The topics provide a systematic and exhaustive analysis. A definition expresses the nature or essence of the subject under discussion by telling to what class or genus it belongs and how it differs from other species within that genus. The contrary or contradictory illuminates by contrast. Comparison of the subject with members of the same species shows it to be greater, equal, or less; with those of a different species, similar or dissimilar. The subject may be considered in its parts, and in relation to its characteristics or adjuncts. One may further consider its causes, its effects, its antecedents, its consequents. Its name may reflect its nature, and related names signify related realities, as for instance, to act justly signifies that one is just or possesses justice.

From these sixteen topics intrinsic to the subject under dicussion— definition, division, genus, species, contraries, contradictories, comparison, similarity, dissimilarity, adjuncts, cause, effect, antecedent, consequent, notation, and conjugates [2]—are drawn artificial arguments, so called because they are discoverable through the art of topical investigation. Besides these there are extrinsic arguments, which are called inartificial because they do not depend upon the art of the investigator, but are furnished to him by the testimony of others.

In the sections of this and the following chapter the theory of the logicians is presented first, then that of the figurists. Through this co-ordination of the topics and forms of logic with the figures related to them it becomes clear that the analysis of composition by the Tudor logicians and figurists was essentially the same. The last two sections of the present chapter illustrate how the topics and figures were applied in genesis or composition and in analysis or reading.

[1] Francis P. Donnelly, S.J., in *Persuasive Speech,* admirably presents the topics and the entire rhetorical tradition in a modern manual of speech-composition, with ample attention to applying the same technique to the reading of speeches ancient and modern.
[2] Cicero considered this list of topics exhaustive. See p. 22, above.

1. Inartificial Arguments or Testimony

Inartificial arguments, which include all forms of testimony, occupy a place of importance in the work of logicians and rhetoricians from Aristotle through the Renaissance. The Tudor theorists explain them clearly.

The witnesses upon whose authoritie proofes are grounded, are either heavenly, earthly, or infernall. Gods word, his wonders, his miracles, and his message, sent to men by angels, and Prophetes, are alledged as heavenly witnesses: Law, custome, othe, bargain, writings, sayings, and so forth, are accompted as humaine witnesses, and such as are taken of the credite of man: Conjuring, witchcraft, appearing of ghostes, oracles and answeres of divels, are infernall and ungodlye witnesses, used onelye of the wicked, and suffered of God for a punishment to deceyve them, that will not beleeve the true meanes that God hath appoynted.

Witnesses are not so muche founde out by the arte and cunning of the spokesman: as they doe arise of the matter it selfe, and are ministred to him by the information of others. (Lever, p. 197)

To these he referred whych the Greekes cal *Symeia* or sygnes: For they also commonlye are not fet by the wytte of hym that disputeth but are ministred otherwyse. They be called signes properlye, whyche rysinge of the thynge it selfe that is in question come under the sences of menne, as threatninges, whych be of the time that is paste, cryinge herde oute of a place, whyche is of the tyme presente, palenesse of hym whyche is axed of the murther, whyche is of the tyme followynge, or that bloud leapte oute of the bodye latelye slayne, when he came that did the murther. Also of signes some bee necessary, as that he liveth whiche dothe breathe, and some probable, as bloude in the garmente, whych myghte also come oute of the nose, or otherwyse. (Sherry, sig. E viii [r])

Mans testimony is eyther of one man, or of many. That of one is eyther obligation or confession. To obligation bee referred pledges or sureties. So in August the two sheepeheards, *Perigot* and *Willy*, for want of better arguments to proove their skill in singing, lay downe wagers, the one a cuppe, the other a spotted lambe . . . The offering of triall and proofe, belongeth to this place . . . (Fraunce, *LL.*, fol. 65 [v], 66 [v])

The testimony of many men, especially that of the wise men of old, was held in great esteem.

Al such testimonies may bee called, sentences of the sage, which are brought to confirme any thing, either taken out of olde Aucthors, or els such as have beene used in this common life. As the sentences of Noble men, the Lawes in any Realme, quicke sayinges, Proverbes, that either have been used heretofore, or bee now used. Histories of wise Philosophers, the judgements of learned men, the common opinion of the multitude, olde custome, auncient fashions, or any such like. (Wilson, *RR,* fol. 49 ʳ)

Fifteen figures related to inartificial arguments provide an analysis even more detailed than that accorded testimony treated as a topic of invention.

Apodixis grounds argument on general or common experience.

Salomon: Can a man take fire in his bosome, and his clothes not be burnt: or can a man go upon coles, and his feet not be burnt? (Peacham, p. 86)

Martyria confirms a statement by one's own experience.

The Evangelist *John* sayth: That which was from the beginning, which we have heard, which we have seene with our eies, which we have looked upon, &c. I Joh. 1.1. (*Ibid.,* p. 85)

Paroemia, better known as an adage or proverb, is a common saying of popular origin.

Whoso toucheth pitch shall be defiled therewith. (Day, p. 358)

Gnome, more frequently called an apothegm or sentence, is a notable saying declaring with apt brevity moral doctrine approved by the judgment of all men.[3] For example,

Prodigalitie is the mother of povertie. (Peacham, p. 190)

Four figures depend upon inartificial argument from authority.

Diatyposis . . . is a forme of speech by which the speaker or Orator commendeth certaine profitable rules and precepts to his hearers and to the posterity. . . . *Peter* geveth good precepts to wives concerning their subjection to their husbands, and their modestie in apparell. 1 Pet. 3. (Peacham, p. 92)

Apomnemonysis . . . is a forme of speech by which the Orator . . . for the cause of better confirmation, confutation, consolation, praise or reprehension reciteth some apt sentence, or fit testimonie of approved Authors, and applieth it to his purpose . . . An example of the Holy Scripture: O hypocrites *Esay,* prophecyed well of you, saying: This people draweth neere unto me with their mouth and honoureth me with their lippes, but their heart is far from me. Matt. 15.7; Esay 29.13. (*Ibid.,* p. 87)

---

[3] Such collections of apothegms and adages as those made by Erasmus went through edition after edition in the sixteenth century. The works of Montaigne, Elyot, Pettie, Lyly, Greene, Bacon, to mention but a few, illustrate their abundant use.

Epicrisis . . . is a forme of speech by which the Orator reciting a sentence or saying of some Authour, addeth and delivereth his opinion or judgement upon it and that either in the praise or dispraise of it, or in giving light to it, which is best performed in a short addition . . . whereby he maketh that plain and evident, which was before darke and hard to be understood. An example of our Saviour Christ saying: Ye have heard that it was sayd to them of old time, Thou shalt not commit adultery, but I say unto you, That whosoever looketh on a woman to lust after her, hath committed adultery with her alreadie in his heart Mat. 5.27 . . . *Philip* enterpreteth a place of *Esay* to the *Eunuch*. Act 8. 35. (*Ibid.*, p. 99)

Chria, a very short exposicion of any dede or saying, with the autours name beyng recited. This is well handled of Cicero in the preface of the third boke of his Offices: that Scipio was wont to saye, he was never lesse ydle then when he was voyde of the common wealthe matters, and never lesse alone, then when he was alone. (Sherry, 1555, fol. lv ᵛ)

Oaths, vows, and pledges are figures of testimony. Orcos is an oath confirming what one has affirmed or denied. "God is my witnesse . . . Rom. 1.9." (Peacham, p. 75). Euche is a solemn promise or vow, such as Jacob made when he awoke from his vision (Gen. 28:21; *ibid.*, p. 67).

Eustathia . . . is a forme of speech by which . . . the speaker promiseth and protesteth his constancie concerning something. . . . An example of *Paul*: Who shall separat us from the love of Christ? shall tribulation, or anguish, or persecution, or famine, or nakednes, or perill, or sword. And by and by after he addeth: I am persuaded that neither death, nor life, nor angels, nor principalities, nor powers, neither things present, nor things to come, neyther height, nor depth, nor any other creature shalbe able to separate us from the love of God, which is in Christ Jesus our Lord. Rom 8. (*Ibid.*, p. 69)

Asphalia . . . is a forme of speech by which the speaker persuadeth a securitie and safetie to his hearer by offering himselfe a suretie for the confirmation of his warrant . . . to ad courage in dreadfull adventures, and to give comfort and assurance in doubtfull causes . . . An example of *Juda* persuading his father *Jacob* to let *Benjamin* . . . go into *Aegypt* with the rest of his brothers . . . saying: I will be suerty for him, of my hand shalt thou require him, if I bring him not to thee, then let me beare the blame for ever. Gen. 49.9. (*Ibid.*, p. 68)

Three figures of testimony prognosticate future events.

Euphemismus . . . is a Prognostication of good . . . the orator either interpreteth an uncertaine thing to the better part, or else declareth before that some good thing shall come to passe afterward, which he speaketh from divine revelation, or else collecteth it by some likely signes and tokens. . . . An example of the Apostle *Paul:* I exhort you to be of good courage, for there shalbe no losse of any mans life among you, but of the ship onely. Act 27.22. . . . But the most generall use of this figure is to collect by probable signes and tokens the likely effectes of good causes, and to foretell them, as by the good towardnesse of youth to prognosticate the vertue and felicity of the future age, for a good beginning doth promise a good end, a good cause a good effect . . . The greatest abuse that this figure may commit is . . . to deceave and seduce by flattery and malice or by the false interpretation of dreames. (*Ibid.*, p. 89)

Paraenesis . . . is a forme of speech by which the speaker expresseth an admonition, or warning to his hearers. . . . Hitherto doth belong . . . the admonition of the Angels to *Lot,* concerning the destruction of *Sodom.* Gen. 19.12, 13. (*Ibid.*, p. 78)

Ominatio . . . is a forme of speech, by which the Orator foretelleth the likeliest effect to follow of some evill cause. . . . By this figure the Orator foresheweth beggery to the slothfull, shame to the proud, mischiefe to the quareller, and the gallowes to the thiefe. (*Ibid.*, p. 90)

2. *Definition*

Of artificial arguments the most fundamental is definition, which is, as Hoskyns says, "the shortest & truest exposicion of the nature of any thinge" (p. 158). Fraunce explains more fully:

A Definition is that which declareth what a thing is: it consisteth of two parts, the generall and the difference. Whereof the first is common to the thing defined, and all his other fellow specials, but the difference is proper onely to the thing defined, and distinguisheth it from all other his fellow specials . . . as, A man is a sensible creature endued with reason, where sensible creature is the generall, and endued with reason is the difference. (*LL*, fol. 60 ͬ)

Lever calls attention to an important point in definition, namely, that

the nexte generall is rather to be answered then that which is further of. For when I am asked what a peach is, I shall come neerer to the matter, if I say it is a frute, then if I say it is a creature or a substance. (p. 159)

Blundeville makes clear how species, which is the term to be defined, differs from genus.

Species . . . of the Greeks . . . is called *Idea*, which is as much to say, as a common shape conceived in the minde, through some knowledge had before of one or two Individuums having that shape: so as after wee have seene one wolfe, or two, we beare the shape thereof continually in our mindes, and thereby are able to know a wolfe whensoever we find him, or (if need be) to paint him. But *genus* extendeth too farre, and comprehendeth too many speciall kindes to bee so easily painted. And note that such shapes or *Ideas* are said also to be perpetuall. . . . Because they continue in the minde, though the things themselves cease to have any being: as the shape of a Rose continueth in our mindes in the cold heart of Winter, when there is no Rose indeed. (p. 7)

Fraunce illustrates the use of definition from Spenser's *Shepheardes Calender*.

By an argument from the definition, *Piers* in May proveth hyrelinges, to be no shepheardes, because the true definition of a shepheard agreeth not with them.
>   Thilke same bene shepheards for the Devils stead,
>   That playen whilest their flockes be unfead.
Where after followeth a definition (a cuntrey definition) of an hirelyng, by application whereof unto them, hee prooveth them to bee hyrelings.
>   Well is it seene their sheepe be not their owne,
>   That letten them run at randome alone:
>   But they bene hyred, for little pay,
>   Of others that caren as little as they,
>   What fallen the flocke, so they han the fleece,
>   And get all the gaine paying but a peece. (*LL*, fol. 60 ʳ)

Puttenham explains the relation between logical definition and the figure horismus, which defines a word by impugning its contrary.

The Logician useth a definition to expresse the truth or nature of every thing by his true kinde and difference, as to say wisedome is a prudent and wittie foresight and consideration of humane or worldly actions with their eventes. This definition is Logicall. The Oratour useth another maner of definition, thus: Is this wisedome? no it is a certaine subtill knavish craftie wit, it is no industrie as ye call it, but a certaine busie brainsicknesse, for industrie is a lively and unweried search and occupation in honest things, egernesse is an appetite in base and small matters. (p. 231)

Peacham describes another rhetorical figure of definition.

Systrophe . . . is when the Orator bringeth in many definitions of one thing, yet not such definitions as do declare the substance of a thing by the general kind, and the difference, which the art of reasoning doth prescribe, but others of another kind all heaped together: such as these definitions of *Cicero* be in the second booke of an Orator, where he amplifieth the dignitie of an hystory thus: An historie saith he, is the testimony of times, the light of veritie, the maintenance of memorie, the scoolemistresse of life, and messenger of antiquitie. (p. 153)

3. Division: Genus and Species, Whole and Parts

Wilson points out the relation between definition and division.

As a definition therefore doth declare what a thing is, so a devision sheweth how many thinges are contained in the same. (*RR*, fol. 14 ᵛ)

There are three kinds of division: the genus into its species, the whole into its parts, the subject into its adjuncts. The first is a classification, the second a partition, the third a distinction between substance and the accidents which inhere in it, as redness inheres in a rose. Fraunce notes that "*Socrates* in *Phaedro Platonis* sayth, that if he finde any man who can cunningly divide, he will follow his steps, and admire him for a God" (*LL*, fol. 57 ʳ).

The rules of good division require that the dividing members be mutually exclusive and that together they constitute the whole that is divided. A proposition which expresses the result of a logical division is called disjunctive. For example:

Whatsoever is a living creature, the same is a thing, that either hath reason, or els that lacketh reason. . . . Either it is day, or els it is night. (Wilson, *RR*, fol. 16 ᵛ, 22 ʳ)

One may argue validly that if the whole be good, the parts must be good, but not conversely, because

One or many parts, whether they be principall or of small importance, are not alwayes of force to prove or to prayse a whole. For a song that standeth of foure parts, that is to saye of the base, the meane, the triple, and the contratenor, is not therefore fine and good, because two or three partes be excellently well song. For in such whole things as song and melody are, all the partes are necessarily required to be good, otherwise there shalbe a discorde and a jarre in the whole. (Lever, p. 159)

The ends served by division are:

First, as *Cicero* saith, it helpeth greatly to teach plainly to define, and to make things that be compound, intricate, or confused, to appear simple, plaine, and certaine: Secondly, by dividing things orderly into their parts, it greatly helpeth memorie: and thirdly, it helpeth to amplifie any kind of speech, and to make it more copious. (Blundeville, p. 62)

Fraunce explains the relation between division and induction.

As the distinguishing of the whole into his parts, is called Distribution: so the collection or gathering together of all the parts to make up the whole, is named Induction. (*LL*, fol. 56 ᵛ)

The foregoing principles of logic are reflected in the eleven figures related to division whereby they are applied to specific problems of composition. Hoskyns comments on the value of division,

which *Bacon* in his [fifth colour] tooke out of the *Rhetoritians*, a way to amplify anything (quoth he) is to breake it & make an *Anatomie* of it into severall parts, & to examine it, according to severall circumstances, he said true, it is like the shewe which Pedlers make of their Packes, when they display them contrary to the German magnificence, that serves in all the good meate in one dish. (p. 136)

The figure diaeresis corresponds to the first kind of division named by the logicians, that of genus into species.

Diaeresis . . . is a forme of speech which divideth the generall kind into the speciall kinds, yet not in a dialecticall forme, but in a rhetorical maner for amplifications sake, whereof this saying of *Job* may be an example: Aske the cattaile, and they shall inform thee, the fowles of the aire & they shal tel thee, the increase of the earth, and it shall shew thee, or the fishes of the sea, and they shal certifie thee, by which answere of *Job* to his frends, he declareth that their wisedome was no other then such as the very brute beastes do daily teach, which he divideth into sundry kinds, whereby he doth pithily & elegantly set forth & amplifie their grosse ignorance. (Peacham, p. 123)

Synecdoche, a trope concerned with division, is of four kinds: the genus is substituted for the species,

put upp your weapon, for your dagger, (Hoskyns, p. 124),

or the part for the whole,

my name is tost & censured by many tongues for manye men where the part of an entire bodye goes for the whole (*Loc. cit.*),

or species may be put for genus, as in the Lord's prayer,

> *Bread* one helpe of life is put for all helps (Fenner, sig. D 2 ᵛ),

or whole for part as,

> nations for the Heathen. (*Loc. cit.*)

Merismus, or partitio, employs the second kind of division, distributing the whole into its parts.

If in generality we said *hee hath consumed al his substance in ryot:* By distribution wee might amplifie thus, Whatsoever patrimony hee had from his father, what private inrichment by his deceased mother, what large assistance by his friends, whereat the world never barked, what dowry soever by his wife, which no doubt was very great, all this hath hee consumed by a most dissolute and wanton living. (Day, p. 385)

Eutrepismus is the arrangement of the parts in an appropriate order.

Eutrepismus . . . is a forme of speech, which doth not only number the partes before they be said, but also doth order those partes, and maketh them plaine by a kind of definition, or declaration. . . . There are three sorts of men which do dispose of all that a man hath, the Lawyer, the Phisition, and the Divine. The Lawyer disposeth of his goods, the Phisition of his bodie, and the divine of his soule. (Peacham, p. 129)

Enumeratio employs the third kind of division,

when the subject is divided into the accidents, the matter into the antecedents, the effect into the causes, and into things annexed and following after the effect. . . . Of the subject into accidents. An example: what may we thinke of man, when we consider the heavie burthen of his miserie, the weakenesse of his patience, the imperfection of his understanding, the conflicts of his counsels, the insatietie of his mind, the brevitie of his life, and the certaintie of his death? (*Ibid.*, p. 125)

The remaining figures represent various rhetorical adaptations of division.

Propositio, which comprehendeth in few words the summe of the matter whereof we presently intend to speake. *Cicero:* I have now to speake of the excellent and singular vertues of *Pompeius.* . . . Now in a proposition, there are three things to be considered . . . First that it absolutely containeth whatsoever pertaineth to the cause . . . Secondly, that it be well divided . . . Lastly that it be disposed in an order, most meete for the same cause. (*Ibid.*, p. 192)

Restrictio, when of the generall word going before, a part afterward is excepted, . . . An example of S. *Paul:* We are afflicted on everie side, yet are we not in distresse: in povertie, yet not overcome of povertie: we are persecuted, but not forsaken: cast downe but we perish not. . . . This exornation is evermore used to these effects, . . . to mingle and temper commodities with their discommodities, as felicitie with miserie, . . . And also to note imperfection, in things whiche seeme perfect. (*Ibid.*, p. 131)

Prolepsis, where something generally first spoken, is afterwardes drawne into parts, as thus, . . . *Men diversely do erre, some by an ignorant simplicity, others by a most perverse folly.* (Day, p. 361)

Puttenham explains that epanodos is similar to prolepsis, since in both there is

the resumption of a former proposition uttered in generalitie to explane the same better by a particular division. But their difference is, in that [prolepsis] resumes but the matter only. This resumes both the matter and the termes, and is therefore accompted one of the figures of repetition. . . . The use of this figure, is seen in this dittie following [from Gascoigne],

> Love hope and death, do stirre in me such strife,
> As never man but I lead such a life:
> For burning love doth wound my heart to death:
> And when death comes at call of inward grief,
> And lingring hope doth feede my fainting breath:
> Against my will, and yeelds my wound relief,
> So that I live, but yet my life is such:
> As never death could greeve me halfe so much. (p. 221)

Synathroesmus has two meanings. One is to heap together many words of different meaning, and this is also named congeries.

Hee was a man wholly malicious, exceedingly proud, utterly arrogant, altogether subtill, by nature cruell, and in speeches contentious. (Day, p. 377)

The second meaning is to gather together by way of recapitulation (the reverse of division) points that have been dispersed throughout the speech in order to give them greater weight and to refresh the memory of the hearers.

The conclusion or lapping up of matter, is an apt knitting together of that, which we have saied before. As thus. If reason can perswade, if examples may moove, if necessitie may helpe, if pitie may provoke, if daungers foreseene may stirre us to be wise: I doubt not but you will rather use sharpe lawes to represse offendours, then with dissolute negligence suffer all to perish. (Wilson, *AR*, p. 183)

Similar to this is epiphonema, a brief summary of what has gone before, often sententious, with a moral note, sometimes expressing joyful approbation as in Vergil's,

> Tanta molis erat Romanam condere gentem. 1 *Aeneid.*
> (Fraunce, *AR*, sig. F 4 ʳ)

It is especially suited to the closing up of an epigram. As Puttenham remarks,

Sir *Philip Sidney* very pretily closed up a dittie in this sort.
> *What medcine then, can such disease remove,*
> *Where love breedes hate, and hate engenders love.* (p. 217)

4. *Subject and Adjuncts*

The distinction between adjuncts and the subject in which they inhere provides the basis for the third kind of division discussed by the logicians in the preceding section. Much more important, however, than the distinction that may be made between these topics is their relationship to each other. This is best understood from the fundamental instance of this relationship, namely, that of a substance and its accidents, which Blundeville explains with his usual clarity.

We cannot see the substance of anything with our bodily eies, but only with the eies of our minde and understanding; but we may see the shape, the quantitie, the colour and such like accidents cleaving to the substance, without the which these accidents have no being at all: and therefore in seeing such accidents, we may assure our selves that there is a substance sustaining those accidents, which doth alwaies remaine, though the accidents doe faile or change never so often. (p. 20)

Fraunce gives a brief but comprehensive explanation of the logical doctrine of subjects and adjuncts, defining subject as a wider term than substance.

[A subject is] not onely . . . an essence, or substance, as the common Logicians usually take it, but also whatsoever can bee imagined or fayned to have any thing adjoyned unto it, in it, or about it: so one quality may bee the subject to another, as in this axiome, Vertue is commendable, where commendation is adjoyned to vertue, being the subject thereof. (*LL*, fol. 39 ʳ)

The subject is that whereunto some thing is adjoyned. The subject receiveth the adjunct, eyther in it, as the minde learning, the place the thing placed: or to it: & this is either affected by the thing adjoyned, as the body receiveth garments to it, and is of them affected: or els it dooth affect the thing adjoyned, as a sicke man receyveth unto him the physitian, and dooth affect him, by occupying and busiying his heade and minde in inventing remedies for him. (38 ʳ)

Explications, illustrations, amplifications, and extenuations are fet from this place: So *Cicero* to his sonne, Thou art at *Athens*, therefore thou shouldest bee learned. . . . From hence are almost all poeticall epithetes deducted. (40 ʳ)

An adjunct is that whereunto something is subject. An adjunct is eyther Inherent in the subject, or adherent to it. The adherent adjunct dooth eyther affect the subject: or is affected by it. So vertues, vices, learning, and all such
qualities are adjuncts to mans minde. And as every place is the subject of the
thing placed: so, time, that is to say, the continuance of every thing, is the adjunct of those thinges which doo continue in time. So all qualities which eyther
bee proper, as laughing to a man: or common, as whitenesse to a stone, and
a wall, are truely called adjuncts. Finally everything which agreeth unto an
other, beeing neyther the cause, nor the effect thereof, is an adjunct of the
thing, whereunto it dooth agree. . . .

In March *Thomalin* argueth the spring to bee at hand, by these adjunctes.

> The grasse now gins to bee refresht
> The swallow peepes out of her nest,
> And clowdy *Welkin* cleareth. (41 ʳ)

Hence are also fet prayses and disprayses, deliberations and consultations.
Herein are contained all those Rhetoricall places concerning the giftes and
qualities of body and soule, as also externall and those of fortune. (43 ᵛ)

Eighteen figures are derived from the relation of subject and adjuncts.

Peristasis, a forme of speech by which the Orator amplifieth by circumstances . . . either of a person or of a thing, a person hath these: Parentage,
nation, Countrie, kinde, age, education, discipline, habite of bodie, fortune, condition, nature of the minde, studie, foredeeds, name, &c. . . . Circumstances
of things: Cause, Place, Time, Occasion: To watch the opportunitie of darke-
nesse to do mischiefe . . . Instrument . . . to murder by poisoning or by
strangling doth argue a deepe and cursed malice of the murderer. . . . *Caution* . . . take heede of long and tedious stay in them, as about who, what,
when, where, how, and such like, which by prolixitie is wont to make the oration barren.[4] (Peacham, p. 164)

Encomion is a forme of speech by which the Orator doth highly commend to
his hearers, some person or thing in respect of their worthy deserts & vertues . . . this [is] the only forme of speech, which both speaketh while the
vertuous man doth live, and also liveth when the vertuous man is dead. (*Ibid.,*
p. 155)

Taxis is a figure . . . which distributeth to everie subject his most proper &
naturall adjunct. . . . The divine wisedome hath assigned Kings to raigne,
Judges to heare causes & give sentence, Advocates to plead, subjects to obey,
the wise to give counsell, and the rich to give almes. (*Ibid.,* p. 60)

Puttenham explains the difference between epitheton and antonomasia.

---

[4] Compare Wilson's list of the places of persons, p. 24, above.

Epitheton . . . giving every person or thing besides his proper name a qualitie by way of addition whether it be of good or of bad . . . as to say.

> *Fierce Achilles, wise Nestor, wilie Ulysses* . . .

But if we speake thus not expressing her proper name *Elizabeth,* videl.

> *The English Diana, the great Britton mayde.*

Then is it not by *Epitheton* . . . but by . . . *Antonomasia,* or *Periphrasis.* (p. 176)

This form of antonomasia substitutes for the proper name a descriptive phrase; another form represents the reverse process whereby a proper name is substituted for a quality associated with it.

When we give to one man the name of another for the affinities sake of their maners or conditions. In praise thus, as when we call a grave man a *Cato* . . . In dispraise, to call . . . a tyrant a *Nero.* (Peacham, p. 23)

Similar to the first form of antonomasia is periphrasis, which substitutes a descriptive phrase for a common name.

If a short ordinarie sence bee odly expressed . . . for kill any maryed man, make his sword accursed by any widdowe . . . (Hoskyns, p. 162)

Metonymy is a trope which sometimes substitutes subject for adjunct or adjunct for subject.

The change of name or Metonymie, where the subject or that which hath any-thing adjoined, is put for the thing adjoined or adjoynt. So the place is put for those or that in the place . . . *It shalbe easier for Sodome and Gomorra,* that is, the people *in Sodome and Gomorra. So Moses chaire is put for the doctrine taught in Moses chaire.* . . .
On the other side, the adjoint is put for the thing to whiche it is adjoyned. . . . So in the Epistle to the Ephesians. *The dayes are evil,* that is, the manner, conversation, and the deeds of men in the dayes. (Fenner, sig. D i ʳ)

Enargia and hypotyposis are generic names for a group of figures aiming at lively description and counterfeit representation,

when the Orator by a diligent gathering together of circumstances, and by a fit and naturall application of them, doth expresse and set forth a thing so plainly and lively, that . . . the hearer . . . rather thinketh he seeth it then heareth it. . . . Now under the generall name of Description, I do not only reckon speciall kindes of description, but also all other figures, which do chiefly respect circumstances and adjuncts . . . (Peacham, p. 134)

The names of the species of counterfeit representation both factual and fictitious exemplify an unflagging zeal for making distinctions which seem to us mere hair-splitting or wearisome pedantry but which men of the Renaissance evidently found interesting and delightful. In *The Lawiers Logike* Fraunce mentions, with a hint of mild amusement, the species which some of the rhetoricians distinguished.

If any person be described, they call it *Prosopographia,* if a place, *Topographia,* if a nation, *Chorographia,* if the earth, *Geographia,* if the water, *hydrographia,* if the wind, *Anemographia,* if a tree, *Dendographia,* if the time *Chronographia,* &c. (fol. 63 ᵛ)

The Tudor figurists omit some in this list, but add others. Because these kinds of description, except for their names, are familiar to us, it will suffice to summarize the figures of this group briefly.

Prosopographia is the lively description of an absent person as if he were present, as when Homer describes Achilles or Chaucer the Pardoner and the rest of his pilgrims. Prosopopoeia is fictional and includes the feigning of persons and the attribution of human qualities to dumb or even to inanimate creatures, as when Cicero represents Rome as reproaching Catiline; another example is Vergil's description of Fame or Rumor. Characterismus is the description of the body or mind; ethopoeia, of natural propensity and affections, manners, arts, virtues, vices; mimesis, of gesture, pronunciation, and utterance; dialogismus, or sermocinatio, of speech, especially when the orator engages in counterfeit dialogue with the feigned person. Pragmatographia is the vivid representation of a counterfeit action, as of a battle, a feast, a marriage. Chronographia describes times; topographia, places. But if the places are fictional, such as the house of envy in Ovid's *Metamorphoses,* the figure is called topothesia. "All Logike," remarks Fraunce, "is generall, and applyable as well to thinges imagined, as things that bee extant in truth." (*Ibid.,* fol. 59 ᵛ).

These figures of counterfeit representations, whether of real or of imaginary persons, places, events, and times, are essentially poetic in the sense of communicating experience by creating an illusion of reality. Through them an author speaks to readers or listeners, not directly, but indirectly by interposing characters and situations which seem real and immediate. This imitation lies at the very heart of epic and of drama, as Aristotle points out in the *Poetics.*

The poet should say very little *in propria persona,* as he is no imitator when doing that. Whereas the other poets are perpetually coming forward in person, and say but little, and that only here and there, as imitators, Homer after a brief preface brings in forthwith a man, a woman, or some other Character—no one of them characterless, but each with distinctive characteristics. (24, 1460 ^{a} 7)

5. Contraries and Contradictories

Often a matter is more clearly understood in relation to its contrary, as Wilson observes.

By contraries set together things oftentimes appear greater. . . . set a faire woman against a foule, and she shall seeme much the fairer, and the other much the fouler. (*AR*, p. 125)

In his "Apologie for Poetrie" Sidney also explains:

Now, as in Geometry the oblique must bee knowne as wel as the right, and in Arithmetick the odde as wel as the even, so in the actions of our life who seeth not the filthines of evil wanteth a great foile to perceive the beauty of vertue. (Smith, I, 177)

Through contraries one may more readily recognize the ambiguity of words, as of *sharp* or *clear*.

Sharp, is a word of double understanding: for his contrarie . . . in voyce is, flat: and in edge, dull. Therefore it must folow of necessitie that it is not one sharpnesse, which is contrarye to flatnes in voyce, and to dulnesse in edge . . . not one and the same clearenes that is sene & heard: the one consisting in colour and the other in sound. (Lever, p. 50)

The Tudor logicians distinguish four kinds of opposites: contraries, relatives, privatives, and contradictories. Contraries are called mediate if there are species between the extremes, as there are between black and white, for

if a cloth be not white, it is no reason to call it blacke. For it may bee blewe, greene, redd, russett, tawnie, yealowe, or any other colour els, as it shall best please the Dyer. (Wilson, *RR*, fol. 52 ^{v})

Contraries are called immediate if there are no species between, but one or the other must be affirmed, as faith or unbelief in a man. Relative terms are opposed to one another, yet each implies the other, as father and son, husband and wife, cause and effect, subject and adjunct. They cannot both be present at the same time and in the same respect: Socrates cannot be father and son to the same man. Yet

that which agreeth with one of the Relatives, commonly agreeth with the other, as if it bee honest to teach, it is no shame to learne. (Fraunce, *LL*, fol. 49 ^{r})

Privative terms represent deprivations opposed to natural perfections, as blindness to sight; hence a stone cannot properly be called blind because sight does not belong to its nature. Of contradictory terms, one is positive, the other negative, as a stone, no stone; righteous, unrighteous. And since the negative term includes everything except its opposite positive, one term must always be affirmed, the other denied.

Besides contrary and contradictory terms, there are contrary and contradictory propositions. Of contradictory propositions, one must be true and the other false.

Therefore if this saying (All fayre women are good) be false: then this saying (Some faire women are not good) muste needes be true. (Lever, p. 206)

But of contraries, both may be false, as

All men are moved with glorie, No manne is moved with glorie. (Wilson, *RR*, fol. 20 ʳ)

but both cannot be true.

The Tudor rhetoricians treat eleven figures based on contraries and contradictories. Litotes is related to what the logicians call equipollence or obversion, which consists in expressing a thought by denying its contradictory. This figure may be used to dispraise another with less offense or to speak well of oneself with greater modesty.

Job saith, that he hath not eaten his meate alone, that he hath not seene any man perish for want of clothing, or any poore for lacke of covering. Here if *Job* had said that he had feasted many, that he had clothed every poore body that should otherwise have perished, he had not spoken so modestly, albeit that he had sayd as truly. (Peacham, p. 150)

Synoeciosis is a composition of contraries.

> *Thus for your sake I dayly dye*
> *And do but seeme to live in deede:*
> *Thus is my blisse but miserie,*
> *My lucre losse without your meede.* (Puttenham, p. 207)

Paradox in the sixteenth century had two meanings: (1) a statement contrary to received opinion, evoking wonder because it is marvelous, strange, incredible; (2) a statement apparently self-contradictory. In Puttenham's illustration of this figure which he calls the Wondrer, Cato, pointing out a young unthrift who had lately sold his patrimony for some salt marshes, seems to find the cause of wonder or incredibility in the apparent contradiction.

> *Now is it not, a wonder to behold,*
> *Yonder gallant skarce twenty winter old,*
> *By might (mark ye) able to doo more?*
> *Than the mayne sea that batters on his shore?*
> *For what the waves could never wash away,*
> *This proper youth hath wasted in a day.* (p. 226)

In contrast to synoeciosis, which is a composition of contrary terms, antithesis [5] is an opposition of them, giving greater light and perspicuity.

For he that alwayes wyll be an enemy to his owne rekenyngs, how should a man trust that he wold be a frind to other mens matters? (Sherry, sig. D iiii ^{v})

Aristotle comments on the value of antithesis.

Such a form of speech is satisfying, because the significance of contrasted ideas is easily felt, especially when they are thus put side by side, and also because it has the effect of a logical argument; it is by putting two opposing conclusions side by side that you prove one of them false. (*Rhetoric*, 3.9.1410 ^{a} 20)

Syncrisis, is a comparison of contrary things, & diverse persons in one sentence. . . . Wise women uphold their house, but a foolish woman pulleth it downe. Prov. 14.1. (Peacham, p. 162)

Antanagoge is a figure whereby something spoken unfavorably is in a measure counteracted, though not denied, by the addition of something favorable which gives another color to the matter. For example, one wishing to encourage youth in study might remark:

> *Many are the paines and perils to be past,*
> *But great is the gaine and glorie at the last.*
> (Puttenham, p. 216)

Inter se pugnantia, is a forme of speech by which the orator reproveth his adversarie, or some other person of manifest unconstancie, open hypocrisie, or in-

---

[5] This is the figure, remarked Hoskyns (p. 151), which Ascham taught the Queen of England and in which she excelled. Writing to his friend Sturm on April 4, 1550, Ascham mentioned that his pupil, the Princess Elizabeth, then sixteen years old, particularly delighted in noting contraries: "She very much admires modest metaphors, and comparisons of contraries well put together and contrasting felicitously with one another. Her ears are so well practised in discriminating all these things, and her judgment is so good, that in all Greek, Latin, and English composition, there is nothing so loose on the one hand or so concise on the other, which she does not immediately attend to, and either reject with disgust or receive with pleasure, as the case may be." (Letter XCIX, translated and quoted in Berdan, *Early Tudor Poetry*, p. 340.)

solent arrogancie. . . . Thou therefore which teachest another, teachest not
thy selfe; thou that preachest a man should not steale, yet thou stealest: . . .
Rom. 2. (Peacham, p. 163)

Irony is a trope which by naming one contrary intends another. It is
used in derision, mockery, jesting, dissembling.

This trope is perceived either by the contrariety of the matter or the manner
of utterance, or both. . . . So the Jewes said unto Christe: Hayle king of the
Jewes. (Fenner, sig. D 2 ⱽ)

Antiphrasis is the irony of one word,

when we deride by plaine and flat contradiction, as he that saw a dwarfe go in
the streete said to his companion . . . See yonder gyant. (Puttenham, p. 191)

Paralipsis is a kind of irony which in the very show of pretending to
pass over a certain matter tells it nonetheless.

I urge not to yow the hope of your friends, though that should animate yow
to answer their expectacion, I lay not before yow the necessitie of the place
which yow are to furnish, wherein to be defective & insufficient were some
shame. I omit the envious concurrencies & some prepared comparisons in your
countrie, which have some feeling with yonge men of fore-sight, I onelie say
howe our owne promises shall give Judgment against us . . . (Hoskyns,
p. 145)

Epitrope is an ironical permission, such as Dido scornfully uttered
to Aeneas.

I, sequere Italiam ventis: pete regna per undas.

Fraunce quotes this from Vergil, and also an example from Sidney's
Arcadia.

If you seeke the victorie take it, and if you list, triumph.
(Fraunce, *AR*, sig. H 5 ʳ)

6. Similarity and Dissimilarity

Contrariety clearly exists between species at opposite extremes within
the same genus, as black and white, but objects of different classes may
be similar or dissimilar in some respect. Consequently argument from
contrariety is fundamental and convincing; that from similarity or dissimilarity is superficial, often adventitious, illuminating rather than compelling. Blundeville observes that

this kinde of reasoning of Like, is more apt to teach and to print in the hearers
minde a lively representation of the thing, then to urge him by any necessitie

of due proofe to beleeve the same, because it is unpossible, that the two things which are to bee compared can be like in all points . . . (p. 111)

Sidney remarks that the force of a similitude is not "to proove anything to a contrary Disputer but onely to explane to a willing hearer" (Smith, I, 203). And Lever asserts:

Learned men in arguing, make small accompt of any similitude. For by a similitude you maye as soone prove a wrong matter as a righte: yet doe men of great judgement use it, but rather to perswade and leade the simple and the ignoraunt, then to force and overcome the wittie adversarie. . . . A similitude is well answered, when an unlikelinesse is shewed in that matter wherein divers things were sayde to bee like. (p. 196)

Induction is a method of argument which from like instances draws a general conclusion. In this manner Socrates, by questioning his adversaries, gathered instances from them and drew conclusions which confounded them. Argument by example is a form of induction.

An example, is a maner of argumentation, where one thyng is proved by an other, forthe likenesse that is founde to be in them both, as thus. If *Marcus Attilius Regulus* had rather lose his life then not keepe promise with his enemie, then should every man beeing taken prisoner, keepe promise with his enemie. (Wilson, *RR*, fol. 33 ʳ)

One may argue also from dissimilitude as Colyn does in "June."

> O happy *Hobbinoll*, I blesse thy state,
> That Paradise hast found which *Adam* lost,
> Here wander may thy flocke early or late:
> Withouten dreade of woolves to beene ytost,
> Thy lovely layes here mayst thou freely boste:
> But I unhappy man whome cruell fate
> And angry Gods pursue from coaste to coaste,
> Can no where finde to shrowde my lucklesse pate.
> (Fraunce, *LL*, fol. 75 ʳ)

This illustration cited by Fraunce in his work on logic would serve perfectly for the figure dissimilitude, which Peacham, using a similar illustration, describes as

a forme of speech which compareth diverse things in a diverse qualitie. An example . . . of our Saviour Christ: The foxes have holes, and the fowles of the aire have nestes, but the sonne of man hath not where to laie his head. Luc. 9.58. (p. 160)

Nine figures are based on similitude. By homoeosis, or the figure of similitude,

we not onely bewtifie our tale, but also very much inforce & inlarge it. I say inforce because no one thing more prevaileth with all ordinary judgements than perswasion by *similitude* . . . which may be thus spoken.

> But as the watrie showres delay the raging wind,
> So doeth good hope cleane put away dispaire out of my mind.
>
> (Puttenham, p. 240)

Puttenham makes homoeosis the genus of icon, paradigma, parabola, and fable or apologue. Icon is the comparison of one person or thing with another, form with form, quality with quality, as

he whets his teeth like a Bore . . . we might compare one man with another, as *Salust* compareth *Caesar* and *Cato* together, or wee might heape many men together, and prove by large rehearsall any thing that wee would, the which of the *Logicians* is called induction. (Wilson, *AR*, p. 207)

By paradigma or example one also proceeds by induction.

We . . . liken one case to another . . . compare the past with the present, gathering probabilitie of like successe to come in the things wee have presently in hand: . . . as if one should say thus, *Alexander* the great in his expedition to Asia did thus, so did *Hanniball* comming into Spaine, so did *Caesar* in Egypt, therfore all great Captains & Generals ought to doe it. (Puttenham, p. 245)

A parable teaches a moral by metaphorical and dark speeches, such as the parable of the laborers in the vineyard. According to Puttenham,

they may be fayned aswell as true: as those fables of *Aesope,* and other apologies invented for doctrine sake by wise and grave men. (p. 245)

Wilson comments on the value of fables.

The feined Fables, such as are attributed unto brute beastes . . . not onely . . . delite the rude and ignorant, but also they helpe much for perswasion . . . because such as speake in open audience have ever mo fooles to heare them, then wisemen to give judgment . . . The multitude (as *Horace* doth say) is a beast . . . use the quiddities of *Dunce,* to set forth Gods misteries: and you shall see the ignorant (I warrant you) either fall a sleepe, or els bid you farewell. The multitude must needes be made merie: . . . The Romaine *Menenius Agrippa,* alledging upon a time, a Fable of the conflict made betwixt the parts of a mans bodie, and his bellie: quieted . . . the uprore of sedicious Rebelles . . . (*AR,* p. 197)

A metaphor is a trope based on similitude. Metaphors

give pleasant light to darke things . . . by the aptnesse of their proportion, and nearnesse of affinitie, they worke in the hearer many effects, they obtaine allowance of his judgement, they move his affections, and minister a pleasure to his wit. . . . they are forcible to perswade. . . . they leave such a firme impression in the memory, as is not lightly forgotten. (Peacham, p. 13)

In Aristotle's opinion,

to be a master of metaphor . . . is . . . a sign of genius, since a good metaphor implies an intuitive perception of the similarity in dissimilars. (*Poetics*, 22, 1459 ^{a} 5)

The figure allegory is a metaphor continued through whole sentences or even through a whole discourse.

The continuance of Tropes called an Allegorie, is when one kinde of Trope is so continued: as, Looke with what kinde of matter it be begunne, with the same it be ended. So in the 23. Psalme, *the care of God towardes his Churche, is set foorth by the woordes proper to a shephearde.* So in the whole booke of Canticles, *the sweete conference of Christe and his Church, is set downe by the wordes proper to the husbande and the wife.* (Fenner, sig. D i ^{v})

Peacham describes onomatopoeia as a figure whereby

we invent, devise, fayne, and make a name, immitating the sownd of that it sygnifyeth, as hurliburly, for an uprore, and tumultuous stirre, thwick thwack, that is blow, for blow, stroake for stroake, and one harder then an other, thwick sygnifyeth the lesser, and thwack the greater, buzzing for the noyse of Bees, . . . and fynally the mooting of beasts, the blating of sheepe, the neighing of Horse, the scriking of Infantes, and al such voyces, as doe resemble the sound, or be straungely fayned. (1577, sig. C iiii ^{r})

Catachresis is the borrowing of a word from its own proper signification to accommodate it to another not proper to it, but somewhat like it, as to say that the sword shall devour, that men's powers are short, or their counsels long, when there is literally no such measure of them. Or, explains Puttenham,

as one said very pretily in this verse.

I lent my love to losse. . . .

Whereas this worde *lent* is properly of mony or some such other thing, as men do commonly borrow, for use to be repayed againe, and being applied to love is utterly abused, and yet very commendably spoken by vertue of this figure.

For he that loveth and is not beloved againe, hath no lesse wrong, than he that lendeth and is never repayde. (p. 180)

7. Comparison: Greater, Equal, Less

Objects of different classes may be similar or dissimilar in some respect, usually in quality. Objects of the same class may be greater, equal, or less with respect to quantity.

This Logicall quantity . . . may bee attributed to any thing incident and convenient to our purpose, as, to dignitie, prayse, reproche, abilitie and power, greatnes, multitude, conveniency, commoditie, opportunitie, facilitie, difficultie, care, neglect, excellencie, vilenes, and in a woorde, to whatsoever may bee saide to bee equall, more, or lesse. (Fraunce, *LL*, fol. 78 ʳ)

Blundeville points out that

of substances one cannot be more or lesse then another; for the greatest Giant, as touching substance, is no more a man then the least Dwarfe that is; neither is a man full growne, more a man then a childe newly borne: for more or lesse appertaineth properly to quantitie, and not to substance. (p. 21)

Lever likewise explains:

Al specials ar partakers of their general indifferently, without respect of more or lesse. For an Egle is no rather nor no more a birde or a foule, then an Oule is, nor an Oule more or lesse then a Wrenne: but they and all other foules equally and indifferently, are named and be in deede birdes, without degree of more or lesse. (p. 151)

Fraunce cautions against fallacy in this kind of argument.

As when you take that for lesse which is not lesse. As if a boy can paynt, then a man can paynt, for although a boy bee lesse then a man, yet a boy may sometimes sooner paynt then a man. (*LL*, fol. 81 ʳ)

One may, however, argue validly from number, as

pardon mee this fault: it is the firste . . . forgeve this second trespasse; for twice is not often. (Lever, p. 164)

An argument may proceed from the greater in any respect, such as the greater in probability, in desirability, in difficulty, or efficacy, as this which Fraunce cites from Vergil.

Counterfayt teares circumvented them, whome neyther the cruell *Diomedes*, nor fierce *Achilles*, nor ten yeares warre, nor a thousand ships could overcome. (*LL*, fol. 79 ʳ)

As an argument from the equal he quotes from Terence.

Sith I meddle not with thine, meddle not thou with mine. (fol. 76 ᵛ)

He presents as an argument from the less:

If God doe not reject the sparrowes, much lesse you: But he contemneth not them: therefore not you. (fol. 80 ᵛ)

The parallelism between the works of the Ramists and the figurists is clearly seen in the similarity of Fraunce's treatment of the logical topics of comparison—greater, equal, less—and Peacham's account of the figure comparatio, whereby

like things are compared among themselves, unlike from the lesse to the greater in amplifying, and from the greater to the lesse in diminishing . . . Comparison of like things, as *Camillus* by his vertue did drive away the Barbarians and set up againe the Romane Empire, being sore opprest, and almost brought to utter destruction: even so *Laurentius Valla* restored the Latine tongue to the former puritie, which through the ignorance of the Barbarians was corrupted, suppressed, and almost quite extinct . . .

From the lesse to the greater: Wherefore if God so clothe the grasse of the field which is to day and to morrow is cast into the Oven: shall he not do much more for you, O ye of little faith? Mat. 6. . . . From the greater to the lesse . . . If God spared not the Angels that had sinned but cast them downe into hell . . . much lesse will he spare the wicked which walke after the flesh in the lusts of uncleannesse. (p. 156)

A number of figures convey a sense of the greater or the less although comparison in them is merely implicit, as in following an order from greater to less or from less to greater in a series; in exaggerating or extenuating; in substituting a stronger for a weaker word; and in iterating the same idea in different words and figures.

Auxesis, as Puttenham and Day call it, or progression, as Hoskyns names it, is a kind of amplification

which by stepps of comparison stores everie degree, till it come to the topp, & [to] make the matter seeme the higher advaunced, sometimes descends the lower; . . . In like sort is this example to abuse the name of god: to make table talke of a meane man's name [were] wrong, to run upon a noblemans tytle were a great scandall, to play with a Princes name were a treason, & what shall it bee to make a vanitie of that name, which is most terrible to tirants & divells, & most reverende even to Monarchs and Angells. (Hoskyns, p. 140)

Such mounting by degrees through words or sentences of increasing weight we would call climactic word order. Peacham names it incrementum, and gives to auxesis a different meaning, that of augmentation accomplished chiefly through hyperbole.

Auxesis is a forme of speech by which the Orator amplifieth by putting a greatter word for a lesse, as to call a proude man *Lucifer*, a dronkard a swine, an angrie man mad, a covetous man a cutthroate: In praising, as to call an honest man a Saint, a faire Virgin an Angell, good musicke heavenly harmonie.

This figure is chiefly set forth by tropes of words . . . but chieflie by *Hyperbole*, which maketh a large and most ample comparison. (p. 167)

That hyperbole exceeds the truth both the speaker and the hearer well know, and therefore its intention is not to deceive but to exaggerate the greatness or the smallness of things by an excessive similitude, as to call an extortioner a wolf, to speak of streams of tears, or to say that a cry reaches to heaven.

The opposite of auxesis is meiosis, whereby one makes a thing appear less than it is by putting a less word for a greater, for various reasons: to bring one's adversaries into contempt, as Hannibal did in his speech to his soldiers; to excuse a fault or an offense, as to call robbery pilfering or a great wound a scratch; to belittle through implication, as to speak of fantastical-minded people whom children and musicians call lovers. When such extenuation tends to flattery or soothing, it is named para-diastole, as for instance to call a prodigal man a liberal gentleman, a miser thrifty, drunkenness good fellowship, insatiable avarice good husbandry, craft and deceit wisdom and policy.

Charientismus mitigates with pleasant words or mocks under smooth and lowly words, as when

wee scoffe a man in his threatning mood, to say, *O good words, I pray you,* or, *Kill us not at the first dash,* or, *Bite not my nose off I pray you,* and such like. (Day, p. 359)

Catacosmesis, like auxesis, expresses degree through word order, but whereas auxesis sets the weightiest word last, catacosmesis sets the word greatest in dignity first, as God and man, sun and moon, life and death.

Epanorthosis, or correction,

is a figure which taketh away that that is said, and putteth a more meet word in the place, . . . written not with inke, but with the spirite of the living God, not in tables of stone, but in the fleshly tables of the heart. 2 Cor. 3.3. (Peacham, p. 172)

Similar to this is dirimens copulatio,

when we bring forth one sentence with an exception before it, and immediately joyne another after it that seemeth greater . . . Wherefore you must needes obey, not onely for feare of vengeance, but also for conscience sake. (*Ibid.*, p. 171)

The figure emphasis, as described by Puttenham, derives its force from substituting for a concrete quality that same quality regarded in its universal abstract essence.

One notable meane to affect the minde, is to inforce the sence of any thing by a word of more than ordinary efficacie, and nevertheles is not apparant, but as it were, secretly implyed, as he that said thus . . .

> O sinne it selfe, *not wretch, but wretchednes*

Whereas if he had said thus . . . O *sinfull and wretched man*, it had bene all to one effect, yet not with such force and efficacie, to speake by the denominative, as by the thing it selfe. (p. 184)

Mere repetition adds weight to an idea, as through the figure synonymia,

when by a variation and change of words that be of like signification we iterat one thing diverse times. An example . . . of *Virgil:* How doth the child *Ascanius?* is he yet alive? doth he eate the etheral foode? and lieth he not yet under the cruell shades? Here through affection he expresseth one thing thrise: for all that he demaundeth is no more but this, is *Ascanius* alive. (Peacham, p. 149)

Exergasia,[6] or expolitio, may be regarded as a figure of augmentation as well as of garnishing,

when we abide still in one place, and yet seeme to speake diverse things, many times repeating one sentence, but yet with other words, sentences, exornations, and figures: it differeth, saith *Melancton* from *Sinonimia*, forasmuch as that repeateth a sentence or thing onely with changed wordes: but this both with like wordes, like sentences, and like things, having also many exornations to the garnishing thereof. (*Ibid.*, p. 193)

In view of their function, three other figures may be regarded as forms of augmentation: an introductory narrative which opens a speech, a digression, and a return from digression.

---

[6] La Rue Van Hook pointed out in "Greek Rhetorical Terminology in Puttenham's 'The Arte of English Poesie,'" *Transactions of the American Philological Association*, XLV (1914), 120, that Puttenham is inaccurate in his definition of exergasia and in some other points. Nevertheless, inasmuch as Puttenham's work had a considerable circulation, his definitions and illustrations, even when inaccurate, represent to some extent contemporary opinion. Puttenham's definition agrees in substance with Peacham's quoted above.

Paradiegesis . . . a form of speech by which the Orator telleth or maketh mention of some thing, that it may be a fit occasion or introduction to declare his further meaning, or principall purpose, which is a speciall and artificiall forme of insinuation. A verie apt example we have in the 17. of the Acts, of *Paul* who tooke an occasion by the Aultar which he saw in *Athens* as he passed by, both to reprove the idolatry of the Athenians, and also to teach them the true worship of the living God . . . (*Ibid.*, p. 94)

By parecbasis, or digression,

we swarve sometimes from the matter, upon just considerations, making the same to serve for our purpose, as well as if we had kept the matter still. As . . . when I shall . . . declame against an hainous murtherer, I may digresse from the offence done, and enter in praise of the dead man, declaring his vertues in most ample wise, that the offence done may be thought so much the greater, the more honest he was, that hath thus bene slaine. (Wilson, *AR*, p. 181)

Concerning reditus ad propositum, coming again to the matter, Wilson remarks:

When we have made a digression, wee may declare our returne. . . . I knewe a Preacher that was a whole hower out of his matter, and at length remembring himself, saied well, now to the purpose, as though all that he had spoken before, had beene little to the purpose, whereat many laughed, and some for starke wearinesse were faine to goe away. (*Ibid.*, p. 182)

8. Cause and Effect, Antecedent and Consequent

The causes include whatever contributes in any way to produce the effect. Logicians distinguish four causes: the efficient, the material, the formal, and the final. Their importance is such that

no man is saide to knowe anye thing throughly afore he know the causes thereof. (Lever, p. 174)

This is pre-eminently true of the formal cause.

The efficient cause is constituted of the agent, for instance, a carpenter, and his instruments, such as axe, hammer, saw. Wilson explains how the efficient cause may be multiple.

In battaille, the Captaine is the efficient commaunder: the Soldiour the efficient obeier: Gunnes, Darts, Bowes and Billes, the instrumentes of doing. (*RR*, fol. 44 ʳ)

Fraunce cites an illustration of the efficient cause from Spenser's *Shepheardes Calender.*

Collyn in the first Egloge maketh loove the efficient of his weale and woe.

> A thousand sithes I cursse that carefull howre,
> Wherein I lov'de the neighbour towne to see,
> And eke ten thousand siths I blesse the stowre
> Wherein I saw so faire a sight as shee.
> Yet all for naught, such sight hath bred my bayne,
> Ah God, that love should breede both joy and payne.
>
> (*LL*, fol. 12 ^{r})

The material cause is that out of which the thing is made, as wood and stone in a house. It is not, however, limited to the corporeal.

The materiall causes, as also all other arguments Logicall, are not to be tied onely to sensible or bodily matters: but generally to bee applyed to any whatsoever, bee it subject to sence, or conceived by reason. As, a man conceiveth in his mind or memory the Art of Logike or any other science, the matter whereof is their severall rules and preceptes, the forme, the due disposition of the same: and yet neither first nor last is subject to sence, but onely understoode by reason, and imprinted in the inward power of mans soule. (*Ibid.*, fol. 22 ^{r})

The formal cause is that which makes a thing to be what it is. Therefore, explains Fraunce,

hath *Aristotle* in the first of his *Topiks* assigned it two properties; The one for giving essence and knowledge of the same essence, the other for causing difference . . . for that especially by the forme things differ one from another . . . So every naturall thing hath his peculiar forme, as a lyon, a horse, a tree, &c. so every artificiall thing also, as a house, a shippe, &c. So things incorporall, as vertue, vice, &c. So in a woord, whatsoever is, by the formall cause it is that which it is, and is different from all other things that it is not. . . .

The forme is eyther internall, or externall: Internall which is not perceived by sence. Externall, which is subject to sence. Externall is eyther naturall, which is ingraven in every thing naturally: or Artificiall, which Art hath framed and performed. The naturall and internall formes of things bee hardly either known and understoode, or expressed and made plaine. The artificiall and externall is much more easily both conceived in reason, and expressed by worde. . . . But now, as the understanding of the formall cause causeth surest knowledge, so hardly can wee understand what the formall cause is . . . So that for the most part things bee not knowne . . . (*Ibid.*, fol. 24 ^{r}, 22 ^{v})

The form is at the root of both identity and change.

The alteration of the forme chaungeth the thing formed, and maketh it another thing: but heere wee must distinguish betweene the universall chaunging of the forme, and the particuler alteration thereof. For if a house bee utterly defaced, though it bee reedified of the selfe same timber and stone, yet it is not the same house, but if it bee but a little decayed and so repayred in part, it remayneth the same house still, though in continuance of time, every stick and stone bee altered by often repayring of it. (*Ibid.*, fol. 24 ^{v})

The final cause is the purpose of the agent which leads him to undertake the enterprise, that is, to produce the effect. Hence it is first in intention, but last in realization.

For first, the finall cause, the end, purpose, intent, drift, marke, or scope, as it were of the whole action, is propounded to the efficient, and so urgeth and moveth him to prepare the matter, and apply the forme thereunto for the full accomplishing of the enterprise: which beeing once performed, the efficient cause now ceaseth, as having obteined that it sought for. As for example, I purpose to sweate, and therefore I daunse: wee neede not take this woord, purpose or deliberation so strictly, as to apply it onely to reasonable creatures, but generally say, that every thing woorketh for some end and purpose whether it bee by nature's instinct, or voluntary consultation. . . . the cause finall is the purpose of God in naturall thinges, and the intent of the artificer in things that bee artificiall. (*Ibid.*, fol. 25 $^{r-v}$)

The first of the following illustrations of final cause has its end in the nature of the thing considered, the second in the purpose of the agent.

Palinode in the fift *Aegloge,*
>   Good is not good, but if it bee spend:
>   God giveth good for none other end.

Thenot in the second *Aegloge.*
>   It chaunced after upon a day
>   Th'usbandman self to come that way.
>   Of custome for to survey his ground,
>   And his trees of state in compasse round.

The ende of goodes is to be spent: the ende of the husbandmans going abroad, was to view his ground. (*Ibid.*, fol. 23 ^{r})

The effect is that which is produced by the operation of all the causes.

Howsoever any thing bee altered, mooved, or changed, the motion, and the thing mooved, or chaunged, belong to this place, and are called effects, or thinges caused: as also sayinges and writinges, thoughtes and all cogitations, although neither uttered nor accomplished. . . . [Thus] were *Lentulus, Cethegus* and other complices of *Catyline* brought to confusion. . . .

Matter of praysing and dispraysing commonly is fet from this place. . . .

Wee commend men . . . especially by reason of their effectes, as for that they did this or this &c . . .

In July, *Thomalin* prayseth Christ the great sheepheard, by his effectes.

O blessed sheepe, O sheepheard great,
that bought his flocke so deare,
And them did save with bloudy sweat
from Wolves that would them teare.

(*Ibid.*, fol. 29 $^{r \cdot v}$, 31 ^{r})

The Ramists carefully distinguish between metonymy of the cause and of the effect, as well as between that of the subject and of the adjunct, discussed above. They subdivide metonymy of the cause into that of the efficient cause and of the material cause. Fenner accordingly explains that the change of name, called metonymy, may be put for the name of either the maker, the matter, or the thing made.

Of the maker, when the finder out, or the author of the thing, or the instrument whereby the thing is done, is put for the thing made. So *Moses is put for his writinges. . . . So faith the cause is put for religious serving for God, the thing caused. Rom.* 1. *So the tounge the instrument of speeche, is put for speech it selfe. Rule thy tongue. James* 3.

Of the matter: *Thou art dust, and to dust shalt thou returne, that is, one made of dust.*

Now on the other side, when the thing caused or the effect is put for any of these causes. *So the Gospel of God is called the power of God to salvation,* that is, the instrument of the power of God. *So Love is saide to be bountifull, because it causeth one to bee bountifull. (Sig. D* 1 ^{r})

Metalepsis is a figure which signifies a present effect by a remote cause,

as *Medea* cursing hir first acquaintance with prince *Jason*, who had very unkindly forsaken her, said:

Woe worth the mountaine that the maste bare
Which was the first causer of all my care.

Where she might aswell have said, woe worth . . . the time that *Jason* arrived with his ship at my fathers cittie in *Colchos,* when he tooke me away with him, & not so farre off as to curse the mountaine that bare the pinetree, that made the mast, that bare the sailes, that the ship sailed with, which caried her away. (Puttenham, p. 183)

Cause and effect are related productively, antecedent and consequent temporally. The conditional or hypothetical proposition states the relation of antecedent and consequent.

If you marry my Daughter I make you myne heire: . . . if you will have warre, looke for cost, trouble, and daunger, for these are incident, and cleave to every person, that will live in warres. (Lever, pp. 69, 192)

Fenner explains important points regarding a hypothetical proposition, or axiom, as the Ramists call it—how it is contradicted and by what principles it is judged true or false or doubtful. The Ramists call a proposition an axiom.

If you were the children of Abraham you would do the workes of Abraham. Whose contradiction is, If the first be, yet the seconde doth not followe. So that when we judge this axiome to bee true, wee must judge the partes to be truly and necessarilye knit together. Whiche may be though the partes be both false: as in this example. The Jewes neither were Abrahams children, neither did the workes of Abraham. This axiome is doubtfull, when the parts and the folowing are doubtfull: As Paule in the shippe: *If you obey my counsell, you shall not perishe* . . . (Sig. C 3 ᵛ)

Fraunce states more forcefully than Fenner that when we judge a conditional proposition to be absolutely true,

wee judge it also to bee necessary. Albeit the necessitie ariseth onely of, or dependeth upon the necessary coupling together of the parts: which may bee when as, notwithstanding, both the parts . . . are false . . . The judgement . . . is certeine knowledge, when the connexion of the parts is necessary, but if the parts be variable, and the connexion onely probable, then our judgement thereof is onely an opinion. (*LL*, fol. 94 ʳ)

Necessity and contingency (which includes the doubtful and the probable) are important logical concepts that have a bearing not only on conditional propositions but on all, for logicians frequently call the subject of any proposition the antecedent, and the predicate, the consequent. If the predicate is the definition of the subject, or a part of the definition, namely, genus or difference, or if it is a property, that is, an invariable characteristic of that subject only, it is necessarily affirmed of the subject. Any other predicate affirmed of a subject is affirmed contingently, as when one says, The servant is crafty. For, as Wilson remarks, "a servaunt maie be, and yet not craftie. Again one maie be craftie, and yet not a servaunt" (*RR*, fol. 48 ʳ), thereby clearly explaining contingency, which he lists among his twenty-four places of logical invention.

Fraunce tells an amusing incident illustrating the status of the contingent in law.

Concerning casuall homicide, I remember an odde historie of a certaine man who falling from the top of a house, lighted on an other mans necke, and crush-

ing him to death, preserved himselfe. The sonne of the dead man, procuring
the revenge of his fathers death, caused him that fell to bee had before the
Judge: Where hee no lesse pretily then reasonably, offered him this faire play:
gett thee up, quoth he, to the top of the same house: I will stand where thy
father did: and if by falling upon mee thou bruse me to death, and save thy
selfe, I promise thee, my sonne shal never seeke to revenge my death. (*LL*,
fol. 20 ͬ)

One figure, antisagoge, depends on the relation of antecedent and
consequent.

The Orator joyneth to a precept, of virtue, a promise of reward, and to the
contempt of a precept, he denounceth a punishment, whereof this example of
Moses may sufficiently shew the forme, where he saith: If thou shalt obey the
voyce of the Lord thy God, and observe and do all his commandements, which
I command thee this day, then the Lord thy God wil set thee on hye above all
the nations of the earth. And all these blessings shall come upon thee, &c. But
if thou wilt not obey . . . then all these curses shal come upon thee, &c. Deut.
28.1, 2; 15, 16. (Peacham, p. 93)

9. Notation and Conjugates

The two topics notation and conjugates are concerned with words as
words in relation to realities and to each other.

Words related to each other by derivation from the same root but differing in termination, as *justice, just, justly,* are called conjugates. Plato's
dialogues often show Socrates skillfully arguing from conjugates. As
Fraunce remarks, Aristotle highly commends this place as a source of
argument in his *Topics*. In his *Rhetoric* he clearly illustrates how argument from conjugates clarifies meanings.

'Just' does not always mean 'beneficial,' or 'justly' would always mean 'benefi-
cially,' whereas it is *not* desirable to be justly put to death. (2.23.1397 ᵃ 20)

Thomas Wilson explains:

I may reason from this place bothe affirmatively, and negatively. If one be not
wise, he hath no wisedome, if one be wise, he hath wisedome . . . We may
learne by this place, to knowe, what thinges are, being considered in other.
. . . If I would knowe what wisedome is, best it were for me to marke their
doinges, that are wise men. (*RR*, fol. 41 ͬ)

Despite Aristotle's authority and also that of Renaissance logicians, including Ramus, Fraunce does not admit conjugates among the topics
of logic, but considers them to be in the province of grammar and rhetoric.

As for Conjugates, I see in them no new different force of arguing, as hee is just, for hee dealeth justly; heere is nothing in effect, but the cause and the effect. For as for the derivation of this woord Juste, from Justice, it seemeth altogether grammaticall: and whereas they both doo fitly allude in the ende and falling, thus, Justice, Just, Justly, that commeth from a Rhetoricall figure, called *Polyptoton*, which concerneth the elegancie that is in the divers fallinges and terminations of woords. (*LL*, fol. 50 ʳ)

Peacham recognizes the logical character of polyptoton, which he calls paregmenon, as is apparent in his comment on the use of the figure.

I will destroy the wisedome of the wise. Esay. . . . The use . . . is twofold, to delight the eare by the derived sound, and to move the mind with a consideration of the nigh affinitie and concord of the matter. (p. 55)

When a word is regarded as a word, it is called a notation, that is, a mark representing a sound. As such it may shed light on the thing it names through its etymology, or it may occasion ambiguity or obscurity. Fraunce quotes Aristotle's illustration of an argument from the name.

Dracoes lawes were a Dragons lawes, for their crueltie. (*LL*, fol. 51 ᵛ)

He gives as an example of false etymology a sixteenth-century favorite.

A woman is a woe man, because shee woorketh a man woe. (56 ᵛ)

To distinguish the various meanings of words was regarded by Renaissance logicians as one of the kinds of division. Aristotle also had set high value on the ability to do this.

The means whereby we are to become well supplied with reasonings are four: (1) the securing of propositions; (2) the power to distinguish in how many senses a particular expression is used; (3) the discovery of the differences of things; (4) the investigation of likeness. (*Topics*, 1.13, 105 ᵃ 21)

From the fact that a word or notation may have a number of different meanings arises ambiguity, sometimes inadvertent, sometimes deliberate, for, says Fraunce,

Quips, taunts, jests, and conceipts are often fet hence. All *Platoes* Cratilus is spent in the interpretation of woords after this manner. (*LL*, fol. 51 ᵛ)

Fraunce, almost alone, denies notation a place among the topics of logic.

So in Notation, the interpretation of the name, seemeth rather the dutie of a dictionary, then of any Logicall institution . . . it seemeth also a Rhetoricall agnomination. (*LL*, fol. 50 ᵛ)

Agnomination, or paronomasia, is a form of pun. The word pun, according to the *Oxford English Dictionary*, appeared first about 1660.[7] What we call puns rhetoricians of the Renaissance subdivided into a number of figures which from ancient times were regarded as adornments. In the opinion of Aristotle,

The liveliness of epigrammatic remarks is due to the meaning not being just what the words say. . . . Well constructed riddles are attractive for the same reason. . . . The effect is produced even by jokes depending upon changes of the letters in a word; this too is a surprise . . . something that gives a twist to the word used. . . . Here again is the use of one word in different senses [as in] the much praised verse of Anaxandrides:

> Death is most fit before you do
> Deeds that would make death fit for you.

This amounts to saying . . . 'it is a fit thing to die when death is not fit for you,' i.e. when death is not the fit return for what you are doing . . . . but the more briefly and antithetically such sayings can be expressed, the more taking they are, for antithesis impresses the new idea more firmly and brevity more quickly. They should always have either some personal application or some merit of expression, if they are to be true without being commonplace— two requirements not always satisfied simultaneously. (*Rhetoric*, 3.11.1412 [a] 21–1412 [b] 26)

Aristotle refers here to paronomasia and antanaclasis, and further cites examples from Isocrates and other Greek writers. Aeschylus, Euripides, and Aristophanes used the figures of ambiguity. Cicero delighted in them, and his discussion in *De oratore* of their use in moving laughter was taken over by Castiglione in *Il libro del cortegiano* and thence by Wilson in *The Arte of Rhetorique.*

Antanaclasis depends for its effect on the two or more meanings attached to the same repeated word.

Care for those things which may discharge you from all care. . . . In thy youth learne some craft, that in thy age thou mayst get thy living without craft.

This figure as it uniteth two words of one sounde, so it distinguisheth them asunder by the diversitie of their sense, whereby it moveth many times a most pleasant kind of civile mirth . . . (Peacham, p. 56)

Peacham directs attention to two characteristics of this figure which caused it to be valued as one capable of dignity: its use in serious thought and its

[7] An earlier instance is noted in John Taylor's "Mercurius Aquaticus," 1643. See *Notes and Queries*, 11 Series, No. 1, p. 425, May 28, 1910.

nature as a form of logical distinction. Antanaclasis can also occasion the fallacy of equivocation.

Syllepsis of the sense, as distinguished from the syllepsis which lacks grammatical congruence in one member, is more subtle than antanaclasis, for in this figure one word serves a double sense but is expressed only once. For instance, in the following illustration concerning a young man who slew the murderer of his father and ravisher of his mother, the verb *requite* means both *to revenge* and *to satisfy.*

> *Thus valiantly and with a manly minde*
> *And by one feate of everlasting fame,*
> *This lustie lad fully requited kinde,*
> *His fathers death, and eke his mothers shame.*
> (Puttenham, p. 166)

Paronomasia, or agnomination, depends for its effect on the different meanings attached to words nearly alike. Wilson cites an interesting illustration of its use by William Somer, King Henry VIII's fool, who,

seeing much adoe for accomptes making, and that the Kinges Majestie . . . wanted money, such as was due unto him: and please your grace (quoth he) you have so many Frauditors, so many Conveighers, and so many Deceivers to get up your money, that they get all to themselves. . . . He should have saide Auditours, Surveighours, and Receivers. (*AR*, p. 201)

Asteismus, like syllepsis, is a subtle figure. It is more lively and witty than antanaclasis or paronomasia, for it is a figure of reply, returning a facetious or mocking answer,

when a saying is captiously taken, and turned to another sense, contrary or much differing from the meaning of the speaker, as in this example: To one demanding of *Diogenes* what he would take for a knocke upon his pate, he made this answer, that he would take an helmet. (Peacham, p. 34)

Cato said to one that had geven him a good knock on the head with a long piece of timber he bare on his shoulder, and then bad him beware: what (quoth *Cato*) wilt thou strike me againe? (Puttenham, p. 190)

Distinction is a figure whereby the ambiguity of words is taken away,

as being charged that yow have brought very light reasons, yow may answeare, if by light, yow meane cleare I am glad yow doe see them, if by light yow meane of noe weight, I am sorry yow doe not feele them. (Hoskyns, p. 156)

The figures of deliberate obscurity include enigma, noema, and schematismus. An enigma is a riddle, a covert and dark speech more obscure than an allegory. Peacham cites as examples the dreams of Pharaoh's butler and baker which were explained by Joseph. In noema the obscurity of the sense lies, not in a single word, but in an entire speech very subtle and dark,

as he that said by himselfe and his wife, I thanke God in fortie winters that we have lived together, never any of our neighbours set us at one, meaning that they never fell out in all that space, which had bene the directer speech and more apert. (Puttenham, p. 230)

The figure schematismus is used

when the Orator propoundeth his meaning by a circuite of speech, wherein he would have that understoode by a certaine suspicion which he doth not speake, and that for 3. special causes. 1. For safetie sake: As when it is dangerous to speake directly and openly. 2. For modestie and good manners sake: As when it is undecent to be spoken plainly. 3. For delectation sake and grace of the hearer, as when it may bring greater delight under the figurative shadow, then by the plaine report and open shew.

   1. If some good man for the love of justice . . . should take upon him to reprehend a tirant . . . he should venture upon a verie dangerous enter-prise . . . Except the manner and forme of his handling the cause be . . . circumspectly delivered. . . . The Orators speech may be shadowed two manner of waies, either by reproving another person, in whom the same evils are . . . or by commending such persons in whom the contraries are . . . by . . . reprehension of that crueltie and tirannie in *Phalaris,* he may make a most bright and resplendent glasse wherein *Dionysius* [the King of *Sicilia,*] must needes behold himselfe and his deformed tirannie. (Peacham, p. 196)

10. Genesis or Composition

   Fraunce explains that the topics of invention provide writer and speaker with plentiful matter for composition, and reader or listener with a technique of analysis for the adequate understanding of what someone else has composed.

If we shall . . . draw any one woord through these generall places of in-vention, it will breede a great plentie and varietie of new argumentes, while wee marke what be the causes, effects, parts, whole, generall, speciall, subjectes, adjunctes thereof, and so foorth in all the rest: and this either in making and enditing our selves, or els in resolving, and as it were dismembring that which others have doone. (*LL,* fol. 81 ᵛ)

An example of genesis or composition is the following from Wilson, who derives from this process a series of notes rather than a finished composition on the chosen subject. Since a few of his names for the topics are strange, as *woordes yoked* for *conjugates,* the more familiar names used by other logicians have been substituted.

And to make this thing more plaine, I will goe through the places, with one certaine worde, and looke what helpe I shall finde there, for knowledge of the same. The worde shall bee (a Kyng) or (a Magistrate.)

The definition.

The definition of a Magistrate. Every King, or Magistrate, is the minister of God, for a good ende, to the punishing of naughtie persons, and the comforting of godly men.

The genus.

The Minister of God.

The Species.

Either a Tyraunt or a godly King, the one ruleth according to his lust, the other according to right and Justice.

Conjugates.

The Officer, the Office, to beare an Office, if the Office can not be spared, the Officer cannot be spared.

Adjuncts necessary.

Wisedome, earnest labour, cunnyng in sciences, skilfull both of warre and peace, these al must needes be in every Magistrate.

Adjuncts contingent.

To be liberall, to be frugall, to be of a temperate life, al these happen to be in good Magistrates.

Deedes necessary.

To defende Religion, to enact godly Lawes, to punish offenders, to defend the oppressed: all these are necessarie in a King, and are never found in a Tyraunt.

Subjects.

Moses, David, Salomon, Ezechias, Josias, Charles the Emperour, Edward the sixt of the name King of England.

The efficient cause remote.

God himselfe, or els the ordinaunce of God.

The efficient cause proximate.

Unquiet subjects, rebelles, disobedient people, are the cause why Magistrates are ordeined, that the rather they may bee ruled, and kept in good order.

The final cause of a Magistrate.

This ende he must needes observe, that alwaies the people live in quietnesse, & in honest conversation passe their whole life.

Effects.

Peace is made, the Realme enriched, all thynges plenteous, but where a Tyraunt ruleth, all thinges are contrary.

Testimony.

The xiii to the Romaines, let every soule be subject to the powers. 1 Peter. ii. Be subject to the King.

Adjuncts contingent.

The Scepter is a token of Justice, even as a Sworde is a signe of revengement, or wrathe, paying of Subsidies, Taxes, Tributes, Rent, or any suche like, Yeomen of the Garde, and al other waiters, Soldiours in warre, the obedience of the subjects, the honour given unto him, triumphes made, running at the Tilt, fighting at the Barriers, fighting at the Tourney. All these are *contingentia* to a King, that is, although these thinges bee not in a Common wealth, yet may there be a King, yea, and although there be no king in some Common weale, yet these thinges may be every ech one of them, as it was in *Athens,* where the people had the rule of the Common weale, and al was referred to their judgement.

Similitudes.

That which the Sheepeheard is to the Sheepe, the same is the Magistrate to his Subjects. That which the master of the Shippe, is to the Shippe, or the master of an household, to his house, or the head to the whole body; the same is the Magistrate to his Subjects.

Comparison.

Servantes must bee obedient, and subject to their Masters with all reverence, as we read in the Scripture: how much more then should the subjects be obedient to their king and soveraigne Lord, which by the ordinaunce of God, is appointed to rule, and to have governaunce over them. (fol. 54 ^{v}–55 ^{v})

As Wilson remarks, he does not search all the places in this example, nor is it necessary to do so in every instance. One ought, however, to search most of them and select the arguments best suited to the purpose. Wilson stresses the fact that the value of this procedure is very great, for

the better able wee shalbe, to confirme our owne cause, and to avoyde all objections, where we knowe surely by this art, whereunto we may leane. For although other shall impeach our doinges, and wrest our wordes, yet we shall be able evermore to keepe our owne, when wee plainely perceive, whereof our argument hath his ground. Many speake wisely, whiche never read *Logike,* but to speake wisely with a judgement, and to know the very fountaine of thinges: that can none doe, except they have some skill in this art. . . .

Therefore, what diversitie there is betwixt a blind man, and him that seeth, the same difference is betwixt a wiseman unlearned, and a wiseman learned. (*RR,* fol. 54 ^{v}–56 ^{r})

11. Analysis or Reading

Fraunce presents an example of analysis or reading which is based on logic.

I have, for examples sake, put downe a Logicall *Analysis* of the second *Aegloge* in *Virgill* . . . I have attempted the interpreting of the same by a poeticall *Paraphrasis*, for the contentation of such as understand no Latine . . . (*LL*, fol. 120 ʳ)

Fraunce's translation, which follows, besides supplying the matter for analysis, is in itself interesting as an illustration of the much discussed quantitative English hexameters, done by one associated with Sidney and Spenser.

Alexis 2. Aegloga Virgilii.

The same in English Hexameters,
verse for verse.

Seelly shepheard *Corydon* lov'd hartily faire lad *Alexis*,
His maisters dearling, but saw no matter of hoping.
Only amid the forest thick set with broad-shadoe beachtrees
daily resort did he make: thus alone to the woods, to the mountains
With broken speeches, fond thoughts most vainly revealing.
   O hardharted *Alexis*: I see my verse to be scorned,
My selfe not pitied, my death by thee lastly procured.
Now do the beasts even seeke for cooling shade to refresh them,
Grene lyzards now too in bushes thorny be lurking,
And for faint reapers by the suns rage, *Thestylis* hastning,
Strong-smelling wilde thime, and garlyke beates in a mortar.
But whilst I trace thee, with sun beams all to bescorched,
Groves by the hoarschirping grashoppers yeeld a resounding.
   Wast not far better t'have borne with surly *Menalcas*,
And sore displeased, disdainfull, prowd *Amaryllis*,
Although thou white were, although but swarty *Menalcas?*
   O thou faire white boy, trust not too much to thy whitnes:
Faire white flowers fall downe, black fruits are only reserved.
Thou carst not for mee, my state thou knowst not, *Alexis*:
What flocks of white sheepe I do keepe, of milke what abundance.
On *Sicil* high mountains my lambs feed more then a thousand:
New mylke in summer, new mylke in winter I want not.
My song's like *Thebane Amphions* song, when he called
His wandring bullocks, on Greekish mount *Aracynthus*.
Neyther am I so fowle: I saw my selfe by the seashore,
When seas al calme were: I doubt not, but by thy censure,
Daphnis I shall surpasse, unles my face do deceave mee.
   O, let this be thy will, to frequent my rustical harbors,
And simple cotages, and sticke in forkes to uphold them,
And drive on forward our flocke of kids to the mallowes:

Wee wil amid the forest contend *Pans* song to resemble:
Pan was first that quils with waxe ty'de joyntly together.
Pan is good to the sheepe, and *Pan* is good to the sheepsman.
Neither think it a shame to thy self t'have plaid on a cornpipe:
For, that he might do the same with skil, what did not *Amyntas?*
Damaetas long since did give me a pipe for a token,
Compact of seven reedes, all placed in order unaequall:
And thus sayd, when he dy'de: One used it onely beefore thee.
Thus sayd *Damaetas,* this greeved foolish *Amyntas.*
Also two pretty kids doe I keepe, late found in a valley
Dangerus: & their skins with mylke white spots be bedecked,
Of dams milke not a drop they leave; & for thee I keepe them.
Thestylis of long time hath these kids of me desired;
And they shalbe her own, for that thou skornst what I give thee.
Come neare, o faire boy, see the nymphs bring here to the lillies
With fullstuft baskets: faire *Nais* now to thy comfort
White violets gathering, and poppies daintily topping,
Daffadil ads to the same, & leaves late pluckt fro the sweete Dill.
Then mingling Casia with divers savory sweet flowrs,
With yelowish Marygold, she the tender Crowtoe bedecketh.

Ile plucke hoare quinces, with soft downe all to besmeared,
And Chessnuts which were loved of my sweet *Amaryllis.*
Add wil I wheateplumbs too: for this fruit will be regarded,
And you laurell leaves wil I plucke, and thee, pretty myrtle
Next to the laurell leaves: for so plast yeeld ye the sweet sent.

Th'art but a foole *Corydon,* for first gifts moove not *Alexis,*
Then, though thou give much, yet much more give wil *Iolas.*
But what alas did I mean, poore foole? I do let go the southwind
Into the flowrs, & boares send forward into the cleare springs.
Whom flyest thou mad man? Many gods have also resorted,
And *Paris* of olde *Troy,* to the woods. Let towers by *Minerva*
Built, by *Minerva* be kept; and woods of us onely regarded.
Grim Lionesse runneth to the wolfe, & wolfe to the yong gote,
And wanton yong gote to the flowring tetrisol hastneth,
And *Corydon* to *Alexis:* a selfe joy draweth on each man.
But see the plow come home hangd fast by the yoke, to the bullocks,
And shadoe by *Phoebus* declining double appeareth:
Yet do I burne with love: for what meane can be to loving?
Ah *Corydon, Corydon,* what mad rage hath thee bewitched?
Thy vin's scarse halfe cut, pestred with leaves of her elme tree:
Leave this churlish boy, and bend thy selfe to thy busnes,
With twigs and bulrush some needefull thing be a making:

Thou shalt find others though th'art disdaind of *Alexis*.

(fol. 121 ᵛ–122 ᵛ)

Fraunce borrows the following analysis of this eclogue from Freigius, a disciple of Ramus.[8]

There bee, saith *Freigius* 2. partes of the Aeglogue.

I. The propounding of the argument, which is of the incontinency of a lover lamenting his love in solitary places.

II. The complaint and lamentation of *Corydon* the lover, speaking

  A. To his love, and that by

    1. Accusing his crueltie, which is argued

      a. By comparison of the unlikes, the proposition consisteth of three unlikes, the beastes, Lysardes, and reapers seeke shade: the reddition is, but yet I burne with love.

      b. By the lesse *Amaryllis* and *Menalcas* are too cruell, but thou more cruel then they.

      c. By the cause of his pride, whiche was his beautie, and that is extenuated by a simily. As white primprint fales, but blacke Violets bee gathered, so beautie decayes, and blacknes remaines.

    2. Enticing him to come to his house to sing, to drive the kids to the Mallowes, &c. and that by praysing of himselfe by his adjunctes. *Corydons* adjuncts be these: he is

      a. Rich, and his riches be proved by specials

        (1) his lambs

        (2) his mylke

      b. Skilfull in singing, and this is prooved

        (1) By a comparison of the equall, in that hee is equall to *Amphion:*

        (2) And heere an objection is prevented by a comparison also of the equall: neither thinke it a shame to play on a pype, for *Amyntas* thought well of it.

        (3) Then the prayse of his singing is continued by his pype, and his pype by the autor that gave it, which was *Damaetas*, and another that envyed it, to wit *Amyntas*.

      c. Faire & comly: it is proved by

        (1) The adjunct of his image in the water

        (2) Comparison of the equall, as was Daphnis

      d. Franke and free, which is proved by his sundry giftes.

        (1) His Kydds, commended by their adjunctes, in that they were white spotted, well sucking, and desired of *Thestylis*.

---

[8] The analysis occupies folios 123 ʳ–124 ʳ of *The Lawiers Logike*. The tabular form has been changed to outline form, letters and numbers have been added, and slight changes in capitalization made to indicate co-ordination and subordination.

     (2) His basket of sweete flowers gathered by the Nymphes, they
        be hearbs and also flowers, as, Lillyes, Violets, Poppy, Dylle,
        Daffadil, Casia, Marigold, Crowtoe.
     (3) His diverse kindes of
        (a) Fruits as Quinces, Chestnuts, wheatplums.
        (b) Boughs as bee The Lawrell, The Myrtle.
  B. To himselfe, by resisting himselfe, as it were, and here is conteyned
    both a
      1. Doble correction or calling backe of himselfe, the first is
      a. Both of the
        (1) Adjunct, pride, and contempt of hys gifts and here is
          (a) A double exclamation: and here
            i. Hee noteth *Alexis* his pride by two similies, the south
              winde, and the boare.
            ii. he entreateth againe, by the equals, as *Paris,* and
              the gods &c.
          (b) A permission by the unlike. Let *Pallace* keep her Pal-
            laces, and wee the woodes which is our delight. The
            reddition is made playne by comparison of lykes: where
            also the generall is concluded by the specialles in a
            Clymax of three degrees, Grimme Lyonesse to the
            Wolfe &c.
        (2) More, or greater, for *Iolas* gave mor largely then hee.
      b. Of the adjunctes both of
        (1) The tyme, where there is a Periphrasis of night, and an
          argument of the divers, albeit the heate of the sunne is miti-
          gated by the comming of the night, yet I burne still with
          love: the reason followeth of the adjunct of love: for love
          hath no meane.
        (2) His businesse neglected, where is a double negligence: of
          (a) His vine halfe cut ⎫
                       for both be naught.
          (b) His elme full of boughes ⎬
      2. Remedy of love by contraries which be:
      a. Businesse in making some needefull thinge of twigs and bulrush.
      b. And hope of some other lover, if *Alexis* should still thus disdaine
      him.

The figurists would have analyzed this poem with similar thorough-
ness, noting precisely the same points as Fraunce but in terms of the
figures and their nomenclature.

The complete Ramist technique of reading, which combines logic and
rhetoric, is exemplified in the analysis of Saint Paul's Epistle to Philemon,

with which Dudley Fenner concludes his work on *The Artes of Logike and Rhetorike*.[9] In this analysis Fenner appears in a threefold role: as a logician exemplifying his precepts; as a rhetorician illustrating the figures; as a Puritan minister of the Gospel elucidating Holy Scripture by the enthusiastic application of the arts of reading.

The Epistle to Philemon

| The entrance of this Epistle hath two partes, | The inscription or title. |
| | Prayers. |

| The inscription setteth downe | The persons which doe write. |
| | The persons to whom it is written. |

The first person which doth write is *Paule* the principal writer, who is described by the adjoint *captive:* which adjoint is declared by the cause *Christ,* that is, by a change of name of the cause for the effect, *Christ leading him to prison by his spirit.* And the second person which doth write is also declared by his proper name, *Timothie:* and an adjoynt of relation, *a brother,* that is by a Metaphor *one of the same Christian religion.*

The persons to whom he writeth, are first	The husband.
	The wife.
Seconde	The Minister.
	The Church.

The *man* is described by his proper name, *Philemon:* by his adjoint *beloved,* & by his effect, *worker togither with us.*

The *woman* is also described by her proper name, *Appia,* & her adjoint, *beloved.*

The *Minister* is also described by his proper name, *Archippus:* and his adjoint, *a fellow souldier:* that is, by a Metaphor, *a felow Minister.*

The *Church* is declared by the subject, which is at *thy house.*

| The prayers are | The salutation |
| | Thankesgiving. |

[9] This work, published in Middelburg in 1584, is attributed to Fenner, although his name does not appear in it. There were at least three editions, two in 1584 and another in 1588. The precepts are avowedly translated from sources unnamed, but they are clearly Ramus and Talaeus, at least ultimately. The illustrations from the Bible are probably Fenner's own selections, unless they owe something to Mulhemius, who, according to Miller (*The New England Mind,* p. 497), published at Frankfort, also in 1584, a Ramist logic with the topics and figures illustrated from the Bible. Miller does not mention Fenner in his brief survey of the literature of the Ramist logic in Europe, including England.

The terminology of Fenner requires a brief explanation: he calls a proposition an axiom; the major premise, the proposition; the minor premise, the assumption. Change of name is metonymy. Fenner is careful to note from which topic the matter for each syllogism is derived.

The *salutation* is set downe, first by the matter of it, which hee wisheth to them. Whereof the parts are *grace,* that is, *ful favour of God, peace,* that is by a Sinechdoche of the special for the general, *al prosperity both of soule and body.* Secondly, by the forme, *from God the father, and from Christ.* All whiche is disposed in a coupled axiome.

The *Thankesgiving* is described, first by the subject, *my God:* that is, *whom only I doe serve and hang upon.* Secondly by the adjoint, *alwaies making mention of you in my prayers.* Thirdly by the efficient cause, *hearing of your love and faith.* Both which are declared by their proper subjectes, *whiche you have towardes our Lorde Jesus Christ, and love towardes al Saintes.* And all these are disposed in a coupled axiome.

In the 6. ver. the adjoint *of thanksgiving, his mention making of them in his prayer,* is set forth by the matter, which he seeketh for in *praier, the communication of faith,* that is, which proceedeth from faith may be effectuall, which is declared by the cause, *by the acknoweledging of al good: which good* is set forth by the subject *which is in you,* and by the cause, *by Christ Jesus.*

The principal matter of this Epistle, which is to intreat for, *Onesimus* is set downe in a simple axiome of the cause & the effect in the 10. ver. *I Paul pray thee for Onesimus,* where the antecedent *Paule,* is declared by the adjoint, *being such a one,* which is declared by the special, *even Paule an old man,* and increased by the greater, and made lightsome by the time, *yea now a bondman of Christ.* The first part of the consequent *pray thee,* is declared by a divers reason, *Although I have liberty to commaund thee, yet I pray thee:* where the first divers, *liberty of commaunding,* is declared by the adjoynt *great:* by the forme, *in Christ,* by the subject, *that which is thy duetie.* The second divers is declared by the moving cause *for loves sake:* and by a comparison of the greater, *rather I pray thee.* The laste part of the consequent, *Onesimus* is described: First by the relation of the cause to the effect, *my sonne,* that is, by a metaphor *one brought to the faith by my ministery:* which is declared by the formal cause, *Whome I begotte:* that is by a Sinecdoche of the part for the whole, and a metaphor *whom God by me did effectually call,* which is declared by the subject of the place, *in my bandes:* that is, by a Sinecdoche of the special for the general, *in prison.* Where in the beginning of the 9. *and* 10. verses, there is a repetition of the same sound in the beginning. *I pray thee, I pray thee.* Secondly, *Onesimus* is described by the adjoint, *unprofitable to thee:* which is made lightsome by the time *once,* and declared by the contrary, *but profitable:* which is declared by the adjoynt of time *now:* & enlarged by a comparison of the greater, *to me also,* and it is garnished by a redoubling of the same sound or Anadiplosis, *thee, me, and thee:* and by a little changing of the name called Paranomasia, *profitable, unprofitable.* This axiome *I pray thee,* beyng thus worthely declared, is confirmed in the 7. verse by the making cause, *bicause*

I have great joy and comfort in thy love, and is disposed in a connexive sillogisme of the first kind.

If I have great joy and comfort in thy love: then I may pray thee for Onesimus:

But I have great joy and comfort in thy love,

Therefore I may pray thee for Onesimus.

The proposition is wanting, the assumption is in the 7. verse, & it is confirmed by the effect of that love, wherein it doeth rejoyce, *because the bowels of the Saints have been refreshed by thee:* And it is concluded in a lesse playne Syllogisme of the second kynd, affirmative speciall.

That love that doth refresh the bowels of the Saints, is to be rejoyced in:

But this love doth refresh the bowels of the Saintes.

Therfore this love is to be rejoyced in.

The bowels, that is by an excessive metaphor, *the inward affections of the Saintes.* Here is set down the special of the former request, in a simple axiome of the cause and the effect *receive thou him,* where the last parte of the consequente *him,* is declared by the adjoynt, *my bowels,* that is, first by a Metaphor, *my love* that is by a chaunge of name of the cause for the effect, *my beloved.* Thys is confirmed by the cause which should move him, and it is concluded in a connexive Sillogisme of the first kind.

If I have sent him for that purpose, receive him:

But I have sent him for that purpose.

Therefore receive him.

This is a preventing of an objection: The objection is wanting, and may be supplied: *If he were so profitable, why diddest thou not keepe him.* The subjection or answere is from the divers reason, *Although I desired to keepe him, yet I would not doe it without thy consent.*

The first divers is declared by the moving cause, *That instead of thee he might minister unto me in the bandes of the Gospel,* that is by a Sinecdoche, in the *afflictions which the Gospel hath brought me.*

The second divers is also declared by the moving cause, *That thy benefits should not be by necessity:* where *necessitie* is declared by the contrary, *but willingly or freely.*

Here is another preventing of an objection, The objection is wanting, & is thus to be supplied, *He was a run away:* The answeare is by the adjoynt of the time, *He went away but for a little time:* which is increased by the moving cause, *But that thou shouldest receive him for ever:* Which is enlarged by a comparison of the lesse, *not so much as a servant, but as more than a servant:* which is garnished by a redoubling or Anadiplosis.

The second part of the comparison, called reddition, is declared by the speciall, *a beloved brother, more then a servant:* which is enlarged by the greater, *especially to me:* which is amplified also by the greater, *much more to thee:* whiche is declared by a distribution of the subject, wherein he was more bound unto *Philemon,* then to *Paule* himselfe, *both in the flesh, and in the Lord,* that is, *things appertayning unto this life, to the Lorde:* By a chaunge of name of the subject for the adjoynt.

Here is a new reason to prove that he should receive him, drawne from the working cause, in a connexive Sillogisme.

If we have fellowship togither in any common blessings, then receive him:
But we have felowship togither in common blessings,
Therefore receive him.

The proposition is the 17. verse, the assumption is wanting: the conclusion is made manifest by a comparison of the like, *receive him as me.*

Here is a preventing of an objection, the objection is wanting, and is thus to be supplied: *He hath hurt me, or done somewhat to me.* The answere is from the divers, *If he owe thee any thing, impute it to me:* which is increased by the greater, *I will pay it:* which is confirmed by a testimony, *I Paule have written it with mine owne hand.*

The last part of the 19. verse is a confyrmation of the second answere from a comparison of the more to the lesse, and is concluded in a connexive sillogisme of the first kind.

If thou doest owe me thy very selfe: then much more thou maiest forgive
    him this debt for my sake.
But thou owest me thy very selfe,
Therefore thou maiest forgive him this debt for my sake.

The proposition is wanting, the assumption is in the end of the 19. verse.

Here is another confirmation drawn from the effects, and is concluded in a connexive Sillogisme of the first kind.

If by this I shal obteine fruite of thee in the Lord, and if thou doest refresh
    my bowels in the Lord: then thou shouldest receive him:
But I shal obteine fruite, &c.
Therefore thou shouldest receive him.

The proposition is wanting, the assumption is in the 20. ver. & is garnished with a crying out of a wishing, *yea, my brother, I would I might obteine.*

Here is an answering of an objection, which might be made against the whole Epistle. The objection is wanting, & must be thus supplied: *why write you so earnestly?* The answere is from the cause, *The perswasion I had of thy readinesse to obey it caused me:* which is proved by a comparison of the lesse to the greater, in a connexive Sillogisme of the first kind.

If thou wouldest do more then this: then thou wouldest do this.
But thou wouldest doe more then this:
Therefore thou wouldest do this.

The proposition is wanting, the assumption is in the 21. ver. and is confirmed by a testimony of *Paule* his owne knowledge, *I know it.*

Here is set downne *a commandement to prepare him hostage,* whereunto is a briefe transition in this word, *Also,* it is confirmed by a reason drawn from the working cause, in a connexive sillogisme of the first kind.

If I hope to be given unto you by your prayers: then prepare hostage:
But I hope to be given unto you by your praiers,
Therefore prepare hostage.

The proposition is wanting, the assumption is in the 22. vers.

Certaine *salutations* are set downe in the 23.24. vers. in a gathering axiome of the cause and the effect.

Epaphras, Marcus, Aristarchus, Demas, and Luke salute thee: whereof the first is set forth by an adjoint, *my fellow prisoner:* which is declared by the cause, for *Christ Jesus,* their other by their adjoints, *my helpers.*

The salutation is set down in a simple axiome affirmative, of the subjecte and adjoynt, *grace be with your spirit,* that is by a Synecdoche, *with you:* The antecedent *grace* is declared by the efficient cause, *Christ,* and is garnished wyth a certaine crying out of wishing. *Amen.*

And this is the particular resolution of this Epistle.

If it makes us somewhat dizzy to follow Fenner through these analytical gymnastics, we must remember that such exercise, like parsing in grammar or noting rhetorical features such as loose and periodic sentences, parallel structure, balance and rhythm, establishes habits of subconscious observation and appreciation which contribute greatly to mature reading even when rapid and preoccupied with content. A habit of logical analysis subconsciously associates itself with one's reading even more deeply than a grammatical or rhetorical analysis, for it is more closely related to the thought itself.

There is ample evidence that boys in the Tudor grammar schools were systematically trained to note both the topics and the figures in their reading. For example, even in a work commonly used as early as the third form, attention was directed to the figures. In the epistle to his edition of *The Floures of Terence* (1533) Nicholas Udall announces:

Where any outstanding or elegant metaphor is used, I have indicated it. Where any figure occurs, I have noted it. Where any fable comes along I am not bored to narrate it rather at length. . . . If any proverb is interspersed, I have exposed it.[10]

[10] Quoted by T. W. Baldwin, *William Shakspere's Small Latine and Lesse Greeke,* I, 745.

CHAPTER VIII

Logos: Argumentation

ARGUMENTATION consists in the orderly disposition of the ideas which have been derived from invention or exposition. In explaining the relation of the two parts of logic Fraunce uses an analogy.

> As in Grammer, *Aetymologie* concerneth severall woords, and *Syntaxis* the due coherence of the same, so Exposition the first part of Logike, declareth the particular affection and nature of every severall argument, and Disposition the second part, by ordering and setling the same, causeth judgement and understanding. (*LL,* fol. 6 ʳ)

According to Ramist terminology, every proposition is an axiom, and every term an argument. The relation of terms in a proposition is axiomatical; that of propositions to one another is dianoetical. The simplest way to relate propositions is merely to join two or more of them. Drawing his illustrations from *The Shepheardes Calender* by Spenser, Fraunce states the principles governing the truth or falsity of such conjunction.

> Hereunto must be referred full comparisons and similitudes, wherein the conjunction is the very relation itselfe, as, *Colyn* in January.
>> And from mine eyes the drizling teares descend,
>> As on your boughs the ysicles depend.
> Heere the judgement is compound, as if hee had sayd, *the ysicles depend on your boughs, and the teares fall from myne eyes.*
> The true judgement of this copulative axiome dependeth on the truth of every part: for if all the partes bee true, it is then a true axiome: false, if any bee false. . . . The contradiction of these, are the denials to every part. . . . The negation in a copulative axiome is not the denying of the partes conjoyned; but the denying of the conjoyning of the partes. (*Ibid.,* fol. 93 ʳ)

Much more important than the mere conjunction of propositions is their coherence and consequence, true or apparent. Accordingly, first to be considered is valid syllogistic reasoning; next fallacious reasoning; and lastly disputation, which may employ either or both in the give and take of argument. The figures related to reasoning and disputation are treated in connection with the logical processes to which they correspond.

1. Syllogistic Reasoning

Fraunce makes clear how syllogistic reasoning derives its matter from the topics of invention.

The arguments in Invention must bee considered severally, singlely, and alone, then after to bee disposed and ordered by certeine precepts, thereby to judge of the truth or falsenesse of the same: as for example.

Paris. A good sheepheard.

These two singly put downe as two arguments, to wit, the subject and the adjunct, are afterwards disposed in an axiome, to judge of the truth thereof, as thus:

Paris is no good sheepheard.

But because this proposition is contingent and doubtfull . . . it is confirmed by another argument, that is to say, by an effect and working of *Paris,* I meane that which *Thomalin* putteth downe in July, in these words.

But nothing such thylk sheepheard was
whome *Ida* hill did beare:
That left his flocke to fetch a lasse,
whose love he bought too deare.

So then, heere bee three severall arguments, or two joyned in the axiome before, and the third following in these verses of *Thomalin;* which third they call, *Medium,* or third argument,

1 *Paris:* 2 A good sheepheard.
3 To leave his flocke to fetch a lasse.

Whereof it is concluded in this wise syllogistically, by disjoyning the two first arguments, the subject and adjunct, *Paris,* and, The good sheepheard.

Hee that leaveth his flocke to fetch a lasse, is no good sheepheard:
But *Paris* did leave his flocke to fetch a lasse,
Therefore *Paris* is no good sheepheard.

That which they call *Medium,* and third argument, is, as it were, an *Arbiter honorarius,* a determiner, a reconciler a daies man: which if it agree with both the other arguments, maketh the conclusion affirmative: but negative, if with one onely, as in the former example of *Paris,* the *Medium,* the arbiter, the determiner, is that effect of *Paris.* To leave his flocke to fetch a lasse: which because it is agreeable with the nature of *Paris,* but is flatly repugnant to the dutie of a good sheepheard, therefore is the conclusion negative, *Paris* is no good sheepeheard. (*LL,* fol. 6 ᵛ)

Fraunce discusses the value of syllogistic reasoning.

In this order, first of single arguments wee make axioms: which axioms, if of themselves they bee perceived and graunted, they bee straightway judged as true or false. . . . if these propositions bee doubtfull, then therof be made questions, which are to bee proved by third arguments, fet from the affections of the other two which were joyned in the axiome, and lastly are to be concluded by syllogisme, the onely judge of all coherence and consequence . . . syllogismes, and onely syllogismes are the true and onely rules of consequence and inconsequence. . . . (fol. 7 $^{r\text{-}v}$) Syllogisme is onely proper and peculiar to man; whereof, no beast dooth in any respect participate. (fol. 112 ^{v})

A syllogism is the relation of three terms in three propositions. The propositions are the major premise, called the proposition; the minor premise, called the assumption; and the conclusion, called the question, because it is that which is to be proved. The subject of the conclusion is the minor term, or antecedent; the predicate of the conclusion is the major term, or consequent. The middle term is that which appears in both premises but not in the conclusion. The relation of the minor term and the major term in the conclusion is determined in consequence of the relation of each of them to the middle term as stated in the premises; in other words, their relation to the middle term determines their relation to each other. It is therefore of the utmost importance that the middle term, the yardstick of reasoning, be understood in its full extension in at least one of the premises. Blundeville emphasizes this fundamental point when he explains the two principles regulative of all syllogistic reasoning, called *dictum de omni et nullo*. The first rule is concerned with affirming the predicate of all the subject (the middle term); the second with denying it of all.

The first rule is, whatsoever is truely affirmed of his naturall and proper Subject, is also affirmed of all those things which are contained under the said Subject: the second rule is thus, whatsoever is denied to bee spoken of any Subject, is also denied to bee spoken of every thing contained under the said Subject. The first rule confirmeth all Syllogismes affirmative, the second confirmeth all Syllogismes negative. (p. 135)

A number of the general and special rules of the syllogism are designed to safeguard the basic rule that the middle term be understood in its full extension in at least one of the premises. Thus it is a corollary that one premise must be a universal proposition, for from two particular premises no conclusion can be drawn. At least one premise must be affirmative, for from two negative premises no conclusion can be drawn, since, obviously, if neither term of the conclusion is related to the middle term in the premises, one cannot thereby determine their relation to each other. Another principle of syllogistic reasoning is that the conclusion follows the weaker part: if one premise is particular, or negative, or contingent, the conclusion can be no stronger than that premise. Moreover, no term may be used in the conclusion in a wider extension than in its own premise, for one cannot validly draw from premises more than is in them; the attempt to do so is an illicit process. There are special rules for each figure of the syllogism, having the same purpose as the general rules, to insure valid reasoning.

A syllogism may be either simple or compound. According to Renaissance logicians, the simple syllogism has three figures, determined by the position of the middle term in the premises. If the middle term is the subject of the major premise, and the predicate of the minor, the syllogism is in the first figure.

> That which bringeth to good, is good.
> Death bringeth to good,
> Therefore Death is good.

Thus Fraunce states in strict logical form the essential thought in the following stanza of Colin's song in "November."

> Unwise and wretched men to weete what's good or ill,
> Wee deeme of death as doome of ill desert:
> But knew wee fooles what it brings us untill,
> Dye would wee daily once it to expert.
>   Faire fields and pleasant layes there beene,
>   The fields ay fresh, the grasse ay greene.
>   o happy hearse:
>   Make hast ye shepheards thither to revert,
>   o joyfull verse. (*LL,* fol. 107 ^r)

In the second figure the middle term is predicate of both premises, as in this syllogism from "May."

> The hyreling letteth his sheepe run at randon:
> The good shepheard letteth not his sheepe run at randon,
> Therefore the good shepheard is not a hyreling. (*Ibid.,* fol. 106 ^r)

In the third figure the middle term is subject of both premises. The Ramists make a special point of showing that a syllogism in this figure is clearer in the contracted form in which it is used in daily life than in the full form, and therefore they call this form the contracted syllogism. Fraunce gives as an example of this contracted form:

Some confidence is not vertue, as Rashnes.

He then expands it and adds his comment.

Rashnes to bee no vertue, yet a kind of confidency,
Therefore some confidency to bee no vertue.

And after this manner, Use, the mayster of syllogisticall judgement, dooth alwaies contract it, and never otherwise expresse it. (fol. 104 ʳ)

Of greatest practical importance is the enthymeme, which although described by Aristotle as the rhetorical counterpart of the dialectical syllogism is nevertheless regularly treated by the Renaissance logicians. Blundeville and Wilson follow Aristotle in their account of its matter and its form. As to its matter, the enthymeme is based on signs or on probabilities. The signs may be infallible, as: He has a fever; therefore he is ill. Or fallible, as: This man is a night-gadder; therefore he is a thief. Probabilities include generally received opinions which in the form of maxims provide a favorite source of matter for enthymemes. As Aristotle remarks, maxims invest a speech with moral character, and people love to hear general statements about practical conduct which voice opinions they themselves hold regarding particular cases. Aristotle explains at length the relation of the maxim to the enthymeme.

A maxim . . . is a statement; not about a particular fact . . . but of a general kind . . . about questions of practical conduct, courses of conduct ·to be chosen or avoided. Now an Enthymeme is a syllogism dealing with such practical subjects. It is therefore roughly true that the premisses or conclusions of Enthymemes, considered apart from the rest of the argument, are Maxims: . . . add the reason or explanation, and the whole thing is an Enthymeme; thus . . .

There is no man among us all is free,

[is a maxim]; but . . . taken with what follows it, is an Enthymeme—

For all are slaves of money or of chance.

[Euripides, *Hecuba*, 864 f]

. . . the maxim may or may not have a supplement. Proof is needed where the statement is paradoxical or disputable; no supplement is wanted where . . . the view expressed is already a known truth . . . or [where] as soon as the view is stated, it is clear at a glance, e.g.

No love is true save that which loves for ever.

[Euripides, *Troades*, 1051]

. . . the best . . . are those in which the reason for the view expressed is simply implied, e.g.

O mortal man, nurse not immortal wrath.

To say 'it is not right to nurse immortal wrath' is a maxim; the added words 'O mortal man' give the reason. (*Rhetoric*, 2.21, 1394 ᵃ 21- ᵇ 23)

As to its form, Aristotle asserts:

The enthymeme must consist of few propositions, fewer often than those which make up the normal syllogism. For if any of these propositions is a familiar fact, there is no need even to mention it; the hearer adds it himself. (*Rhetoric*, 1.2. 1357 ᵃ 16)

Fraunce agrees.

Strict syllogismes bee never lightly used among authors, but eyther contracted or amplified, or els inverted, . . . The quicknes of mans wit is such, that it conceaveth the whole sometimes without any proposition, another while without any assumption, and now and then it preventeth and foretaketh the conclusion. (*LL*, fol. 112 ᵛ)

In the first of the following enthymemes the minor premise is omitted; in the second, the major.

That is not good whiche bringeth a man to mischief. Therefore money is not good. Pleasure bringeth endlesse paine after it. *Ergo* pleasure is to be eschued. (Wilson, *RR*, fol. 31 ʳ)

The figure which the rhetoricians call aetiologia is identical with what the logicians call an enthymeme. It is a cause given to a sentence uttered:

I mistrust not the Judges, because they are just. (Wilson, *AR*, p. 205)

Puttenham calls aetiologia the Reason rendrer, and composes a

dittie . . . where the lover complaines of his Ladies crueltie, rendring for every surmise a reason, and by telling the cause, seeketh (as it were) to get credit, thus.

> *Cruel you be who can say nay,*
> *Since ye delight in others wo:*
> *Unwise am I, ye may well say,*
> *For that I have, honourd you so.*
> *But blamelesse I, who could not chuse,*
> *To be enchaunted by your eye:*
> *But ye to blame, thus to refuse*
> *My service, and to let me die.* (p. 229)

The rhetoricians reserve the name enthymeme for a figure whereby a cause is given to things contrary. Their limitation of the word enthymeme to a striking antithesis of thoughts in opposition is apparently due to the fact that Cicero and Quintilian (8.5.9) regarded this as the pre-eminent type of enthymeme. But Aristotle too recognized its outstanding character.

The Refutative Enthymeme has a greater reputation than the Demonstrative, because within a small space it works out two opposing arguments, and arguments put side by side are clearer to the audience. (*Rhetoric*, 2.23, 1400 [b] 25)

Sherry and Peacham offer these examples of the figure enthymeme.

If it be a great praise to please good men, surely to please evyl men it is a greate shame. (Sherry, sig. F vii [r])

They which may do me good, wil not, and they which are willing cannot, therefore my distresse remaineth. (Peacham, p. 163)

Syllogismus is a figure even more contracted than the enthymeme. According to Peacham it expresses a sign or token from which the whole meaning is gathered.

Virgill speaking of *Poliphemus*, saith he held a pine tree in his hand to stay himselfe, and walked through the sea: by this we conjecture what a great bodie he had. (p. 180)

The full syllogism implicit in this single proposition may be stated thus:

Whoever walks through the sea holding a pine tree in his hand to stay himself has a great body.
But Poliphemus does this.
Therefore Poliphemus has a great body.

Hoskyns calls this figure intimation, because it suggests more to the mind than to the ears.

It exceedeth speech in silence, & makes our meaning more palpable by a touch, then by a direct handling, as he that should say (yow must live many yeares in his companie, whome yow shall accompt for your friend) sayth well, but he that saith yow had need eate a bushell of sault with him, saith more, & gives yow to reckon more then many yeares. (p. 139)

This figure of intimation by vivid detail is essential to poetic composition in the Aristotelian sense as contrasted with exposition. A man who is frightened trembles; he who repents weeps. Given the situation, only the action need be stated. The reader or listener supplies the rest.

A sorites is a chain of enthymemes. Fraunce cites one attributed to Themistocles.

My sonne ruleth my wife; my wife commaundeth mee: I the Athenians; the Athenians all Graece: Therefore my sonne ruleth all Graece. (*LL,* fol. 99ᵛ)

Two figures of repetition are frequently employed in syllogistic reasoning.[1] Anadiplosis may express an enthymeme and climax or gradatio a sorites. In his work on rhetoric, Hoskyns explains:

Climax is a kinde of *Anadiplosis* leadinge by degrees and makynge the last word a stepp to the further meaninge, if it be turned to an Argument it is a Sorites . . . yow could not injoy your goodnes without government, nor goverment without a magistrate, nor a magistrate without obedience, & noe obedience where every one uppon his private passion doth interpret the doeings of the Rulers, Nowe to make it a *Sorites* or Clyming Argument, joyne the first & last with an *Ergo,* as *Ergo* yow cannot enjoy your goods where every man uppon his private passion doth &c: this in pennd speech is too Accademicall, but in discource more passible & plausible. (p. 126) [2]

Discussing sorites in *The Arte of Logick,* Blundeville observes:

The Rhetoricians use another kinde of Argument, called *Gradatio,* which is much like to *Sorites,* saving that the Subject of the first Proposition is not rehearsed in the Conclusion, for they use it rather as an ornament of speech, then as a proofe. (p. 177)

The compound syllogism is either hypothetical or disjunctive, or a combination of these called the dilemma.

The sign of the hypothetical or conditional proposition is *if, unless,* or an adverb of time, such as *when.* A hypothetical syllogism is valid if the minor premise either affirms the antecedent or denies the consequent of the major premise, which is a hypothetical proposition. Fraunce quotes from Spenser:

Willy in March.

>   But see, the Welkin thicks apace,
>   And stouping *Phebus* steepes his face,
>   It's time to haste us homeward.

He then formalizes the argument.

---

[1] See above, p. 306, where anadiplosis and climax are discussed among the figures of repetition.

[2] Hoyt Hudson, in the notes to his edition of Hoskyns, *Directions for Speech and Style,* Princeton, 1935, states: "This relation between the figure of climax and the sorites . . . is mentioned in Claude Minos's gloss to Talaeus (*Rhetorica,* Frankfort, 1587, p. 109) with a reference to the *Rhetorica ad Herennium,* lib. 4."

When night drawes on, it's time to goe homeward,
But now night drawes on,
Therefore it's now time to get homeward. (*LL,* fol. 109 ᵛ)

The figure epilogus is related to the hypothetical syllogism. Sherry explains it as a figure

which by a brief argumentacion of these thinges that be spoken before or done, inferreth that thynge that necessarilye shulde folowe, thus: And if a revelacion wer geven to the Trojanes, that Troy myght not be taken without the arowes of Philectetes, and thei did nothing else but strike Alexander, to kyl him, that in dede was Troy to be taken. (Sig. D iiii ʳ)

In a disjunctive syllogism the minor premise affirms one of the two alternatives presented in the disjunctive major premise, and the conclusion denies the other, or contrariwise. Thus:

He is eyther good or evill;
but he is good:
Ergo not evill. (Blundeville, p. 157)

The figure apophasis, or expeditio, is equivalent to the disjunctive syllogism of the logicians and is consequently grounded upon division. It is used

when many reasons being reckoned by which somthing may be done or not done, one reason is left which the Orator standeth unto & concludeth upon, and the other are taken away, thus: Seeing this ground was mine, thou must needes shew, that either thou diddest possesse it being void, or made it thine by use, or bought it, or else that it came to thee by heritage: Thou couldest not possesse it voide when I was in possession: also thou canst not make it thine by use: Thou hast not to shew that thou diddest buy it, it could not come to thee by inheritance, and I alive: it followeth then that thou wouldest put me from mine owne ground, before I be dead. (Peacham, p. 186)

Prosapodosis, which also depends on a disjunction of alternatives, differs from apophasis in that it

overthroweth noe parte of the *Division,* but returneth some reason to each member . . . affirmes & keepes all sides upp . . . your silence must carrie with it a construccion of contempt, unkindness or displeasure, If yow take me not for your friend, yow offer unkindnes, if you deeme me unworthie of an answeare it comes of contempt, if your passion differrs a reply, it argues your displeasure. (Hoskyns, p. 160)

In its full form the dilemma consists of a compound hypothetical proposition as the major premise, a disjunctive proposition as the minor, and a simple or a disjunctive proposition as the conclusion. Fraunce gives as an example of the dilemma and its rebuttal the oft-repeated one concerning the rhetorician Protagoras and his pupil Euathlus.

Euathlus gave some money in hande to his Rhetoricall Doctor *Protagoras*, and covenanted to pay the rest when *Euathlus* should win the first cause that ever hee pleaded for. *Protagoras* suing *Euathlus* for his money, saide, if *Euathlus* overcome mee, then by bargaine & composition hee must pay mee the money; if hee loose, then by the course of Law. Nay quoth *Euathlus*, if I loose, then by covenant you get nothing: if I winne, then will the judgement discharge mee. (fol. 99 ᵛ)

Such rebuttal is possible when each of two opposites has both a good and a bad consequence opposite, respectively, to each other. A dilemma open to rebuttal is an invalid argument. A correct dilemma is, however, a valid form of reasoning.

The figure dialysis or dilemma is like the dilemma of the logicians except that it usually states only the major premise and leaves the rest to be understood. According to Sherry, this figure by

dividing one thyng, from another, endeth them both by shewing a reason, thus . . . what shuld I speake of myne owne good turnes towarde the. If thou do remember them, I shuld not trouble you: If you have forgotten them, when by deede I have profited nothyng, what good can I do in wordes? (Sig. D iiii ʳ)

Fraunce insists that all argumentation is syllogistic.

The schoolemen have commonly foure kindes of Argumentations, Syllogisme, Enthymeme, Induction, Example, to the which some adde *Sorites* and *Dilemma* . . . and all these, . . . come all to one. For an Enthymeme is but a contracted and short syllogisme: An example, but an argument from the like or equall . . . and no argumentation of it selfe without the helpe of a syllogisme: An Induction, which is called the *Socraticall* Argumentation, is but an argument concluded by a syllogisme, from the enumeration of the partes: A *Sorites*, but an Enthymematicall progression by certainy [*sic*] degrees. (*LL*, fol. 99 ʳ)

The relation between the example, induction, and the syllogism is clearly explained by Blundeville.

An Example is a kind of Argument, wherein wee proceed from one particular to prove another particular, by reason of some likenes that is betwixt them . . . an Induction out of many particularities gathereth an universalitie . . . Notwithstanding *Aristotle* saith, that it may be reduced partly to an Induction, and partly to a Syllogisme: for in taking the first particular, you may by an unperfect induction imply an universal Proposition. And so from that universall Proposition to proceed by order of Syllogisme unto the other particular implyed in the conclusion of the Example, as in this Example: *Judas* died evill; *Ergo*, *Pilate* also died evill: it may be first reduced to an unperfect Induction thus: *Judas* dyed evill, because hee was the author of Christs death, and did not repent: *Ergo*, Every man that was author of Christs death, and did not repent, died evill. Into a Syllogisme thus: Every man that was author of Christs death, and did not repent, died evil; but *Pilat* was author of Christs death, and did not repent: *Ergo*, *Pilate* died evill. (p. 175)

Blundeville warns that for validity in this kind of argument the similitude of the particulars must be the very cause why the predicate of the antecedent belongs to its subject. And Lever remarks:

A reason by example allureth the ignorant: a reason by rule forceth the learned. (p. 102)

The method of applying syllogistic reasoning to the writing of themes as practiced in Tudor grammar schools is exemplified in the instructions dictated by Christopher Johnson, master of Winchester school, in the autumn of 1566. These instructions were recorded in the notebook of William Badger, a pupil in the sixth form.[3]

He who is about to treat a theme, ought at the very beginning to examine thoroughly what is its *sententia*, to what common place it must especially be referred, and whether it must be restricted by some added word. (185 ^{v}) . . . in proof two kinds of arguments are used: either enthymeme or syllogism. Of the enthymeme the parts are the proposition, the reason, the confirmation of the reason, the embellishing, the conclusion. Of the proposition and conclusion the *sententia* should be the same with the theme itself. The embellishing serves rather for ornament than proof. The confirmation of the reason is not of the form of the enthymeme, but proves its assumption. For example, let the theme be this, "Virtue being praised increases."

By love of praise all things are governed and especially stimulated, therefore virtue also.

There is no animal so stupid which does not permit itself to be petted, there

---

[3] Quoted by T. W. Baldwin, *William Shakspere's Small Latine and Lesse Greeke*, 1944, I, 334 ff.

is no man so barbarous who does not permit himself to be praised, therefore all are captivated, etc. Here now the oration should run on into similitudes, examples, apothegms, and other ornaments, and thence concludes (186 ʳ).

Of the rhetorical syllogism, which is the other part of explaining the theme, six parts are enumerated, the proposition, the major, the proof of the major, the minor, the proof of the minor, and the conclusion. Let the theme be, "A philosopher should never be an avaricious person."

Proposition	No one doubts, I think, that especially disgraceful in a philosopher is that avidity for riches which we call avarice. For ava-
Major	rice (that I may say it in one word) as it is the contrary of virtue, so certainly it fights directly against wisdom. For wisdom
Proof of the major	is a kind of right habit of the mind lifting itself to celestial and eternal things. But avarice is what other than depravity depressing the mind in itself immortal to the enfeebled members of this money, that is, earthly dregs? So that no one does not clearly see what is the difference between avarice and wisdom.
Minor	Further, since the philosopher teaches others wisdom, so too he himself should also be a participator of the same in his life. For
Proof of the minor	wherefore that boast, wherefore the name of philosopher unless as he professes to love wisdom, so also he can follow it and live according to its prescript? Wherefore, since this is now manifest that wisdom does not at all couple with avarice, but a philosopher both in fact and in name is a wise man, how disgrace-
Conclusion	ful in a man of this kind would even a slight suspicion of avarice be. Those of whom I speak this ought to appear wise (186 ᵛ).

What in the proof of themes we have omitted must here be added that nothing may be lacking. For there are certain propositions so general and universal that it is possible for each one to be demonstrated a priori (as they say). These are to be proved by enumeration, which is accustomed to be called induction by the dialecticians, and confirmed by multitude. Let the proposition be one in Aristophanes that all obey money. But this, what enthymeme? What syllogism? will so appositely establish it as if one by running through all orders of men, arts, inventions, labors should show with Chremulus that nothing is done except for money? Therefore in these three ways all themes must be treated, by enthymeme, syllogism, and enumeration (188 ʳ).

2. Fallacious Reasoning

Sophistry ostentatiously employs the forms of reasoning but hides underneath them a fallacy which must be detected by the art that teaches true reasoning. The sophist wishes to appear wise, to win an argument, to put down his adversary. He is little concerned with truth. Aristotle describes him as one who asks as if for information while he draws from his adversary statements against which he himself is well supplied with arguments; he shows the discrepancy between his opponent's hidden and professed opinions; he puts to him many questions at once. As Blundeville observes,

Aristotle saith, that the fraudulent disputation of the Sophister, tendeth alwayes to one of these five Ends or Marks; that is, either by force of argument, to bring you into some absurditie, which he calleth Elench; that is to say, a reprehension or reproofe, or else to make you to confesse that which is manifestly false, or to grant some Paradox, which is asmuch to say as an opinion contrary to all mens opinions: or to allow of incongrue speech contrarie to the rules of Grammar, called in Latine, *Solecismus,* or to admit some vaine repetition, called in Latine, *Nugatio.*

Of the first marke, let this be your example: If in disputing of Vertue, you have perhaps granted, that the meditation of Vertue doth make a man sad, the Sophister will force you by argument, to denie againe that which you before granted, thus: all things that bee contrarie, have contrarie effects: but it is proper to vice to make the minde of man sad: *Ergo,* vertue maketh his minde glad . . .

Of the second Marke, let this be your example: Every Dog hath power to barke; but there is a certaine Starre called the Dog: *Ergo,* that starre hath power to barke. . . .

Of the Paradox: . . . Whosoever is subject to sin, is wretched: but all rich and happy Kings are subject to sinne: *Ergo,* all rich and happy Kings are wretched and miserable . . .

Of the fourth . . . The Sophister will make you to allow of this false Latine, *mulier est candidus,* by force of argument, thus: *Omnis homo est candidus, at mulier est homo, ergo mulier est candidus* . . .

Of the fift . . . The Sophister will make you to allow of this vaine repetition . . . *Plato* is learned, but *Plato* is a man learned: *Ergo, Plato* is learned; a man learned: heere the premisses and the conclusion are all one thing, and therefore contrarie to the rules of Logick. (p. 188)

Aristotle explains the value of knowing how to deal with sophistic arguments.

The use of them, then, is, for philosophy, two-fold. For in the first place, since for the most part they depend upon the expression, they put us in a better condition for seeing in how many senses any term is used, and what kind of resemblances and what kind of differences occur between things and between their names. In the second place they are useful for one's own personal researches; for the man who is easily committed to a fallacy by some one else, and does not perceive it, is likely to incur this fate of himself also on many occasions. (*De sophisticis elenchis*, ch. 16, 175 ª 5)

Falsity arises from an erroneous relation of terms; a fallacy from an erroneous relation of propositions. A premise may be false; a syllogism may be fallacious. One may flatly deny a premise as false

by shewyng the faulte to bee in the definition, in the devision, in the causes, or in some other place: As thus.

> I had good cheere in suche a mans house.
> *Ergo*, he is an honest man.

Here the fault is in the definition, for, if I would goe about to define an honest man, every bodie would laugh me to scorne if I would thus define him. That man, whosoever he be, that maketh mee good cheere at his house, is a very honest man. . . . For vertue is gotten by long practise, and by well doing of many good thinges, not by making a good dinner. (Wilson, *RR*, fol. 83 ʳ)

A syllogism is fallacious when the conclusion does not follow from the premises, even though both premises may be true; their lack of coherence may be due to a formal or to a material fallacy.

The fallacy is formal if it violates a rule of the syllogism. For example:

Every covetous man doth violate the lawes of liberalitie; but every prodigall man doth violate the lawes of liberalitie; therefore every prodigall man is a covetous man. (Blundeville, p. 184)

Here the middle term is not understood in its full extension in either premise, since it is predicate in both of them and both are affirmative. Consequently the conclusion does not follow from the premises and in this instance it is false. Wilson offers an example of another formal fallacy.

> All ryot is an offence.
> No covetousnesse is riot.
> *Ergo*, no covetousnesse is any offence.

Thus we see a false conclusion, made of two undoubted true propositions . . . (fol. 85 ʳ)

In this syllogism there is an illicit process of the major term: *offence* is used in its full extension in the conclusion and in only part of its extension in the major premise.

A material fallacy is one that vitiates an argument which on the surface appears to be formally correct. Blundeville and Wilson, following Aristotle, group material fallacies into two classes: those arising from ambiguity in the language, and those arising from a hidden assumption in the matter.

Six material fallacies have their root in ambiguity of language and therefore common to all of them is the formal fallacy of four terms; for if the middle term has a different meaning in each premise, it merely appears to be one term whereas it is really two and consequently cannot serve to establish a true coherence between the premises. The ambiguity may be in one word or in a conjunction of words.

The fallacy of equivocation arises from the ambiguity of one word.

The Prophet saith that there is no evill in the Citie, but God doth it; but there be horrible evils in the Citie; *Ergo*, God is the Author of evill: the Conclusion is to be denied, because in the Major this word evill signifieth punishment, and in the Minor it signifieth sinne: (Blundeville, p. 190)

Wilson remarks:

Of no one thyng riseth so muche controversie, as of the doubtfulnesse, and dubble taking of a worde. Scholars dispute, wise men fall out, Lawyers agree not, Preachers waxe hot, Gentlemen strive, the people mutter, good men give counsaile, women have their wordes, this man affirmeth, the other denieth, and yet at length, the dubble meaning being once knowne (when al things are quiet) endes the whole matter. (*RR*, fol. 65 ᵛ)

He cites as an amusing instance of equivocation the story of Will Somer, King Henry VIII's fool, who

in commending a bishop of his acquaintaunce, declared to a noble personage, that this Bishop had a goodly base voice, and made at one time (quoth he) as base a Sermon, as he never heard the like in all his life before, and therefore, worthie to be coumpted a great Clerke, in his foolish judgement. Who will not say, that this Bishop was basely praised. (66 ʳ)

Amphibology is ambiguity in construction, as in the oracle prophesying that

Craesus going over the flood *Halim,* shal overthrow a great Empire. Here is not mentioned, whether he shal overthrow his owne, or an other mans. By the which Oracle in deed, he being deceived, lost his owne Kingdome, when he thought to subdue his enemies, and bring them under subjection. (Wilson, *RR*, fol. 66 ᵛ)

Wilson also quotes in full, with evident relish, the two love letters from Nicholas Udall's *Ralph Roister Doister* in which meanings quite opposite are given by different punctuations. He himself composes two verses to illustrate the same point.

> A robberie doe not feare: thy God, thy maker
> Will punish not one: God spareth, be thou sure.
> *Otherwise*
> A robberie doe not: feare thy God, thy maker
> Will punishe, not one God spareth, be thou sure.
>   (*Ibid.*, fol. 66 ᵛ)

The fallacies of composition and division are the reverse of each other.

Composition or conjunction, is the joyning together of things that are to be severed. As for example, two and three be even and odde, but five maketh two and three, therefore five is both even and odde:

Division is, when things are severed, which should be joyned together, as, all the wise men of Greece are seven; *Solon* and *Periander* are wise men of Greece, therefore *Solon* and *Periander* are seven: heere the Consequent is to be denied, because *Solon* and *Periander* are severed from the rest whereunto they should be joyned. (Blundeville, p. 191)

The fallacy of form of speech results

when words are falsely supposed to be like either in signification, in Case, or in Gender, or to be of one selfe Predicament, because they are like in termination . . . coloured and numbred are like in termination: *Ergo*, they are of one selfe Predicament, and yet the first belongeth to the Predicament of Qualitie, and the other to Quantitie. . . . when a word hath not his proper signification, or is not used according to the true phrase of speech in which it is uttered, as thus: Whatsoever thou hast not lost, thou hast still, but thou hast lost no hornes: *Ergo*, thou hast hornes. Heere this word, to lose, hath not his proper signification, for wee are said to lose properly that which we had, and not that which we never had. (*Ibid.*, p. 192)

As an example of the fallacy of accent whereby the true signification of a word is altered, Blundeville, as a true Englishman, offers

this old jest of a Master that said to his servant: Go heate this Capons legge, who immediately did eate it: then his Master being angry, said, I bade thee heate it, with an h: no Sir (said the servant) I did eate it with bread. (p. 191)

Seven fallacies have their source outside the language in a hidden assumption.

In the fallacy of accident it is falsely assumed that whatever is attributed to the substance of some thing, is attributed also to some accident of the said substance, and contrariwise, as thus: Whatsoever thou hast bought, thou hast eaten, but thou hast bought rawe flesh: *Ergo,* thou hast eaten rawe flesh: heere the Consequent is to be denied, because the Major hath respect to the substance, and the Conclusion to the qualitie. Another example, What I am, thou art not, but I am a man: *Ergo,* thou art none. (*Ibid.,* p. 193)

Wilson gives this illustration of the fallacy of accident.

> This man is a wittie fellowe.
> This man is lame.
> *Ergo* this same man hath a lame wit.

This is evidently false, because the accidentes of the bodie are referred to the substaunce of the mynde. (*RR,* fol. 71 ᵛ)

The fallacy of speech respective instead of speech absolute rests on the false assumption that what is true in a qualified sense is true absolutely.

The Fallax *A dicto secundum quid ad dictum Simpliciter,* chanceth when we goe about to make a thing to seeme absolute, that is spoken in some respect . . . by reason of time, place, person, comparison, and such like. Of time, as thus: I saw *John* yesterday, but I saw him not today: *Ergo,* I did see him, and not see him. Of place thus: It is not good to buy and sell in the Church: *Ergo,* it is not good to buy and sell. Of person thus: A Magistrate may kill a theefe: *Ergo,* every man may kill a theefe. Of comparison, thus: Riches are not good to him that cannot use them: *Ergo,* Riches are not good. (Blundeville, p. 194)

Wilson explains how hyperbole may have a bearing on the fallacy of *secundum quid.*

There is a figure in Rhetorike, called *Hyperbole,* that is to say, when a thing is spoken beyond measure uncredibly, and yet is not so largely meant. . . . Therefore, we must diligently take heede, when such speaches are used, that we take not them as they bee spoken, but as they are ment. . . . A noble man had a childe, which was very towarde in learnyng, and partly for such worthinesse as was in the childe, and partly to get favour of such a Peere, as the father was, divers commended the childe wonderfully well, and one above all other, thinking to say the most, not content with right excellent, or marveilous wittie, or toward, sayd thus after other mens judgement, and report given: Surely in my mynd, the childe is even a very monster. With that the noble man laughed, to heare his folly, and all the other likewise that were there. (*RR,* fol. 74 ʳ)

The fallacy of ignorance of the elench differs little, in Blundeville's opinion, from that of *secundum quid*, except that it is more general and inclusive.

An Elench . . . is a Syllogisme rightly gathering a Conclusion contrary to the assertion of the respondent, which contrarietie consisteth of foure principall points or respects, whereof, if any be wanting, then the contrarietie is not perfect. . . . First, that it be one selfe thing. Secondly, in one selfe respect. Thirdly, in one selfe manner. And fourthly, in or at one selfe time: for if you be deceived at any time by some false Elench, in thinking that it rightly gathereth a Conclusion meere contrarie to your assertion, when it is not so indeed, by reason that it faileth in some part requisite and incident to a true Elench: then it may be rightly said that you are deceived by ignorance of the Elench . . . Of the first, let this bee your example: foure is double to two, but not to three: *Ergo*, foure is double and not double; this is not to one selfe thing. . . . Of the third thus: This Prince ruleth mightily, but not mercifully: *Ergo*, he ruleth, and not ruleth; this is not in like manner. . . . (p. 194)

The fallacy of consequent arises from the assumption that a proposition is convertible when it is not. A universal affirmative proposition is convertible only when the predicate is the definition or a property of the subject. In the following argument the implicit major premise, Whoever is pale is in love, is not convertible.

> He is pale in countenaunce.
> *Ergo* he is in love.

Palenesse may come of studie, or care, and thought, of abstinence, of watching, of some distemperature in the body, and manie other wayes besides. (Wilson, *RR*, fol. 78 ʳ)

The fallacy of consequent also occurs when one thinks that upon the contrary of the antecedent the contrary of the consequent must needs follow.

It is a man: *Ergo*, It is a sensible body. It is no man: *Ergo*, it is no sensible body. Heere you see that this Proposition, It is no man, is the contrary of the first Antecedent, which saith, It is a man. Of which contrary, the contrary of the Consequent doth not necessarily follow: for though it bee no man, yet it may be some other sensible bodie. (Blundeville, p. 196)

The fallacy of false cause results

when a cause that is not able to prove the matter, is brought in, as though it were of force and strength, but the grounde being considered the faulte easely espied,

> Dronkenesse is evill:
> *Ergo* wine is naught. . . .

In all such argumentes, wherein good thinges are reproved, because evil bodies abuse the same, the evill will and the naughtie enclination of the man, which abused, such thynges is to bee rebuked: and therefore when it is otherwise, it may be saied, that a cause which is not, is put for a cause. . . .

Now a daies they will say, I cannot tell, here is much preaching, much teachyng of Gods word, but I see fewe folowers of it, it was a better worlde, when we had not halfe so many preachers, Heresies were never more ripe, naughtinesse never more abounded, therefore geve us the old learning again, and take you the newe.

This reason is not worthe a strawe. The wickednesse of the Preachers cometh not of their learning, but of their vicious natures, and naughtie desires: for out of one and the same flower the Bee sucketh Hony, and the Spider draw-eth poyson. . . .

This deceiptfull argument is much used in this our life, & made a buckler for divers maters. . . . when one that is rich should helpe a poore man, to say: God helpe you sir I have a great charge my self, I can not doe for you. . . . And the using of such excuses among the Rhetoricians, is called *translatio*, that is to say a shifting of the fault from one to an other. As we reade that *Demades* used a wonderfull good shift, when it was laied sore to his charge, that he had written a verie naughtie decree and unhonest, for the obteyning of the peace at *Alexanders* hand. He answered that the same decree was not written with his owne writing penne but with *Alexanders* warring speare, which is asmuch to say, feare did drive him to take such, & such condicions of peace. (Wilson, fol. 76 ^{r}–77 ^{r})

The fallacy of begging the question is present when the proof is as lit-tle known as the thing to be proved, or when it is less known, or when the proof is the same as the conclusion.

Every sensible bodie sometime sleepeth: *Ergo,* Man sometime sleepeth. Heere it is more to be doubted whether all sensible Bodies, all Beastes, Fowles and Fishes, doe sometimes sleepe or not, then whether man doth sometime sleepe: for it is an easier matter to know the nature and propertie of one speciall kinde, then of all, or many kindes. Of the third way, thus . . . The soule doth live ever: *Ergo,* it is immortall. (Blundeville, p. 195)

Wilson calls the first kind utis, and the last kind the "Cuckoes song," of which he remarks:

Self willed folke that followe lust, and forsake reason, use oft the Cuckowes song. As being asked why they will do this and that, they answere streight, Mary, because I will doe it, or because it pleaseth me best so to doe: . . . Some women are subject to this aunswere, which in wit doe excell, though in the eight partes of reason, fewe Schollers can hardly finde them. (*RR,* fol. 80 ^{r})

The fallacy of many questions consists in demanding a simple answer to a complex question.

The seventh and last Fallax, is when unadvisedly, and without using any distinction, you make an answere to manie questions, as though they were but one; as for example, The Sophister, seeing two men standing together, whereof the one is blinde, and the other hath his sight, will aske you, perhaps, whether they see, or not; whereunto if you answere directly, either yea, or no, you are by and by taken: for if you say that they see, then you grant that the blind man also seeth, and if you say, that they doe not see, then you grant, that he which seeth, is blinde; but if you answere, that the one seeth, and the other not, you shall by such distinction easily avoid the Sophisters cavillation: for divers questions hudled up in one, doe always require divers answeres. (Blundeville, p. 196)

The fallacies lend themselves to jesting, of which Aristotle remarks:

As to jests. These are supposed to be of some service in controversy: Gorgias says that you should kill your opponents' earnestness with jesting and their jesting with earnestness; in which he was right. (*Rhetoric*, 3.18, 1419 ^{b} 3)

Wilson concludes his treatment of the fallacies with a group of seven captious arguments which he introduces zestfully.

And nowe the rather to delight the Reader, I will ad here certaine wittie questions and arguments, which can hardly be avoyded, being very pleasant, & therfore not unworthie to be knowne.

They are called trapping arguments, because fewe that aunswered unto them, can avoyde daunger, and thus they are named in straunge wordes. *Crocodilites, Antistrephon, Ceratinae, Asistaton, Cacosistaton, Utis, Pseudomenos.* (*RR*, fol. 85 ^{r})

Utis, an argument in which the proof is as uncertain as the thing to be proved, is identical with the first form of begging the question illustrated above.

Antistrephon, is nothing els, then to turne a mans saying into his owne necke againe, and to make that which hee bringeth for his owne purpose, to serve for our purpose . . . There is in *Aristophanes* a wonderfull pretie talke, betwixt the father and the sonne . . . For where as the sonne had beaten his father, contrary to all order and honestie: yet notwithstanding, the soonne thought he had as good authoritie to beate his father, if he did amisse, as the father had to beate him. And therefore he sayd, wherefore should my father beate me? His father made answere. Mary (quoth he) because I love thee, and would thou shouldest do wel. Mary therfore (quoth the sonne) will I beate thee to, because I love thee also good father, and would thou shouldest doe well: & with that layd on strokes surely, till he made his father graunt that it was as lawfull for the sonne to beate his father, as for the father to beate his soone. (Wilson, *RR*, 85 ᵛ)

As another example of antistrephon, Wilson cites Euathlus' reply to Protagoras, the rebuttal which has been quoted on p. 363.

Cacosistata are such arguments, that being proponed betwene two persons, they serve aswell for the one part, as the other, as thus. . . . Alas, saith one, it is pitie such a man should be hanged, considering he is a gentleman. And why not gentlemen, aswel as other poore men, if they deserve it? Yea, why not they rather then any other, if they more deserve it then any other. (*Ibid.*, fol. 87 ᵛ)

Of the four remaining captious arguments Blundeville remarks that they are intricate kinds of reasoning comprehended under dilemma.[4] He and Wilson illustrate them with the same examples.

Pseudomonos. This is called a lying argument, for whatsoever ye shall say, must needes say amisse. *Epimenides* a man borne in *Crete*, sayd that the people borne in *Crete*, were lyers, sayd he true or no? (Wilson, fol. 87 ᵛ)

Assistation, is a kinde of cavelling, not consisting of any sure ground, as if a man did say, that he doth hold his peace . . . another by and by might cavill thereof in this sort: *Ergo*, He that holdeth his peace, speaketh . . . (Blundeville, p. 179)

[Ceratin or] The horned Argument is, when by some subtile and craftie manner of questioning, we seeke to have such an answere, as we may take vantage therof, as the Pharises did, when they questioned with Christ touching the payment of Tribute to *Caesar*. (Blundeville, p. 179)

Crocodilites, is such a kinde of subtiltie, that when we have graunted a thing to our adversarie, being asked before what he will say: the same turneth to our harme afterward, and causeth an inconveniencie, thereupon to ensue. Aucthours doe feigne, that the Crocodile . . . did take a womans childe from her, and spake with the mother in this wise: woman, I will give thee thy childe againe, if thou wilt say trueth to me, and tell me assuredly, whether I will give thee thy child againe or no: She aunswered, I know assuredly, thou wilt not give me my childe againe, and therefore it is reason I have my childe againe, because I have sayd trueth. Nay, sayd the Crocodile, I will not give thee thy childe againe, because thou mayst be seene to have sayd trueth: least that if I give thee thy childe again, thou shouldest have made a lye: neither yet would I have given thee thy child again, if thou haddest not sayd otherwise, because then thou haddest not sayd trueth. And hereof this argument hath his name, called *Crocodilites*. (Wilson, fol. 85 ᵛ)

---

[4] Blundeville makes no mention of utis, antistrephon, and cacosistaton.

3. Disputation

In distinguishing four kinds of disputation Blundeville follows Aristotle.

> Disputation is a contention about some question taken in hand, either for finding out of truth, or else for exercise sake, and there be foure kindes of disputation, whereof the first is called doctrinall, because it appertayneth to Science.
> The second is called Dialecticall, which belongeth to probable opinion.
> The third is called Tentative, which serveth to trie another mans knowledge, in any kinde of Science. The fourth is Sophisticall, which tendeth onely to deceive. (p. 187)

Disputation most often deals with the probable, which has the inherent capacity to generate arguments on both sides of a question. There are five ways in which a proposition may be probable.

> Things probable, according to *Aristotle*, are these that seeme true to all men, or to the most part of men, or to all wise men, or to the most part of wise men, or else to the most approved wise men. (*Ibid.*, p. 169)

Because dialectic and rhetoric have as their subject matter the probable, they are by that very fact arts of disputation, as Aristotle explains:

> No other of the arts draws opposite conclusions: dialectic and rhetoric alone do this. Both these arts draw opposite conclusions impartially. Nevertheless, the underlying facts do not lend themselves equally well to the contrary views. No; things that are true and things that are better are, by their nature, practically always easier to prove and easier to believe in. (*Rhetoric*, 1.1., 1355 [a] 34)

Fraunce gives this brief picture of the ancient seeker after truth.

> *Socrates* in this sort cogged with the olde *Graecian* Sophisters, making them say and unsay, and therefore say this, that hee was a wrangler, an inchaunter, a dissembler, a deceiver. (*LL*, fol. 114 [r])

One savors a keen relish of disputation in Wilson's account of it.

> That is called a disputation, or reasoning of matters, when certaine persons debate a cause together . . . whereupon after harde holde and long debating, the trueth either appeareth, or els they rest both upon one point, leaving the matter to bee adjudged of the hearers . . .
> In al debating of causes, warines is ever thought great wisedome. And therefore, he that wil shew wit and learning, must . . . evermore have some cheefe ground in his head, whereunto he mindeth to leavell all his reasons before hand,

that upon the graunt of them, a weightier matter may evermore be obteyned. And whereas the aunswerer perhapps shall smell where aboutes he goeth, and therfore will seeke starting holes to escape, and flee such daunger: The disputer must alwaies keepe him in, and suffer him at no hand to slippe away, but force him still, to aunswere the propouned argument directly, that either he graunt the argument to be true, or denigh it to be good, or els shewe wherein the fault is, by either opening the doubtfulnesse of some worde, or declaring plainely the wrong knitting and lapping up of the whole reason. (fol. 61 $^{r-v}$)

The maner of confutation, two waies considered.

For the first, either we purpose by disputation, to aunswere fully to the matter, or els secondly (if power want to compasse that) we seeke some other meanes, to satisfie the man, and that three maner of waies, either by making the objection seeme lesse then it is, or by bringing some other example against it, or els by seeking some meanes, to goe from the matter.

We make the argument appear slender, when we receive it laughingly, and declare by wordes, even at the first, that it is nothyng to the purpose, and so abash the opponent.

Again, we turne an other argument in our adversaries neck, when we bring an other example against him. Or els when wee charge him, with a like fault, and lay some greater matter in his dish. Lastly, wee shift away from the violence of our adversarie, by making some digression, or giving occasion of some other talke, whereby the adversarie, either is driven to forget his argument, or els being blinded with too much matter, is forced either to goe no further, or els to thinke himself content. (63 ^{v})

Objections are then used, when wee doe not dissolve the argument, by the rules of Logicke, or directly avoyde the daunger, but bryng an other thing, as an example, to overthrowe that, which was spoken before, and this maner is fower waies used.

i. By takyng occasion of the selfe same thyng, that is put forth and wresting it otherwise . . . riches are good, because they bring pleasure. The answere: Nay Marie, richesse are evill, because they bring woe. . . .

ii. By using the same example in an other matter . . . Such a one is an honest man, for, I saw him once give almes to the poore: I aunswere: Such a one is no dronkard, for I sawe him once sober. . . .

iii. By makyng a cleane contrary example. . . . Such an honest man hath once received a great displeasure, of his frend and neighbour. *Ergo*, he may hate him deadly for ever. Nay, not so, for the wicked man will sometimes forgive, receivyng displeasure, and therfore, the good man must much more forgive. . . .

iiii. By standing to authoritie, or using sentences of the sage. . . . Forgive him, because he is a childe. Nay, not so, for *Salomon* biddeth, that the rodde should not goe from the childe, therefore, it is good to beate him, when he offendeth. (82 $^{r-v}$)

Fraunce gives a more detailed outline of the technique of disputation, after warning against faults manifest in Vergil's clowns.

In every syllogisticall conflict and controversie, there is a defendant & an opponent. The first is to urge, prove, conclude; the other to repell, avoyd, and drive backe. The disputation being once begon, it is an unorderly confusion for the same man sometimes to aunswere, sometimes to reply, and never constantly to playe out his owne parte: much like the two clownes in *Virgill*, which, when they could not aunswere what was propounded, begin a freshe with a new doubt on the necke of the olde: *Dic, quibus in terris*, quoth the one, and *Dic, quibus in terris*, quoth the other, Arreede me a riddle, sayth *Damaetas*: and Arreede me a riddle replyeth *Menalcas*, thincking it a faire conquest, to have taken and given blowe for blowe, as Bakers and Butchers use to doe, who never care for any curious wardes, but lay on loade like good fellowes, one for one, till both begin to stagger, with their valiant blood about their brused pates. I have therefore in a word or two, layd downe some generall instructions and directions for orderly disputations.[5]

Logicall exercise is that which expresseth that in particular practise which is generally put downe in art. For as art followeth nature, so exercise followeth art. Herein let us consider

 I. The adjuncts & affections of it, for it is performed either by
  A. Writing, or
  B. Speaking, & eyther of these is eyther
   1. Continued as in long discourses & tractates, or
   2. Interrupted as, in
    a. Dialogues
    b. Disputations. Vide B B.
 II. The specials of it. Vide A A.

B B. Disputation is an argumentable discussing of a doubtfull proposition, where note.
  1. The Disputers
   a. The proponent, who defendeth the proposition or position: whereunto also the moderator and determiner of the disputation is referred, who commonly mainteineth the position.
   b. The opponent, whoe defendeth the contrary.
  2. The duties of the disputers, eyther,
   a. Common to both of them as in
    (1) preparation and furniture

[5] What follows has been changed from tabular to outline form by supplying numbers and letters in place of braces to indicate subordination and co-ordination. Fraunce here outlines his whole theory of composition and of reading. Although *logos* naturally predominates, he gives some attention to *ethos* (by recommending courtesy) and to *pathos* (by remarks on scorning).

(a) of instruments for the disputation, as bee
    i. Logike
    ii. Rhetorike
(b) things requisite for the same, it must be noted there-
    fore.
    i. What may confirme or confute the position.
    ii. What sect of philosophy the adversary followeth.
    iii. They must have in memory the generall heades of
        artes, which are commonly used in disputations.
(2) Conflict and assault: they must neither
    (a) Wrangle about trifling wordes,
    (b) Nor make long and impertinent excursion and va-
        garies.
    (c) Nor seeke starting holes.
    (d) Nor bring in any such thing as may rather make
        against them, then with them.
    (e) Nor seeke to supplant or circumvent one another in-
        juriously.
    (f) Nor overweene themselves, or be obstinate and singu-
        lar in conceipt.
    (g) Nor fal to threatning and railing with undecent
        tearmes.
b. Proper to eyther of them.

C C. The proper dueties of the
  1. Opponent be
    a. To have his weapons in a readines, that is, to have his objections
      framed artificially with syllogisticall disposition.
    b. Not to cast his argumentes confusedly on a heape, but to use
      them distinctly, one after another.
    c. To have Prosyllogismes in a readynes, for the confirmation of
      such parts of his syllogismes, as may by likelyhood, be denied.
    d. To bring in nothing which hath not some probabilitie or shew
      of truth in it.
    e. Sometimes to deale directly & openly: sometimes covertly, and
      by bringing his adversary to an absurditie or impossibilitie.
    f. Never to choppe in impertinent matters, which make nothing at
      all to the matter in controversie.
  2. Defendent be
    a. In choise of his position, that it be not
      (1) Repugnant to sence.
      (2) Contrary to equity & honesty.

(3) Too hard and difficult.
  b. Both in
    (1) Repetitions of the objections made, & that either by the selfesame words, or with the selfe same sence, in the like order as they were propounded: with a kind of courteous preface: that both himselfe may have some meane-space of conceaving a solution, and the auditors better understand what was objected.
    (2) And also in aunswering of the same.

D D. The objections be aunswered
  1. Either
    a. By skorning, and rejecting, if absurd fooleries be objected, or such as no man understandeth.
    b. By graunting and confessing, when such thinges bee brought in, as make nothing against the position.
    c. By affirming or denying, when any interrogation is made: or els by asking what he meaneth by his interrogation, if it be ambiguous and sophisticall
  2. Or by direct solution, & that either
    a. Perfect, when the very cause is shewd, why the conclusion is not sufficient, and it is
      (1) By denying either of
        (a) The premisses and prosyllogisms when they be false
        (b) Or the consecution & consequence, when the fault is in the forme of conclusion: for the conclusion it selfe must never be denied.
      (2) Eyther
        (a) By distinguishing when eyther
          i. The questions and interrogations be captious and doubtfull,
          ii. Or the premisses bee true not absolutely, but in part. And here fryvolous distinctions must be avoyded.
        (b) Or conditionall graunting, as I graunt, if you so understand it. Sometimes the defendent doubteth of the truth of some one of the premisses, and doth therefore leave it, of purpose to aunswere to the other that is more plaine, Thus, Let the Major passe for a whyle, I now aunswere to the minor.
    b. Imperfect by bringing in some instance, that is by taking a particular exception to a generall proposition.

A A. So much of the affections of this logicall exercise the specials now follow which bee

1. Analysis, in undoing & examining that which is already made, & is
   a. eyther belonging to Invention: as
      (1) to search and invent the question it selfe.
      (2) to picke out the arguments and proofes.
      (3) to refer every one to their several heads, & there to inquire of their sufficiency, as whether that be used for a Cause which is no cause, &c
   b. or to Disposition & that either
      (1) Axiomaticall, where all the axiomes must be also brought to their heads, and their truth or falsnes diligently examined.
      (2) Dianoeticall which is eyther
         (a) Syllogisticall, for the examination and triall of conseqution, what followeth or not followeth
         (b) Methodicall, for proofe of order and Methodicall handling of the matter discoursed upon.

2. Genesis, in making or framing of any thing by our owne industrie, & that eyther
   a. By way of imitation and that either
      (1) Of the whole worke ⎫ eyther of these is
      (2) or of some part   ⎬
         (a) in wordes, called Translation
         (b) in things called properly imitation. Wee must Imitate
            i. neyther all autors, but the best of al:
            ii. nor al things but the best, & that freely, not servilely, as bindyng our judgment to othermens fancie.
   b. Or by proper Invention, where we must
      (1) First peruse every place of Logicall invention for the inventing of proofes and arguments.
      (2) Then dispose them artificially both by judgment
         (a) Axiomaticall
         (b) and Dianoeticall & that both
            i. Syllogisticall
            ii. Methodicall

                          (*LL*, fol. 101 ^{r}–103 ^{r})

The twenty-one figures of disputation represent a rhetorical analysis of its techniques which closely parallels the logical analysis. Among these figures are included all that have any sort of reference to an opponent or to judges, even when the speaker himself takes both parts, as in arguing with himself, or in anticipating and answering beforehand questions or objections which his adversary may put to him.[6]

The figure aporia is a doubting or deliberating with oneself, when

the speaker sheweth that he doubteth, either where to begin for the multitude of matters, or what to do or say, in some strange and doubtfull thing. *Cicero* for *Roscius;* Of what shall I first complaine O Judges? or where shall I first begin? Of what or of whom shall I call for helpe, of the immortall gods, or of the Romane people? or shall I most pitifully crave your defence, who have the highest authoritie? (Peacham, p. 109)

Anthypophora is a reasoning with ourselves.

Then we reason the matter with our selves, when we aske questions of our selves, and aunswere thereunto. As thus. . . . Seing thou art so basely borne, so poore in state, so smally learned, so hard favoured, and hast no witte at al, what meanst thou to vaunt thy selfe so much, and to make such bragges as thou doest. What doth make thee to waxe so proud? Thy stocke whereof thou did-dest come? Why man they are very base folke. Thine owne wealth? Tush, thou art as poore as *Job.* Thy learning? Marie thou never camst yet where any learning did growe. Thy beautie? Now in good soth, a worse favoured man can there not be upon earth againe. Thy witte? Now God he knoweth, it is as blunt as many bee. What other thing then is all this thy bragging, but plaine mad-nesse. (Wilson, *AR,* p. 207)

Anacoenosis is used when

the Orator seemeth to aske counsell of his adversary, or to deliberate with the Judges what is to be done, or what ought to have bene done. . . . the Apostle *Paul:* This would I learne of you, received ye the spirit by the workes of the law, or by hearing of faith preached? Gal. 3. (Peacham, p. 110)

By the figure synchoresis,

the Orator, trusting strongly to his cause, giveth leave to the Judges or to his adversaries, to consider of it with indifferencie, & so to judge of it, if it be found just and good, to allow it, if evil to condemne and punish it. . . . *Peter:* Whether it be right saith he in the sight of God, to hearken unto you more then unto God, judge ye. Acts 4. (*Ibid.,* p. 111)

Eight figures illustrate more specific methods of meeting an opponent's arguments than those outlined by logicians.

[6] These figures are concerned with points similar to those dealt with by Aristotle in his *Rhetoric,* Bk. III, ch. 15, and those dealt with by Wilson and Fraunce in their treatment of disputation quoted above.

By an apt similitude Puttenham conveys the spirit of the figure pro-catalepsis, which confutes what an adversary may object even before he has uttered it:

for by reason we suppose before what may be said, or perchaunce would be said by our adversary or any other, we do prevent them of their advantage, and do catch the ball (as they are wont to say) before it come to the ground. (p. 232)

Puttenham offers no illustration. Fraunce quotes an example from Cleophila's speech to the inconstant multitude, in Sidney's *Arcadia*.

An unused thing it is, and I thinke not heretofore seene, *Arcadians*, that a woman should give publike counsaile to men, a stranger to the countrey people, and that lastlie in such a presence a private person, as I am, should possesse the regall throne. But the strangenes of your action makes that used for vertue, which your violent necessitie imposeth. For certainlie a woman may well speake to such men who have forgotten all manlike government; a straunger may with reason instruct such subjects, that neglect due points of subjection, and is it mervaile this place is entred into by an other, since your owne Duke, after thirtie yeares government, dare not shewe his face to his faithfull people? (*AR*, Sig. H 3 ᵛ)

Paromologia is a figure by which the speaker admits and grants to his adversary many things unfavorable to his own position, and then suddenly brings in a point which overthrows all that was granted.

Suppose you have omitted nothing in your owne person, of a friend to be performed, that you were no partaker with him of these evill counsels, that you abstained to accompany him in the execution of his mischiefes, yet are you not therefore cleared: For it is not sufficient for a man not to do evill of himselfe, but that by too much lenity he become not occasion of anothers mischiefe. (Day, p. 384)

Concessio is used

when we jestinglie admit of anie speach or argument. . . . This figure delighteth very much when we grant that which hurteth him to whom it is graunted, as it manie times falleth out in contentious disputations. (Fraunce, *AR*, Sig. H 5 ᵛ)

Fenner gives this example of concessio.

Eccle. 11. *Rejoyce young man in thy youth, and let thy heart cheare thee in the dayes of thy youth, and walke in the wayes of thy hearte, and in the sight of thine eies: but knowe that for al these thinges God will bring thee to judgement.* (Sig. E 2 ᵛ)

Metastasis is a forme of speech by which we turne backe those thinges that are objected against us, to them which laid them to us . . . 1 Kings 18: When *Ahab* likewise charged *Elia,* that it was he which troubled all Israel, nay saith *Elia* it is not I that trouble Israel, but thou and thy fathers house, in that you have forsaken the commandements of the Lord, and thou hast followed Baal. (Peacham, p. 181)

Apodioxis, when the Orator rejecteth the objection or argument of his adversaries as thinges needlesse, absurde, false, or impertinent to the purpose, as proceeding from follie, or framed by malice, or invented by subtiltie. . . . To the Sadduces captiously inquiring of Christ, concerning the state of mariage in the resurrection, he answered: you do erre, not knowing the Scriptures, neither the power of God: by which answere he rejecteth their captious objection, by noting their ignorance. (*Ibid.,* p. 185)

Diasyrmus is a Trope by which the arguments of an adversarie are either depraved or rejected. . . . This figure is for the most part made either by some base similitude, or by some ridiculous example, to which the adversaries objection or argument is compared, whereby it is either made ridiculous, or at least much disgraced.

As for to shew examples of this figure I judge it needlesse and superfluous, considering the dayly plentie of them almost everie where, both private and publike. (*Ibid.,* p. 39)

The last two of these eight figures, namely, antirrhesis and aphorismus, involve reprehension. By antirrhesis,

the Orator rejecteth the authority, opinion or sentence of some person: for the error or wickednesse of it. . . . This same forme of speech Christ useth against Satan Mat. 4, where he rejecteth the subtil attempts and false allegations of Satan by the mightie power and truth of his answeres. (*Ibid.,* p. 88)

Aphorismus is a form of reprehension which raises a question about the proper application of a word, as,

your councellors, if such may be called counsellers as draw unto mischiefe, are utterlie unmeet to such kind of assemblies. (Day, p. 380)

Two figures of argument depend on an insistent return to one point. Commoratio consists in dwelling upon and frequently returning to one's strongest argument, supporting it with varied pleas or with varied expression.

When wee are earnest in a matter, and feele the weight of our cause, we rest upon some reason, which serveth best for our purpose. Wherin this figure appeareth most, and helpeth much to set forth our matter. For if we stil kepe us to our strongest hold, and make often recourse thither, though we be driven through bytalke to goe from it now and then: we shall force them at length, either to avoyd our strong defence, or els to yeeld into our hands. (Wilson, *AR*, p. 178)

Epimone is the persistent repetition of the same plea in much the same words.

There is a good example hereof in *Abrahams* praier or sute to God for the *Sodomites,* saying: if there be fiftie righteous within the Citie wilt thou destroy, and not spare the place for the fiftie righteous that are therein? . . . and thus he continueth perseverantly . . . Gen. 18. (Peacham, p. 70)

Puttenham describes epimone as a refrain in a poem, repeated often at intervals. He calls it the Love-burden, because it bears the whole burden of the song. A refrain obviously has the qualities of persistence and repetition, characteristics of this figure.

Apoplanesis is a figure of evasion through digression. The logicians mention digression as one of the recognized forms of defense in disputation. By apoplanesis,

the speaker leadeth away the mind of his hearer, from the matter propounded or question in hand, which maketh much against him. . . . when the cause of the Orator is weake, and not able to abide the uttermost triall. . . . *Cicero* when he should have answered to an accusation, in which it was objected that *Caelius* poysoned *Metellus* . . . he digressed by and by to *Metellus* death . . . he sigheth, weepeth and bewaileth that death, whereby he staieth and appeaseth his adversaries, and causeth them to mourne with him . . . turneth the mindes of the Judges from the cogitation of the fact . . . it may be compared to the subtiltyes of war called stratagems. (*Ibid.,* p. 117)

Three figures of excuse represent another refuge in disputation. By proecthesis,

the speaker defendeth by his answere, conteining a reason of that which he hath said or done, proving thereby that he ought not to be blamed. . . .

In this forme of speech our Saviour Christ doth many times defend his doings against the accusation of his enemies: as, for healing the man with the withered hand on the Sabboth. (*Ibid.,* p. 102)

The figure dicaeologia, or anangeon, is used

when we confesse the thynge to be done, but excuse it by necessitye, eyther of the person or tyme, thus: I confesse that thys I dyd. But the woman that thou gavest me dyd deceyve me. (Sherry, Sig. D vi ᵛ)

By pareuresis,

the speaker alledgeth a premeditated excuse conteining reasons of such might as are able to vanquish all objections. A most artificiall example hereof is found in the answere of *Aeneas* to *Dido*, in the *4.* booke of *Aeneidos*, wherof I have gathered the summe both of the [3] objections of *Dido*, and of the [9] answeres & excuses of *Aeneas*. (Peacham, p. 95)

Questions should be used skillfully in disputation. Pysma is a figure by which

the Orator doth demaund many times together, and use many questions in one place, whereby he maketh his speech very sharpe and vehement . . . *Cicero* for *Roscius:* In what place did he speake with them? with whom did he speake? did he hire them? whom did he hire, and by whom? To what end, or how much did he give them? . . .

This figure . . . is mighty to confirme, to confute, to provoke, to cause attention, to moove affections. . . . Plaine meaning & just dealing would that this figure should not be used to deceave the hearer by the multitude of questions . . . as doth the fallace in Sophistrie, called *Plures interrogationes.* (*Ibid.*, p. 106)

Lastly there are two general figures of persuasion and dissuasion. Peacham asserts of these that dehortatio needs no further explanation than that it is the contrary of adhortatio, or protrope, of which he remarks,

that forme of speech which deserveth the name of *Protrope* or *Adhortatio,* hath not only the forme of a commandement or of a promise, but also sundry & mightie reasons to move the minde and understanding of man not only to a willing consent, but also to a fervent desire to performe the thing adhorted. . . . The greater power that this figure hath, the more mischiefe it may worke, if it be perverted and turned to abuse . . . as by moving of sedition, tumults, or rebellion. (p. 78)

CHAPTER IX

PATHOS AND ETHOS

1. Pathos

ARISTOTLE gave the name *pathos* to that form of persuasion which
endeavors to put the audience into a certain frame of mind. He
thus describes its importance.

When people are feeling friendly and placable, they think one sort of thing;
when they are feeling angry or hostile, they think either something totally different or the same thing with a different intensity: when they feel friendly
toward the man who comes before them for judgement, they regard him as
having done little wrong, if any; when they feel hostile, they take the opposite
view. Again, if they are eager for, and have good hopes of, a thing that will be
pleasant if it happens, they think that it certainly will happen and be good for
them: whereas if they are indifferent or annoyed, they do not think so. (*Rhetoric*, 2.1.1377 ^b 31)

The orator must accordingly know how to appeal to the emotions,
which so change men as to affect their judgments. He must know how
to arouse or quiet them according to his purpose, for the emotions or passions come and go, and therein lies his opportunity.

Passion is a sudden motion of the minde or body, that endureth not long, and
therefore easie to be removed. Passion of the minde is a sudden feare or joy conceived of some evill or good that is offered: and of the body, as palenesse . . .
blushing, or trembling. (Blundeville, p. 32)

It is particularly in the conclusion of a speech that the orator should

stirre the hearers to bee sorie, to bee glad, or to bee offended . . . vehemently
enlarging that, which before was in fewe wordes spoken to set the Judge or
hearers in a heate: or els to mittigate, & asswage displeasure conceived with
much lamenting of the matter, and moving them thereby the rather to shewe
mercie. (Wilson, *AR*, p. 114)

The response of the hearer is the effect at which every speaker aims; his
efforts are vain if he does not put his audience into the frame of mind
he desires.

And assuredly nothing is more needfull, then to quicken these heavie loden wittes of ours, and much to cherish these our lompish and unweldie Natures, for except men finde delite, they will not long abide: delite them, and winne them: wearie them and you lose them for ever. And that is the reason, that men commonly tarie the ende of a merie Play, and cannot abide the halfe hearing of a sower checking Sermon. . . . Thus we see, that to delite is needfull, without the which weightie matters will not be heard at all. (*Ibid.*, p. 3)

In *The Arte of Rhetorique* the traditionalist Wilson speaks of moving the affections, of moving to pity, and of moving to laughter. The moving of affections, he explains, is

none other thing, but a stirring or forsing of the minde, either to desire, or els to detest and loth any thing, more vehemently then by nature we are commonly wont to doe. . . . Neither onely are wee moved with those things, which wee thinke either hurtfull, or profitable for our selves, but also we rejoyce, we be sorie, or wee pittie an other mans happe. . . .

In mooving affections, and stirring the Judges to be greeved, the waight of the matter must be set forth, as though they sawe it plaine before their eyes, the report must be such, and the offence made so hainous, that the like hath not bene seen heretofore. (*Ibid.*, p. 130)

To move the hearers to pity, the speaker should feel in his own heart the sorrow he recounts, then lead them to share in it either through memory or through imagination.

Now in moving pitie, and stirring men to mercie . . . the best were to wil them, to remember their owne state . . . if the like hath not happened unto the hearers of this cause, yet it were meete to shewe them that the like may happen . . . Neither can any good bee done at all . . . except we bring the same affections in our own harte, the which we would the Judges should beare towards our owne matter. For how can he be greeved with the report of any hainous act . . . in bewayling the miserable misfortune of the thing, or in fearing much, the like evill hereafter: except the Oratour himselfe utter such passions outwardly, and from his heart fetch his complaints . . . such men . . . will force a man to be sory with them, and take part with their teares even against his wil. Notwithstanding when such affections are moved, it were good not to stand long in them. For though a vehement talke may moove teares, yet no arte can holde them. For as *Cicero* doth say, nothing drieth soner then teares, especially when we lament an other mans cause, and be sorie with him for his sake. (*Ibid.*, p. 133)

Moving the audience to laughter serves two purposes: it gains their attention and it puts them into a favorable frame of mind.[1]

---

[1] Wilson's discussion of moving to laughter is derived from *Il cortegiano* of Castiglione, who borrowed it from Cicero's *De oratore*.

Assuredly it behoveth a man . . . evermore to have regarde to his audience . . . And now because our senses be such, that in hearing a right wholsome matter, we either fall a sleepe . . . or els are wearied with still hearing one thing, without any change . . . the wittie and learned have used delitefull sayings, and quicke sentences, ever among their waightie causes, considering that onely good will is got thereby (for what is he that loveth not mirth?) but also men wonder at such a head, as hath mens hartes at his commaundement, being able to make them merie when he list . . . Againe, we see that men are full oft abashed, and put out of countenance by such taunting meanes, and those that have so done are coumpted to be fine men, and pleasaunt fellowes. (*Ibid.,* p. 136)

The figurists also understood the value of appealing to the feelings. Concerning this form of persuasion, Peacham remarks:

the Orator . . . may prevaile much in drawing the mindes of his hearers to his owne will and affection: he may winde them from their former opinions, and quite alter the former state of their mindes, he may move them to be of his side, to hold with him, to be led by him, as to mourne or to marvel, to love or to hate, to be pleased or to be angry, to favour, to desire or to be satisfied, to feare or to hope, to envy, to abhorre, to pittie, to rejoyce, to be ashamed, to repent, and finally to be subject to the power of his speech whither soever it tendeth. (p. 121)

In discussing pathopopoeia, the generic figure of *pathos,* Peacham emphasizes the same points as Wilson.

The Orator moveth the minds of his hearers to some vehemency of affection, as of indignation feare, envy, hatred, hope, gladnesse, mirth, laughter, sadnesse or sorrow: of this there be two kindes.

The first is when the Orator being moved himselfe with anie affections (sorrow excepted) doth bend & apply his speech to stir his hearers to the same . . . to which diverse vehement figures do belong, as *Exclamatio, Obtestatio, Imprecatio, Optatio, Exuscitatio, Interrogatio,* and such like. And to move mirth, formes of speech serving to that purpose, as *Asteismus,* and others of that kinde. . . . Examples hereof are common in Tragedies, but of mirth and laughter in Comodies.

The other kind of *Pathopeia,* is when the Orator by declaring some lamentable cause, moveth his hearers to pitie and compassion, to shew mercy, and to pardon offences. . . . A serious and deepe affection in the Orator is a mightie furtherance and helpe to this figure, as when he is zealous, and deeply touched himselfe with any of those vehement affections, but specially if he be inwardly moved with a pitifull affection, he moveth his hearers to the same compassion and pitie, by his passionate pronuntiation. (*Ibid.,* pp. 143–45)

Exuscitatio is the stirring up of others to like or dislike, through the vehement affection of the speaker himself.

Doth it not abhor you to heare and understand of a rabble of so great and unaccustomed lewdnesse, a man every way so vile, to go thus freely unpunished? Surely I do thinke no honest mind but would bee of this opinion, that of all creatures living he were most worthy to be extirped. (Day, p. 389)

In a few figures of *pathos* the form of the language reveals the speaker's emotion. This is true of aposiopesis, by which

the Orator through some affection, as either of feare, anger, sorrow, bashfulnesse or such like, breaketh off his speech before it be all ended. *Virgil:* How doth the childe *Ascanius*, whom tymely *Troy* to thee: breaking off by the interruption of sorrow. (Peacham, p. 118)

Concerning ecphonesis, or exclamation, Hoskyns observes:

Exclamacion is not lawfull, but in extremity of mocion, as *Pirocles* seeing the milde *Philoclea* innocently beheaded, cryed out, oh Tyrant heaven. Traitor earth, blind providence, noe Justice, howe is this done? howe is this suffred? hath this world a government? (p. 147)

Fraunce and Fenner give examples of many species of the figure exclamation, which, they say, is an excellent means to the forcible stirring up of divers affections, such as wonder and admiration, despair, wishing, cursing, indignation, disdain, derision, scorn, mocking (often joined with irony), detestation, protestation, grief and misery, pity and commiseration. Thus the Ramists present under the one figure exclamation many species which the figurists treat as distinct figures, giving to each its own peculiar name. Thaumasmus is a figure by which one utters an exclamation of wonder.

O the deepenes of the riches, of the wisedome and knowledge of God &c. Rom. 11, . . .
By this figure the Orator sometime wondereth, at the boldnesse and impudency of wicked deedes . . . at the negligence of men, in not preventing danger, or at their brutish security when the battel axe of destruction hangeth over their heads . . . at impunitie, when he seeth great wickednes passe free without punishment or rebuke . . . at the accusation of some person, in whom he hath a good opinion. (Peacham, p. 72)

Erotema, or interrogatio, although expressed in the form of a question, does not ask for information but is rather a device whereby the Orator doth affirme or deny something strongly, Job 8.3.11: Doth God pervert the thing that is lawful, or doth the Almighty pervert justice? can a rush be green without moisture, or may the grasse grow without water? that is to say it cannot.

This figure giveth to speech not onely life and motion, but also great strength and a coragious countenance, which is much commended in the supporting of good causes. (*Ibid.*, p. 106)

Apostrophe often employs prosopopoeia, exclamation, or interrogation. Hoskyns thus explains it:

Apostrophe, is a turning of your speech to some newe person, as to the people, when your speech before was to the Judge. . . . Sometymes the occasion is to some quallitie, or thing, that your selfe gives shewe of life to as hope tell me, what hast thou to hope for? Love be ashamed to be called Love. (p. 162)

The figures of vehemence and affection sound the whole gamut of the emotions.

Three of them have as their purpose to recall and lament sorrow.

Anamnesis is a forme of speech by which the Speaker calling to remembrance matters past, doth make recitall of them. Sometime matters of sorrow, as did *Dido* a litle before her death . . .

An example . . . of the prodigall sonne: Then he came to himselfe and said, how many servants at my fathers house, have bread inough, and I die for hunger. Luke. 15.17. (Peacham, p. 76)

Threnos is a forme of speech by which the Orator lamenteth some person or people for the miserie they suffer, or the speaker his owne calamitie. . . . The greatest part of *Jeremies* lamentations, is framed by this forme of speech. . . . O that my head were full of water, and mine eyes a fountain of teares, that I might weepe day and night, for the slaine of the daughter of my people. Jeremy 9. (*Ibid.*, p. 66)

Apocarteresis is a forme of speech by which the speaker signifieth that he casteth away all hope concerning some thing, & turneth it another way. *Job* . . . signifieth that he hath no more hope of worldly prosperitie and comfort, and therefore he turneth the eye of his hope to heaven, saying: I know that my redeemer liveth, &c. Whereby he comforteth himself the better to indure & suffer so great and heavy a burthen of misery. Job 19.25. (*Ibid.*, p. 83)

Three figures express desire or supplication.

Optatio is a forme of speech, by which the speaker expresseth his desire by wishing to God or Men. An example of *Cicero:* I would the immortall Gods had granted that wee might rather have given thankes to *Servius Sulpitius* being alive, then now to examine his honours being dead. (*Ibid.*, p. 72)

Deesis, when for God, or for mannes sake we vehemently desyre to have any thynge. As Cicero for Publius Sestius: O I praye you, & for the Gods sakes most herteli besech you, that as it was your wylles to save me, so you wyl vouchsaf to save them thorow whose helpe you received me agayne. (Sherry, Sig. D ii ʳ)

Mempsis is a forme of speech by which the Orator maketh a complaint, and craveth helpe. . . . King *David:* Why standest thou so farre O Lord, and hidest thy selfe in the needfull time of trouble? the ungodlie for his owne lust doth persecute the poore. . . . The poore committeth himselfe unto thee, for thou art the helper of the friendlesse, breake thou the power of the ungodlie and malicious. Psal. 10 (Peacham, p. 65)

Three figures are designed to console or to placate.

Paramythia is a forme of speech which the Orator useth to take away, or diminish a sorrow conceived in the minde of his hearer. An example of *Aeneas* in *Virgil,* and thus translated,

O mates (quoth he) that many a wo have bid, & borne ere this,
Worse have we seene, and these also shall end, when Gods will is.
(*Ibid.,* p. 100)

Medela, when seeing the offences of our friends, or of them whom we defend, to be so great that we cannot honestly defend them, or so manifest that we cannot well deny them, we seeke to heale them with plastures of good words . . . The Apostle *Paul* giveth a verie good example of this figure in his Epistle to *Philemon,* where he useth sundry reasons & diverse meanes to salve and cure the fault of *Onesimus,* and to appease and pacifie the displeasure of *Philemon.* (*Ibid.,* p. 176)

Philophronesis . . . is a forme of speech by which the speaker perceiving the might of his adversary to be too great and too strong against him, useth gentle speech, faire promises, and humble submission, to mitigate the rygor and crueltie of his adversary: we have a notable example hereof in *Jacob:* who fearing the malice and might of his brother *Esau,* used this meanes to appease his rage and crueltie. . . . assoone as he saw *Esau,* he shewed a signe of dutiful submission, he bowed himselfe seven times most humbly before he came neare to him, calling him his Lord . . . his family also children came likewise in seemly and suppliant order, and humbled themselves at his presence . . . by meanes whereof the fiery and flaming wrath of *Esau* was turned into teares of compassion. (*Ibid.,* p. 96)

Mocks and taunts, not only in words but also in gesture, were treated in Renaissance rhetoric as figures. Puttenham calls mycterismus the fleering frumpe and defines it as a mock given with scornful countenance, as for example by drawing the lip awry. Sherry decribes it as a skornyng by some jesture of the face, as by wrythinge the nose, putting out the tonge, pointyng, or such lyke. (Sig. C vii ^{v})

Peacham considers mycterismus to be a subtle mock with words and gives this example:

To one that demanded of *Demonax* the philosopher, if Philosophers did use to eate sweete cakes, *Demonax* made this answer, Doest thou thinke (quoth he) that bees gather their hony for fooles onely? (p. 39)

Without naming it, Blundeville makes a logician's natural comment on mycterismus in discussing what he calls confutation of person.

There be some that make two kinds of Confutation, the one belonging to person, the other to matter. Confutation of person is done either by taunting, rayling, rendring checke for checke, or by scorning, and that either by wordes, or else by countenance, gesture and action: which kinde of Confutation, because it belongeth rather to scoffing then to true order of reasoning, I will leave to speake thereof. (p. 183)

Sarcasmus, more open than mycterismus,

is a bitter sporting a mocke of our enemye, or a maner of jestying or scoffinge bytynglye, a nyppyng tawnte, as: The Jewes sayde to Christ, he saved other, but he could not save hym selfe. (Sherry, Sig. C vii ^{v})

Chiding, reprehension, accusation, or abhorrence characterize five figures. Epiplexis, or percontatio, is asking questions, not in order to know, but to

chide, and set forth our griefe with more vehemencie . . . *Tullie* enveighing against *Catiline* . . . beginneth his Oration chidingly . . . How long (*Catiline*) wilt thou abuse our sufferaunce? How long will this rage and madnesse of thine goe aboute to deceive us? (Wilson, *AR*, p. 184)

Onedismus . . . is a form of speech by which the speaker upbraideth his adversary of ingratitude, and impietie. . . . *Dido* . . . upbraiding *Aeneas* with the great and manifold benefites which he had received of her . . . exclaimeth . . . No Goddesse never was thy Dam . . . Some Tigers thee did nurce . . . it tendeth most specially to reprove and rebuke ingratitude. (Peacham, p. 73)

Categoria . . . is a forme of speech by which the speaker openeth and detecteth some secret wickednesse of his adversary, and laieth it open before his face. An example of Christ detecting *Judas:* He that dippeth his hand with me in the dish, he shall betray me. Mat. 26.23. (*Ibid.*, p. 80)

Proclees . . . is a forme of speech by which the Orator provoketh his adversary to the conflict . . . either by a vehement accusation, or by a confident offer of justification. By accusation, this of *Eliphaz* provoking *Job* . . . Is not thy wickednesse great? and thine ungratious deeds abhominable? for thou hast taken the pledge from thy brother for nought, and spoyled the clothes of the naked. . . . By offer of justification, this example of Christ . . . Which of you can rebuke me of sinne? (*Ibid.*, p. 83)

Bdelygmia . . . is a forme of speech which the speaker useth to signifie how much he hateth and abhorreth some person, word, deed, or thing, and it is used commonly in a short forme, and in few words. Against a person thus: Out upon him wretch . . . Against an odious deed, thus: Fie upon it. (*Ibid.*, p. 82)

The vehement figures of threatening and cursing Peacham illustrates from the Bible.

Cataplexis is a forme of speech by which the Orator denounceth a threatening against some person, people, citie, common wealth or country . . . declaring the certaintie or likelihood of plagues, or punishments to fall upon them for their wickednesse, impietie, insolencie, and generall iniquitie. . . . Jonas 3. Yet fortie daies, and Ninivy shall be destroyed. (p. 79)

Ara is a forme of speech by which the Orator detesteth, and curseth some person or thing, for the evils which they bring with them, or for the wickednesse which is in them. Psalm 109. Let the ungodly have dominion over him, and let Sathan stand at his right hand. (p. 64)

In contrast, two figures express blessing and rejoicing.

Eulogia is a forme of speech by which the Orator pronounceth a blessing uppon some person for the goodnesse that is in him or her. . . . Psal. 41. Blessed is the man which considereth the poore and the needie. (*Ibid.*, p. 65)

Paeanismus is a forme of speech which the . . . speaker useth to expresse his joy, either for the cause of some good thing obtained, or some evil avoyded. . . . To this forme of speech perteineth this saying in the song of the virgine *Mary:* From henceforth all generations shal call me blessed. . . . He hath filled the hungry with good things, and the rich he hath sent emptie away. . . . This figure after a sort is lively represented in the Larkes song, which she singeth everie morning, in joy that the darknesse is gone and the light come. (*Ibid.*, p. 81)

2. *Ethos*

That mode of persuasion which Aristotle calls *ethos* is, in a sense, included in *pathos,* for the attitude of the audience toward the personal character of the speaker, their confidence in him and in his good will toward them, constitutes part of their feelings or frame of mind as they listen. And *logos*, the sum of the ideas in the speech, helps not only to inspire in the audience confidence and good will toward the speaker but also to affect their feelings favorably or unfavorably toward the persons or matters being discussed. Consequently, although each of these three modes of persuasion, *ethos*, *logos*, and *pathos*, has special reference either to the speaker, to the speech, or to those spoken to, they are, nevertheless, closely interrelated; all three are intrinsic to the speech, all are under the control of the speaker, and the measure of success of all three is the effect on the hearers, as Aristotle succinctly explains.

Since rhetoric exists to affect the giving of decisions . . . the orator must not only try to make the argument of his speech demonstrative and worthy of belief; he must also make his own character look right and put his hearers, who are to decide, into the right frame of mind. (*Rhetoric*, 2.1.1377 [b] 21)

In his *Rhetoric* Aristotle gives a clear and illuminating account of the mode of persuasion which he calls *ethos*.

Persuasion is achieved by the speaker's personal character when the speech is so spoken as to make us think him credible. We believe good men more fully and more readily than others . . . This kind of persuasion, like the others, should be achieved by what the speaker says, not by what people think of his character before he begins to speak. It is not true . . . that the personal goodness revealed by the speaker contributes nothing to his power of persuasion; on the contrary, his character may almost be called the most effective means of persuasion he possesses. (1.2.1356 [a] 4)

It adds much to an orator's influence that his own character should look right and that he should be thought to entertain the right feelings toward his hearers. (2.1.1377 [b] 25)

There are three things which inspire confidence in the orator's own character—the three, namely, that induce us to believe a thing apart from any proof of it: good sense, good moral character, and good will. False statements and bad advice are due to one or more of the following three causes. Men either form a false opinion through want of good sense; or they form a true opinion, but because of their moral badness do not say what they really think; or finally, they are both sensible and upright, but not well-disposed toward their hearers, and may fail in consequence to recommend what they know to be the best course. These are the only possible cases. It follows that anyone who is thought to have all three of these good qualities will inspire trust in his audience. (2.1.1378 [a] 6)

In the *Poetics* Aristotle treats character and thought as two of the six formative elements of drama, which has as its essential function to arouse pity and fear in order to purge the audience agreeably of an excess of those emotions.[2] Here again is the combination of *ethos*, *logos*, and *pathos*. Aristotle thus defines the two elements of character and thought.

Character in a play is that which reveals the moral purpose of the agents, i.e. the sort of thing they seek or avoid, where that is not obvious—hence there is no room for Character in a speech on a purely indifferent subject. Thought, on the other hand, is shown in all they say when proving or disproving some particular point, or enunciating some universal proposition. (*Poetics*, 6.1450 [b] 8)

Not only in their speeches but even in their actions the characters of drama employ *logos* and *pathos* to convey their thought.

The Thought of the personages is shown in everything to be effected by their language—in every effort to prove or disprove, to arouse emotion (pity, fear, anger, and the like), or to maximize or minimize things. It is clear, also, that their mental procedure must be on the same lines in their actions likewise, whenever they wish them to arouse pity or horror, or to have a look of importance or probability. The only difference is that with the act the impression has to be made without explanation; whereas with the spoken word it has to be produced by the speaker, and result from his language. What, indeed, would be the good of the speaker, if things appeared in the required light even apart from anything he says? (*Poetics*, 19.1456 [a] 36)

It is particularly at the beginning of a speech that a speaker endeavors to win for himself the confidence and favor of his audience. Consequently in treating of the exordium Wilson touches upon *ethos* as a means of persuasion.

We must advisedly marke the men, before whom we speake, and al the circumstances which belong unto the matter. If the matter be honest, godly, and such as of right ought to be well liked, we may use an open beginning . . . If the cause bee lothsome, or such as will not be well borne with all, but needeth much helpe and favour of the hearers: it shalbe the speakers part prively to get favour & by humble talk to win their good wils. First requiring them to give him the hearing, . . . Wee shall make the people attentive, and glad to heare us . . . if we promise to tell them things concerning either their owne profit, or the advancement of their countrie . . .

We shall get the good willes of our hearers fower maner of waies, either beginning to speake of our selves, or els of our adversaries, or els of the people and companie present, or, last of all, if we begin of the matter it selfe, . . .

---

[2] Lane Cooper, in *An Aristotelian Theory of Comedy*, shows reason to think that Aristotle, in a part of his work now lost, considered the function of comedy likewise to be a catharsis, one to be wrought through laughter. Aristotle remarks (*Rhetoric*, 3.18.1419 [b] 5): "Jests have been classified in the *Poetics*." But they are not treated in the extant *Poetics*.

Wee shall get favour for our owne sakes, if we shal modestly set foorth . . .
our service done, without al suspition of vaunting . . . and lastly, if wee shewe
without all ostentation, aswell our good willes towards the Judges there, as also
pleasures done for them in tymes past. . . . in most humble wise to seeke favour . . .

We shall get favour by speaking of our adversaries, if wee shall make such
reporte of them, that the hearers shall either hate to heare them, or utterly envie
them, or els altogether despise them . . .

We shall get good will, by speaking of the Judges and hearers: if wee shall
commend their worthie doings, and prayse their just dealing . . . and tell
them in what estimation the whole countrey hath them . . .

We shall finde favour by speaking of the matter, if in handling our owne
cause, we commende it accordingly, and dispraise the attempt of our adversary. . . .

A privie beginning, or creeping in . . . must then, and not els be used,
when the Judge is greeved with us, and our cause hated of the hearers.

The cause selfe oftentimes is not liked for three divers causes, if either the
matter selfe be unhonest . . . or els if the Judge himself by a former tale be
perswaded to take parte against us, or last if at that time we are forced to speake,
when the Judge is weried with hearing of other. . . . evermore nothing
should be spoken at the first, but that which might please the Judge . . . when
the hearers are some what calmed, we may enter by little and little into the
matter, and say that those things, which our adversary doth mislike in the person accused, we also doe mislike the same. And when the hearers are thus
wonne . . . it were not amisse for the furtherance of our owne causes, closely
to speake our phantasie, and so, streight to aulter their hearts . . . But if the
adversarie have so tolde his tale, that the Judge is wholly bent to give sentence
with hym . . . we may take advantage, of some part of our adversaries tale,
and talke of that first, which he spake last: or els begin so, as though wee
doubted what were best first to speake . . . wondering . . . at the strange-
nesse of his reporte, and confirmation of his cause. For when the standers by,
perceive that the answerer (whome the adversaries thought . . . wholly
abashed) feareth so little the objections of his adversarie, and is readie to answere *Ad omnia quare* with a bolde countenance: They will thinke that they
themselves, rather gave rash credite, and were overlight in beleeving the first
tale. (*AR,* pp. 99–104)

It is evident that *ethos* is a pervasive quality running through a speech.
Yet there are four figures which seem designed to inspire confidence in
the speaker's goodness and in his good will toward the hearers and may
therefore be classified under *ethos*.

Comprobatio, when we see some good thyng eyther in the Judges or in our
hearers, or in any other. And therefore declare that we doo well allowe of it,

and also commende them for it. *Cicero.* I commende and prayse you, you Judges, for that most lovingly ye do advance the name of so famous a young man. (Peacham, 1577, Sig. L ii ᵛ)

Parrhesia, is a forme of speech by which the Orator speaking before those whom he feareth, or ought to reverence, & having somewhat to say that may either touch themselves, or those whom they favour, preventeth the displeasure and offence that might be taken, as by craving pardon afore hand, and by shewing the necessitie of free speech in that behalfe, or by some other like forme of humble submission and modest insinuation. An example of *Cicero* . . . I feare judges after what sort you may take my words, but for my continuall desire that I have to maintaine and augment your dignitie, I pray and beseech you, that if my speech be either bitter or incredible unto you . . . yet that you would accept it without offence . . . Neither that you will reject it before I have plainlie declared the whole unto you. . . .

This figure doth best beseeme a man of wisedome and gravitie, who is best able to moderate the forme of this speech . . . which is the onely forme that boldly delivereth to great dignities and most high degrees of men, the message of justice and equitie, sparing neither magistrates that pervert lawes, nor Princes that abuse their kingdomes. (Peacham, 1593, p. 113)

Eucharistia . . . is a forme of speech by which the speaker geveth thankes for benefites received . . . Sometime it is joyned with a confession of the unablenesse of the receiver to requite the giver . . . Psal. 16. What shal I give unto the Lord for all the benefites towards me? (*Ibid.*, p. 101)

Syngnome . . . is a form of speech by which the . . . speaker being a pacient of many and great injuries, or of some one great and greevous wrong, pronounceth pardon and forgivenesse to his adversary, who was the worker of all his miserie . . . An example of . . . *Steven* the Martyr at his death, who cryed with a loud voice, saying: Lord laie not this sinne to their charge. (*Ibid.*, p. 98)

In addition, a few figures which have been classified under other headings are likely to engender a favorable opinion of the speaker by revealing his courtesy or his goodness: anacoenosis, asking counsel of the adversary or of the judges; synchoresis, confidently asking one's adversary or judges to judge of one's cause; eustathia, promising constancy in purpose and affection; asphalia, becoming surety for another; philophronesis, gentle speech and humble submission; eulogia, pronouncing a blessing. Even prosopographia, as Aristotle shows, may contribute substantially to *ethos*.

With regard to the element of moral character: there are assertions which, if made about yourself, may excite dislike, appear tedious, or expose you to the risk of contradiction; and other things which you cannot say about your opponent without seeming abusive or ill bred. Put such remarks, therefore, into the mouth of some third person. . . . So . . . Sophocles makes Haemon appeal to his father on behalf of Antigone as if it were others who were speaking [*Antigone*, 688–700]. (*Rhetoric*, 3.17.1418 ^{b} 23)

3. Conclusion

Part III is a reconstruction, essentially complete, of the general theory of composition and of reading current in the Renaissance as it is embodied in extant sixteenth-century English texts on logic and rhetoric. Some passages from Aristotle have been included, because his work had an influence both direct and indirect on the Tudor logicians and rhetoricians, who frequently refer to him and sometimes use his very illustrations.

Careful study of the Tudor texts, which were based directly on Renaissance Latin texts used in the schools, discloses beneath obvious superficial differences the same fundamental doctrine among the traditionalists, the Ramists, and the figurists: all of them take account of the three modes of persuasion, *logos, pathos,* and *ethos;* all build on the topics of invention and recognize the same forms of reasoning and disputation. Logic was clearly regarded as the most important factor in composition not only by the Ramists and the traditionalists but also by the figurists. As has been shown in Chapters VII and VIII, one hundred and twenty-two of the two hundred figures of speech which the figurists distinguished are derived from the topics and forms of logic, a fact which they often explicitly pointed out. The figure diaeresis, for example, is equivalent to logical division, litotes to obversion, aetiologia to the enthymeme of the logicians, climax to sorites, epilogus to the hypothetical syllogism, apophasis to the disjunctive syllogism, dialysis to the dilemma.

The Renaissance theory, basically the same for all three groups, contains little that is altogether new to us, although the names of the figures and the sixteenth-century concept of figure, astonishing in its inclusiveness, present an initial obstacle. The precepts of all the arts are ultimately only codified good sense—rules derived by critics from the practice of creative artists whose native genius has produced results that have been admired, approved, and imitated throughout the ages.

The ancient classification of the figures, which the Renaissance rhetoricians retained, tends to obscure the simple and coherent functional pattern underlying their meticulous and comprehensive analysis of thought, emotion, and expression. It is hoped that the correlation of the works of the logicians and rhetoricians here undertaken and the reclassification of the figures according to their functions under the headings grammar, *logos*, *pathos*, and *ethos* will both clarify the theory and contribute to a fuller understanding of Renaissance literature.

BIBLIOGRAPHY

A. Primary

Aristotle. Works; tr. into English under the editorship of W. R. Ross. Oxford, 1928, 1924. "Organon," Vol. I; "Rhetoric" and "Poetics," Vol. XI.

Blundeville, Thomas. The Arte of Logick [1599]. London, 1617.

Butler, Charles. Rhetoricae libri duo [1598]. London, 1629.

—— Oratoriae libri duo. Oxford, 1629.

Cicero, Marcus Tullius. Brutus and Orator; tr. by George Lincoln Hendrickson and Harry Mortimer Hubbel. Loeb Classical Library. Cambridge, Mass., 1939.

—— De inventione rhetorica; texte revu et traduit avec introduction et notes par Henri Bornecque. Paris, 1932.

—— De oratore, De fato, Paradoxo stoicorum, De partitione oratoriae. 2 vols., tr. by E. W. Sutton and H. Rackham. Loeb Classical Library. Cambridge, Mass., 1942.

—— The Orator; tr. by E. Jones. London, 1808.

—— Rhetorica; recognovit brevique adnotione critica instruxit A. S. Wilkins. 2 vols. Oxford, 1901–1903.

—— Orations; tr. by C. D. Yonge, Vol. IV. Bohn's Classical Library. London, 1894–1903. "Rhetorical Invention" and "Topics."

Cox, Leonard. The Arte or Crafte of Rhethoryke [ca. 1530]; a reprint edited by Frederic Ives Carpenter. Chicago, 1899.

Day, Angel. The English Secretorie; with a Declaration of Tropes, Figures, and Schemes [1592]. London, 1635.

Fenner, Dudley. The Artes of Logike and Rhetorike. Middelburg, 1584.

Fraunce, Abraham. The Arcadian Rhetorike; or, The Praecepts of Rhetorike Made Plaine by Examples, Greeke, Latin, English, Italian, French, Spanish. London, 1588.

—— The Lawiers Logike; Exemplifying the Praecepts of Logike by the Practise of the Common Lawe. London, 1588.

Hoskyns, John. "Direccions for Speech and Style" [ca. 1599]; printed from MS Harley 4604, in The Life, Letters and Writings of John Hoskyns, 1566–1638, pp. 114–166, by Louise Brown Osborn. New Haven, 1937.

—— Directions for Speech and Style; ed. by Hoyt H. Hudson. Princeton, 1935.

Lever, Raphe. The Arte of Reason, Rightly Termed Witcraft; Teaching a Perfect Way to Argue and Dispute. London, 1573.

Melanchthon, Philippus. Opera, Corpus Reformatorum, ed. by Bretschneider et Bindseil. 28 vols. Brunswick und Halle, 1834–60. Vol. XIII, "Institutiones rhetoricae" (Haganoa, 1521), "Elementa Rhetorices" (Wittenberg, 1531), "Erotemata Dialectices" (Basel, 1521).

Peacham, Henry. The Garden of Eloquence. London, 1577.

—— The Garden of Eloquence; corrected and augmented by the first author. London, 1593.

Puttenham, George. The Arte of English Poesie [1589]; ed. by Gladys Doidge Willcock and Alice Walker. Cambridge, 1936.

Quintilian, M. Fabius. Institutio oratoria; with an English translation by H. E. Butler. 4 vols. Loeb Classical Library. London and New York, 1922.

—— Institutes of Oratory; tr. by J. S. Watson. 2 vols. Bohn's Classical Library. London, 1891.

Rainolde, Richard. A Booke Called the Foundacion of Rhetorike. London, 1563.

Ramus, Petrus. Dialecticae institutiones. Paris, 1543.

—— Institutionum dialecticarum libri III. Paris, 1547.

—— Dialecticae libri duo, et his e regione comparati Philippi Melanth. Dialecticae libri quatuor cum explicationum et collationum notis, ad utramque . . . auctore Frederico Beurhusio, Meinertzhagense Scholae Tremoneanae Rectore, 1586.

Ramus, Petrus. Dialecticae libri duo; cum commentariis Georgii Dounami annexis. London, 1669.

Rhetorica ad C. Herennium; texte revu et traduit avec introduction et notes par Henri Bornecque. Paris, 1932.

Shakespeare, William. Complete Works; ed. by George Lyman Kittredge. Boston, 1936.

Sherry, Richard. A Treatise of Schemes & Tropes. London, 1550.

—— A Treatise of the Figures of Grammer and Rhetorike. London, 1555.

Susenbrotus, Joannes. Epitome troporum ac schematum et grammaticorum et rhetoricorum [Zurich, 1540]. London, 1621.

Talaeus, Audomarus. Rhetorica e P. Rami praelectionibus observata [1544?]; per Claudium Minoem. Frankfort, 1579.

Wilson, Thomas. The Arte of Rhetorique; a reprint of the edition of 1585 [1553]; ed. by G. H. Mair. Oxford, 1909.

—— The Rule of Reason; Conteining the Art of Logike [1551]. London, 1567.

B. Secondary

Abbott, E. A. A Shakespearian Grammar. 3d ed. London, 1871.

Abelson, Paul. The Seven Liberal Arts; a Study in Medieval Culture. New York, 1906.

Anders, H. R. D. Shakespeare's Books. Berlin, 1904.

Ascham, Roger. The Scholemaster. London, 1570.

—— The Whole Works of Roger Ascham; ed. by Giles. 3 vols. in 4. London, 1865.

Baldwin, Charles Sears. Ancient Rhetoric and Poetic. New York, 1924.

—— Medieval Rhetoric and Poetic. New York, 1928.

—— Renaissance Literary Theory and Practice. New York, 1939.

Baldwin, T. W. William Shakspere's Small Latine and Lesse Greeke. 2 vols. Urbana, 1944.

Berdan, John. Early Tudor Poetry 1485–1547. New York, 1931.

Boethius, Anicius Manlius. "De differentiis topicis," in Patrologiae cursus completus, series prima, ed. Jacques Paul Migne, Vol. LXIV.

Brinsley, John. Ludus literarius; or, The Grammar Schoole; ed. by E. T. Campagnac. Liverpool, 1917.

Cameron, Kenneth Walter. Authorship and Sources of "Gentleness and Nobility." Raleigh, 1941.

Campbell, Lily B. Shakespeare's Tragic Heroes, Slaves of Passion. Cambridge, 1930.

Campbell, Oscar James. Comicall Satyre and Shakespeare's 'Troilus and Cressida.' San Marino, 1938.

—— Satire in Shakespeare. New York, 1943.

Castiglione, Baldassare. The Book of the Courtier; tr. by Sir Thomas Hoby, 1561. New York, 1928.

Chambers, R. W. "Shakespeare and the Play of *More*," in Man's Unconquerable Mind (London, 1939), pp. 204–49.

Chapman, George. Works; ed. by R. H. Shepherd. London, 1874–75.

Clark, Donald Lemen. Rhetoric and Poetry in the Renaissance. New York, 1922.

Cooper, Lane. An Aristotelian Theory of Comedy; with an Adaptation of the Poetics and a Translation of the 'Tractatus Coislinianus.' New York, 1922.

Craig, Hardin. The Enchanted Glass. New York, 1936.

—— "Shakespeare and Formal Logic," in Studies in English Philology: a Miscellany in Honor of Frederick Klaeber (Minneapolis, 1929,) pp. 380–396.

—— "Shakespeare and Wilson's *Arte of Rhetorique;* an Inquiry into the Criteria for Determining Sources," *Studies in Philology*, XXVIII (October, 1931), 618–30.

Crane, William G. Wit and Rhetoric in the Renaissance. New York, 1937.

Curry, Walter Clyde. Shakespeare's Philosophical Patterns. Baton Rouge, 1937.

Dekker, Thomas. Dramatic Works; ed. by R. H. Shepherd. London, 1873.

—— Satiro-Mastix; ed. by Hans Scherer. Louvain, 1907.

Donnelly, Francis P., S.J. Literature, the Leading Educator. New York, 1938.

—— Persuasive Speech. New York, 1931.

Faral, Edmond. "Les Arts poetiques du XIIᵉ et du XIIIᵉ siècle," in Bibliothèque de l'École des Hautes Etudes, Paris, 1924.

Franz, Wilhelm. Die Sprache Shakespeares in Vers und Prosa. Halle, 1939.

Frasure, Louise D. "Shakespeare's Constables," *Anglia*, LVIII (1934), 384–392.

Gascoigne, George. Complete Works; ed. by John W. Cunliffe. 2 vols. Cambridge, 1907.

Gilbert, Allan H. "Logic in the Elizabethan Drama," *Studies in Philology*, XXXII (October, 1935), 527–45.

Gordon, George Stuart. "Shakespeare's English," in Society for Pure English, *Tract* 29 (Oxford), 1928, pp. 255–75.

Graves, Frank Pierrepont. Peter Ramus and the Educational Reformation of the Sixteenth Century. New York, 1912.

Greene, Robert. The Life and Complete Works in Prose and Verse of Robert Greene; ed. by A. B. Grosart (The Huth Library). 15 vols. London, 1881–1886.

Greenewald, Gerard M., O.M.Cap. Shakespeare's Attitude towards the Catholic Church in "King John." Washington, 1938.

Groom, Bernard. "The Formation and Use of Compound Epithets from 1579," in Society for Pure English, *Tract* 49 (Oxford), 1936, pp. 293–322.

Hart, Alfred. "Shakespeare and the Vocabulary of *The Two Noble Kinsmen*," in Shakespeare and the Homilies, (Melbourne, 1934), pp. 242–56.

—— "Vocabularies of Shakespeare's Plays," *Review of English Studies*, XIX (April, 1943), 128–40.

Hart, H. C., ed. Love's Labour's Lost. 3d ed., revised. The Arden Shakespeare. London, 1930.

Haskins, C. H. The Renaissance of the Twelfth Century. Cambridge, Mass., 1928.

Henderson, W. B. Drayton. "Montaigne's *Apologie of Raymond Sebond* and *King Lear*," *Shakespeare Association Bulletin*, XIV (October, 1939), 209–25.

Hermogenis. De ratione inveniendi oratoria, libri IIII; latinitate donati & scholis explicati atque illustrati a Jonane Sturmio, 2 vols., ed. by J. Cocin. [Argentorati], 1570.

Herrick, Marvin T. The Poetics of Aristotle in England. New Haven, 1930.

Hubbell, H. M. The Influence of Isocrates on Cicero, Dionysius, and Aristides. New Haven, 1913.

Hultzen, Lee S. Aristotle's "Rhetoric" in England before 1600. Unpublished dissertation presented to Cornell University, 1932.

Johnson, Francis R. "Two Renaissance Textbooks of Rhetoric: Aphthonius' *Progymnasmata* and Rainolde's *A Booke Called the Foundacion of Rhetorike*," *Huntington Library Quarterly*, VI (August, 1943), 427–444.

Jonson, Ben. Ben Jonson; ed. by C. H. Herford and Percy Simpson. 7 vols. Oxford, 1925–41.

—— Discoveries; a critical edition with an introduction and notes by Maurice Castelain. Paris, n.d.

—— The English Grammar [written *ca.* 1630–35]; ed. with introduction and notes by Alice Vinton Waite. New York, 1909.

Kellett, E. E. "Some Notes on a Feature of Shakespeare's Style," in Suggestions (Cambridge, 1923), pp. 57–78.

Kennedy, Milton Boone. The Oration in Shakespeare. Chapel Hill, 1942.

Kempe, William. The Education of Children. London, 1588.

Lever, Katherine. "Proverbs and *Sententiae* in the Plays of Shakspere," *Shakespeare Association Bulletin*, XIII (July and October, 1938), 173–83; 224–239.

Lewis, C. S. The Allegory of Love. Oxford, 1936.

Lodge, Thomas, and Robert Greene. A Looking Glasse, for London and Englande. London, 1598.

Lyly, John. The Complete Works of John Lyly; ed. by R. W. Bond. 3 vols. Oxford, 1902.

—— Euphues, the Anatomy of Wit, and Euphues and His England; ed. by Morris W. Croll and Harry Clemons. London, 1916.

Marlowe, Christopher. Works; ed. by C. F. Tucker Brooke. Oxford, 1929.

Massinger, Philip. Plays; ed. by William Gifford. 3d ed. London, 1845.

McBurney, James H. The Place of the Enthymeme in Rhetorical Theory. Reprinted from *Speech Monographs*, III (October, 1936), 49–74. An abstract of a dissertation presented to the University of Michigan.

McKeon, Richard. "Rhetoric in the Middle Ages," *Speculum*, XVII (January, 1942), 1–32.

Miller, Perry. The New England Mind. New York, 1939.

Milton, John. Artis logicae plenior institutio, ad Petri Rami methodum concinnata. London, 1672; in The Works of John Milton, Vol. XI, New York, 1935, ed. and tr. by Allan H. Gilbert.

Montaigne, Michel Eyquem de. Essayes; tr. by John Florio; ed. by Thomas Seccombe. 3 vols. London, 1908.

Moore-Smith, G. C. Gabriel Harvey's Marginalia. Stratford-upon-Avon, 1913.

Mulcaster, Richard. Elementarie [1582]; ed. by E. T. Campagnac. Oxford, 1925.

Nashe, Thomas. Works; ed. by R. B. McKerrow. 5 vols. London, 1904–10.

Osborn, Louise Brown. The Life, Letters, and Writings of John Hoskyns 1566–1638. New Haven, 1937.

Paetow, Louis John. The Arts Course at Medieval Universities; with Special Reference to Grammar and Rhetoric. Champaign, 1910.

The Pilgrimage to Parnassus with the Two Parts of the Return from Parnassus [three comedies performed in St. John's College, Cambridge, 1597]; ed. by W. D. Macray. Oxford, 1886.

Plato. Phaedrus, Ion, Gorgias, and Symposium; tr. into English with an introduction and prefatory notes by Lane Cooper. New York, 1938.

Rubel, Veré L. Poetic Diction in the English Renaissance from Skelton through Spenser. New York, 1941.

Rushton, William Lowes. Shakespeare and 'The Arte of English Poesie.' Liverpool, 1909.

Sidney, Sir Philip. Complete Works; ed. by Albert Feuillerat. 4 vols. Cambridge, 1912–26.

Skelton, John. The Poetical Works of John Skelton; ed. by Alexander Dyce. 2 vols. Edinburgh, 1843.

Smith, G. Gregory, ed. Elizabethan Critical Essays. 2 vols. Oxford, 1904.

Spencer, Theodore. Shakespeare and the Nature of Man. New York, 1942.

Spenser, Edmund. Poetical Works; ed. by J. C. Smith and E. De Selincourt. London, 1935.

Spingarn, Joel E. A History of Literary Criticism in the Renaissance. New York, 1899.

Spurgeon, Caroline F. E. "Imagery in the *Sir Thomas More* Fragment," *Review of English Studies*, VI (July, 1930), 257–70.

—— Shakespeare's Imagery and What It Tells Us. Cambridge, 1935.

—— "Shakespeare's Iterative Imagery," *Proceedings of the British Academy* (London), Vol. XVII (1931).

Taylor, Warren. A Dictionary of the Tudor Figures of Rhetoric. [Chicago], 1937. Distributed by the University of Chicago libraries.

—— The Tudor Figures of Rhetoric. Unpublished dissertation presented to the University of Chicago, 1937.

Tilley, Morris Palmer. Elizabethan Proverb Lore in Lyly's *Euphues* and in Pettie's *Petite Pallace* with Parallels from Shakespeare. New York, 1926.

Tuve, Rosemond. "Imagery and Logic: Ramus and Metaphysical Poetics," *Journal of the History of Ideas*, III (October, 1942), 365–400.

Van Hook, La Rue. "Greek Rhetorical Terminology in Puttenham's 'The Arte of English Poesie' " in *Transactions of the American Philological Association*, XLV (1914), 111–28.

Wagner, Russell H. Thomas Wilson's 'Arte of Rhetorique.' Unpublished dissertation presented to Cornell University, 1928.

Whiting, B. J. "The Nature of the Proverb," *Harvard Studies and Notes in Philology and Literature* (Cambridge, Mass.), Vol. XIV, 1932.

Willcock, Gladys Doidge. "Shakespeare and Rhetoric," *Essays and Studies by Members of the English Association* (Oxford), XXIX (1943), 50–61.

—— "Shakespeare as Critic of Language," *The Shakespeare Association Publications* (London), No. 18, 1934.

Wilson, Frank P. "Shakespeare and the Diction of Common Life," *Proceedings of the British Academy* (London), Vol. XXVII, 1941.

Wilson, Harold S. "Nature and Art in 'Winter's Tale,'" *Shakespeare Association Bulletin*, XVIII (1943), 114–19.

INDEX

ALL THE figures of speech and the vices of language are alphabetized under Figures of speech and vices of language. All the fallacies and the captious arguments are alphabetized under Fallacies and captious arguments.